The Last Days of the Ottoman Empire

RYAN GINGERAS

The Last Days of the Ottoman Empire

ALLEN LANE
an imprint of
PENGUIN BOOKS

ALLEN LANE

UK | USA | Canada | Ireland | Australia
India | New Zealand | South Africa

Penguin Books is part of the Penguin Random House group of companies
whose addresses can be found at global.penguinrandomhouse.com

First published in Great Britain by Allen Lane 2022

003

Set in 10.5/14pt Sabon LT Std
Typeset by Jouve (UK), Milton Keynes
Printed and bound in Great Britain by Clays Ltd, Elcograf S.p.A.

The authorized representative in the EEA is Penguin Random House Ireland,
Morrison Chambers, 32 Nassau Street, Dublin D02 YH68

A CIP catalogue record for this book is available from the British Library

ISBN: 978-0-241-44432-0

Contents

List of Illustrations

Maps

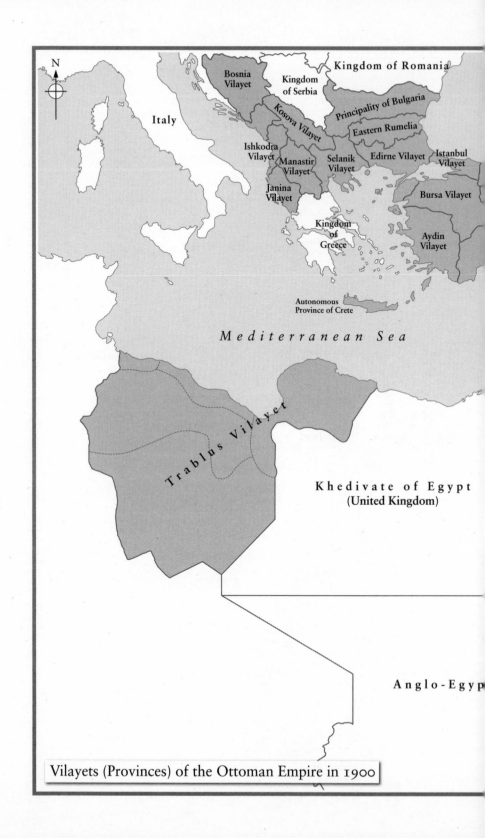

N

Italy

Kingdom of Romania

Bosnia
Vilayet

Kingdom
of Serbia

Principality of Bulgaria

Kosova Vilayet

Eastern Rumelia

Ishkodra
Vilayet

Manastir
Vilayet

Selanik
Vilayet

Edirne Vilayet

Istanbul
Vilayet

Janina
Vilayet

Bursa Vilayet

Kingdom
of
Greece

Aydin
Vilayet

Autonomous
Province of Crete

Mediterranean Sea

Trablus Vilayet

Khedivate of Egypt
(United Kingdom)

Anglo-Egyp

Vilayets (Provinces) of the Ottoman Empire in 1900

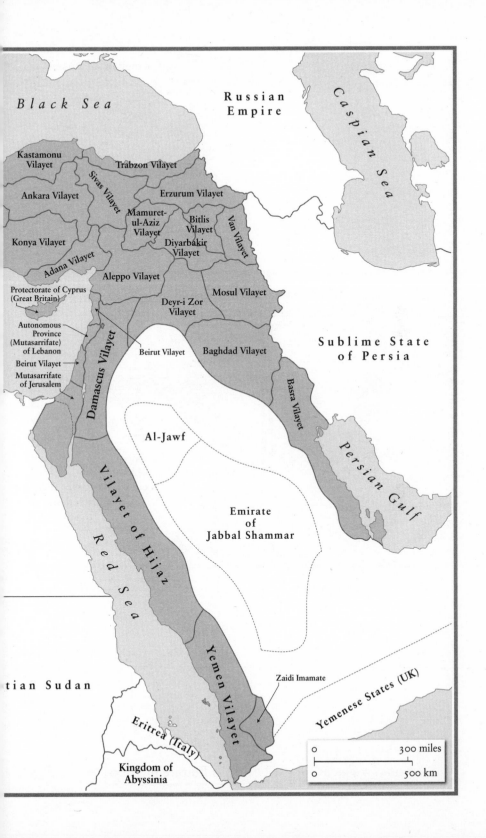

Black Sea

R u s s i a n E m p i r e

Caspian Sea

Kastamonu
Vilayet

Trabzon Vilayet

Ankara Vilayet

Sivas Vilayet

Erzurum Vilayet

Mamuret-
ul-Aziz
Vilayet

Bitlis
Vilayet

Van Vilayet

Konya Vilayet

Diyarbakir
Vilayet

Adana Vilayet

Aleppo Vilayet

Protectorate of Cyprus
(Great Britain)

Mosul Vilayet

Autonomous
Province
(Mutasarrifate)
of Lebanon

Deyr-i Zor
Vilayet

Beirut Vilayet

**S u b l i m e S t a t e
o f P e r s i a**

Beirut Vilayet

Baghdad Vilayet

Mutasarrifate
of Jerusalem

Damascus Vilayet

Basra Vilayet

Al-Jawf

Persian Gulf

Emirate
of
Jabbal Shammar

Vilayet of Hijaz

Red Sea

Zaidi Imamate

Yemenese States (UK)

tian Sudan

Yemen Vilayet

Eritrea (Italy)

**Kingdom of
Abyssinia**

| 0 | | 300 miles |
| 0 | | 500 km |

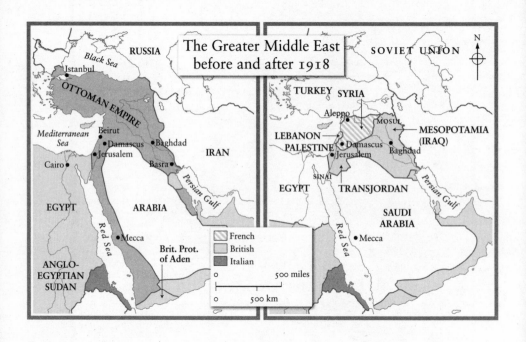

The Greater Middle East before and after 1918

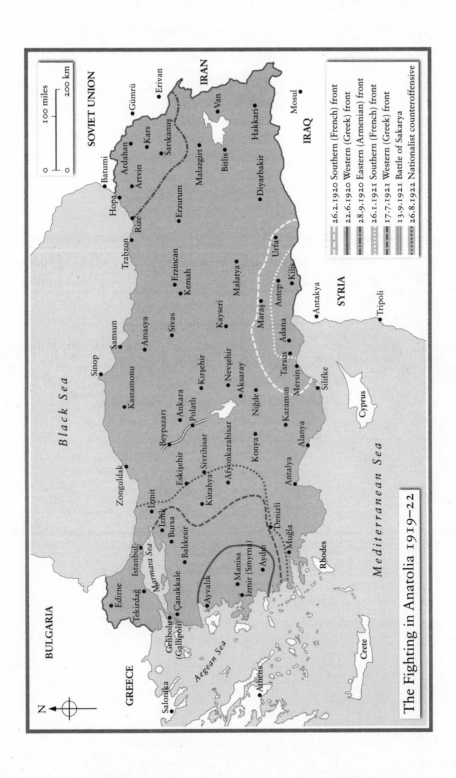

The Fighting in Anatolia 1919–22

26.2.1920 Southern (French) front
22.6.1920 Western (Greek) front
28.9.1920 Eastern (Armenian) front
26.1.1921 Southern (French) front
17.7.1921 Western (Greek) front
13.9.1921 Battle of Sakarya
26.8.1922 Nationalist counteroffensive

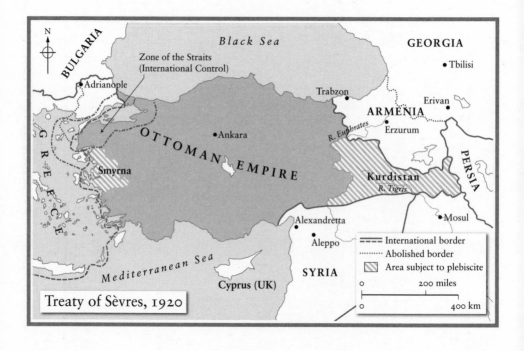

Treaty of Sèvres, 1920

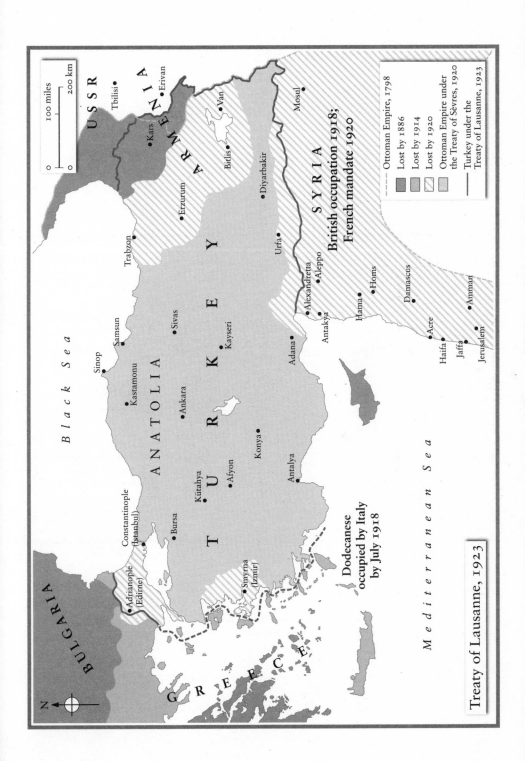

Treaty of Lausanne, 1923

Introduction

By the last week of October 1918, there was every reason to believe that the Great War had approached its end. News from all points spoke of dramatic events. Since the start of the month, Allied forces had made steady progress all along the line in Flanders. With German troops retreating into Belgium, Kaiser Wilhelm II sanctioned efforts to secure an armistice with the Allies. Erich Ludendorff, who had commanded the German army through much of the fighting, resigned in anger as October came to a close. Although he and other ranking generals stood willing to 'fight to the bloody end', a different sort of bitterness reverberated through the ranks.[1] Before the month was out, mutinous soldiers took to the streets of Berlin calling for an end to Wilhelm's rule. Similar scenes of revolution were unfolding to the south in the Habsburg lands as well. By the 30th, Vienna betrayed signs of insurrection as thousands of demobilized soldiers joined demonstrators demanding the royal family's abdication. Events were moving even faster in Budapest. There, lawmakers had already commenced efforts to break away from the Habsburg crown. As Hungary lurched towards independence, separatism had taken root in Poland, Czechoslovakia and among the south Slavs. In Bulgaria, the least of the Central Powers, political uncertainty reigned. After abandoning the war early in the month, peasants and soldiers rose up outside the capital, Sofia, forcing Tsar Ferdinand to vacate the throne.

It was on 30 October that the Central Powers' most eastern member, the Ottoman Empire, conceded its own defeat. Like other members of the alliance, fortune had long deserted the empire on the battlefield. Earlier in September, British forces had broken through Ottoman defenses outside Nablus in Palestine. Over the following weeks, the

Ottoman army's flight north through Syria degenerated into a rout. After taking Damascus, British troops marched on Aleppo, seizing it after only a brief fight. The disintegration of Ottoman forces in the Levant accentuated the hopelessness felt in Istanbul. For some officials, the horizon had appeared dark well before summer's end. The capital itself stood on the brink of chaos. Basic foodstuffs had long been in short supply. Fuel stocks of every type were rationed, and electricity cuts were a frequent occurrence. City residents competed for these resources alongside tens of thousands of war refugees. Istanbul, one minister admitted to his diary, was 'completely soiled, an open sewer flowing from every side'. Rampant lawlessness and banditry in the countryside, more than anything, revealed the ultimate truth. 'The government', the minister conceded, 'was left with absolutely no influence and no dignity'.[2]

And yet, with the signing of an armistice at the end of October, the imperial government offered no signs that it feared revolution or dissolution. Speaking before the press the day after the empire's surrender, Istanbul's chief negotiator declared that he returned to the capital with joy and pride, not sadness. 'Our country's rights', he proclaimed, 'and the future of the Sultanate have been wholly saved as a result of the armistice concluded'. The British delegation had publicly avowed that they did not seek to destroy the nation. Nor, he assured journalists, would a foreign army come to occupy the capital. 'Yes', he exclaimed, 'the armistice we have concluded is beyond our hopes'.[3]

Very few would retain such optimism as the days passed. Within a week of the armistice, the sitting government dissolved itself in consultation with the sultan. The resignation of the grand vezir, the country's highest civilian official, came as the empire's only political party agreed to disband. After a decade in power, the collapse of the reigning Committee of Union and Progress tore at the very fabric of the Ottoman political establishment. The iron rule of the CUP – or Young Turks, as they were so often called – had long polarized both state and society. During its ten years in power, the CUP had fought and lost three wars and had driven all dissent underground. Young Turk leaders assumed office in 1908 championing the principles of liberty and equality under the law. A decade later, the CUP had methodically disenfranchised vast numbers of citizens, most of them Christians.

Hundreds of thousands were killed in the process. With the party now gone, and its leaders driven into exile, doubt and animosity weighed heavily over the capital. Contrary to earlier assertions, the first contingents of an occupying army arrived in Istanbul in mid-November. The prospect of the capital under occupation, as one senior official remembered, exposed a deep rift within society as a whole. In Beyoğlu, the capital's historic foreign quarter, the appearance of British and French ships docked offshore was greeted with wild excitement. 'All the houses, the shops, hotels and restaurants were decked out like it was a grand celebration', he remembered. Rather than rue the coming occupation, locals there, most of them Christians, embraced the British, French and Greek presence as a moment of redemption. The mood across town, however, could not have been more somber. In predominately Muslim neighborhoods such as Eminönü, Topkapı and Eyüp, the streets were decidedly dark and empty. Save for the 'meowing of hungry cats and the hopeless barking of stray dogs', one rarely heard voices. Amid wet weather and grieving families, the official, and others like him, were left 'trembling with a sense of catastrophe and mourning'.[4]

Images such as these are often interpreted as the Ottoman Empire's last signs of life. Most accounts from the fall of 1918 tend to accentuate what seems like an obvious truth: the Ottoman state was meeting an end in keeping with the times. Each of the old houses of Eastern Europe, the Romanovs, Habsburgs and Hohenzollerns, had been banished from power before the winter of 1918 was out. Revolution hung thick in the air as new states took their place. Republics championing the national will instead ruled the day. Given what had happened and what was to come, 30 October 1918 appears a fitting time to mark the Ottoman Empire's final hours.

It is equally tempting to see the fall of the Ottoman Empire as an event long overdue. For generations, commentators in Europe talked of the empire's demise as an eventual possibility, one predicated upon what seemed like a *longue durée* marked by disaster. For some, the Ottoman state's collapse began with its defeat before Vienna in 1683. The timely arrival of a Polish relief column outside the Habsburg capital that September forced an Ottoman retreat from which they ultimately never fully recovered. Through the nineteenth century, European statesmen and journalists regularly foretold Istanbul's demise. The evidence, depending upon the times, was as clear as day. With the start of a new century, the empire continued to cede territory across the continents of Europe, Asia and Africa. Istanbul struggled to fight civil disorder within its borders. The state treasury wavered between austerity and bankruptcy. This long list of failings, many observers came to conclude, was what brought the Ottomans to the brink in 1918.

Yet to see the Ottoman Empire's fall as inevitable requires one to ignore a series of signs to the contrary. Despite decades of territorial contraction, the legitimacy of the Ottoman royal family remained remarkably intact. Citizens throughout the empire continued to answer the call to service in spite of repeated reversals in war. Elite and popular support for the monarchy grew particularly entrenched with the spread of nationalism. Ottoman nationalism, as large numbers of citizens conceived it, proved loose enough to capture their loyalties. One did not need to natively speak Turkish, the lingua franca of the state, to embrace it as the common language of the nation. Albanians, Arabs, Armenians, Turks, Greeks and Bulgarians regularly proved themselves dedicated to the survival of the empire despite disagreements over a variety of issues. Peoples of various faiths could similarly embrace the sultan in his dual capacity as a ruler of the Ottoman lands and caliph of the Islamic world. In the Great War, Muslim, Christian and Jewish citizens demonstrated a shared willingness to fight and die in what the sultan's government termed a jihad against the enemies of Islam. War and insecurity most certainly shook the confidence of large numbers of citizens in the years leading up to 1918. There is no denying that large numbers of erstwhile citizens contemplated the possibility of the empire's dissolution. And it is also true that many Ottomans cursed their government for a variety of wrongs, including violence against them. Yet, as one closely surveys the history of the empire through to the end of the First World War, one is struck by the resilience of the Ottoman state and the durability of its legitimacy in the eyes of its diverse citizenry.

Still, one must address the central fact that the Ottoman Empire *did* fall. That story is typically told as a grand narrative, one that spans decades, if not centuries. In this traditional retelling, the events after 1918 are often presented as a postscript. The Great War, it would seem, rendered a final verdict on the Ottoman state's viability. With the loss of its Levantine and Arabian provinces, only Asia Minor and a small sliver of European Thrace remained in its grasp. Neither the sultan nor his closest supporters offered much resistance to the pressing demands of the Allies. Istanbul's acquiescence, however, proved critical for the establishment of a new state, the Republic of Turkey, to take the empire's place. Born after the advent of nation-states in Eastern Europe, Turkey's founding is often seen as reflective of a more legitimate and more viable consensus taking hold in Anatolia. The events that followed after October 1918 allowed Turks – the oft-presumed majority of Turkey – to form a state of their own. With Turkey's birth, people outside the empire's old borders moved on from the Ottoman collapse. The world after the Treaty of Versailles was evolving. History ultimately would prove that the rule of empires, monarchs and caliphs was a relic of the past.

Two intentions lie at the heart of this book. It is, first and foremost, an attempt to re-center the story of the Ottoman Empire's last years. In truth, the autumn of 1918 did not result in the fall of the Ottoman sultanate. It instead marked the beginning of an exceedingly complex period of warfare and negotiation over the empire's uncertain future. In the four years that followed, imperial officers and statesmen fought mightily, and against long odds, in the hopes of restoring the empire's sovereignty and good name. By 1922, this struggle had attained a relevance that was no longer limited to the confines of the sultan's dwindling lands. Former citizens of the empire in Europe, the Middle East and North Africa, as well as peoples much further afield, actively followed and supported the Ottoman struggle in Anatolia. For a time, at least, it was a conflict that resonated within a broader struggle among colonized peoples to resist rule under the British, the French or the Russians. Ironically, the success of this independence campaign proved fatal to the sultan and his family's claim to the throne. When the end finally arrived, it was the empire's most esteemed servants, its generals and soldiers, who decided that the time had come for the Ottoman state to pass into history.

To understand this turn away from empire and sultan, one must also appreciate the profundity of loss witnessed during this period.

For those who remained citizens of the Ottoman Empire in 1918, hardship and heartache had long been fixtures of daily life. What was to come after the armistice of 1918 proved, for many, that much more trying and defining. The severity of the fighting in Anatolia between 1918 and 1922 reaped a staggering toll, leaving millions dead, maimed or displaced. Far more difficult to calculate are the cultural and social costs born out of this period of time. Large swaths of the empire's remaining lands were emptied of people, utterly destroying communities that had endured for many centuries. The horrors of this era nurtured the political disillusionment harbored by growing numbers of citizens. By 1922, events appeared to have left little room for nostalgia. An empire representing many faiths and languages no longer seemed viable. And for its perceived sins, both past and present, the Ottoman royal family was overthrown and repudiated. Much of this book endeavors to give clarity to these dark times.

One may be forgiven for seeing this history as primarily relevant to Turks. It is, after all, a period that features the ascendancy of Turkey's heroic founder, Mustafa Kemal Atatürk. More than that, it is a time still celebrated as Turkey's moment of conception. The National Struggle (*Milli Mücadele*), as this period is often called, continues to be remembered as both the blackest and the most illuminating hour in the country's history. As an era marked by foreign occupation and unspeakable violence, it represents Turkey's greatest fears and humiliation. At the same time, the victory won by Atatürk and his supporters is hailed as a moment of hard-earned salvation, laying the foundation for a state genuinely worthy of national and international admiration.

A deeper inspection of this time reveals a history possessing still greater relevance. While Turks may observe the years between 1918 and 1922 as their 'War of Independence' (*İstiklal Harbi* or *Kurtuluş Savaşı*), this time yielded far more bitter results for other peoples. The fighting that marked the era was the last in a succession of violent waves that all but destroyed the Christian peoples of Anatolia. It was a time that featured the rise and fall of a movement to build an independent Kurdish state, an outcome that remains elusive to this day. The prospect of an Ottoman collapse impacted peoples and states beyond the empire's borders as well. Affairs in Anatolia catalyzed the imagination and activism of nationalist movements ranging from

Morocco to India. For Great Britain and France, the struggle over the future of the Ottoman sultanate offered a stern warning regarding the future of their own empires. For the United States, the period proved to be an early tutorial in the politics of the modern Middle East.

The object of this book, in short, is to breathe new life into a subject that is often treated as relatively obscure. It is an effort to bring greater context to events that preface the broader evolution of the Middle East in the twentieth and twenty-first centuries. The tensions documented in this study are meant to provide a vantage point for understanding critical challenges still at play in the old Ottoman world, particularly those related to identity and to relations with the West. It lastly intends to give weight and significance to voices and experiences often overlooked in the retelling of the empire's end. The Ottoman Empire's collapse is not merely a Turkish story, nor is it one solely germane to the lands it once ruled. It is a history that encapsulates an important moment in the making of modern international affairs, one that still resounds in the headlines of today.

UNRESOLVED QUESTIONS: WHAT PRECISELY HAPPENED BETWEEN 1918 AND 1922?

Once secure, the leaders of the Russian Revolution were eager to portray the fall of the Romanov dynasty as the natural result of history. Russian society had long toiled under the tsars and the imperial aristocracy. The empire itself, as Lenin famously declared, was a veritable 'prison of peoples' that stretched across Eurasia. The dire conditions brought on by the Great War, as well as the precise planning of the Bolsheviks, assured the end of the old regime. Yet, in his epic retelling of events leading up to October 1917, Trotsky was careful to note that the revolution did not lead to instantaneous change. Attendants in the tsar's Winter Palace, each dressed in 'blue with red collars and gold braids', continued to go about their duties on the morning the Bolsheviks seized power. Elements of the official press similarly maintained the façade of control, an act Trotsky likened to when 'nails and hair continue to grow on a corpse'.[5]

Historians have since added a considerable amount of nuance to our understanding of the consequences of the Russian Revolution. The fall of the Romanov dynasty certainly prompted radical changes within state and society. Key pillars of imperial rule, such as the nobility and the clergy (be it Orthodox or non-Christian), gave way as the Bolsheviks consolidated power in the months and years that followed. On the other hand, clear continuities span the rupture that occurred in 1917. Lenin's forces continued to lay claim to much of the old Russian Empire, albeit under the auspices of promoting revolution among workers and peasants everywhere. The initial stages of this transition from Russian to Soviet rule were not necessarily neat. After Red troops occupied Georgia in 1921, Lenin criticized Stalin's role in imposing a new Communist administration, claiming that elements of the old regime endured in Tbilisi after being 'anointed with a little Soviet oil'.[6] The challenge of refashioning the empire along the lines of a Communist state was eased with the eventual adoption of what one scholar has famously likened to a general policy of 'affirmative action'. By 1923, Moscow had committed itself to developing national movements among the many peoples of the Soviet Union in the hope that citizens would grow to embrace Communism and abandon the bourgeois trappings of nationalism. 'We are undertaking the maximum development of national culture', as Stalin put it, 'so that it will exhaust itself completely and thereby create the base for the organization of international socialist culture'.[7] As time passed the Soviet government made its peace with other apparent trappings of the old imperial order. The building of an expansive surveillance state was largely based on Russian imperial models and methods. Experiences, and even personnel, from the tsarist era provided the inspiration for ending 'banditism' among Cossacks and Central Asian rebels.[8] By the outbreak of the Second World War, elements of imperial culture were rehabilitated and even applauded. Stalin himself saw no ideological contradiction in the production of *Alexander Nevsky* and *Ivan the Terrible*, two films that celebrated the great predecessors of the Romanovs. Even though he went on to ban *Ivan the Terrible* for its veiled criticisms of his reign, the principle of commemorating Russia's imperial past endured well after his death. These and other incongruities would lead some to suggest that a Russian Empire of some kind endured under Soviet rule.

Ambiguities abound in other cases of imperial collapse. In February 1912, Longyu, the Chinese empress dowager, conceded to popular pressure and endorsed the abdication of the Qing dynasty. The end of Manchu rule in China, however, did not mean that the empire they constructed completely vanished as well. Like the Soviets, successors to the Qing committed themselves to retaining the territories previously ruled by the empire. The affirmation, or reassertion, of rule from Beijing raised important questions over the meaning of the revolution that overthrew the Qing. Sun Yat-sen, founder of the first Chinese republic, felt more than justified in maintaining Beijing's claims to the empire's old borders. The state and people, as he saw it, had always been in harmony (or were in fact one 'race') since the days of the classical Qin dynasty.[9] Mao Zedong similarly accepted the principle that China as a state, and to some degree a nation, was born out of millennia of dynastic rule. His government openly embraced the multinational character of Chinese identity, a belief that echoed the policies of both the Soviets and, ironically, the Qing.

Iran's evolution through the twentieth century offers a more modest, but no less striking, set of paradoxes. Unlike the case of the Ottoman dynasty, Iran's monarchy survived the First World War in spite of foreign occupation and mass violence. With the 1925 overthrow of Iran's reigning house, the Qajars, dynastic rule endured for another half century under the Pahlavi royal family. However, beginning with the reforms of the 1930s, Iran ceased to distinguish itself as an empire. Reza Shah's decision in 1935 to officially change the name of the state of Persia to Iran denoted a pretense that he ruled over a nation-state comprising one people with one culture (a position that clashed strongly with his Qajar predecessors). Iran's formal repudiation of its status as an empire, and as a monarchy, came much later, with the establishment of the Islamic Republic in 1979.

Like the fall of the Romanovs or the Qing, the end of the Ottoman dynasty is an event beset by contradictions and quandaries. There is no simple explanation, for example, for exactly when the Ottoman state ceased to exist. It is entirely plausible to point to a combination of dates. The empire ended, one could argue, when its elected assembly endorsed a new constitution in January 1921. With this document, which endured as the Turkish Republic's constitution until 1924, the

Ottoman royal family was formally stripped of all powers and prerogatives with reference to the state. Further still, it was with the 1921
constitution that the name 'Turkey' was formally adopted. The 30th of
October 1922 arguably stands as a second and historically more res-
onant date with respect to the empire's collapse. It was on this day that
the Turkish Grand National Assembly voted to abolish the office of the
sultan. In doing so, the assembly rendered its verdict that 'the Ottoman
Empire, with its autocratic system, has altogether collapsed'.[10] The
decision to institutionally dissolve the sultanate, however, did not
mean the complete end of Ottoman rule. Two days after the vote, the
assembly agreed to retain the services of the royal family and allowed
its most senior member to hold the title of caliph. Although invested
with no political authority, Mustafa Kemal personally vowed that an
Ottoman caliph would continue to sit as 'an exalted figure who is fundamental to the State of Turkey'.[11] This arrangement, fatefully, lasted
just over a year. By the winter of 1924, the National Assembly moved
not only to formally declare a republic but also to terminate the office
of the caliph altogether. By then, there was no doubt that the Ottoman
Empire had come to a complete end.

Identity politics makes the Ottoman collapse even more difficult to
interpret as a historical event. Conventionally speaking, what happened
between 1918 and 1922 appears clear: a multinational empire broke
apart. In its wake, ethnically defined nation-states came into being. In
this light, the overthrow of the Ottoman sultanate appears similar to
the revolutions that splintered the Habsburg Empire. As with the case
of Austria, one may see Turkey as the consolidation of a Turkish majority
within lands that were historically theirs. Drawing such a comparison,
however, flies in the face of certain realities. Anatolia's demography, for
example, had long been fiercely debated in the years leading up to the
armistice. To contend in 1918 that Anatolia was undisputedly Turkish
required one to dismiss the claims of visibly large numbers of peoples
who did not consider themselves Turks. Despite the eventual outcome,
contemporary evidence also shows that there was a great deal of popular confusion as to what 'being Turkish' precisely meant. As late as
1922, there were considerable disagreements over the meaning of
'Turkishness' among Atatürk's own supporters.

The name 'Turkey' itself adds the greatest amount of convolution. For centuries, the lands ruled by Istanbul were never known by one single moniker. In official parlance, imperial representatives moved between various names, the 'Sublime State' (*Devlet-i Aliyye*) or, somewhat later, the 'Ottoman State' (*Osmanlı Devleti*) being the most common. Foreigners, and to some degree locals, also referred to the empire as 'Turkey', a reflection of the fact that the lingua franca of the government was Turkish. Adding further complication was the amended use of 'empire' (*imparatorluk*) in reference to the state. Exactly when and why Ottomans took to calling the country an empire is not clear. Speculatively, one may say it is an affectation of the nineteenth century. If other great states or houses – Britain or the Habsburgs, for example – possessed large empires, would that not also apply to the Ottoman government? Ironically, the name 'Turkey' also took on greater resonance by the late nineteenth century. By then, use of the word tended to be favored by nationalists who believed the country's national core or spirit resided among Muslims who spoke Turkish. Still, as late as 1922, ambiguity reigned. 'Turkey' and the 'Ottoman Empire' remained interchangeable and did not always carry an explicit ethno-nationalist connotation. This, above all, is what makes events after 1918 all the more complex. Even among the most diehard Turkish nationalists, the significance of the immediate postwar years remained something of a muddle in the decades that followed. Years after the dynasty's overthrow, some Turkish ideologues would argue that Atatürk's republic was a re-manifestation of the state once ruled over by the Ottoman royal family. The post-facto difference was that the republic was a thoroughly legitimate state, one that had been reformed and had become more modern.

To limit talk of the Ottoman collapse solely to politics, however, would be a mistake. Personal accounts from this period make it clear that the empire's final years featured things that were far more painful and traumatizing than the end of a regime. In social terms, the violence that accompanied the breakdown of the Ottoman order was apocalyptic in scale. As a result, comparatively few who lived through the empire's end saw events in a nuanced light. What happened between 1918 and 1922 was not so much the dismantling of a state as the destruction of cultures and whole communities. In this respect, one may be able to tell a relatively inclusive history of the empire's end. The violence of this era was typically unforgiving and left very few communities unscathed. In principle, this is a story Turks, Greeks, Armenians, Arabs and Kurds could and should share equally.

THE END OF THE OTTOMAN EMPIRE AND THE CHALLENGE OF SOURCES

Like many survivors of the Armenian Genocide, J. Michael Hagopian experienced the end of the Ottoman Empire as a time punctuated by departure and abandonment. He estimated that he was around nine years of age when the last Ottoman sultan was deposed. Up until then, he had been spared the worst of the horrors that had wracked Harput, his hometown. Having witnessed the arrival of refugees forced from their homes, he knew that war had raged in various parts of the country. Speaking decades later, he professed that he was aware that he, as an Armenian, lived a life that was distinct and subordinate within the Ottoman Empire. And yet, he also knew that his father, the town's most prominent doctor, allotted him comforts and security that few enjoyed. Speaking before his death at the age of ninety-seven, Michael Hagopian could recall no personal calamity that scarred his recollections of the country he abandoned. Save for an early brush with illness, his childhood years had largely been filled with warm memories. When he and his family left Harput for good in 1922, it was in the relative comfort of a Ford Model T. The opportunity to ride in an automobile made his leaving more of an adventure. 'I [didn't] have any sad feelings', he admitted in 2010. 'The sadness comes now or has come later that you have left your home'.[12]

Michael Hagopian would spend most of his adult life recording the memories of others who lived long enough to remember the Ottoman Empire's fall. Over the course of a forty-year career, he traveled across the world filming and interviewing others who had survived the violence of the First World War and its aftermath. By the time of his death, he had collected the testimony of more than 400 survivors and witnesses. Those who agreed to be filmed retold their life stories in English, Turkish, Armenian, Greek, Arabic and other languages.[13] Most of the interviews, it must be said, are very difficult to watch. Despite the passage of decades, Hagopian's subjects were still pained by the terrible things they witnessed and experienced: murders, rapes, torture and starvation. Most of those who agreed to be filmed were children at the time of the empire's collapse, a fact that does not necessarily detract from the details or clarity of their memories. Despite the violence many witnessed or experienced, interviewees often prefaced their accounts with recollections that were sentimental. Many continued to hold onto warm memories of old homes, neighborhoods, villages, friends and relations. Collectively, the revelations of the Hagopian collection offer the contemporary viewer something that most histories fail to impart. Through them, the empire and its demise appear far less abstract or detached from the present. Seeing the faces of men and women who were once Ottoman citizens allows the viewer to empathize and commiserate with the history in ways that feel authentic and real.

J. Michael Hagopian's film collection is one of a handful of oral history archives dedicated to the last years of the Ottoman Empire. Arguably the largest and oldest is to be found in Athens in Greece. Like the Hagopian collection, the researchers who first accumulated interviews housed in the Centre for Asia Minor Studies did so with the intention of documenting the horrors that accompanied the empire's collapse. Most of the records in the collection, which number in the thousands, are significantly older than Hagopian's recordings, with some from as early as the 1930s. Though diverse with respect to the respondents' points of origin and social background, virtually all of the accounts found in the Centre for Asia Minor Studies come from Greeks forced to leave Anatolia after 1922. The weight of this collective experience presents a challenge similar to the sort of limitations found in Michael Hagopian's films. Hagopian's goal was to expose and commemorate the genocidal campaign waged against Ottoman Armenians. The tragedies detailed in his collection, and others like it, are confined to those endured by Christians. The experiences of brutality and exile they detail collectively render the Ottoman government in extremely dark terms. Although one may find comparably warm memories of old neighbors and former town quarters, the tenor of the interviews is usually one of sadness, loss and betrayal. Ottoman society consequently comes across as one set along a stark divide. As an era that culminated with the near-total expulsion of Greeks and Armenians from Anatolia, the empire's end represented an unmitigated disaster for Christians. In spite of whatever hardships they bore, Muslim Turks emerged from this period the unquestioned transgressors and victors. If seen solely through the eyes of Greek and Armenian deportees, the politics of the sultan's overthrow tends to be stripped of its complexity. Other oral history collections, in their construction, also tend to underscore Turkish gains at the expense of dead or deported Christians. Records found at the Zoryan Institute located in Toronto and Boston are relatively expansive (numbering 800 interviews on tape and video), but they are similarly limited to oral histories left by Armenians who survived the 1915 genocide.

Counterbalancing the strengths and weaknesses of these oral history sources remains a daunting task. Aside from a few small private efforts, there is currently no Turkish equivalent to the sort of oral history archives found in Athens or the Zoryan Institute. To date, Turkish scholars have produced only one volume composed of oral testimony related to events between 1918 and 1922. The book, which comprises excerpts from sixty-five interviews, largely explores the history of Greece's occupation of Izmir (or Smyrna) after the First World War.[14] An even more grim set of conditions presides in the empire's former Arab territories. Although one may point to various studies based on interviews with witnesses to the empire's end, no state in the Arab Middle East possesses resources akin to the archives amassed by J. Michael Hagopian or the Centre for Asia Minor Studies. Save for the perspective provided by regional newspapers, far less is known about how local residents understood the end of the Ottoman state in Jerusalem, Damascus, Kirkuk, Medina or Baghdad.

Needless to say, the absence of oral history sources has not limited the sheer number of studies on the end of the Ottoman Empire. To the contrary, an immense corpus of books and articles on the period has been produced in the last century. The vast majority of these studies are in Turkish and were published largely for the benefit of a Turkish-speaking audience. Worldcat, for example, lists more than 3,500 books as covering the history of Turkey's 'revolution' between 1918 and 1922 (of this number, more than 3,000 are listed as printed in Turkish). Not accounted for in this estimate are the large number of memoirs, or articles in the popular press, that also address the Ottoman collapse. This body of literature, more than any other source of influence, remains the backbone of how many popular histories of the empire's end are written. To comprehend many of the tensions and gaps discussed in the pages ahead, it is essential to first explain how Turkish-language sources and histories have come to dominate the retelling of the empire's end.

In spite of a few personal accounts dating to the years in or around 1922, most Turkish-language works covering the empire's collapse were published a decade or more after the end of the First World War. By then, the Turkish government had imposed a strict regime laying out how this history was to be told. Setting the tone for how the empire's end was to be interpreted were imperatives established by Mustafa Kemal Atatürk. In his famous 1927 speech delivered before his governing party, Mustafa Kemal related his own version of the events that transpired between 1918 and 1922. The narrative of 'The Speech' – or 'Nutuk', as it was called – laid out both a historical and a moral set of lessons to be learned by each of the republic's citizens. Two main transgressions, he maintained, deservedly condemned the empire to collapse. First, the Ottoman government failed to truly represent the interests and aspirations of Turks, who, Atatürk asserted, constituted both the demographic and historical marrow of the Ottoman state and nation. As the seat of a multinational empire, Istanbul had instead allowed itself to be undermined by the interests of 'minorities' such as Greeks and Armenians. Second, the royal family, headed by the last sultan, Mehmed VI Vahideddin, betrayed the Turkish nation in ceding territory and sovereignty to the victorious Allies. Rather than dedicate himself to fighting the French, British and Greeks, the sultan had attempted to stifle Mustafa Kemal's National Movement (*Hareket-i Milliye*) in the hopes of retaining his throne. For these and still other offenses, the empire and ruling dynasty had to be dismantled and repudiated. Allowing an heir to the dynasty to stay in Turkey, as sultan, caliph or citizen, would 'never', Kemal insisted, 'simply never, be compatible with reason, patriotism or nationalism'.[15]

In the years that followed the Nutuk, an official history that adhered to Atatürk's retelling began to take on a more refined shape. By the time of Kemal's death in 1938, Ankara funded the work of multiple academic bodies tasked with embellishing the core conclusions of 'The Speech'. One of the most important forums devoted to this official narrative was the Institute of Revolutionary History. Founded in 1934 on the campus of Istanbul University, the institute sponsored the formulation of an official course, the 'History of the Revolution' (*İnkılab Tarihi*), dedicated to explaining the significance of the empire's fall and its immediate aftermath. In addition to endorsing Mustafa Kemal's version of events, the 'History of the Revolution' presents the post-1918 period as a struggle that pitted the loyal Turkish nation against a great host of internal and external enemies. In addition to Europe's victorious powers, a long list of traitors and rebels sought to undermine Turkey's National Struggle. Greeks, Armenians, Kurds, Arabs and reactionaries loyal to the Ottoman crown were equally responsible for the pain and humiliation endured by Turks. 'The Turkish revolution', as Turkey's second president, İsmet İnönü, put it, 'began as a mere military-political struggle' for Turkish liberation from foreign occupation. 'But it instantly became a fundamentally national and political revolution against the Ottoman order'.[16] It was this revolution that enabled Atatürk's rise and gave birth to the reformist republic he established.

The full weight of this government effort continued to influence the writing of history well after Mustafa Kemal's death in 1938. In the decades that followed, those who served alongside Atatürk remained faithful to the Nutuk's main conclusions in presenting their own accounts of events. Arguably, most memoirs explicitly echoed the narrative arc found in the 'History of the Revolution'. Memoirs that questioned Kemal's leadership or decisions were either suppressed or banned. Meanwhile, early studies published by Western scholars helped to reinforce Ankara's doctrinal approach towards the past. Enthusiasts of Atatürk's revolution, such as German orientalist Ernst Jaeckh, were among the first and most important writers to introduce Turkey's official interpretation of its history to larger audiences. The 1961 publication of Bernard Lewis's *The Emergence of Modern Turkey* marked an especially important moment in the validation of Ankara's historical orthodoxy. Lewis, one of the leading scholars of Middle Eastern studies of the postwar years, detracted very little from the overall narrative of the Nutuk. His reputation as one of the first Western historians to explore the Ottoman archives lent particular credence to his findings.

Challenges to this historical canon have been comparatively recent. Instrumental to this revisionist push has been the increased openness of the Turkish national archives. Over the last several decades, scholars have been granted increased access to the Prime Minister's Ottoman Archive (*Başbakanlık Osmanlı Arşivi*), which houses the largest collection of government records from the imperial era. The loosening of restrictions on the collection has led to a broader renaissance in Ottoman studies. What has emerged in recent years is a much more granular understanding of the empire's political and social diversity, a trend that has helped affirm the cosmopolitan character of Ottoman history. This new bearing on the field has allowed for historical perspectives that stand in defiance of the traditional narrative produced and promoted in Ankara. Now more than ever, it is possible to appreciate insights into the empire's end that do not exclusively privilege Turks. In principle, Atatürk's version of events is no longer sacrosanct or beyond reproach.

Arguably an even more influential source of change has come as a result of recent political events. Since the election of Recep Tayyip Erdoğan as Prime Minister in 2003, popular interest in Ottoman history has surged to unprecedented levels. Be it through Erdoğan's use of historical references in campaign speeches, or the flood of television dramas set in the Ottoman past, the empire no longer invokes the sort of negativity or condemnation often heard during the time of Atatürk. Though never going so far as to mourn the establishment of the republic, Erdoğan has often touted the Ottoman past as a golden era for Turkey and other nations born out of the empire. It was the 'excellent administrative system' of the Ottomans, he has posed, that long kept peace in the lands now shared by Israel and the Palestinian Authority. 'The First World War occurred and the Ottoman state withdrew from these lands', he has argued. 'And from that moment on, this region began to be remembered with blood, tears and persecution'.[17]

Renewed interest in and affection for Ottoman history has by no means fully undermined the old orthodoxies associated with the Nutuk. To the contrary, new revisionist histories have barely altered Turkey's educational landscape. The 'History of the Revolution' remains a compulsory course at all levels of Turkish state education. Doctrinally, the history presented in the course remains faithful to the narrative devised in 1934. For many people in Turkey, escaping the conservatism of this history remains difficult. Part of this hesitancy is rooted in Atatürk's continued deification within Turkish politics and society. In addition to laws barring any insult levied against him (a statute first passed in 1951), there is still a clear reluctance among a broad spectrum of Turks to explicitly question his dictates. The Turkish Historical Association, an official body which still lords over much of Turkish academia, plays an especially outsize role in maintaining this cultural reticence. Equally important is the extent to which Turkish officials and everyday citizens refuse to accept 'minority' accounts of the empire's end. To comprehend this resistance, one need only observe the extent to which the Armenian Genocide remains an unacknowledged fact in Turkey. According to a 2014 poll, only 9 percent of Turkish respondents believed the government had an explicit obligation to take responsibility for the genocide. An overwhelming majority rejected such a proposal, with almost 24 percent stating categorically that the government should offer no specific recognition to the suffering of Ottoman Armenians during the First World War.[18] This broad consensus, naturally, cannot be divorced from the consistency with which state officials have rejected the charge of genocide. The 1915 mass deportation of Armenians, as Erdoğan once put it, was 'the most reasonable act that could have been done during such a period of time'. Those who were exiled, he added, were deserving of such a penalty given the acts of 'Armenian gangs who murdered Muslim women, children and the elderly'.[19] Erdoğan's insistence upon Armenian guilt and Muslim suffering reflects a long-standing trope within Turkish popular history. It is the Turks, as opposed to Armenians, Greeks and other 'minorities', who endured the greatest amount of pain in the years that led to the empire's collapse. To argue otherwise is to distort the truth.

Such abiding taboos have had a tangible effect on the writing of late Ottoman history. Beyond influencing the editorial tone of many works, Turkish sensitivities have led to fierce debates over the reliability of historical sources. A scholar's decision to highlight or neglect specific historical records, depending on the circumstances, may speak volumes about one's political sympathies. There is a strong tendency among scholars, for example, to embrace the Ottoman archives as the most reliable resource for documenting the empire's end. To some extent, such leanings are warranted. As an institution that only recently opened its doors to researchers, the Ottoman archives remain relatively novel and exotic territory. Naturally, the insights to be gleaned from such a collection are indispensable for any scholar seeking to understand the imperial government from the inside.

Yet use of the Ottoman sources has served as a litmus test in other ways. Both scholars and politicians in Turkey regularly assert that imperial documents represent the final word on a great host of issues, especially the persecution of Armenians and other charges of violence. This contention has led to bitter debates over the existence of incriminating evidence within the Ottoman documentary record. In spite of the work of a number of scholars, large numbers of Turkish historians remain convinced that the Ottoman archives contain no proof of a genocidal campaign waged during or after the First World War. The fierceness of this debate has had consequences for other historical resources as well. Those who deny the genocide often dismiss the Western diplomatic record – particular British and French consular reports – as unreliable or of marginal value. Given the prejudices often found in such accounts (particularly contempt for Muslims), some degree of wariness among scholars is not without cause. Such observable flaws, however, have also served as a catch-all defense for many of the dogmas of Turkish history. How can one trust such accounts if they derive from Western diplomats or missionaries with such discernable prejudices? Accounts from Armenian and Greek survivors are typically tarred with the same brush. Rather than countenance the experience of victims, Turkish officials and sympathetic scholars have made the case that such testimony is either flawed or fictitious.

The sum result of all of these internal strains is a body of literature that bears a conspicuous set of traits. The history of the Ottoman collapse is one typically told from the perspective of governments and officials. The communal experience, particularly that of everyday people, is minimized unless it relates to perpetrators or victims or both. Save for relatively recent developments in the field, most surveys present the empire's last years almost entirely through the prism of Turkey's birth. In this light, the fall of the Ottoman Empire is merely the backdrop to Atatürk's spectacular rise to power. How the empire came apart is thus told as a series of battles and political confrontations that enabled his rule to begin. Those who defied Mustafa Kemal, particularly those who sought to preserve the old order, typically appear as traitors and reactionaries. The principal losers in this struggle, such as the Greek army, expelled Christians and representatives of Europe's Great Powers, are similarly treated as ill-fated antagonists. For all of the blood and suffering wrought by this period, the empire's end is only partly related in sorrowful terms. As prologue to Turkey's founding, it is instead a story marked by defiance and triumph.

This present book differs from previous histories in both its tone and content. What follows is not a history that simply serves to explain and elevate Atatürk's final victory. Rather it is an attempt to retrace the political and social factors that led to the empire's demise after 1918. From the perspective of the war's end, a total collapse of Ottoman rule was not inescapable. Large numbers of citizens shared the basic hope that the empire would survive beyond the winter of 1918. This belief endured among various parties well after the signing of the October armistice. The resumption of fighting between the Allies and Ottoman forces in the spring of 1919 stands as a testament to this consensus. Yet as the next three years passed, partisan politics steadily eroded all signs of unanimity among the empire's foremost leaders. By 1922, a fatal rupture within the imperial elite came clearly into view. At the heart of this breach was the question of who was to rule: members of the former governing party – the Young Turks – or those who had opposed them since the Great War. Galvanizing these separate camps were two distinct personalities, Mustafa Kemal and Sultan Mehmed VI. Ironically, despite their bitter differences, both sides in this struggle expressed a desire to preserve the Ottoman state (at least in some form). It was only in the very late stages of the conflict, when an Allied defeat seemed all but certain, that the empire's dissolution was openly contemplated.

Amid the fighting that marked the empire's final years, a more profound struggle unfolded, one that was not defined by any single moment or confrontation. Since the early nineteenth century, citizens had wrestled with the fundamental question of what it meant to be Ottoman. Officially speaking, being Ottoman had long been defined in relatively inclusive terms. Anyone, regardless of their language or creed, could be counted as an Ottoman patriot so long as they remained loyal to the sultan and devoted to the *vatan*, or fatherland. In reality, the looseness of these terms left nationalists of various stripes dissatisfied. By the end of 1918, the question of what it meant to be Ottoman reached a critical moment of catharsis. The war, in the minds of many citizens, ended the possibility of reconstituting a society capable of accommodating peoples of various faiths. In a time that featured the collapse of old empires and the rise of new nation-states, the rhetoric of national belonging in the empire began to change, albeit slowly. It is during this period that the notion of Turkey as a nation-state began to take definite shape. Though the meaning of 'Turkishness' remained less than precise, the 'Ottoman' moniker was steadily abandoned. Rather than an empire, 'new Turkey', as it was called, was conceived along the lines of other states that emerged in the postwar era. At the core of this shift was the belief that a dominant demographic majority of 'Muslims and Turks' commanded the country's future. All others who resided in this state, be they Arabs, Armenians, Greeks or Kurds, were to accept this or leave.

The struggle over the empire's destiny influenced events well beyond the eventual borders of the Turkish Republic. A variety of people who had once been Ottoman citizens, including those that lived in the Levant, the Balkans and the Caucasus, proved willing to fight on behalf of the empire long after 1918. For a time, some even favored restoring some semblance of the prewar imperial map. For a great many others, there was no going back. Events after 1918 served as a breaking point and a pretext for calls for independence or greater national rights. In the wider world, would-be revolutionaries in Europe, Asia and Africa viewed Ottoman politics in the armistice era in more ennobled terms. For them, the fight to re-establish the sovereignty of the sultan's government echoed their own aspirations to resist European imperialism. Officials in Paris and London were also conscious of the broader implications of the fight over the Ottoman Empire's future. While the Great War may have resulted in rich territorial gains for both France and Britain, statesmen in both countries quickly came to recognize that there were limits on how far they could impose their will upon the Ottoman lands. For many in the West, the resumption of war in the Middle East was symptomatic of far more dubious influences at play, namely Communism and Islamic fanaticism.

The story presented here, more than anything, places greater focus on people and places. Painfully few studies of the post-1918 years delve into the experiences of those who were not generals or great statesmen. Even fewer attempt to distill this history with an eye to the diversity of the empire's communal politics. To tell of the empire's fall without deference to local conditions ultimately is a disservice to the richness of the Ottoman experience as a whole. In taking on the social dynamics that governed these final years, this work hopes to go beyond the banalities of documenting battles and massacres. Here the available historical record, including more personal accounts like those of the Hagopian collection and others, allows for the inclusion of greater perspective on the significance of the empire's end. In doing so, it will make plain the more tangible things lost with the empire's fall.

I

'Our Policies Have Failed'

The Ottoman Empire by 1918

When the nation mobilized for war in 1914, Kalusd Sürmenyan and Hüseyin Fehmi were young men bound by very little. They differed considerably in terms of background and fortune. Hüseyin, unlike Kalusd, was not a native of the empire. He was born in the Crimea, the youngest of five sons. We know nothing of his parents or the reasons why they elected to leave imperial Russia. As a Tatar native to the Crimea, Hüseyin likely left with his family seeking opportunity and a better life. By the time they settled in Adapazarı, east of Istanbul, the Ottoman Empire had welcomed as many as 400,000 migrants and refugees from the Crimea.[1] Hüseyin, like many children of his time, did not attend school. Yet, remarkably, he taught himself how to read and write, a skill that allowed him to accede to some formal education once he entered the army.

Kalusd, by all accounts, was born into a certain amount of privilege. Like Hüseyin, he was a child of the 1890s, born in Erzincan in the far east of Anatolia. Records suggest that his family and kin ranked highly among the citizens of the town. Given what is known, it appears likely that Sürmenyan could have followed other relatives into a life of trade, as either a cobbler or a moneychanger. He instead embraced a military education and entered the prestigious Harbiye, the empire's academy for officers. Patriotism, and the promise of a better future as an Armenian citizen, inspired him to take such an extraordinary step. By the time he entered the Harbiye, the school had admitted 1,200 students into its ranks. When Kalusd graduated in 1912, he was one of only five Armenians in his class who received a commission in the Ottoman army.[2]

Both men went to war in 1914 intent on defending the empire. Their memoirs offer snapshots of the multiple fronts upon which Ottoman soldiers fought: Gallipoli, the Balkans, Iraq, Syria and the Anatolian east. Unlike so many, both survived long enough to bear witness to the war's end. By the time of the armistice, however, the two assumed two very different paths. Hüseyin ended the war in a British internment camp in India alongside thousands of other Ottoman prisoners of war. In spite of his years in the army and the hardships of his imprisonment, he left India's tropical south determined to return home and fight on. Kalusd was also presented with the choice of remaining an officer in the Ottoman army. He instead relocated with his family across the empire's eastern border and dedicated himself to the defense of Armenia, which had only recently achieved its independence from Russia. Why he chose to abandon the Ottoman army is clear once one reads of his own ordeal during the war.

To understand the things that bind and divide these two men, one must take into account the broader history they share. Both were Ottoman citizens who matured as the empire entered the twentieth century. Both inherited a collective past beset by loss and a contemporary politics driven by the promise of reform. Their most striking personal differences, their respective religions and points of origin, were representative of the rifts that set Ottoman society against itself. Their respective decisions to serve in the Ottoman army, and endure the worst horrors of the Great War, underscore the extent to which society, in principle, could overcome its internal fractures. What brought Hüseyin and Kalusd together as comrades, and what eventually made them adversaries, provides several instructive lessons critical to understanding the empire's collapse. Their experiences, and the historical burden borne by both of them, get to the heart of the Ottoman demise and its incongruities.

IMPERIAL ILLS AND NATIONAL QUESTIONS: THE OTTOMAN EMPIRE ENTERS THE TWENTIETH CENTURY

In the summer of 1893, Chicago invited the world to exhibit its wealth and sophistication. Like other great fairs of the nineteenth century, Chicago's Columbian Exposition was meant to be a celebration of every participating nation's past, present and future. Attending states were allowed the opportunity to present their histories and cultures in the most romantic of terms. In essence, each exhibit was intended to be a demonstration of national dignity and ingenuity. Japan, for one, spent a fortune recreating an exact replica of an eleventh-century temple in Kyoto. The Krupp corporation, pride of the German arms industry, offered demonstrations of their latest artillery pieces. As hosts of the fair, American participants treated visitors to a variety of wonders, such as cowboy shows, a railway exhibit and the world's first Ferris wheel.

Such an opportunity to display the nation's refinement was eagerly seized upon by representatives of the Ottoman Empire. Until then, Istanbul had either overlooked such events or had failed to receive an invitation (as was the case of the Paris Exposition in 1889). The chance to join the community of nations in Chicago came at a time when the empire was in need of more positive exposure. Evidence of the treasury's threadbare state had become glaring, often to the point of embarrassment. In 1890, a long-planned naval tour of Asia went awry when the government found itself struggling to finance the expedition's sole ship. Affairs proved so dire that the vessel, the *Ertuğrul*, found itself stranded in Singapore for months with no money to buy supplies or pay the crew. News items closer to home cast an even greater shadow over Istanbul. Beginning in 1890, the government began a crackdown on what it termed a widespread conspiracy among Armenian revolutionaries. With stories of massacres of innocent civilians mounting in the international press, other signs of popular discontent and violence in the Balkans and on the island of Crete provided still more fodder to foreign critics. Europe, the *New York Times* supposed in 1890, was outraged at the 'barbarism, the misgovernment and the chaos which prevailed in every branch' of the Ottoman government.[3]

It was against this backdrop that Ottoman ministers and representatives threw themselves into their American plans. With the help of a private Ottoman trading company, the government endorsed the building of an enclosed pavilion and concourse. Dubbed by local promoters the 'Turkish village', the Ottoman display featured a bazaar, a theater, and an ornate fountain modeled after one that sat before the Topkapı Palace in Istanbul. Government representatives also insisted upon the construction of a mosque which, despite keen interest from fairgoers, was largely reserved for Muslims aiding with the exhibition. The pavilion as a whole proved a popular attraction (despite one local critic claiming that it appeared 'less authentic' than the nearby Egyptian, Persian and Algerian displays).[4] Privately, the fair's heavy financial costs tempered Ottoman exuberance over the exhibit's success. Expenditure on construction, upkeep and other needs quickly exhausted the official budget set for the effort in Chicago, leaving Ottoman contractors begging Istanbul for more money. Refusal to invest in the exhibition, officials at home were warned, would lead to losses of a different kind. The fair was an event 'at which all the civilized nations of the world are represented, and even obscure states such as the Kingdom of Johore from the Malaca peninsula, and some small Central American republics whose very names are unknown, [were making] great sacrifices to show themselves'. 'It would be unthinkable', a representative concluded, 'for the Sublime [Ottoman] State not to do the same . . .'[5]

The fear that Istanbul would be upstaged by Guatemala was more than a matter of imperial vanity. Ottoman participation in the Chicago Fair was deeply revealing of insecurities that plagued the empire at home. Since the start of the 1880s, the government's finances had been at the mercy of European creditors. With the nineteenth century coming to a close, the Ottoman economy labored to expand and industrialize. Western investors and firms tended to dominate the country's major export industries, particularly tobacco, textiles and tea. Rural poverty grew more rampant while most citizens went without basic schooling and healthcare. These difficult conditions, however widespread, did not leave the government, or the economy at large, completely dysfunctional. Most of the empire's major cities benefited from greater amounts of private and public investment. European trade and commerce utterly transformed towns across the empire. Beirut, once a small hamlet by the sea, quadrupled its population to more than 100,000 after sixty years of sustained growth.[6] Regardless of the benefits, the commanding influence of foreign investors and creditors picked at Istanbul's pride and well-being. To counter signs that the empire was a European colony in all but name, officials endeavored to demonstrate the government's own role in growing the imperial economy. In 1900, workers began construction on a railway which eventually linked the capital to the holy cities of Mecca and Medina. Despite initially threatening to swallow up to 19 percent of the state's budget, work on the railway soldiered on with the help of a worldwide fundraising campaign conducted among devout Muslims.[7] To operate and maintain the railway, however, officials were nonetheless forced to employ foreign (largely German) engineers and other experts.

Market forces alone did not produce these hardships and imbalances. They were instead symptomatic of a broader existential crisis confronting the state. By the turn of the twentieth century, Ottoman citizens were universally familiar with the consequences of war. It was, to some extent, the central axis of all things. By the time Hüseyin Fehmi and Kalusd Sürmenyan were born, the Ottoman Empire had not known a decade without war in a hundred years. As in any country, war resulted in a recurring set of difficulties for the bulk of the population, such as conscription, higher taxes and shortages. For tens of thousands of citizens, the likelihood of foreign occupation was not a distant possibility. By 1914, the empire housed millions of refugees from territories once claimed by the sultan. The largest contingent of these migrants came from the North Caucasus (a group generally referred to as 'Circassians' in the Ottoman Empire). For many like Hüseyin Fehmi, the personal experience of conflict and flight was fundamental to how they saw the world around them. War, above all things, posed grave implications for the empire itself. Since the end of the seventeenth century, the empire had ceded vast amounts of land to foreign foes. With a new century approaching, the loss of once rich provinces, such as lower Egypt and the Danubian valley, left the empire visibly far weaker and poorer. One may say the psychological damage wrought by conflict was just as devastating. For the generations who bore the personal consequences of repeated Ottoman defeats, anxiety over the state's future was inescapable.

There was nothing organic about the conflicts waged on the empire's borders. More often than not, they were an outgrowth of Europe's own internal struggles. With Napoleon's invasion of Egypt in 1798, the strategic significance of the Ottoman domain loomed ever larger within many European capitals. After Egypt's brief occupation, Britain grew more watchful over the politics of the Levant for fear of being outmaneuvered in India and beyond. France's subsequent conquest of Algiers in 1830 provided still more evidence of the fragility of Istanbul's hold on North Africa. Meanwhile, Russia's territorial gains against the Ottomans assumed new implications for Europe as a whole. By the early 1800s, the mere thought of a Russian fleet from the Black Sea seizing Istanbul and the Turkish Straits was enough to reconcile British and French leaders in their shared opposition. Germany's unification in 1871 only complicated these geostrategic tensions. Although Chancellor Otto von Bismarck touted himself as an honest broker in negotiating a peace between Russia and the Ottomans in 1878, British, French and Russian leaders grew concerned that Berlin was just as capable of assuming undue influence over Istanbul's affairs. At times, these apprehensions led European leaders to act in defense of Ottoman sovereignty (as in Britain's and France's intervention on Istanbul's behalf during the Crimean War). In most cases, however, wars tied to Europe's competing interests forced the Ottoman Empire to cede land, economic privileges or other legal concessions.

As time passed, European hegemony and the threat of conflict bore direct consequences on the fundamental meaning of Ottoman identity. With its conquest of the Crimea in the late eighteenth century, Russia attained the right to intervene on the behalf of Orthodox Christians living in the empire. Between 1774 and 1878, this concession granted by Istanbul served as a *casus belli* for multiple wars which resulted in the partition of Ottoman territory. Britain, Austria and France soon followed Russia's lead and became self-appointed patrons of other peoples in the empire. St Petersburg's role in fostering Greek, Serbian and Bulgarian independence, coupled with other acts of European intervention, raised an obvious set of questions for Ottomans of all walks of life. How durable was the state if it could not exercise jurisdiction over all its citizens? What was the value of Ottoman citizenship if some citizens enjoyed the benefits of European patronage while others did not? Above all, was it even right to call those under European protection loyal Ottomans?

Each of these questions brought to the fore the overlapping importance of sectarian identity in foreign and domestic politics. From the earliest stages of the Ottoman Empire's development as a state, its rulers had used religion as a tool of governance. Highly practical concerns, as well as certain taboos, led to the institution of this order. For administrators, creating separate legal, social and political standards on the basis of religion allowed the state a means of incorporating diverse groups of people while limiting disturbances of the communal status quo. Under this arrangement (often referred to as 'the *millet* system'), non-Muslims were guaranteed religious freedom and a degree of administrative autonomy under the authority of their respective clergy. However, it was understood that Muslims enjoyed the full benefits and responsibilities of the sultan's rule. In real terms, Jews or Christians were liberated from the burden of military service (often looked upon as a veritable death sentence). In exchange, they were obliged to accept political and legal constraints that made them subordinate to Muslims. Ottoman administrators often took for granted the inherent precedence that favored Muslims, even though the imperial government depended upon the loyalty and services of bishops, rabbis and their congregations.

By the nineteenth century, new social and political pressures compromised this system and forced it out of existence. With the development of the first national movements in the Balkans, the old system, predicated on hierarchy and subjugation, faced challenges from within. For young and newly educated Christians, nationalism gave license to question the authority of both the clergy and imperial officials. In claiming to represent the will of the nation, upstart Serbian, Greek and Bulgarian leaders equally set their sights on other bastions of the *ancien régime*, such as large landowners and provincial lords. Nationalism's growth, to a large extent, reflected growing economic disparities seen within society as well. At a time of increased trade and consumption, non-Muslims living in urban centers often attained greater prosperity despite having limited recourse to power. Achieving national recognition, and perhaps independence, appeared to many to be a logical strategy for forcing a shift in the political balance of power. The development of these national movements was in keeping with the revolutionary waves that were sweeping through much of the world. In an era that witnessed the proliferation of national movements across Asia, the Americas and Europe, powerful voices in European politics and society helped to nurture nationalist dissent in the empire. By the end of the nineteenth century, many opinion-makers throughout the West came to consider Ottoman rule over Christian peoples as inherently illegitimate. As competition among the Great Powers intensified, European statesmen attempted to leverage the concerns of Ottoman Christians to suit their own national interests.

The consequences of nationalist revolution left few in the empire unscarred. Beginning with the Serb insurrection early in the nineteenth century, the intervention of one or more of the Great Powers proved instrumental for the success of aspiring national movements. For nationalist leaders, this trend incentivized the use of violence. As a result, armed rebellion – and fierce campaigns of suppression – became endemic to Ottoman politics. The devastation left by these killings is often difficult to fathom. Within the first weeks of the Greek War of Independence in 1821, it is estimated that rebels massacred 20,000 Muslims inhabiting the Peloponnese.[8] Ottoman efforts to crush Armenian separatism in the 1890s left an even larger wake of destruction. Although estimates vary, scholars today place the death toll in a range between 100,000 and 300,000.[9] Numbers alone fail to convey the full extent of the damage. In the century that passed after the first revolutions in the Balkans, untold thousands of architectural monuments associated with the Ottoman past, including mosques, graveyards and whole town quarters, were demolished in the spirit of 'national rebirth'. Within what remained of the Ottoman Empire, imperial officials and Muslim neighbors harbored ever-deeper suspicions towards native Christians. The attempted assassination of Sultan Abdülhamid II in 1905 represented an especially critical point of reckoning among elements of the Ottoman elite. Even though many would remember him as a tyrant, Abdülhamid's brush with death came to represent the broader Armenian treason at large. Taking aim at the sultan, as one former minister later argued, was not simply the product of 'a people's dream of freedom'. It was, in his estimation, an attempt at 'elevating a small minority' at the expense of the state and of Muslims as a whole.[10]

European statesmen also understood that certain risks accompanied the spread of nationalism and revolt in the empire. Even though artists, politicians and activists bade Christian rebels to rise up and seize their freedom, European proponents of revolution often held Ottoman insurgents in low regard. The poet Lord Byron, in spite of his enthusiasm for the Greek national cause, found the peoples and culture of the Peloponnese boorish and backward. There was a difference, as one French poet saw it, between Greece's 'past greatness and present debasement'.[11] Instead of embracing peace, European diplomats often feared that Balkan nationalists would continue to destabilize the empire both from within and from without. As the nineteenth century came to an end, Greece, Bulgaria and Serbia actively worked to subvert Ottoman authority in what remained of its Balkan provinces, each hoping to gobble up portions of territory. Such brazen acts of irredentism, many believed, chiefly benefited Russia, long the political patron of Orthodox Christian rebels. The prospect of revolution and imperial collapse in the Balkans fueled wider apprehension that the Ottoman Empire as a whole could come apart, prompting war between Europe's Great Powers. For this reason, many senior European statesmen urged what they believed was prudence. Forcing Istanbul to cede control over its Balkan lands, William Gladstone observed, was acceptable so long as unanimity prevailed among the Western powers. Wiser still was 'to avert, or at the very least postpone, as long as we honourably can, the wholesale scramble, which is too likely to follow upon any premature abandonment of the principle of territorial integrity' for the Ottoman Empire.[12] The 1914 killing of Archduke Franz Ferdinand by Serb nationalists in Sarajevo eventually rendered this line of European thinking moot.

The politics of nationalism and revolt tended to blur the deeper complexities of provincial life in the Ottoman Empire. Upon closer inspection, tensions were often rooted in conditions that did not necessarily conform to the beliefs of activists and politicians. Denial of land rights and the rule of law, for example, often helped catalyze popular mobilization around national causes. For much of the nineteenth century, Armenian leaders in Anatolia's east lobbied government officials for protection from provincial Kurdish lords who indiscriminately took possession of their fields and homes. In the absence of formal deeds, many Kurdish chiefs utilized loopholes in an 1858 law to appropriated vast tracts of Armenian land without compensation. The settling of Muslim refugees en masse instilled similar anxieties along the Anatolian coast and in the western interior. Among native Orthodox Greeks on the Sea of Marmara and the Black Sea, crimes committed by migrants displaced from the Balkans and the Caucasus aroused acute fears. Other grievances, such as the state's refusal to appoint Christians to the civil service or abuses committed by local gendarmes or officials, pushed peasants to see nationalist agitators as allies. And yet, such shared hardships also led Armenians and Greeks to find common cause with their Muslim neighbors. In these cases, nationalist politics was secondary to more common concerns over personal safety and the well-being of society.

Demography added still more complications to Ottoman provincial politics. By the end of the nineteenth century, activists and foreign observers regularly framed nationalism as a contest between majorities and minorities. Beginning with the first Serbian insurrection in 1804, European statesmen predicated multiple interventions into Ottoman affairs on the basis of protecting the rights of oppressed nations. Europe's final recognition of independence, be it in Serbia or elsewhere, was equally grounded in assertions that certain peoples constituted dominant majorities within their historic lands. In practice, assessing the size and territorial extent of provincial populations was fraught with challenges. It was not until 1831 that the first-ever census was conducted in the Ottoman Empire. Although imperial surveys grew more comprehensive over time, confidence in the accuracy of these population estimates varied considerably. From the start, Ottoman census-takers tabulated Muslim populations without deference to ethnic identities. All Muslims, in official terms, were counted the same, regardless of whether they identified as Sunnis, Shiites, Turks, Arabs, Kurds or Albanians. Discerning the scope or character of Christian groups could be equally daunting. At various times, administrators treated Orthodox Christians as a single community under the leadership of the patriarch in Istanbul. Yet, with the establishment of an independent Serbia, Greece and Bulgaria, pressure mounted upon Ottoman congregations to identify with their 'national' Churches and states. As decades passed, nationalist Serbs, Greeks and Bulgarians clashed with one another over the right to build churches and claim souls throughout the Ottoman Balkans. By the early twentieth century, it became commonplace for families and whole communities to convert from one Orthodox rite to another under the threat of violence.

Efforts to count or even create Bulgarian, Greek and Serb Orthodox communities in the Balkans reflected a deeper truth regarding identity politics in the Ottoman Empire. Since the state's founding, heterogeneity had long defined life in both town and country. Centuries of migration and intermingling created communities that rarely fitted neat groupings. Use of a specific language, for example, often transcended sectarian divides. For generations, the Orthodox Church in Istanbul claimed hundreds of thousands of parishioners who spoke Bulgarian, Greek, Serb or Albanian. There were even large numbers of Christians in Anatolia and the Levant who spoke Turkish, Arabic or Kurdish. Similarly, large numbers of Muslims spoke Greek or Slavic languages after generations of exposure, intermarriage or conversion. In areas where literacy and education were lacking, rigid ideas about national belonging lacked genuine relevance. Frustrated nationalists frequently came across Muslims and Christians who did not understand why they should call themselves Turks or Greeks. Why, after all, should one identify oneself in exclusively ethnic or national terms when other traits, such as religion, profession, place of birth or family, mattered more in their daily interactions?

No census of the Ottoman Empire ever sought to capture these sorts of nuances. As nationalism grew into an ever more potent force, population surveys drew increased amounts of controversy. Leaders from the Greek and Armenian Churches frequently charged imperial statisticians with deliberately undercounting Christian communities. Albanian nationalists denounced surveys that depicted their communities as broken up into Muslims, Catholics or Orthodox Christians (since, they believed, Albanians were bound together regardless of their religion). Meanwhile, Ottoman administrators decried census data showing Muslims as regional minorities. By 1914, Istanbul asserted that all provinces of the Ottoman Empire contained Muslim majorities. For many respondents, how one officially identified oneself to state administrators came with dire risks. Intense nationalist competition in Macedonia frequently led to acts of intimidation towards peasants officially registering as Greeks, Bulgarians or Serbs. 'Villagers', one community was told, 'open up your beautiful eyes. Don't have yourselves registered Rum [Greek], because no good will come to your children, your goods and your animals . . .' Those who resisted, they were warned, were liable to be hunted down and killed, even if they fled as far away as America.[13]

When assessing the empire's political climate during the nineteenth century, some European visitors found attitudes to be somewhat fatalistic when it came to the future. 'The blood destined to be shed cannot be retained in the artery', was one popular aphorism heard by a traveler who visited in the 1850s.[14] There was another side of Ottoman life, however, which was not bound by pessimism. As crushing as many of the empire's problems were during the nineteenth century, there was an equally evocative spirit of reform harbored in large numbers of citizens. Rather than succumb to internal strife and foreign influence, several generations of Ottoman civic leaders preached a gospel of progress and of strength in the face of adversity. Fortifying this forward-looking attitude was a wave of official measures that transformed the nature of the Ottoman state during the course of the century. In the years preceding the First World War, the nature of government and society changed rapidly. Embodying this positivistic spirit was the political party that came to govern the Ottoman Empire during its last two decades, the Committee of Union and Progress (or CUP). For the party's leaders and most devoted supporters, there was little doubt that the empire was capable of both surviving and thriving in the modern era. Their collective experiences, as well as the dogmas they embraced, gave them this confidence.

Ultimately, the CUP's fierce determination to see the empire set on the right course contributed mightily to the state's undoing. Although the party relied partly on elections and promises of greater liberty to retain power, few CUP leaders possessed genuinely liberal or democratic instincts. The party proved ferociously uncompromising and was often brutal in its pursuit of greater power. More importantly, despite maintaining a nominal commitment to fostering a spirit of brotherhood among the empire's many peoples, senior leaders tended to be chauvinistic in their outlook. At the root of this chauvinism was a virulent and ever more narrow conception of the Ottoman nation. While dissident nationalism certainly helped destabilize the empire, it was the CUP's own concept of the nation that ultimately brought it to the point of collapse.

A CULTURE OF REFORM: THE POLITICS OF STATE AND NATION IN THE LATE OTTOMAN EMPIRE

Kalusd Sürmenyan offers us little in the way of first impressions of Istanbul in 1910. Given what we know of him and his times, it was likely an overwhelming experience. In departing Erzincan, he embarked on a journey that was undoubtedly long and at times dangerous. The roads leading west were most probably rough and poorly maintained. It was also a route long plagued by bandits or kidnappers. In making his way to the capital, Kalusd left behind a life that was provincial and remote. As a stopover on the main road to the Russian border, Erzincan was a signpost for those heading east towards the garrison town of Erzurum or travelers bound for Trabzon or Sivas to the north and west. Yet for a place that resided on the way to more important points beyond, it did offer Kalusd opportunities that prepared him for his entrance into the imperial military academy. Erzincan possessed several schools that boasted curricula in line with European educational standards. As a graduate of the prestigious private Central School (*Getronagan Varjaran*), it is likely he received a broad exposure to geography, mathematics, history, natural science and the arts. To be assured entrance into the Harbiye, he chose to continue his high-school education at a local public school. Attending the state school, he later explained, allowed him to attain a better grasp of Turkish as well as Arabic and Farsi, languages that were essential for mastering the full Ottoman Turkish lexicon.

When Kalusd settled in Istanbul, it is likely he boarded at least part of the time in the dormitories that overlooked the Bosphorus straits. The stunning view from the academy's campus was only one of the attractions of his new surroundings. Just a short walk from the school was the famed Rue de Pera, Istanbul's premier thoroughfare. Like the Harbiye, the apartment buildings and shops that lined the boulevard would have been like nothing he would have seen in Erzincan. Pera's architecture, and to some extent its culture, tended to echo the tastes and aesthetics of Paris and Europe at large. Unlike most cities in the empire, Pera's nightlife was lively and exuberant, a feature driven by its many cafés, restaurants and shops. The free time Kalusd may have spent there, however, was probably limited by the rigors of life at the academy. Most required classes were oriented towards the practical challenges of being an officer in the Ottoman army. Other courses, such as military history and French, were intended to broaden the students' intellectual horizons. Above all, Kalusd would have encountered an education that was doctrinally uncompromising. As an institution that purposely mirrored the German military education system, the Harbiye inculcated its students with the belief that they, as officers, were the natural leaders of a nation of warriors. War had always been integral to the fame and successes of the Ottoman state. The empire's survival, they learned, now depended upon them and their willingness to lead others into battle. Given the political circumstances of the times, war was presented as an inevitability.

Even without Kalusd's first-hand impressions, one may be certain that he understood his experiences in Istanbul with an eye towards history. The Harbiye, at the time of his arrival, was less than a century old but nonetheless revered as a storied institution. As the empire's first military academy, it had been established by Sultan Mahmud II in concert with other ambitious reforms during the first half of the 1800s. The academy's first graduates went on to redefine the organizational and professional culture of the Ottoman military. Famed generals, including the German theorist Colmar Freiherr von der Goltz, came to teach there. In spite of the defeats the army weathered over the decades, the Harbiye's instructors and students embodied a spirit that lay at the heart of imperial politics for much of the nineteenth century. They, collectively, were testament to the empire's ability to adapt and persevere. They represented a prevailing culture that championed progress, action, service and intellect. Perhaps most of all, Kalusd and his peers believed they exemplified a new, more ardent form of patriotism. These principles, as many had it, placed them firmly among, if not above, the empire's old elite.

To fully grasp the context of the empire's final years, it is essential to understand the many forces that the Harbiye, and its graduates, encapsulated. On the one hand, there was nothing exceptionally novel about the reformist politics that gave birth to the academy in 1835. As early as the eighteenth century, sultans and their attendants generally agreed that the empire needed to adopt new methods and technologies in order to remain competitive on the battlefield. What made the establishment of the Harbiye different was the growing belief that reform could not be cosmetic. Over the course of the nineteenth century, Ottoman officials took on an increasingly trenchant attitude towards matters of governance and administration. Unlike past eras, when administrative challenges were approached extemporaneously or by committee, the new Ottoman order was entrusted to established institutions staffed by trained professionals. The inspiration for this shift in thinking largely derived from European models. European strength, it was widely believed, resided in the West's supposed mastery of science and industry. As a consequence, the power of European states appeared to flow from the application of scientific reasoning in matters of politics. In drawing upon French, British or German ideas and institutions, Ottoman reformers were confident the empire could recapture its vitality if it adopted more 'modern' governmental institutions. It was this reasoning that led to the establishment of both military and civil service academies, as well as the creation of formal ministries of state, health and education. Students of the academies and ministry officials were to look the part of more 'modern' gentlemen as well. Trousers and frockcoats replaced the more traditional robes of the Ottoman elite. Each man was made to wear a fez: a headpiece, reformers believed, that looked contemporary, while still conforming to the strictures of devout Muslims.

An essential element of this new approach towards government was the conviction that the state lay at the center of everything. It was the obligation of every citizen, not simply the sultan and his retainers, to serve the state and make it stronger. Acquiring knowledge from the West, or establishing more effective institutions, was understood to be crucial to the state's defense. In this regard, the military assumed an especially central place within modern Ottoman life. Building a modern army required a government materially capable of arming itself with advanced weaponry and equipment. It was also the government's duty to conscript soldiers and train the army's officers. Accomplishing such tasks was no mean feat. It demanded a state that was independent of any constraints placed upon it by elites or society at large.

This reformist spirit was not confined solely to officials in the capital. By the end of the nineteenth century, it was possible to find evidence of the state's growing visibility and effectiveness in virtually every corner of the empire. From the Balkans to Arabia, new government institutions assumed an ever-larger place within provincial towns and villages. Historically remote districts like Erzincan gradually acquired new barracks, police stations, transport services, telegraph offices and hospitals, all staffed by government employees. By 1900, state-run schools proliferated literally by the thousand. Religious leaders, like those who opened Erzincan's Central School, regularly augmented efforts backed by the state. Local conditions often affected the quality and nature of government services. Especially poor districts often struggled to find qualified candidates to serve as teachers or clerks. On the island of Crete, for example, it was possible for high-school students to be taught both French and Greek. At the same time, in the city of Mecca, local schools refused to teach French since Western languages were deemed to be forbidden in the birthplace of Muhammad.[15] Regardless, social attitudes gradually changed as government reform manifested itself in the provinces. Before 1800, it would have been difficult to speak of popular or public opinion across the Ottoman Empire. By 1900, both townspeople and rural folk actively wrestled with issues of citizenship and civic responsibility. Aided by advances in literacy, as well as the growth of the consumer economy and the greater ease of travel, people throughout the empire became more engaged in the intellectual trends shaping affairs in the capital and countries abroad.

From the beginning, structural reform in the Ottoman Empire raised deeper questions about the relationship between the state and the population at large. Reformation of the army, for one, was predicated on the government's ability to marshal the energies of willing young men who were capable of going to war. A variety of events, particularly rebellions in the Balkans, underscored the dangers of such assumptions. So long as national movements continued to spread, popular loyalty to the empire, particularly among non-Muslims, appeared broadly at risk. This anxiety, more than any other factor, drove officials to reconsider what it meant to be a citizen of the Ottoman Empire. In 1839, the newly crowned Sultan Abdülmecid I issued a formal proclamation aimed at addressing the state's relationship to its people. In it, he declared that all his subjects, be they Muslims or non-Muslims, were now recognized as equal before the law. In doing away with legal parameters that had upheld the old *millet* system, the Rose Garden Decree, as it was called, promised a regime that did not cater to religious bias or social hierarchy. Dissident national movements, it was hoped, would lose their appeal in favor of a new shared sense of belonging and responsibility. 'Cordial bonds of patriotism', as Abdülmecid I put it, would eventually replace the old communal divisions that separated Muslims and non-Muslims. In recognizing one another as equals, each of his subjects would find 'the means of making the prosperity of my empire grow from day to day'.[16]

The legal consequences of the Rose Garden Decree were basic but profound. Jews and Christians could become soldiers, officials and bureaucrats, professions that were hitherto inaccessible to many. A unitary judicial system also emerged from the decree, assuring that rules governing testimony in court and the judge's decision applied equally to Muslims and non-Muslims alike. Ultimately, something much more elemental emerged out of this revised legal system. After 1839, intellectuals and officials spoke of the decree as the basis of a new national identity. Generally referred to as 'Ottomanism' (*Osmanlılık* or *Osmancılık*), this new national vision offered all citizens an incentive to invest themselves in the state's welfare. Ottomanism, in principle, was an invitation for all to dedicate themselves to the empire's preservation. In exchange, each citizen could now count upon the promise of equal protection under the law. Intrinsic to this proposition was the belief that every citizen, regardless of religion or language, shared a natural affinity with the sultan and the fatherland (*vatan*). The sultan's command to peoples of the empire, as one famed intellectual declared, could not be clearer: 'Unite and Progress'.[17]

A great many challenges beset this reformist surge right from the start. Primarily there was the matter of money. From the start of the nineteenth century, the imperial treasury struggled to finance the massive expenditure that accompanied the first reforms. Matters grew worse as the century drew to a close. Ongoing rebellions and a succession of wars sapped much of the empire's fiscal strength. An even greater set of burdens came with increased Western intervention in Ottoman domestic affairs. Early in the century, Britain had led the way in forcing the government to abolish all state monopolies and slash custom duties, eliminating rich sources of imperial revenue. By the 1880s, the state verged on total insolvency, a predicament that allowed European diplomats and bankers to dictate the country's financial policies up until the First World War. All told, the Ottoman government would secure more than £370 million in loans from European investors between 1854 and 1914. The extent of these debts, as well as the invasiveness of foreign influence over investment and fiscal policies, created an environment akin to what one scholar has called 'colonization through lending'.[18] Like the governments of Iran and China or much of Latin America, Istanbul never fully succumbed to Western imperialism. Foreign creditors, however, saw to it that its political and economic sovereignty remained under Western supervision.

An equally daunting challenge to reform resided in the ability and instincts of Ottoman administrators themselves. Among the conceits of state policy during the nineteenth century was the belief that an increasingly professionalized civil service and officer corps would lead to dramatic improvements in administration. A variety of human failings, however, regularly diluted these hopes. Graft was a pervasive problem, one that grew worse amid economic or financial difficulties. Nepotism and deference to the power of prominent families or landed elites frequently led to popular impressions that there was little difference between the old order and new institutions. Conservatism constituted a more subtle, but no less consequential, source of resistance. Both the pace of the reforms, as well as their philosophical underpinnings, came as a great shock to various elements of society. Confusion and anger as to what new laws and regulations fully entailed led to unsettling results among Muslims and non-Muslims alike. The Rose Garden Decree undermined the traditional authority of Christian and Jewish clergymen, leading many to demand some return to the old way of life. Among Muslim elites and everyday citizens, the abolition of the *millet* system challenged what many believed was society's natural order. Even leading statesmen at times cast doubt on the benefits of borrowing European or 'Frankish' methods. 'Forgetting our religious loyalty in all our affairs' was a matter of grave concern for one senior reformer. In a state where 'following Frankish ideas was now the fashion', and where Islam no longer held a position of privilege, the empire appeared to risk losing both its character and its soul.[19]

It was the reign of one sultan, Abdülhamid II, that brought many of these internal tensions to a boiling point. At the time of his coronation in 1876, the power of the Ottoman monarchy had reached a low ebb. His brother, Murad V, had been deposed three months into his reign after he was ruled psychologically unfit. With rebellion and war again threatening in the Balkans, senior reformers pressed Abdülhamid II to allow for the drafting of a constitution. In giving his blessing, the new sultan sanctioned the opening of an elected parliament comprising representatives from throughout the empire. Bureaucrats and intellectuals in the capital broadly heralded the constitution's passage as a triumph for both reform and Ottoman nationalism ('Yesterday', one newspaper headline declared, 'was, for all Ottomans, a felicitous beginning' of a new era).[20] Within two years, these airs of achievement and enthusiasm gave way to despair. Russia's invasion of the empire in 1877, which sealed the loss of Bulgaria and other territories, gave Abdülhamid II a pretext to suspend the constitution and close the parliament. A harsh regime of censorship and political oppression soon descended over the whole of the empire. In the place of more independently minded reformers, the sultan appointed relatives, loyalists and palace favorites to oversee the government. Although Abdülhamid did not demur from policies geared towards making the state stronger and more centralized (a core objective of most reformers), he did so with a noted disdain for liberalism and Western sensibilities. Affairs across the empire turned especially sour by the century's end. It was at the height of his reign in the 1880s that the empire formally declared bankruptcy. Nationalist movements continued to gain strength in the Balkans and, most notably, among Armenians in Anatolia. For whatever publicity his participation in the Chicago Fair gained him, it was not remotely enough to reverse his international reputation as the 'Red Sultan', killer of Armenians and other Christians.

The violence of Abdülhamid II's reign was, to some extent, indicative of deeper rifts registering within the population as a whole. By 1900, the legal reforms associated with the Rose Garden Decree had resulted in only modest changes in terms of the composition of the imperial administration. Christians and Jews, despite the new regime, largely refrained from serving in the military or state bureaucracy. The growth of the state education system did little to dent the appeal of private academies, such as Erzincan's Central School, which catered specifically to non-Muslims. For many observers, Christians and Jews were more intimately linked to private industry and commerce (and, by extension, the West). Critical to this perception was what many believed was a deep divide defined by wealth and class. Those who served in the army or the bureaucracy were typically poorly paid. Among Muslims in various levels of the imperial services, the hardships that accompanied imperial employment contrasted with what appeared to be the ease and wealth enjoyed by Christians and Jews. Neighborhoods most synonymous with affluence and European tastes, such as Pera in Istanbul and Frank Street in Izmir, were largely inhabited by foreigners and native non-Muslims. To see a theater show in Istanbul, one Muslim man remembered, one was forced to endure a humiliating trudge across town. After the long climb up the hills of Galata, and having braved the muddy streets, one could lose oneself in the performance and forget 'all that trouble, difficulties, your hurt personal pride'. There was, as he remembered it, 'something twisted in your heart as you thought, your heart aching about the foreigners, the Greek Rum [or native Greeks], the Armenians and Jews on the other side of the bridge leading a very pleasant life in their own magnificent mansions . . .' He, as well as many other Muslims, was obliged to pull 'the blanket of his deprived life . . . over his head to sleep, only to awaken the following day to see the sun turbid once again'.[21]

Abdülhamid II was conscious of this discord and, as the nation's sovereign, exploited it. Though he had been educated in French and was familiar with European culture and philosophy, the sultan possessed strong convictions with regards to Islam and the role of the Ottoman dynasty in the world at large. For Abdülhamid, Westerners falsely demonized Muslims as bloodthirsty in spite of the violence wrought by Christian militants across the Balkans. He especially loathed the activism of Western missionaries, who, he believed, 'attributed to the Muslims all the outrages committed by the Crusaders against the people of our country and did not hesitate to slander the Muslims in every way in order to incite the Christians to rebellion'. He noted what many saw as a stark economic and social rift between Muslims and non-Muslims in the country. Christians, he argued, were always 'thinking, working and progressing while we [Muslims] remain spectators [to world progress]'.[22] The solution to these challenges, he countered, lay in unifying Muslims in the empire more securely with the state. More than any other Ottoman sovereign before him, he actively promoted the duality of his office – as both the empire's sultan and the caliph of Islam – as a source of solidarity for the nation's Muslims. Though never formally repudiating Ottomanism, his government accentuated the notion that the country's culture and national spirit derived from Islam. Throughout history, Abdülhamid maintained, the Ottoman royal family had championed and defended Muslims the world over. His august claims were not solely directed at Ottoman audiences. Through a number of demonstrative acts, such as the building of a railway to Mecca and Medina, or his support for Uighur rebels in China, the sultan availed himself as the representative and voice of all the world's Muslims, particularly those in distress.

For many citizens who came of age during the reign of Abdülhamid II, the politics of the era left an indelible mark. The sultan was neither popular nor much beloved. As the new century opened, the empire appeared no closer to freeing itself from the influence of Europe's Great Powers. Rebellion was rampant in what remained of the Ottoman Balkans. After an attempt on Abdülhamid II's life in 1905, Armenian nationalists appeared more daring and dangerous than ever. Even if one proved oneself capable and loyal, the sultan's nepotistic preferences limited the opportunities for most young officers and officials to rise in his service. For those entering the middle ranks of the bureaucracy or military, these and other signs of the sultan's failings were more than apparent. For this reason, many came to remember this period as the 'reign of tyranny' (*istibdat idaresinde*).

And yet there were aspects of Abdülhamid's rule that resonated strongly among elements of Ottoman society. The sultan's contempt for Western imperialism, as well as his acute loathing of foreign missionaries, were widely shared among Muslim elites. For state officials, both young and old, violence perpetrated by nationalist rebels was indicative of broader conspiracies harbored by the empire's Christian population. Above all, there was something fundamental and true in the way that Abdülhamid II talked about the Ottoman nation. The empire was indeed a land of many peoples – that no one could deny. But for many senior and aspiring officials, Islam was seminal for the concept of Ottoman nationality. So much of what had defined law, philosophy and morals in the country derived from Islam. The glories of the empire's past, as well as the contemporary make-up of the imperial bureaucracy and officer corps, appeared to speak directly to Muslim fealty and fortitude. For some, however, history and contemporary politics underscored the unique service rendered by Muslims who spoke Turkish. The founders of the dynasty, after all, were the direct descendants of Turkic nomads from Central Asia. The language most spoken by Ottoman elites was Turkish. Even so, like the sultan, many leading intellectuals believed that all Muslims, regardless of their ethnicity, were bound together as brothers in faith and nations. 'Arabs', as one famed commentator put it, 'made our nation Muslim . . . Now, we will assist the Arabs to be able to recover from their misery. They [in turn] will help us to protect our nationhood and advance in the path of civilization in the future'.[23]

Such contentions, however, were largely the product of debates emanating from the capital. How citizens outside Istanbul grappled with issues of nationality and administration under Abdülhamid II is far more difficult to grasp. Though the sultan lived a relatively public life, most citizens lacked access to any sort of popular press. In the absence of newspapers and elections, it is possible that large numbers, regardless their ethnicity or religion, failed to absorb the controversies that divided imperial elites. The empire, after all, was still primarily a nation of peasants and pastoralists as the new century began. According to government statistics, 15 percent of Anatolia's population made a living from professions or in occupations other than trade and agriculture by the year 1895. Dersaadet, the province encompassing Istanbul and other outlying districts west of the capital, had the highest number of professionals and non-agrarian or commercial workers, with 38 percent.[24] Though difficult to verify, it is likely that nationalist activism was similarly restricted to a comparatively narrow stratum of individuals (most often relatively well-educated men and women who lived and worked in sizable urban centers). Given these conditions, large numbers of the empire's citizens remained unengaged in debates involving identity or sovereignty. This appears to have been at least partially the case among those interviewed by Greek anthropologists after the empire's end. Though their memories were no doubt colored by the horrors endured thereafter, at least some former Ottoman Greeks remembered the reign of Abdülhamid II as a relatively simple time, one not plagued by the sectarian tensions of the war years. 'If you gave a Turk a glass of water, he cherished it', one recalled. 'And if a Turk insulted you with swear words, under [Abdülhamid] you could obtain justice'.[25]

In the end, Abdülhamid II's perceived excesses would condemn him. The harshness of his rule, coupled with the many hazards facing the nation, inspired a slew of intrigues against him. In the three decades that followed the closure of the parliament, desperate cliques of Ottoman dissidents strove to unite like-minded activists in the hopes of restoring the constitution. Some favored a path that forced him to reinstate the parliament. Others wished him removed altogether. Regardless of the strategy, dissidents inside and outside the empire believed that the state would right itself once the constitutional order was restored. This aspiration was what ultimately carried the empire's last ruling party to power. The Young Turks, as they more affectionately came to be known, did not necessarily look the part of conspirators. Most were young officers and officials, men who stood to lose everything if they failed in forcing Abdülhamid's hand. Their most senior leaders, particularly those who lived and plotted abroad, were not iconoclasts. Most held the Ottoman monarchy in high regard but believed a restored constitution and parliament were essential to the empire's future. 'We believe that to maintain order', an early Young Turk newspaper declared, 'there is no need to overthrow the existing dynasty'.[26] As a political movement, and ultimately a party, they conceived of their Committee of Union and Progress as representative of all Ottomans. When the CUP launched itself into domestic politics in July 1908, it boasted Muslim and non-Muslim supporters from throughout the empire. In taking command of the government, 'brotherhood and unity' – the party's most popular slogan – remained its official creed.

The CUP took power by means of insurrection and revolution. In doing so, it promised to promote parliamentary governance and peace among the empire's diverse peoples. These appeals roused large numbers of citizens to support the CUP's coup against Abdülhamid II's regime. By the end of 1908, voters went to the polls across the Balkans, Anatolia and the Arab lands and overwhelmingly endorsed a Young Turk-led government. Fundamentally, the CUP's promises were in keeping with the times. By then, virtually all the states of Europe, including Russia, had constitutions and parliaments. Even Iran, despite its weakened condition, had adopted a parliament that checked the authority of the shah. Despite all that happened thereafter, it is hard to minimize the joy and expectation many in the Ottoman Empire felt as 1908 came to a close. The CUP's political arrival that summer offered tangible proof that the reforms of the last centuries had borne fruit. The spontaneity that drove such broad support for the parliament's return suggested that a more inclusive politics, one devoid of violence, was possible in the empire. Voters elected a genuinely diverse body to sit in the parliament. Out of 288 members, the 1909 parliamentary session included more than four dozen Christians and Jews.

This consensus, however, would soon dissipate. Within months, the CUP revealed itself to be less tolerant of debate or opposition than many first assumed. Crackdowns on dissent, and the resumption of violence in the provinces, gave cause for fears that nothing had really changed. Outwardly, the Young Turk administration remained committed to the principle of Ottomanism. Yet, like Abdülhamid II, many senior CUP leaders abided by a far more constrained understanding of what truly constituted the core of the Ottoman nation. This tendency towards exclusion grew more aggravated as subsequent disasters in the Balkans unfolded. As the First World War drew near, there were already signs that the CUP was abandoning its faith in a pluralistic society. The wartime horrors that would plague the Ottoman Empire to the very end – be they massacres, starvation or forced flight – were already occurring in advance of the Great War.

THE YOUNG TURKS IN POWER, 1908–1914

The empire's first and last ruling party arose from a melange of would-be reformers and revolutionaries. The individuals who first conceived of the Committee of Union and Progress were largely men of letters and some refinement. As expatriates living in Europe, most were former officials who fancied themselves both intellectuals and servants of the fatherland. The party's founder, Ahmet Rıza, studied at the Sorbonne in Paris and wrote widely on topics ranging from agriculture to political philosophy. When the Young Turks held their first congress, in the French capital in 1902, the large cast of attending dissidents proved antagonistic towards one another on a variety of critical issues. All could agree on the need to reinstate the constitution, but sharp divisions emerged over whether to overthrow Abdülhamid or seek the aid of the Great Powers in starting a revolution. For Rıza and other partisans, foreign intervention was tantamount to suicide. 'The history of Poland, the affairs of Crimea lie before us', one congress member declared. It was necessary instead that Ottomans undertake their 'own reform without the intervention by the deceitful and usurping hand of Europe'.[27] What Rıza and his supporters abroad lacked, however, was an immediate means of affecting any such change.

The ultimate vehicle for the CUP's rise to power came from a parallel cohort of conspirators. While not personally given to direct action, Ahmet Rıza and other exiled Young Turks helped inspire the imagination of a young generation of activists living within the empire. The majority were imperial officials and officers stationed in the provinces. Many were graduates of the Harbiye or the product of other esteemed schools. Unlike expatriates like Rıza who enjoyed the pleasant environs of Paris, this aspiring faction of Young Turks endured the hardships and perils of Abdülhamid's reign. It was in the empire's war-torn provinces in Macedonia that the CUP found its strongest following. After a devastating insurrection in 1903, an international agreement forced Istanbul to accept British, French, Austrian and Russian oversight of the region's provincial administration. The presence of foreign officers, as well as Istanbul's commitment to reform, did little to ameliorate the violence. In the five years that followed, rival guerrilla groups left as many as 8,000 people dead in attacks on other militants and civilians alike.[28] For Ottoman officers in Macedonia, the CUP's campaign against the sultan represented a practical and appealing solution to the imminent dangers facing the region. By 1907, small cabals of party devotees began to organize among officials and prominent citizens throughout the Balkans. In a matter of months, the CUP's leadership in Macedonia assumed control of a now vast network of activists operating throughout the empire, thus eclipsing the influence of the exiled Young Turks based in Western Europe. The sudden and rapid growth of this movement tapped a deep well of enthusiasm and pride in large numbers of young officers. As they plotted to force the sultan to restore the constitution, many converted officers to the Young Turk cause drew upon their belief that they were the natural leaders of the movement. 'We are the most responsible members of the nation', one declared to his fellow soldiers. As officers, they had long been complicit in protecting Abdülhamid II's reign, 'this source of tyranny'. Now it was the duty of all officers to do their part 'in the arena of the struggle for freedom'.[29]

This explicit sense of purpose ultimately drove the Young Turks of Macedonia to take action in the summer of 1908. Over the course of several days in late July, junior officers assigned to the empire's Third Army abandoned their posts and led detachments of troops and civilians into the hills and onto the streets. With thousands of villagers and townspeople threatening to join the insurrection, officials in Istanbul were left with little recourse to stem the revolt, save for the initiation of civil war. On 24 July, three weeks after the first stirrings of the Young Turk plot, the sultan admitted defeat and announced the restitution of the constitution. News of Abdülhamid's concession swept quickly through the empire, leading to dramatic displays of elation from Shkodra to Jerusalem. For some citizens, the revolution, as it came to be seen, offered a potential end to the violence that had plagued the Balkans and eastern Anatolia. For others, it presented an opportunity for a more liberal empire, one that would allow provincial leaders greater influence over local and national affairs. Kalusd Sürmenyan, for his part, saw the events of 1908 as the reason why he and other Armenians chose a career in the military. In the wake of the revolution, the government acted sincerely and amicably towards Christian peoples, and especially Armenians. As in all areas, 'all of the doors inside the military were opened'.[30]

Senior CUP leaders came to understand their success, to a large degree, in much more personal terms. Forcing the sultan to abandon absolute rule was greeted as validation of their valor and patriotism. To achieve what many had considered impossible or too risky, Young Turk officers had proved their mettle as selfless warriors. Within their correspondence and speeches, many would frequently refer to themselves as *fedai*, a term historically associated with fighters or guardians of the Islamic faith. Others spoke of themselves as *komiteci*. Like the French revolutionaries of a century earlier, or the Balkan paramilitaries that tormented Macedonia, Young Turk activists romanticized their clandestine origins as a secretive organization or *comité*. To be a *komiteci* meant to be someone willing to plot or kill in the name of the party. Despite its victory, and its decision to stand for elections as a national party, the CUP retained its secretive nature. Over time, those most tied to its clandestine elements, particularly those willing to murder at the party's behest, grew in authority at the expense of intellectuals and theorists in the mold of Ahmet Rıza and others. This wing of the CUP would have the greatest effect upon the empire's fate in the decade to come.

The tumultuous year that followed the Young Turk Revolution proved decisive in solidifying the CUP's hold over the Ottoman Empire. Before 1908 was out, the party's candidates won an overwhelming majority in the imperial 'Chamber of Deputies' (*Meclis-i Mebusân*) and took hold of senior positions in the imperial ministries. The speed with which the Young Turks consolidated power, in turn, roiled most conservative circles. Religious figures, particularly junior members of the Islamic clergy, were aghast at the prospect of a government run by Jacobins and secularists. Rank and file soldiers, and members of the provincial elite, tended to share this disdain, leading to rumors that the Young Turks made up a party of Freemasons, Jews and atheists. Meanwhile, senior generals in the army bristled at the impetuousness the party encouraged among young officers. The mere thought that 'yesterday's school children', as one conservative commentator put it, were now deciding the empire's future struck many senior military leaders as a form of insubordination. All of these internal tensions came to the fore in April 1909 with the launching of a counter-coup in the capital. Led by mutinous soldiers and Islamic seminary students, the counter-coup leaders stormed the Chamber of Deputies and empowered the few sitting opposition members to form a new government. This sudden change of regime, however, proved short-lived. Within two weeks of the first disturbances, an army led largely by Young Turk loyalists marched on Istanbul and put an end to the rebel government. The restored CUP-led cabinet wasted little time thereafter in punishing those suspected of instigating or abetting the counter-coup. In addition to the arrest and forced exile of CUP opponents, the Young Turks secured a decree from the empire's chief Islamic jurist deposing Abdülhamid II. The sultan, despite playing no role in the CUP's ouster, acquiesced to the ruling, leaving the throne to his brother Mehmed Reşad. In the new sultan, the party found a rather pliant and unobtrusive monarch. 'To be sure', one of his attendants confessed, 'Sultan Reşad was not a man of scholarly education. He had not researched the different regions of the country, or studied world history or devised solid opinions on foreign policy'.[31] The fact that few in the royal family possessed such refinement added that much more to the strength and influence of the CUP. Until his death in 1918, Mehmed V, as he was crowned, proved more than willing to allow the Young Turks to rule in his stead.

As the events of April 1909 passed into memory, Young Turk ministers moved steadily to clamp down on sources of political opposition. Heavy restrictions were placed on public demonstrations and political gatherings. A new regime of censorship was imposed, leading to a dramatic curtailing of opposing voices in the press. Perhaps the most chilling display of Young Turk distrust came in reaction to a series of violent events in Adana, in Anatolia's south. In the midst of the coup, rioters went on a rampage through the town's Armenian quarter, killing thousands. Although the authorities would try scores of Muslims for their complicity in the attacks, Young Turk commentators charged Armenians with provoking the violence. After all, one local editor suggested, Armenians had brought a 'huge calamity on the head of the country' through their long-held demands for national recognition and provincial autonomy.[32] In the year that immediately followed, other issues pertaining to language, religion and national representation drained the CUP's patience and interest. Despite banning the formation of political parties with ethnic affiliations, the Young Turk government was repeatedly compelled to weigh in on issues deemed locally or nationally critical to Kurdish, Albanian, Greek, Armenian and Arab community leaders. Conversely, CUP initiatives meant to strengthen the authority of the central government tended to arouse stiff opposition from provincial activists. The most polarizing of these proposals was an effort to mandate the use of the Turkish language in matters of local government and education. Although Ottoman Turkish was specifically identified in the 1876 constitution as the state's one official language, the move inspired a fierce backlash across the empire's ethnic and political spectrum. To force citizens who spoke only Arabic, Greek, Albanian or Bulgarian to conduct their business in Turkish struck many as fundamentally impossible. Critics of the government's intentions countered that any effort to promote Turkish was nothing less than an act of national chauvinism. What the CUP desired, one prominent Albanian dissident insisted, was not a union of 'different races under the flag of the Ottoman constitution'. The Young Turks instead aimed to 'absorb the nationalities' and render them 'docile and common Ottomans' with no knowledge of their ethnic origins.[33]

What the CUP's genuine position was on matters of nationality is somewhat hard to ascertain during the early stages of its rule. Until its dissolution in 1918, the party never disabused itself of Ottomanism. Nor did it ever, as a matter of imperial policy, advocate any revision of Ottoman citizenship laws along ethnic lines. Yet early on, there were clear signs among senior Young Turk leaders that party members held strong views on ethnic pluralism. Most prominent members of the party were Muslims from either the Balkans or western Anatolia. Though it attracted a smattering of notable supporters who spoke Greek or who came from Arab-speaking provinces, it became increasingly evident that the CUP possessed little patience for what eventually came to be termed 'minority' politics. For some, at least, insistence upon a single national language was simply a matter of practical sense. 'To allow different languages in government', one CUP pundit commented, 'would be setting up a Tower of Babel'.[34] For others, continued demands for greater national rights among the empire's diverse population revealed a bitter truth. The 1876 constitution, one senior CUP minister declared, had failed in its promise to deliver true equality between Muslims and Christians. Resistance from both sides made such a principle an 'unrealizable ideal'. Christian reluctance to conform to the new era, and become 'loyal Osmanli [Ottomans]', was the greatest of obstacles. 'There can therefore be no question of equality', he insisted, 'until we have succeeded in our task of Ottomanizing the Empire', thus stifling 'the agitation and propaganda of the Balkan States'.[35] While it is not entirely clear what was meant by 'Ottomanizing the Empire', this address, delivered before the CUP general congress in 1910, offers an early indication of the disillusionment that swept over the whole of the party. Lessons from the past appeared to drive many in the CUP to see the continued spread of nationalist activism in the Balkans as an ill omen. The empire's future, it seemed to many, depended upon the willingness of citizens, particularly Christians, to conform and to demonstrate their loyalty. For this reason, the CUP would continue to insist that only the central government – with them in charge – held the right to enforce these standards. Allowing provincial autonomy or pluralism to flourish unchecked was to contemplate the end of the empire.

Still, before the First World War, there was no clear consensus within the CUP as to what a truly 'Ottomanized' empire meant. For the majority in the party, Abdülhamid II's vision of the nation still held true: while the empire was indeed diverse, Muslims, more than any group, embodied the empire's origins, allegiances and ideals. There were some Young Turks, particularly in positions of leadership, who believed that even this conception of the nation was not sufficient. In the wake of the 1908 revolution, the writings of a small circle of activists garnered greater attention within CUP circles. Led most prominently by Muslim émigrés from Russia, the group organized itself around a social club entitled the 'Turkish Hearth' (*Türk Ocağı*). As a homage to the bivouac encampments found among Turkic nomads in Central Asia, the Turkish Hearth dedicated itself to 'the national education of the Turkish people and raising its intellectual, social and economic level, for the perfection of the Turkish language and race'.[36] The group's main publication, *Turkish Homeland (Türk Yurdu)*, lavished praise upon the great conquerors of the steppe, such as Genghis Khan and Tamerlane. It celebrated the cultural traits of all Turkic people, from the Aegean to Xinjiang, as the basis for a shared civilization. Above all, it advocated the need to promote and refine the Turkish language as key to the future of the Ottoman Empire. Taken as a whole, the views expressed in *Turkish Homeland* amounted to a general re-evaluation of the terms of Ottoman nationalism. Turkish-speaking Muslims, the group maintained, resided at the core of the empire's history, culture and politics. For members and followers of the Turkish Hearth, recognizing the prominence of Turks was a matter of accepting reality as it appeared. The goal of Ottomanism, as one thinker put it, was to create a new nation, one that spoke and used the Ottoman language (often referred to as *Osmanlıca*). As a consequence, that 'new nation would be a Turkish nation', since Ottoman was, at its root, a Turkish idiom.[37]

Writers and activists associated with the Turkish Hearth often disagreed over the nuances their goals entailed. Some of its senior members, particularly those from Russia, saw the organization as part of a global effort aimed at liberating Muslims from European imperialism. Others limited their interests to Ottoman affairs alone. In addition to other challenges, such as money and personality conflicts, members of the group struggled early on with several fundamental issues. Though they were confident as to what constituted the soul of the Ottoman nation, contributors to the *Turkish Homeland* were often somewhat ambiguous about what precisely it meant to be a Turk. For some, it was a matter of cultural choice. If one was a Muslim (preferably Sunni), and spoke Turkish by birth or by way of education, one could be counted as a Turk regardless of parentage. For others, Turkishness was biological. After all, Turkic nomads and warriors had settled across Europe, Asia and North Africa, leaving behind descendants throughout the Ottoman lands and beyond. For this reason, one could imagine Albanians, Kurds or Arabs sharing a common Turkish ancestor. Left largely unaddressed within this framework was the role of non-Muslims. Christians were excluded from all musing about the past and present glories of the Turks. By omission, their future within the empire appeared uncertain.

Before 1912, political events offered few opportunities for advocates in the Turkish Hearth to advance their views. Beset by a variety of provincial crises, the central government in Istanbul was increasingly overwhelmed. Measures meant to strengthen administrative control over the western Balkans drove thousands of Albanian peasants to revolt. Ongoing popular resistance similarly exposed the government's weakness in Yemen. In 1911, after decades of fighting in the province, Young Turk negotiators conceded to rebel leaders north of Sanaa a number of political privileges in exchange for declarations of loyalty. By far the gravest threat, however, emanated from North Africa. Italy's invasion of Libya represented a decades' long effort by Rome to colonize the territory. Italian troops assumed quick control of the main ports of Benghazi and Tripoli, with some local authorities greeting the occupation with enthusiasm. Despite limited means of reinforcing or resupplying local forces, the CUP remained undaunted. Hundreds of officers and civilians, large numbers of them party members, volunteered to aid the resistance, stealing across the Mediterranean by any means available. With the start of spring in 1912, the Italian advance was brought to a complete halt. Young Turks in the field interpreted this early indication of success as testament to their command over state affairs. For a time, at least, the war appeared to bolster the courage and resolution of Muslims inside and outside of the empire. Even if the Libyan provinces were lost, one senior CUP officer wrote in his diary, he remained committed to the fight. The struggle was, in his words, 'a moral obligation to fulfill, one that the whole of the Islamic world expects from us'.[38] The efforts expended by the Ottoman volunteers ultimately brought little reward. Italy pressed the war beyond Libya, attacking Beirut and seizing the island of Rhodes. Istanbul eventually sued for peace in the fall of 1912. Though local troops and Ottoman agents continued to fight for several more years, Italian rule over Libya would endure for the next three decades.

While imperial volunteers struggled to hold onto North Africa, the Young Turks faced even more difficult challenges closer to home. In April 1912, citizens in the Ottoman Empire returned to the polls to elect a new Chamber of Deputies. Unlike the election four years earlier, the CUP faced increased opposition in a variety of provinces. Large numbers of religious conservatives, as well as a slew of independent candidates with other grievances, competed against the Young Turks in districts across the empire. To stave off defeat, CUP supporters staged attacks on voters and candidates both before and during the ballot. The 'election with a stick', as the 1912 campaign was called, returned a CUP majority to the Chamber of Deputies, but at a cost. Later in the summer, a mutiny among army officers in the CUP's historic stronghold of Macedonia cast still further doubt on the party's legitimacy as a governing force. Fearing damage to his own credibility, Sultan Mehmed V convened a new cabinet, one containing ministers known for their anti-Young Turk views. By summer's end, a sense of foreboding undermined the confidence of at least some in the party's leadership. It seemed the case, one former CUP minister admitted, that 'we go through one crisis after another without ever overcoming it. I keep asking myself the question are *we* ruining the country?'[39]

Events turned even more sharply with the beginning of fall. After months of secret talks, each of the empire's Balkan neighbors mobilized for war in early October. An invasion by the armies of Greece, Serbia, Bulgaria and Montenegro was something Istanbul had long contemplated but not necessarily believed possible. All of these states had looked enviously at one another as they schemed to acquire what remained of the Ottoman lands in the Balkans. But when this newfound alliance struck that October, Ottoman forces were quickly overwhelmed. By the end of the month, imperial troops had suffered two massive defeats at the hands of Bulgaria and Serbia, routs from which the empire never recovered. An armistice signed in early December all but sealed the near-total collapse of imperial rule west of the capital. Though Ottoman troops continued to hold Edirne (or Adrianople), roughly 240 kilometers west of Istanbul, into the spring, it was clear that the empire would be forced to relinquish control over Thrace, Macedonia and the Albanian highlands. Sensing an opportunity to reverse their political fortunes, and perhaps set affairs right, CUP leaders took drastic measures. In late January 1913, a mob of Young Turk officers stormed into the Sublime Porte, the empire's main administrative offices, and forced the cabinet to resign at gun point. With the government's central ministries back under CUP control, Ottoman armies resumed the offensive in the hopes of saving the besieged city of Edirne. Though the spring campaign would fail to break Bulgaria's encirclement of the city, the outbreak of a second Balkan War between Bulgaria and its neighboring states allowed Istanbul another chance by summer. In July, with Bulgarian troops now fighting on four fronts, Ottoman forces faced little resistance in recapturing Edirne. The retaking of the city, which had once been the capital of the Ottoman Empire, allowed the government to claim a much-needed victory. With Ramadan beginning at the close of the month, the sultan declared a national festival marking 'a day of rejoicing for the Ottomans in particular and the Muslims in general'.[40]

War's end, however, brought very little respite for hundreds of thousands of citizens. On multiple levels, the loss of the Ottoman Balkans was devastating. The region was arguably the empire's economic heartland. Its towns, such as Salonika, Ohrid, Ioannina, Serres and Manastir, were the homes and birthplaces of much of the imperial elite, especially the officer corps and bureaucracy. Of the thirty-one members of the CUP's secretive central committee, at least eleven were born in the Balkans (by contrast, seven are known to have been born in Anatolia).[41] In historical terms, the Balkans were long the main arena of Ottoman politics. It was where the empire was first forged during the fourteenth and fifteenth centuries. Most of the wars that had defined its greatest periods of strength and weakness were fought over Balkan towns and provinces. Now, with virtually all of that gone, the government appeared to have lost more than just territory. The empire's eastward retreat stripped it of much of its heart and being.

The human costs of the war were the source of still greater uncertainty. Well before the first armistice in December 1912, tens of thousands of refugees fled by boat and by foot for Anatolia. The exodus continued well after a formal peace treaty was signed in London in May 1913. According to a 1920 census, Ottoman officials would tabulate the number of refugees from the Balkan Wars to be 509,922.[42] The sheer volume of migrants overwhelmed the limited capabilities of government agencies. Tens of thousands remained poorly sheltered or starving months after the war was over. Amid the enormous scale of the crisis, a great wave of pessimism crashed over society. The war, in the words of one prominent editor, was 'an examination, an examination our nation took and failed'.[43] Many European commentators were even more convinced that the empire's defeat had revealed a terrible truth. When the Young Turks took power, one German editor observed, many in Istanbul believed the country would cease to be a 'patriarchally, despotically governed half-Asian empire'. It would become instead 'a constitutionally based state and a modern European great power' in a matter of time. 'That was a dream', the editor now concluded, 'a beautiful, youthful and, for the time, a pardonable dream'.[44]

Among the CUP's senior leaders, there was simply nothing pardonable in how events had unfolded. In the four years that led to the Balkan Wars, the party had seesawed from great heights to a moment of profound uncertainty. With the empire teetering on the edge of ruin, CUP agitators and theorists strained for lessons. For many, the war had exposed one point of clarity. Although the displaced came from every walk of life, virtually all who suffered as a result of the conflict were Muslims. Many of those who fled the Balkans were victims or witnesses of terrible atrocities, including the burning of villages, massacres, rapes and forced conversions. Though many of these crimes had been documented by local and international observers, the perpetrators of these acts – soldiers and fighters in the service of the Balkan states – generally escaped the war unpunished. The brazenness of the violence committed against Muslims did more than add further humiliation to the loss of the Balkan provinces. Defeat at the hands of 'milkmaid Bulgarians, Serb pig-herds and Greek barkeepers' appeared to raise important questions for the future of the nation.[45] With nearly 2 million Orthodox Christian citizens still living in the empire, could the state still count upon the loyalties of native Greeks, or indeed other Christians living in the empire?[46] Having been dealt such a defeat by states that had once formed integral portions of the country, just how secure was the remainder of the sultan's domain? Above all, were the Balkan Wars a harbinger of a still greater crisis, one that could bring an end to the empire as a whole? And, if so, was there anything that could be done to prevent such a catastrophe from occurring?

In the months ahead, the Committee of Union and Progress vacillated between defiance and conciliation. After executing their January 1913 coup, Young Turk ministers conducted a thorough purge of the imperial army and bureaucracy, forcing thousands of suspected opponents into retirement or exile. With the retaking of Edirne, Istanbul reached an agreement with Sofia to 'exchange' its respective Bulgarian Orthodox and Muslim populations on either side of their shared border. By the start of 1914, provincial officials went beyond the terms of the accord and forcibly expelled 50,000 native Bulgarian Orthodox Christians from their homes in Ottoman Thrace and western Anatolia. That winter, negotiators hoped that a similar compromise could be reached with Athens, one that would allow the empire to oust all Greek Orthodox Christians from its western territories. As talks with Greece proceeded over the first half of 1914, administrators and CUP supporters in western Anatolia took matters into their own hands. Party offices throughout the region imposed a popular boycott of all Orthodox Christian businesses. Though it was never officially sanctioned, government administrators turned a blind eye as party supporters and armed thugs ransacked shops, assaulting and intimidating patrons and owners alike. By June, attacks escalated into a broader campaign of terror which gripped the whole of the Aegean coastline. With the help of armed gangs led or organized by CUP agents, tens of thousands of Orthodox Christian peasants were driven from their homes under threat of death, arson or sexual assault. Despite denying any involvement in fomenting the attacks, government officials embraced their results. Banished Ottoman Greeks, according to one estimate, left behind 33,000 abandoned homes in their wake.[47] Once expatriation had happened, local administrators took charge of the dwellings, selling them off or distributing them to displaced Muslims from the Balkans. The benefits of the campaign, as one official put it, could not have been clearer. Non-Muslims in Anatolia's west were 'internal tumors' that needed to be removed for the state to survive.[48]

And yet the government also evinced signs that it was willing to mollify the fears and concerns of other non-Muslim citizens. During the party's annual congress in 1913, the CUP vowed to address the 'expansion of responsibilities and distribution of obligations' among the provinces, a pledge many assumed would lead to a softening of the government's position on matters pertaining to language, education and greater provincial autonomy. The Young Turk regime followed up these assurances with even more concrete steps in Anatolia's east. In early 1914, the government announced that it would institute a general set of reforms aimed at tackling long-held grievances among provincial Armenian representatives. As in Macedonia before the Balkan Wars, the empire accepted the creation of a new autonomous administration for the region. More Armenians were also to be recruited into local administrative posts, a step partially overseen by European advisors. The agreement won plaudits from international commentators, leading one Russian diplomat to declare that the plan was 'the dawn of a new and happier era in the history of the Armenian people!'[49] In private, however, CUP officials seethed. It was with great reluctance that many in the government acceded to these demands for greater autonomy. Several influential officials saw the decision as a repeat of earlier steps in Macedonia. Promises of reform, it seemed, only accelerated the eventual loss of the region in its entirety. In the wake of the Balkan Wars, the empire was now that much weaker. With the Kurds 'sitting on one side and the Armenians on the other', one minister declared that the reform plan at best promised a reign of oppression against the 'majority', presumably Muslim Turks.[50]

The July Crisis, and the first signs of mass mobilization in Europe, led to an abrupt pause in the government's conflicting domestic policies. At first, Istanbul was a hapless spectator of the maelstrom. Having never been included in the Bismarckian system of alliances, the empire faced the prospect of a war among the Great Powers alone. With history as their guide, most senior ministers saw neutrality as a potential death sentence. It was likely that Russia would force a passage through the Turkish Straits or incite dissident Armenians or Kurds in Anatolia to rebel. Britain and France both possessed economic and strategic interests in the eastern Mediterranean, a fact that likely could lead one or both powers to lay claim to Ottoman territory. Such prospects lent greater weight to those who argued for stronger ties with Germany. Since the time of Abdülhamid II, Berlin had courted Ottoman favor through investment and military aid. Unlike Europe's other powers, Germany had never sought territorial concessions from Istanbul (though some in Berlin quietly savored plans to colonize Ottoman land). Above all, Germany's military prowess was a thing few were willing to underestimate. To have Berlin as a guarantor for Ottoman security was, for many, ideal.

Though it would take months for Ottoman and German negotiators to finalize the terms of their alliance, the empire began preparing
itself for war in August 1914. A general call to arms brought hundreds of thousands into the ranks of the military by the end of the
summer. Mobilization orders extended to all male citizens, a charge
that was accepted by Muslims, Christians and Jews alike. State offices
did much to make the occasion a celebration of youth and national
pride. Strong desires to 'gloriously expunge all the abasements' stemming from previous conflicts infused the empire's rush to war.[51] Even
before the first calls to mobilize, schools and newspapers frequently
implored citizens to remember the horrors witnessed in the Balkans.
As early as 1913, geography textbooks for children had included
passages detailing the extent to which 'innocent Muslim and Turkish
blood was shed' during the Balkan Wars. Students were commanded
to remember that 'it is our children's and grandchildren's national
duty to right this wrong and to prepare for taking revenge for the
pure and innocent blood that flowed like waterfalls'.[52]

It is somewhat difficult to assess the genuine feelings and perceptions
of the likes of Kalusd Sürmenyan and Hüseyin Fehmi at the start of the
Great War. Even in hindsight, neither related how they understood the
political gravity of the empire's decision to mobilize. Kalusd, who was
already under arms as an officer, professed that Muslims and Christians
in Erzincan both 'rushed to assume their patriotic duties'.[53] For his part,
Hüseyin Fehmi opted not to take a one-year deferment and eagerly
went to his local recruiting office in Adapazarı. After detecting apprehension from him and his friends, the recruiter went out of his way to
reassure them. 'You will all be deployed but be glad', he explained.
Hüseyin and his friends would each become telegraph operators, leaving open the possibility that they would all serve together.[54]

How Kalusd and Hüseyin experienced the war eventually left little
room for political ambivalence. The cruelties both men would
encounter created, or perhaps reinforced, profound feelings of enmity
and distrust in them. Yet it would be a mistake to overlook the patriotism and shared sense of duty that led them to take up arms in
1914. If the outbreak of the Great War revealed anything, it was
the belief among large numbers of Ottoman citizens that the empire
was indeed alive. Though doubt and apprehension may have been

inescapable in the months and years before the war, there was still enough cause for peoples across the Ottoman lands to stand in the empire's defense. The reasons for this sudden rush of enthusiasm and love of country were complicated. Given the empire's profound diversity, Ottoman citizens tended to see the nation they were defending in profoundly different ways. The shared commitments made by young men like Kalusd and Hüseyin suggest that the empire's collapse was something most citizens, regardless of their background, did not foresee or desire.

THE GREAT WAR AND
THE OTTOMAN DEFEAT

How the Ottoman Empire entered, and eventually lost, the Great War is in part the story of two senior officials. The alliance that brought Istanbul in on the side of Germany and the Central Powers was the defining moment in the life of the empire's Minister of War, Enver Pasha. Just over a decade before, he was a newly minted graduate of the Harbiye. Like other officers of his generation, he spent his first years in the imperial army fighting guerrillas in his native Macedonia. Enver's early experiences of combat, as well as the corruption he witnessed under Abdülhamid II, made him an early convert to the Young Turk cause. When the revolution began in July 1908, he quickly made a name for himself as a spokesperson for the party and its cause. Cementing his place within popular consciousness were postcards printed and distributed by the CUP during this time. His youthful looks, and his avowed commitment to the restored constitutional order, made him the face of the Young Turk movement. Efforts by military superiors to sideline Enver and his ambitions ultimately proved fruitless. After playing a prominent role in suppressing the counter-coup of 1909, he ranked among the leading volunteers sent to Libya. By the time of the Balkan Wars and the CUP's seizure of power in January 1913, he was counted as one of the most esteemed members of the party's inner circle. For Enver, the opportunity to enter the Great War in coalition with Germany was a personal triumph of the highest order. After years of retreat and isolation, here was the Ottoman

Empire, now a major ally of Europe's most dynamic country. He made no secret of his deep admiration for German culture and martial elan. He understood the prospect of war with the Entente as a chance to prove the empire's vitality and avenge the 1912 disaster in the Balkans. His thirst for vengeance, as well as his personal magnetism, won him the undying devotion of officers and political lackeys in the capital and beyond. However, at the tender age of thirty-two, Enver had never commanded large armies in the field. Though he had served as a junior member of the Ottoman general staff and enjoyed the confidence of his German advisors, very little in his earlier experiences prepared him for the challenges that lay ahead as the empire's chief strategist.

Enver's counterpart in the Ottoman Interior Ministry, Talat Pasha, came into power with a somewhat less illustrious reputation. Though he also ranked as an early organizer of the CUP's efforts in Macedonia, Talat did not fit the image of a romantic hero. Somewhat older than Enver, and lacking his youthful looks, he entered imperial service as a postal clerk after a far more modest education. His humble roots were well compensated for by his drive and attention to detail. He earned a fierce reputation as a party administrator in advance of the 1908 revolution. Though lacking any military training, he openly fetishized the violent proclivities and militancy found among many of the CUP's early faithful. 'Spiritually', as one friend remembered him, 'he was a *komiteci*'.[55] With the revolution achieved, Talat was appointed Minister of the Interior, a position he held on and off for more than half of the CUP's years in power. Though possessing friends and acquaintances who were Armenian, he did little to hide his distrust of non-Muslims, who he believed were prone to treason and rebellion. The Balkan Wars proved critical in laying bare his fears and his antipathy towards Christians as a whole. In overseeing the empire's provincial administration, he was the primary architect of the mass cleansing of native Greeks from western Anatolia. Though he would deny any government involvement, he privately helped direct the CUP's violent effort to drive Orthodox Christians from their homes. 'Talat Bey prioritized cleansing the country from the population elements that had revealed themselves as treacherous during the Balkan War', one minister remembered.[56] As Interior Minister, and then grand vezir, he demonstrated even greater mercilessness in his management of the Ottoman home front.

After binding the empire to the Central Powers in early August 1914, neither Enver nor Talat expected the fighting to last long. Despite feverish appeals from Berlin, CUP ministers were hesitant to join the conflict too early, believing the war would be over in a matter of weeks. Yet as the German advance stalled north of Paris, Berlin put the Ottoman government on notice: enter the war or risk losing German financial support. The majority of the cabinet, led by Enver, acceded to German pressure, and in late October the government commenced hostilities with the Entente. In doing so, Enver committed the empire to a relatively limited set of strategic goals. The war, first and foremost, provided a pretext for Istanbul to repudiate all the old trade treaties it deemed unequal and exploitative (known generally as the dreaded 'capitulations'). On the battlefield, Enver hoped, a swift Ottoman drive into the Caucasus would help return territory previously lost to Russia in 1878. To further this cause, Istanbul deployed thousands of paramilitaries, organized into guerrilla bands or çetes, in the hopes of goading native Muslims in Russian territory into rebellion. Similar tactics were deployed later in areas much further afield, such as in French North Africa, Russian Central Asia and British India. Compelling Muslims living under British, French or Russian colonial rule to rebel, it was reasoned, aided both Ottoman and German grander strategic interests. Such efforts, which included a formal declaration of global jihad by the sultan in November 1914, largely came to naught. The notion of globalizing the Ottoman war effort, however, established a precedent that became critical to imperial politics after 1918. From 1914 onward, Ottoman agitators, and fellow travelers abroad, would work diligently to cast the fate of the empire as a matter relevant to all peoples under European colonial rule.

Events during the first six months of the war, however, quickly put all of Istanbul's aspirations in grave jeopardy. An early winter offensive against Russian positions in the Caucasian foothills ground to a halt amid heavy snowfall and impassable roads. With temperatures dipping below −40 °C, Ottoman troops froze to death by the thousands. When Enver called for a withdrawal in early January, thousands more surrendered to the Russians rather than brave the trek westward. The

Battle of Sarıkamış, as the campaign would be remembered, did irreparable damage to Ottoman forces in Anatolia's east. According to one contemporary estimate, as many as 90 percent of the troops who began the campaign were either killed, wounded, captured or succumbed to disease or the elements.[57] A second Ottoman offensive, against British-held Egypt, similarly met with defeat. After an arduous journey across the Sinai, attempts at forcing passage across the Suez Canal proved ineffectual. After briefly holding the west bank of the waterway outside Ismailia, Ottoman forces withdrew under a torrent of artillery fire and aerial assault. The most fearful news came in February, as a massive fleet made up of British and French ships approached the Dardanelles. The attack which followed over the next two months, it was generally agreed, was simply the prelude to an inevitable amphibious assault. With Istanbul in their sights, British and French troops, many of them from the colonies, waded ashore on 25 April 1915. The months of fighting that followed were bloody and unrelenting. While Ottoman soldiers demonstrated great resolve in holding the high ground along the narrow Gallipoli peninsula, casualties among them chewed up the army's reserves well into the fall. The tempo of the fighting ebbed and flowed into winter as trench warfare took hold on the battlefield. The summer's heat, followed by early snow, inflicted a terrible toll upon Ottoman troops. By the time the campaign ended, as many as a third of the 80,000 Ottoman soldiers killed at Gallipoli had died as a result of disease. It was only in January 1916 that Allied forces, after gaining little ground since first landing on Ottoman soil, gave way and withdrew entirely from the Gallipoli peninsula.

The CUP and their supporters naturally relished the British and French defeat at Gallipoli. Beyond the implications it held for the war, the fact that Ottoman troops had bested the world's two largest empires was deemed an achievement of historic proportions. As one prominent editor put it, Ottoman forces had hurled back an army of Western imperial and colonial troops comprising the 'wild, semi-wild, civilized and not civilized, the colored and the white'. 'A new phase in world history had begun' with Gallipoli, banishing, at long last, all the 'misfortune and anxiety' of past eras.[58] Writers and advocates aligned with the Turkish Hearth endorsed this view but added still greater national significance to the victory. Gallipoli, for many, was primarily a Turkish achievement of arms. Most of the empire's soldiers, perhaps as many as three-quarters of the Ottoman army as a whole, came from Anatolia and spoke some variant of the Turkish language.[59] Although prominent thinkers associated with the Turkish Hearth did not minimize the battle's significance for all Muslims (be they Ottoman citizens or not), leaders of the CUP tended to agree that Gallipoli was a triumph enjoyed by what they believed were the empire's truest sons. The struggle, in the words of Talat Pasha, was the 'immortal masterpiece of Muslim Anatolia'.[60]

This new emphasis in the CUP's rhetoric reflected a sea change taking place within Ottoman society as a whole. As early as the first stages of mobilization, there were signs that the government could no longer trust non-Muslims with the nation's defense. Military authorities, for example, preferred Armenian recruits to be assigned to help build roads, as opposed to carrying arms. By the early spring, government apprehension towards its Christian citizens hit fever pitch. It was widely believed that Russia had recruited Armenian defectors as shock troops in its offensive against the Ottoman east. Isolated cases of opposition to conscription, as well as the belief that Armenian and Greek border communities were welcoming the Entente's successes, fed the suspicions of Talat Pasha and the Interior Ministry. Anxieties in Istanbul spiked with the attack on the Dardanelles, followed by the fall of the eastern town of Van in early April 1915. With the empire giving ground, and the capital in peril, Talat and other ministers arrived at a dramatic, though not necessarily sudden, conclusion: Armenians, as well as perhaps other groups, constituted a mortal threat to the state's survival. Talat's intended solution to this problem, however, derived in part from the prewar campaign against Ottoman Greeks. During that time, his ministry had developed a broad strategy for the mass cleansing of unwanted peoples. In forcing hundreds of thousands to flee, state agents secured vast tracts of land and thousands of dwellings and businesses. Herein, Talat believed, the government had found a remedy for a number of ills tormenting the empire. Cleansing the land of treasonous peoples made the country more secure. With their expulsion, the homes and estates of displaced Armenians could house and employ hundreds of thousands of Muslim refugees, particularly those from the Balkans. The nation, and its economy, would be the greatest beneficiaries. Once the land was emptied of unwanted 'minorities', Muslims would retain a far larger stake in the country's industry, agriculture and commerce. Searing debates over linguistic, religious and national rights would dissipate. And with proper oversight by local officials, the government could make the empire more nationally homogeneous as a land of loyal citizens who spoke Turkish. These goals, ultimately, were what framed the implementation of the Armenian Genocide.

The exact process by which the genocide was contemplated or debated is not entirely clear. Due to the absence of the CUP's internal records (which were purposely destroyed at the end of the war), we are not privy to the discussions that guided the government's decisions. Recent discoveries from the Ottoman archives suggest that Talat launched his plans in coordination with more radical subordinates operating in the provinces. By mid-April 1915, it had become one governor's opinion 'that we will no longer be able to live with the Armenians as brothers in this country'. 'If we do not crush them', he added, 'they will obliterate us without mercy and at the first opportunity'.[61] The first public indication of the government's plans came with the mass arrest of Armenian intellectuals, politicians and other community leaders in Istanbul in the last week of April. Under the watchful eyes of guards, the men were sent south and east of the city. Along the road, most were summarily executed and their bodies secretly discarded. The scale of the arrests and deportations grew dramatically over the following weeks. Between May and June 1915, provincial gendarmes and paramilitaries forced hundreds of thousands of Armenians from their homes in districts to the rear of the Ottoman army. Early on in their displacement, men were often separated from their families, only to be massacred out of public view. As they were led away from their towns and villages, women and children also faced the threat of execution, as well as the possibility of rape, abduction or starvation. By the end of May, legislators in the Chamber of Deputies ratified the government's actions with the passage of the Temporary Deportation Law. In it, the parliament charged all Armenians living in 'areas of warfare' with 'collaboration with the enemy' and 'armed attacks against the armed forces and innocent civilians'.[62] Though the Chamber mandated the protection of Armenian life and property, the law allowed the seizure of Armenian lands and homes for the 'settling of immigrants and [nomadic] tribes'. By then, Istanbul's German allies had grown aware of the scale of the violence and sought an official explanation. The policy, as Talat explained 'without reservation' to a German diplomat, 'was not motivated by military considerations alone'. The government 'wanted to use the world war in order to thoroughly sweep up [*gründlich aufzuräumen*] internal enemies, the native Christians, without being disturbed by foreign diplomatic intervention'. It was 'also in the interest of the German alliance', Talat concluded, that the empire 'be strengthened in this way'.[63]

The extent of the deportations continued to broaden in the second half of 1915. By the end of the summer, Armenians living in districts far removed from any fighting were ordered to leave their homes. By then, Talat's Interior Ministry had developed a complex system for the relocation of Armenians and for their replacement with Muslim refugees and settlers. A band of territory was set aside in the Syrian desert for Armenians who survived their initial ordeal. Local officials overseeing the establishment of barebones encampments were obliged to minimize congregation (it was stipulated that Armenians not exceed 5–10 percent of the overall population of most districts). Agents tending to the care of orphans were directed to provide for the welfare of Armenian children. Talat decreed that children also be 'raised and assimilated' as Muslims.[64] As the war progressed, the scope of the Interior Ministry's deportation program grew by leaps and bounds. Between 1915 and 1916, Istanbul renewed its efforts to expel peaceable native Greeks from villages in the north and west of Anatolia. Though largely spared the targeted killings that afflicted tens of thousands of Armenians, Orthodox Christians died by the thousands from hunger, disease and exposure after their relocation to the interior of the country. Before the war's conclusion, hundreds of thousands of other suspect populations, such as Assyrians, Chaldeans, Levantine Arabs, Kurds, Circassian immigrants and many others, were forcibly relocated at the hands of government agents. A full accounting of the victims of these varied efforts, particularly the numbers killed, remains elusive. Talat appears to have kept careful record of the properties left behind by many of these deportees (according to one tabulation, his ministry laid claim to more than 61,000 Armenian and Orthodox homes after 1915).[65] Estimates of the death toll from the 1915–18 deportations vary considerably. While current scholarly approximations of the numbers of Armenians who perished range between 600,000 and 1.2 million, other studies have put the total numbers of deaths among Assyrian, Orthodox Greek and other Ottoman Christians during the war in the hundreds of thousands.[66]

Kalusd Sürmenyan was both an observer and a victim of the very worst of the wartime deportations. He began the war as a unit commander on the eastern front. In the midst of the Sarıkamış campaign, he and his men found themselves deployed along the army's left flank, outside the town of Oltu. The fighting proved fierce as his regiment pressed forward, at one point taking fire from both the Russians and frightened Ottoman troops. Wounded in the calf, he was evacuated to the rear, where he nearly succumbed to illness. With his return to duty he was reassigned to oversee the movement of supply trains in the vicinity of his native Erzincan. The first indications of the horrors to come arrived with the nearby deployment of work battalions made up of disarmed Armenian and Greek soldiers. A few days after he had helped to feed and house the men for a night, Kalusd discovered that a band of Ottoman paramilitaries had slaughtered them, an act supervised by the ruthless governor of the province. As an officer, he was legally spared from deportation, an exemption that was generally granted to imperial officials and Armenians with 'essential' skills. His family, including his wife, were not so lucky. With the permission of his commanding officer, he frantically searched for them over the course of several days. During this time, he encountered dozens of soldiers and civilians who openly bragged of killing, robbing and abducting displaced Armenians. Through it all, he worked to maintain his composure (as an Armenian wearing the uniform of an Ottoman officer, he became, as he put it, 'a lamb in wolf's clothing').[67] He eventually found most of his immediate family in a village west of Erzincan, alive but in terrible health. After securing approval to have them return home, he was accused by a local officer of inciting rebellion among Armenians and court-martialed. Fortunately for Kalusd and his family, his service as a wounded veteran, as well as his rank as a first lieutenant, afforded him an early release and a transfer back to Erzincan. Over the following two years, he and his family lived on the precipice of mortal danger. Miraculously, in spite of repeated threats to their lives and visible evidence of murder all around them, he and his relatives saw out the war in Zile, hundreds of kilometers west of the front lines. For his service there as a training instructor, he received both a promotion and a commendation. Still, he could hardly count himself as happy or at ease. 'No matter how materially comfortable we were in Zile', he later explained, 'we were spiritually distressed. We too possessed no hope regarding our survival'.[68]

By the time Kalusd arrived in Zile in 1916, there were still few signs that the war was approaching its climax. Along the eastern front, Ottoman forces slowly ceded ground to Russian troops pressing deeper into Anatolia. A British offensive in Iraq made even greater headway through much of 1915, only to be halted just south of Baghdad in late November. With winter approaching, British forces withdrew down the Tigris to the stronghold they had fortified at Kut. Sensing a moment of opportunity, Ottoman troops seized the initiative and laid siege to the British encampment. Mounting casualties, flooding and starvation eventually took its toll on the beleaguered troops, leading the British commander to surrender in April 1916. The victory, along with the capture of 13,000 British and Indian prisoners, was hailed as a triumph second only to Gallipoli. German emissaries who visited Istanbul during this time took some heart in the victory in Iraq as well. 'Had we not entered into the war', Talat told one visitor from Berlin, 'we would have lost everything. [Up to this point,] we have salvaged, at the very least, something'.[69] German observers tended to agree that affairs in the empire had improved and moved beyond the crisis of a year earlier. Moreover, as one representative noted, the Ottomans appeared to have 'almost attained national or much more religious cohesion through the Armenian massacres'.[70]

Largely left unaddressed within German evaluations of the Ottoman war effort was the state of affairs in the Levant. Although there had been little change at the front since the failed Suez offensive, traces of discontent and anxiety were visible through much of Syria, Lebanon and Palestine. A plague of locusts in the spring of 1915 devastated the interior's fragile wartime economy; by the conclusion of the war, famine would have claimed an estimated half a million lives in the region as a whole.[71] A series of arrests and show trials staged by Syria's governor, Cemal Pasha, added to the gloom that hovered over the Levant. Between 1915 and 1916, Cemal – nicknamed *al-Saffah* (or 'the Bloodshedder') – arrested scores of prominent citizens in Beirut and Damascus, charging them with sedition and other crimes. Although several were known dissidents who had entertained French overtures before the war, no evidence of a forthcoming rebellion was presented before the court. Regardless, dozens were executed in the central squares of Damascus and Beirut. Meanwhile, in Mesopotamia, local authorities struggled to maintain order. In late 1916, deserters from the front swarmed into several central Iraqi towns and expelled local administrators. In retaliation, officials executed over a hundred men and exiled thousands more north to Anatolia.[72] An even graver challenge to state legitimacy emerged from Arabia in the summer of 1916. After secretly negotiating an alliance with British forces, Sharif Hussein, the ancestral guardian of the holy cities of Mecca and Medina, called upon all Arabs to rise up and overthrow Ottoman rule. Under the military leadership of his son Faisal, this self-declared 'Arab revolt' initially struggled to maintain allies and secure supplies. Yet as Ottoman fortunes faded into the next year, the strength of Faisal's forces cast a pall over the Arab lands as a whole.

These and other events greatly influenced how common soldiers like Hüseyin Fehmi came to perceive the war. Hüseyin, unlike most soldiers, recorded his experiences and impressions in a diary (although it is likely that he later augmented his memories with observations written after he left the army). His impressions about the state of the war and the empire can be found among his earliest entries, during his deployment on the Gallipoli front. Amid the terror of artillery barrages and the threat of an Allied breakthrough, Hüseyin's notes from this period also tell of his frequent attention to news from elsewhere. It was at Gallipoli, Hüseyin claimed, that he first heard of the Armenian deportations and the mass hanging of dissidents in Syria. The government, he believed, was right to resort to such measures. After all, Hüseyin argued, British blood money, and Sharif Hussein's promise of independence, had 'deceived all the Arabs and prompted the cowardly attacks on the Ottoman army'.[73] After leaving Gallipoli, he and his comrades were dispatched to the Balkans to serve in an Ottoman unit supporting a Bulgarian offensive in Greece. Fighting alongside former enemies in a land only recently ceded by the empire was a bewildering experience for him. As he journeyed to the front, he and fellow soldiers were mobbed by local Muslims who praised the sultan and offered them kisses and gifts. 'Friends', one officer declared, 'two years earlier we went to war with the Bulgarians. For the reasons that are known, they defeated us and turned us out of our homes'. Although the 'infidel' Bulgarians were now their allies, the officer bade the men not to forget 'our old and eternal enmities'.[74] Another senior officer later intoned a similar message, emphasizing that they were serving their country as both Ottoman soldiers and Muslims. 'We are soldiers', Hüseyin remembered him saying; 'do not forget our jihad in the name of religion, nation and fatherland. Our service will please our ancestors'.[75]

By his own account, Hüseyin remained faithful to these ideals with his subsequent redeployment to the Iraqi front. After crossing the length of the empire in early 1918, he and his unit found themselves in the trenches outside Ramadi, west of Baghdad. There he endured a final three months of bitter fighting. By then, the British had consolidated their hold over much of Iraq and had taken Jerusalem. Hüseyin Fehmi's own participation in the war came to an end after a heavy British assault in late March. After surrendering on the battlefield, he endured a hard and hungry six months' journey from Iraq to Madras (modern Chennai), on India's Coromandel coast. The months of captivity that followed solidified Hüseyin's views of the empire and the world at large. When news reached him in September of the Allied seizure of Damascus and Kirkuk, he and other prisoners fell into a deep depression. After many years, 'the whole of the Christian world', in his estimation, had landed a blow 'it had wanted to strike against the Turkish and Muslim world'.[76] The implications of this struggle took on a more definite shape with his transfer to Bellary, north of Bangalore. As one of between 6,000 and 7,000 soldiers interned in the historic fortress above the town, Hüseyin was surrounded by Muslims from all parts of the empire and the world at large. Among the many Muslims from the Balkans, Central Asia, North Africa and the Ottoman interior, 'there was', in his estimation, 'a genuine warmth towards one another'. It was only those prisoners who were CUP members 'who behaved in a very partisan way'.[77] His impressions of India heightened this sense of collective belonging and antagonism. As a nation of many Muslims living under harsh British rule, colonial

India itself appeared no different to the fort where he was interned. His awareness of calls for Indian independence, as well as the movements taking shape around Gandhi and the Muslim League, echoed his own desire to resist. As the months passed, the struggle over India's future, as well as nationalist movements in the wider colonial world, nourished Hüseyin Fehmi's newfound consciousness and sustained his will to return home.

As late as September 1918, Enver and Talat continued to believe the empire could salvage some gains from the war. Though the lines in Syria and Iraq might have crept northward, the fighting against Russia had yielded genuine gains. The Bolshevik seizure of power in the fall of 1917 led to the total dissolution of Russian forces in Anatolia, allowing Ottoman troops to retake all that had been lost since 1914. Rather than send reinforcements south to Iraq or Palestine, Enver chose to press on, and he ordered an advance on the Caucasus in the spring of 1918. Like Germany's own spring offensive on the western front, Enver conceived of his invasion of the Caucasus as a final gamble worth the risk. With a free hand to alter the political landscape along the empire's eastern frontier, advancing Ottoman troops lent support to breakaway regimes in Azerbaijan and Dagestan. For propagandists in Istanbul, the Ottoman seizure of Baku in Azerbaijan in September 1918 was heralded as a moment of 'great consequence for the whole of the Turkish and Muslim world'.[78] But the glee among the CUP's senior leaders faded within days of Baku's fall. At the close of September, Bulgaria withdrew from the war and sued for peace, an act that effectively severed the land bridge connecting Istanbul to Germany. The British seizure of Damascus, and the total collapse of Ottoman control over Syria in early October, provided the final proof that the war was indeed lost. In the weeks that followed, Enver and Talat resigned from the cabinet and proposed the formation of a new government, to be tasked with seeking an armistice. With the commencement of negotiations between Ottoman and Allied officials, both men, as well as a number of other high-ranking Young Turks, were already making plans to flee the capital.

On 1 November, Talat delivered a final speech before a congress of fellow CUP members. He began his address defiantly, claiming the government was innocent of any wrongdoing during the course of the

war. The decision to enter the conflict had not been of Istanbul's making, but the result of German and Austrian pressure. The mass removal
of Armenians had been entirely justified, given what he believed was
the pervasiveness of Armenian attacks upon imperial supply lines and
troop movements. 'Evil', Talat conceded, had been done, but it was
'by no means anticipated'. However, any inquiry into official malefi-
cence had to wait until the war's end. Attempts to halt any of the
cruelties towards Armenians, or to punish those responsible, would
have been inappropriate, since it was 'a time when we had wished to
create men out of stone to send them to the front'. All of this now, he
concluded, was irrelevant. Bulgaria's withdrawal from the war, and
the collapse of the Syrian front, made the empire's defeat inevitable.
'Our policies', he admitted, 'have failed', leading him and others from
the wartime cabinet to abandon politics altogether.[79] With the conclusion of the congress, CUP members voted to dissolve the party once
and for all. Later that evening, both Talat and Enver, alongside a
handful of other notable senior officials, left aboard a German tor-
pedo boat bound for exile. What was to come of the empire, ultimately,
was left to others to decide.

2

'A Comedy of Mutual Distrust'[1]

The Politics of Surrender and Occupation

When tasked with finding a peace in harmony with the president's designs, American Secretary of State Robert Lansing harbored more than a modicum of dread. The source of his unease was the fundamental notion of 'national self-determination'. Encouraging subject nations to seek recognition and independence was central to President Woodrow Wilson's agenda at the Versailles peace conference. For Wilson, the national enmity that drove Gavrilo Princip to kill Archduke Franz Ferdinand was the match that had ignited the continent in 1914. To set Europe aright, he deemed it sensible to settle all of Central Europe's 'national questions' at the 1919 conference, thus eliminating a critical source of animus and instability. Lansing foresaw a very different set of outcomes. National self-determination, he privately confided, was bound to trigger a tidal wave of upheaval. 'What effect', he mused, 'will it have on the Irish, the Indians, the Egyptians and the nationalists among the Boers? Will it not breed discontent, disorder and rebellion?' These and other questions raised an obvious, troubling conclusion. National self-determination was a phrase 'simply loaded with dynamite', something that would dash hopes and cost thousands of lives.[2]

As talks at Versailles commenced, negotiators were presented with a deluge of petitions and queries regarding the status of territories that had belonged to each of the war's combatants. Among the many places in need of redress were the environs of Izmir or Smyrna, the main Ottoman port on the Aegean. Greece, a late addition to the Allies, held an interest in the city, as well as the surrounding countryside. Situated at the heart of the ancient Greek lands of Ionia, the district housed tens of thousands of Orthodox Christians. For Athens, history and demographics, as well as what they charged was the harshness of Ottoman rule, demanded the region be awarded to Greece. Officials in the British Foreign Office acknowledged these desires but remained wary of their repercussions. Before the coming of spring 1919, at least some in Whitehall sought alternative opinions on the matter. In performing what they believed was their due diligence, officials entertained the perspectives of private British citizens who lived in Izmir.

By early March 1919, officials in London received correspondence from two of Smyrna's long-time residents. Erwin Hansen Freshfield submitted his assessment of the city's postwar status as one of its 'principal private English landlords'. As such, he cast a great deal of doubt upon Izmir's annexation by Greece. The problems reigning over the town were severe. Agricultural production had been stagnant for many years, a fact made worse by the violence and loss of population witnessed during the war. Izmir, in his estimation, required a more capable and professional administration if good order and economic activity were to be restored. To that end, neither Greece nor Italy – the other aspirant to Smyrna – appeared to possess such a capacity. What was needed along Anatolia's Aegean coast, as far as Freshfield was concerned, was a 'special administration' akin to the British protectorate of Egypt. Any Greek attempt at annexing Izmir's countryside further depended upon the pacification of the provincial Muslim majority. That challenge, however, could be mitigated with depopulation. 'I might add', he commented, that 'past experience shows that where Greeks enter into and administer a country populated by Mahomedans[,] the Mahomedans migrate'.[3]

The second letter received in early March reinforced these points with greater detail and conviction. Lieutenant Langdon Rees was the scion of another prominent merchant family, one that had lived and worked in Izmir for three generations. Like Erwin Freshfield, he extolled the potential wealth of the town. Smyrna and its surrounding districts were among the finest parts of the Ottoman Empire: 'White Man's country', in Rees's words. He acknowledged that it was neither practical nor likely that the town and its outlying districts would remain in Istanbul's hands. All signs appeared to point towards partition, a likelihood made possible by years of poor Ottoman administration. Greece's designs upon the region were undeniable, but he warned that such a turn would lead to disaster. Muslims would never accept rule from Athens. As a state 'lacking the necessary colonial experience', Greek rule would face 'continual troubles and disorder throughout the country'. Like Freshfield, he endorsed an Egyptian model of administration. Only a 'strong Power', be it Britain, France, the United States or all three combined, was capable of delivering good government and 'fair play for all'. These were not simply his views, Rees stated, but those of other British and French expatriates in town as well.[4]

In the end, neither of these surveys had much bearing upon British policy. In spite of widespread misgivings within his government, Prime Minister David Lloyd George was adamant in his support for Greece's claims in Anatolia. Woodrow Wilson and French Prime Minister Georges Clemenceau also tended to sympathize with Athens and its interests in Izmir. Only Italy, which occupied Rhodes and other islands in the Aegean, stood opposed to Greece. As the Allies deliberated, affairs in Izmir and the surrounding province of Aydın continued to deteriorate sharply. Reports of isolated killings bolstered rumors of impending massacres beyond the town. Food shortages and the return of refugees added further complications to daily life. The perilousness of the situation in Smyrna was visible in other parts of the country as well. By January 1919, French and British troops had pressed beyond the armistice line and occupied the towns of Adana, Antep and Marash. The arrival of thousands of Armenian refugees, including many who had returned as soldiers in the French occupying army, further heightened tensions in the region. Similar anxieties were visible along stretches of the Black Sea coast. With contingents of British troops garrisoning key ports there, and activists clamoring for Greek annexation, communities throughout Anatolia's north braced themselves for the worst.

Perhaps the greatest source of instability was the uncertain state of the Ottoman government itself. With the signing of the armistice in October 1918, politics in the capital was thrown into chaos. The dissolution of the CUP, and the flight of its senior leaders, created a void at the core of the administration. As winter set in, a great host of actors jockeyed for power in Istanbul. Emerging from this contest was a fragile coalition led in part by the new sultan, Mehmed VI Vahideddin. Amid the flurry of challenges facing the future of the empire, the sultan and his supporters focused much of their attention upon what remained of the CUP. Before the opening of spring, hundreds of Young Turks, including noted members of the wartime government, were arrested under charges of corruption and murder. This dramatic rupture within the Ottoman political establishment reverberated throughout what remained of the empire. Across Anatolia, divisions resulting from the war and the CUP's conduct divided local elites and communities at large. For many former Young Turks, the imperial government was as grave a threat to the country's future as any foreign power.

Nevertheless, many citizens were not planning upon the empire's immediate collapse. For the bulk of the population, other concerns, such as starvation, crime and displacement, outranked more abstract questions regarding the country's future. These and other strains made the winter of 1918–19 an exceedingly hard time.

MAKING PEACE:
THE OTTOMAN EMPIRE
IN THE SHADOW OF VERSAILLES

Eleftherios Venizelos was a man who left few people with a dull impression. At the time of the Paris peace conference, he was fifty-five years old, making him younger than Woodrow Wilson, Georges Clemenceau and David Lloyd George. Yet his life story, which he told with alacrity, was arguably far richer and more extraordinary than that of any other senior statesman present at Versailles. He was born on the island of Crete, then an increasingly restless province of the Ottoman Empire. His name Eleftherios (meaning 'free man' in Greek) reflected his pedigree as the descendant of rebels. His grandfather and father prided themselves on being revolutionaries in the service of Greek independence. After studying law in Athens, his political ambitions led him to return to Crete, where he helped lead an anti-Ottoman insurrection in 1897. His reputation as an ardent nationalist and advocate

for reform ultimately catapulted him to the heights of the Greek kingdom. After his election as Prime Minister in 1910, Venizelos oversaw
the country's participation in the Balkan Wars, which resulted in the
acquisition of much of Ottoman Macedonia. With the outbreak of the
Great War in 1914, he advocated Greece's entrance into the conflict on
the side of the Entente despite the country's initial policy of neutrality.
The utility of such an alliance, to his thinking, was clear: an Allied victory would allow for the acquisition of more Ottoman land. A larger,
greater Greece was destined to be a dominant Mediterranean state. Yet
conservatives, particularly the country's reigning monarch, King Constantine, opposed Venizelos, leading to the dissolution of the Greek
government in 1915. Undaunted, and with the backing of both Britain
and France, Venizelos muscled his way back into power at the head of
nationalist factions within the Greek army. By the summer of 1917, his
allies in the military secured full control of the country and forced
Constantine to abdicate the throne in favor of his son, Alexander.
Greece's subsequent involvement in the war, followed by the Allied
victory in 1918, eliminated any remaining doubts as to the weight and
influence Venizelos bore. Upon his arrival in Paris, he delighted in
entertaining other attendees with the story of his unlikely rise to power.
Guests marveled as he told of how he learned English by reading *The
Times* of London while hiding from Ottoman troops in Crete's mountains. He openly delighted in his ability to recite verses from Homer or
relate his impressions of other leaders from the Balkans. The whole of
Venizelos, as one British diplomat put it, 'gives us a strange medley of
charm, brigandage, welt-politik, patriotism, courage, literature', all
packed in a 'large muscular smiling man'.[5]

With the victors of the Great War assembled in Paris, Venizelos
used his charisma and newfound status to advance his aspirations to
make Greece a regional power. His first formal opportunity to make
his case before the conference came in early February 1919. Armed
with a detailed memorandum outlining his government's interests,
Venizelos laid out an ambitious vision for what he believed were
Greece's just claims over Ottoman territory. Population statistics, he
maintained, served as the most reliable indicator for changes to the
empire's borders. More than 2.5 million Greeks were spread out
across Ottoman Thrace and Anatolia. Though not always comprising

outright majorities (such as in Constantinople), each and every enclave inhabited by Greek Orthodox Christians was evidence of an ancient birthright. There were some places, Venizelos admitted, where Athens was willing to abandon certain claims. Trabzon, Anatolia's largest Black Sea port, as well as Adana in the south, appeared more deserving of rule under an Armenian state (despite, he argued, the presence of tens of thousands of Greeks in both districts). Smyrna, along with the rest of the hinterland facing the Aegean, was another matter. Statistical data, he maintained, demonstrated clear Greek majorities all along Anatolia's western periphery. These realities, as well as the horrors of the war years, made any return to the old status quo simply inconceivable. 'After the tragic experience of a whole century', Venizelos declared, 'it is impossible to entrust the future of the Christian populations of the Ottoman Empire to fresh attempts at reform'. No matter what Istanbul promised in terms of remediation or good government, history, he contended, was apt to repeat itself. The maintenance of Ottoman sovereignty in Thrace and western Anatolia was bound to lead to 'massacring on a vast scale the Christians who were to benefit' from any change to imperial law.[6]

Venizelos advanced his claims on Ottoman territory knowing that the Greeks were not alone in demanding compensation. By the opening of the Paris peace conference, it was widely understood that any settlement concerning Istanbul had to address Armenian interests. Long before any armistice, Armenian suffering had registered strongly with European and American observers. With the Allies' sympathy at their backs, two representatives arrived in Paris to deliver a general appeal on behalf of both the Republic of Armenia and the Armenian diaspora at large. Like Venizelos, the Armenian delegation invoked both the past and reason in laying its own demands before the conference. 'The history of Armenia', they asserted, 'has been one of continuous, obstinate and unequal battles to defend its individuality, its culture and its faith against powerful enemies and races which attacked it on all sides'.[7] Their deliverance from what they called an 'alien yoke' was only half achieved with the end of the war. The establishment of the Armenian Republic in the wake of the Russian Revolution created a state that accounted for only a part of the lands historically inhabited by Armenian majorities. Armed with their own array of maps and population statistics, the delegation put forth a bold vision for a large Armenian state occupying much of eastern and central Anatolia. Though willing to admit that much of this territory was also home to native Turks and Kurds, the delegation posed that Armenian majorities had endured in the region until the deportations of 1915. Awarding these lands to the Armenians, they argued, would do more than redeem a people long subjugated and brutalized. Liberating the full breadth of their ancestral lands from Ottoman rule would allow an industrious and vibrant Christian nation to finally blossom. 'The time has indeed arrived', the representatives concluded, 'for the Armenians to be given the opportunity to put their talents and their abilities at the disposal of their own country'.[8]

Also present in Paris was the Arab leader Emir Faisal. As the commander of Arab rebel forces in the Levant, Faisal did not come to France as an official envoy of any state. Nevertheless, as a guest of Great Britain, he did his best to present himself as every bit the regal statesman. Arriving at the conference clad in flowing silk robes, he was, as one participant put it, 'one of the picturesque figures' of the talks.[9] Unlike those representing Greek or Armenian interests, Faisal appeared before Allied negotiators without having to make the case against the resumption of Ottoman rule. The British conquest of Mesopotamia and the Levant all but guaranteed an end to Istanbul's hold over the Arab lands. Instead, as head of an aspiring government sitting in Damascus, he attended talks in Versailles in the hopes of securing some sort of state for Arabs. For Faisal, validating his people's desire for independence did not require census data. All of the Ottoman territories south of Anatolia, he maintained, were Arab in race and culture. And, like Armenians and Greeks, Arabs too could claim to have been subjected to oppression under the Ottoman government. To grant a unified Arab nation its independence would not only comply with the principle of self-determination, it would also stand in recognition of 'our splendid past', as he put it, and 'the tenacity with which our race has for 600 years resisted Turkish attempts to absorb us ...' Faisal, however, was willing to concede a certain amount of foreign control over Palestine. In recognition of British support for a Jewish homeland there, he offered to accept 'the effective super-position of a great trustee' in order to maintain a fair administration between Arabs and Jews. 'The Jews are very close to the Arabs in blood', he assured the Allied Powers, 'and there is no conflict of character between the two races. In principles we are absolutely at one'.[10]

Faisal presented his appeal to the supreme council of victors knowing that his position was likely tenuous. Though he had led a revolt in the name of all Ottoman Arabs, he did not attract the admiration or loyalty of every citizen living in the Levant and Mesopotamia. With the war over, the opinions of provincial leaders in Beirut, Aleppo, Baghdad and Jerusalem varied with regards to the future. Faisal's relationship with British and French occupation authorities posed an especially daunting challenge. His appearance in Paris alone was an act of desperate political negotiation. For much of the winter, France had resisted British efforts to invite Faisal as an official representative. Despite his proud assertions before the conference, Faisal understood that he would likely become the vassal of one empire or another. The Ottoman provinces of Syria and Lebanon had long been the focus of France's imperial ambitions. Despite the comparatively limited role played by the French in the Allied campaign to take the Levant, they loudly embraced the victory in 1918 as a vindication of their interests in the eastern Mediterranean. It was equally unlikely that the British would afford Faisal any real independence. Despite the backing of Faisal by T. E. Lawrence (whose exploits in Arabia made him a celebrity), Lloyd George and his cabinet were just as committed to retaining British interests in Palestine and Iraq. Woodrow Wilson proved willing to listen, but America alone was unlikely to stand as guarantor to a united Arab kingdom.

Faisal's predicament was emblematic of the broader politics of Versailles. In principle, settling 'national questions' was broadly seen as inseparable from the task of sealing a peace between the warring powers. Before the opening of spring 1919, Paris played host to delegations from throughout the world, with each asking for their sovereign rights. China and Czechoslovakia both sent representatives to Versailles in the hopes of achieving national and territorial recognition. Other governments, such as those of Albania and Iran, were not allowed an official hearing. Emir Faisal was but one of a handful of welcomed participants who did not represent a formal state. A great many others, including petitioners from Ireland, Tunisia and French Indochina, were largely ignored as proceedings began. Among all those who placed their faith in the negotiations, few had any illusions as to the main dynamics governing the whole affair. The wider imperial interests of the war's victors, most notably Britain and France, would likely decide the final terms of any agreement. The power most apt to entertain the appeals of subject peoples was the United States. Months before the talks began, Wilson's insistence upon self-determination had forced London and Paris to rein in some of their territorial ambitions. Rather than redistribute German and Ottoman imperial lands as outright spoils, the victors instead agreed to serve as trustees over 'mandate' states which eventually would be granted independence. For the peoples of the Ottoman Empire, many anticipated that much, if not all, of the sultan's lands would become mandates under the steward-ship of one power or another. The principal challenge at Versailles was how the powers would arrive at such an agreement.

As the state most responsible for securing Istanbul's surrender, Great Britain possessed a unique advantage in redrawing the Otto-man map. The sheer presence of thousands of troops deployed across the region seemed to ensure the construction of mandates tailored to London's interests. By the spring of 1919, British officials were already exercising considerable influence in the formation of local administra-tions in Basra, Baghdad and Jerusalem. British patronage underwrote Sharif Hussein's claim that he was the true king of western Arabia. France, however, was a force not to be denied. Throughout the war, Paris remained undeterred in its insistence upon occupying territories inland from the Levantine coast. In addition to the lands of greater Syria, French interests also extended into Cilicia, north of the original armistice line, inside what was still generally recognized sovereign Ottoman territory. Each of these claims clashed with British backing for Faisal's Arab state as well as London's endorsement of a Jewish homeland in Palestine.

Then there were the fickle demands of the United States. Woodrow Wilson entered the Great War without ever declaring open hostilities towards the Ottoman Empire. While the American public tended to be sympathetic to the plight of Ottoman Christians, many in the Wil-son administration believed any campaign beyond the western front was too risky ('surely if Armenia were as near to us as Cuba', one official avowed, 'we would have fought Turkey as we did Spain').[11] At Versailles, the American president's attitudes towards Ottoman affairs remained somewhat obscure. While having pledged his support for the 'absolutely unmolested opportunity of autonomous development' for all Ottoman citizens, Wilson betrayed an early ambivalence to British and French plans of occupation. He loathed the secret treaties reached by British and French officials during the war. As Clemenceau and Lloyd George clashed over their respective claims in the Levant, Wilson suggested the Allies dispatch a special commission to ascertain the opinions of peoples in the region. Clemenceau agreed to the commission so long as it extended to Palestine and Iraq, areas sought by Great Britain. Lloyd George reluctantly consented, but warned that the inquiry could potentially stir up trouble. It was possible, he advised, that such an investigation would lead to false conclusions, since 'Oriental peoples are suspicious and do not easily open up to newcomers'.[12] In the end, the commission formed that spring included no British or French participants, a fact that all but ensured the inquiry's ultimate failure.

There were, however, topics upon which Clemenceau, Wilson and Lloyd George did firmly agree when it came to the settlement of Ottoman-related questions. The American president saw the Ottoman Empire, like other members of the Central Powers, as an extension of Germany's malevolence. France and Britain, of course, interpreted the war as having eliminated a serious rival for influence in the Middle East and beyond. With the withdrawal of German troops from Ottoman lands, as well as the stiff penalties meted out to Berlin at Versailles, both London and Paris eyed a series of opportunities for expansion and influence. Before the war's end, British troops had been dispatched to the Caucasus and Iran to counter a suspected German drive to seize oil fields in the region. Despite Germany's withdrawal of several thousand troops from the newly declared Republic of Georgia, British forces remained in the region following the armistice. With Syria potentially in its grasp, Paris stood prepared to expand France's role in developing rail networks across the Middle East, an ambition long hindered as a result of the German-financed Baghdad Railway.

A more immediate and concrete source of mutual concern stemmed from Soviet Russia. Anger towards Moscow's decision to exit from the war in March 1918, as well as the broader fear of Communism, had not dissipated by the time a final armistice was reached. That summer, both Britain and France had sent small military expeditions to occupy vital ports in the former Russian Empire. With the peace conference set to begin, other Allies had joined in the intervention. Before the war was over, both Japan and the United States deployed troops to Siberia in the hopes of encircling Soviet forces. Talks at Versailles commenced without Soviet representatives present. Although Moscow denounced the proceedings as an imperialist farce, it was widely believed a lasting peace could not be reached in the absence of Soviet consent. Central to these reservations was the future security of Poland and other states in Eastern Europe. A Communist uprising in Germany in the winter of 1918–19, followed by a revolution in Hungary in March 1919, made the possibility of a Bolshevik surge across Europe appear particularly likely.

For Britain, Russia cast an equally large shadow over its imperial interests in Asia. Before the armistice, British troops found themselves embroiled in a confusing set of conflicts in the Caucasus and Central Asia. In northern Iran, a small force of British and colonial regulars supported a motley alliance of 'White' insurgents against pro-Bolshevik nationalists. Affairs appeared more ominous further east, between the Caspian coast and Afghanistan. There, contingents of British and Indian troops faced what many believed was the beginnings of a Bolshevik offensive southward. By the spring of 1919, this tenuous defensive line began to give way. In the Caucasus, British forces vacated their positions, save for a lonely garrison in Batum, the disputed port on the Georgian–Ottoman border. In Afghanistan, British observers suspected a Russian hand in the rise of pro-independence forces under the Pashtun leader Emir Amanullah. The worst of these anxieties appeared realized in May 1919, after a dramatic Afghan assault on British positions along the Indian border. Iran, too, seemed in danger from what one official long suspected would be 'hordes of triumphant Bolsheviks'.[13] London took heart, for a time, after reaching new terms with Tehran in the summer of 1919, an agreement that made Persia a virtual British protectorate. But the threat of Soviet influence in the wider Middle East still loomed.

For many in London and in the British colonies, Communism was a harbinger of something that much more ominous. The 1917 revolution, at its core, was a global call for unity among the downtrodden, one aimed at overthrowing the power and hegemony of European empires. Among many outside Russia, the Bolshevik takeover echoed a cause long associated with the Ottoman Empire. Since the mid-nineteenth century, activists from throughout the colonial world had appealed to Muslims living everywhere to unite in defense of their religion and their independence. The implications of this movement, for many British and French officials, were as clear as they were dire; be it in Asia, Africa or imperial territories in between, the loyalties of Muslim colonial subjects could not be taken for granted. It was this fear that made Istanbul's entrance into the Great War appear especially menacing. With Sultan Mehmed V's declaration of a global jihad against members of the Entente, London and Paris labored to forestall any sign of Muslim discontent or revolt within their empires. In French Morocco, senior officials were wary of transferring local troops to the western front for fear 'that a general revolt would arise under our feet, on all our points . . .'[14] Fear of losing the support of Indian Muslims, particularly among conscripts fighting against the Ottomans, was among the chief factors that led British officials to cultivate a relationship with Emir Faisal and his father Hussein. Such an intervention was seen early on in some quarters as politically risky. Critics warned that imperial Britain's decision to support the Arab revolt fundamentally weakened the movement's legitimacy (after all, as one Indian detractor pointed out, the lords of Mecca and Medina were 'not strong enough to stand without alien support and therefore could not fill the role of an Islamic king').[15] Ironically, the war passed with few signs that the sultan's jihad was heeded. Still, as negotiators went about their business in Versailles, doubts over the loyalties of British and French Muslims lingered within London and Paris.

All of these hazards cast a long shadow as the Allies contemplated the occupation of Istanbul and what remained of Ottoman territory in Anatolia. According to the terms of the armistice reached at the end of October, the Entente secured the right to occupy places of strategic importance in the interest of public security. This concession soon became a license used liberally by the Allies. Before the close of

December, contingents of British and French troops took hold of multiple towns north of the armistice line, including Adana, Mersin, Antep and Mosul. After assuming possession of forts along the Dardanelles, an Allied fleet passed into the Sea of Marmara and came to anchor off Istanbul's Golden Horn. Commanders overseeing the landing of British and French troops in the capital did not move immediately to usurp the authority of Ottoman officials. Control over the city, all agreed, was a matter fraught with political, cultural and geostrategic considerations. This did not, however, preclude them from privately expressing disdain for their hosts. 'That the Straits will be open is certain', one British consular official wrote that December, 'but I could bear to see the town under almost any Government you can mention so long as it is not Turkish for they truly are not fit to administer a pigsty even'.[16]

There was little harmony among Allied leaders dispatched to Istanbul. As troops took up residence in the Ottoman capital, a large and unwieldy collection of British, Italian, American and French officials came in tow. With regional politics growing more complex by the day, the question of who among the Allies was in charge, as well as how the occupation was to proceed, became less clear. Istanbul's British garrison, for example, fell under the command of France's Army of the Orient, led by General Franchet D'Espèrey. With the general dividing his time between affairs in the city and a French invasion of Ukraine, D'Espèrey's leadership regularly served as a source of irritation among British representatives. More vexing was the question of what was to become of Istanbul once a final settlement was reached. On one issue Great Britain was resolute: neither the Dardanelles nor the Bosphorus was to return to Ottoman hands. Yet precisely how the Turkish Straits were to be administered was a more difficult matter. At Versailles, the powers tended to agree that an international regime was best suited to the task of overseeing both bodies of water. Settling the land borders of such an entity, however, was tricky. In laying his case before the peace conference, Venizelos had demanded virtually the whole of Ottoman Thrace, up to Istanbul's city limits, as well as parts of the Sea of Marmara's southern shores. Such claims, if accepted, would effectively put the Straits in Greek hands.

Venizelos, for his part, did his best to downplay such ambitions.

'Great international interests' had to be considered in determining Istanbul's future. And of course, he added, any international regime placed over the city had to include 'a sufficient hinterland' to genuinely ensure the freedom of all maritime traffic.[17] He was far more forceful when it came to Greek claims in the Aegean. From the outset of the conference, Venizelos was tireless in lobbying the Allied Powers, underscoring the natural rights and benefits that would accompany Greece's seizure of Smyrna. His confidence in the matter was accentuated thanks to the backing of Lloyd George. In the midst of the Great War, the British Prime Minister had fallen under the spell of Venizelos. He became convinced that a larger Greece, one allied with Britain, would guarantee the security of London's interests in the eastern Mediterranean. Wresting the Aegean and Thrace from Istanbul's control appealed to his basic sensibilities. The Ottomans, as he put it, had been a source of 'distraction, intrigue and corruption in European politics' for nearly 500 years.[18] Not everyone in his cabinet, or within the British government, agreed. In addition to questions over Greece's capacity to defend a potential exclave in Anatolia, there were fundamental doubts about the legitimacy of Venizelos's claims. Intelligence and diplomatic reports, such as those submitted by British residents in Izmir, cast doubt upon the statistical data the Greek premier presented at Versailles. More worrying was the possible effect Greece's actions would have upon Muslim opinion within the British Empire. Foreign Secretary Lord Curzon, a man who embodied Britannia's commitment to empire, cast Izmir's annexation as a disaster in waiting. Representatives of the India Office in London concurred. The thought of Greek soldiers lording it over Muslim civilians, let alone any challenge to Ottoman sovereignty in Istanbul, would fan British Muslim anxieties over the future of the caliph and his royal dynasty. British diplomats in Versailles, however, dismissed such concerns. 'Our India Office people are over-nervous about the Khalifat', one negotiator confided to his diary. 'I do not believe our Indian Moslems care a hoot for the Khalifat as such. What they like is to be able to exercise pressure upon the British Government on behalf of the soldier of Islam'.[19]

It was not until 1 June 1919 that the Ottoman Empire was officially invited to present its case before the peace conference. When representatives were finally granted an audience at Versailles, they begged senior heads of state for understanding. All faults stemming from the war, the delegation maintained, resided with the Committee of Union and Progress. There was no denying that the Young Turk regime had killed a great number of Christians (at least 3 million Muslims, they added, were also killed upon the CUP's orders). To tar the empire with such shame, however, was unjust. 'It would be fairer to judge the Ottoman nation', they argued, 'by its long history as a whole rather than by a single period which shows it in the most disadvantageous light'.[20] Once the delegation was excused from the chamber, Wilson and Lloyd George indicated that they found the presentation contemptible in its tone and content. Ottoman assertions of innocence were ridiculous, Wilson spat. 'We have not allowed that sort of discussion in what concerns Germany'.[21]

The Ottoman delegation, by their own account, understood that there was little margin for error in appealing to the Allies for leniency. 'This is our first and last opportunity', one representative told the sultan; 'let us not lose this as well'.[22] And yet, by the time the representatives from Istanbul arrived in Paris, Greek soldiers had already seized Izmir, touching off fierce fighting in the Aegean interior. Meanwhile, in the Ottoman capital, a different kind of struggle was continuing to play out. In the six months that followed the armistice, much of the imperial administration remained in disarray. Rather than confront the harsh realities of coming to terms with the Allies, many in Istanbul looked inward.

RESTORATION AND VENGEANCE: ISTANBUL'S CRISIS OF LEADERSHIP

The man tasked with overseeing the Ottoman government's surrender to the Allies possessed an exemplary career of service. For nearly thirty-five years, Ahmet İzzet Pasha distinguished himself both on the battlefield and as a minister of state. His commitment to the empire, he later explained, often came at the expense of his conscience. Under Abdülhamid II, he shared the dismay of many loyal officers who served in spite of the sultan's mismanagement of state affairs. His faith in the CUP was similarly tested in the years after the 1908 revolution. He found its politics manipulative and unscrupulous. Its ideology, particularly ideas stemming from the Turkish Hearth, was also too divisive for his tastes (not to mention the fact that he found the Hearth's principal leaders men who genuinely 'did not know their parentage or nationality').[23] İzzet was opposed to entering the Great War but served nevertheless on the eastern Anatolian front. The depredations of the war, in and beyond the fighting, he found deplorable. While he deemed the mass removal of Armenians unfortunate but necessary, he disapproved of the brutality of the Young Turk administration in the Arab provinces. 'People', he later argued, 'should not solely be thought of as grass or pebbles'.[24] Even so, he remained in the field until the war's last year. Then, as it happened, fate suddenly intervened.

In the summer of 1918, Sultan Mehmed V succumbed to illness. The slow decline of his health was, in many ways, a reflection of his household's own dwindling fortunes. Like many wartime residents in the capital, attendants in the palace struggled to find basic commodities such as rice. The situation at some point grew so desperate that Enver Pasha, who had married into the royal family before the war, requisitioned food bound for the front on the sultan's behalf. Amid frightful losses of men and territory, the palace sustained a terrible blow in 1916 with the death of Yusuf İzzeddin, the crown prince. İzzeddin had long suffered from anxiety and depression, a fact that had often set the whole of the royal family on edge. 'All of us could see we were dealing with a sick man', one attendant remembered, 'all of us down to the servant who came back with his coffee and fruit drinks and could tell he'd refused them because he was afraid of being poisoned'.[25] When the crown prince committed suicide in February 1916, Reşad's fifty-five-year-old brother, Mehmed Vahideddin, became the heir to the throne. Mehmed, according to some, had long pined for his place in line. He had clashed repeatedly with his cousin Yusuf over the years and, it is said, had privately urged the sultan to disqualify the prince as heir apparent on the grounds of insanity.

History has made an intimate retelling of Mehmed's life somewhat difficult. Despite being the empire's last reigning sultan, only so much can be said about him with great confidence. He was born in 1861, the last of Sultan Abdülmecid I's forty-two children.[26] He became an orphan at a young age and was largely self-taught. In recounting his ultimate ascension to the throne, many contemporary sources tend to emphasize those qualities that eventually led to his downfall. To his critics, he was unmistakably conniving, suspicious and without any true shrewdness or fortitude. Mustafa Kemal Atatürk personally boasted that once, when he was serving as an aide-de-camp, he had to remind Mehmed to wave to the crowds of onlookers as the then crown prince passed on a train. Rather than resist or reprimand the young officer for his insolence, Vahideddin sheepishly complied. One of the most damaging charges levied against Mehmed VI was his affection for Great Britain. To some extent, the historical record attests to this. 'My dear father Abdülmecid', he is quoted as saying, 'was friends and connected with France and England. I have always loved England myself . . . The noble English nation and government, emblazoned with feelings of humanity and justice, will help us to achieve our rights'.[27] In his more private moments, there are indications that he was not so easily won over by Great Britain or any other foreign power. 'The mentality of the foreigners', he said on more than one occasion, 'does not suit us'.[28]

Though Mehmed VI's true character remains elusive, all available accounts testify to his personal enmity towards the CUP. He cultivated his disdain for the Young Turks as a prince, long before the passing of Reşad's first chosen heir, Yusuf İzzeddin. His primary fear, as one attendant remembered, 'was the danger of being dismissed as second *veliahd*', or heir to the heir apparent. 'He was aware how much the CUP opposed him and they held all power in their hands'.[29] With his coronation as sultan and caliph in the summer of 1918, the war offered him an opportunity to assert his imperial rights. Bulgaria's decision to sue for peace in September 1918 placed the Young Turk government in an impossible position. With the resignation of Talat Pasha, then the sitting grand vezir, the responsibility fell upon Vahideddin to approve a new cabinet. Efforts to find a replacement for Talat and his ministers were initially fraught with infighting and disagreement. It was then that Ahmet İzzet was brought before the sultan to discuss the crafting of a new government. Sensing his chance to make his opinions felt, the general was unbridled in denigrating Talat and the CUP as a whole. Since the time of the Young Turk seizure of power in 1908, he declared, 'the old strength of the sultanate has been lost'. Throughout the war, the Ottoman dynasty had served the interests of Enver and Talat, reducing itself to nothing more than a symbol of the 'sultanate's spiritual strength'. İzzet urged his sovereign to seize the moment and form a government that would secure the dynasty's 'legitimate rights' and restore justice in the nation.[30] Moved by these words, Vahideddin embraced the general as his preferred grand vezir. Ahmet İzzet took up his new responsibilities with gusto, cobbling together a cabinet of officials who either had never joined the Young Turks or were largely disassociated from the party's wartime conduct. According to his own recollections, he also offered posts to two well-respected bureaucrats of Armenian and Greek extraction. Both refused for reasons that were never fully revealed, leaving İzzet to assume that they, as Christians, had disabused themselves of the Ottoman state.

As Ahmet İzzet worked to reach a truce with the Allies, senior CUP leaders looked to their own safety. It was widely suspected that any peace with the Entente would also include demands that Talat, Enver and others be apprehended. As early as May 1915, Britain, Russia and France vowed to 'hold all members of the Ottoman Government' responsible for what they characterized as crimes against 'humanity and civilization'.[31] When asked whether he would comply with any such request, Ahmet İzzet offered a less than reassuring answer. 'As long as I am in the cabinet', he told Talat Pasha, 'I will never turn you over to the enemy. But who knows how long I will remain in the cabinet?'[32] It was for this reason that Talat and other heads of the CUP elected to flee the country following the armistice. In their absence, what was left of the party chose to abandon the Young Turk moniker all the same. Days after Talat's and Enver's departure, the CUP dissolved itself, only to be reorganized under a new name, the Renovation (or Renaissance) Party (*Teceddüd Fırkası*). The founding bylaws of the party made it clear that its current members rejected their 'Unionist' or Young Turk roots. 'With the name "Renovation"', they declared, '[the party] is introducing a more liberal program. In that regard, this is a revolution. It wants to renew its structures and transform itself into "Renovation"'.[33] Such claims, as well as promises to bar former officials from the wartime government, failed to convince anyone of the party's sincere intentions. From the perspective of the press, foreign observers and everyday citizens, the reinvention of the party did little to cleanse members of their former allegiances and actions. 'The newspapers are ushering in a hitherto unseen era', one CUP leader noted in his diary. 'They say in the country there is only the sultan ... They almost give no weight to the government. Those who want to take advantage of current events and take vengeance upon Union and Progress are slowly forming a web around the sultan'.[34]

In the months that followed, great waves of disaffection washed over the politics of the capital. Among the first signs of this turn in Istanbul's political climate came with the loosening of government censorship. After years of rigid controls over dissent and social activism, writers and agitators were now undeterred in denouncing the CUP on a variety of counts. 'In the last session of the Union and Progress congress', one paper reported, 'the party's name was changed: Renovation. But is it possible the party's leading men changed their mentalities?' The answer, according to the editor's reading of the past, was clear. 'The nation will eternally denounce the name "Union and Progress" because the memories this name arouses are so painful: blood, fire, torture and pillage'.[35] As weeks turned to months, articles condemning the CUP's tenure in power regularly filled the pages of the Istanbul press. The party's conduct of the war effort drove only some of this coverage. Some newspapers printed accusations dating back to the years before the war (such as the case of Hacı Adil, prewar governor of the province of Thrace, who purportedly appropriated five large estates through illicit means).[36] The greatest amount of venom, however, was saved for the CUP's most senior leaders, Talat, Enver and Cemal Pashas. 'I am tired of all the Talats', one journalist declared. 'One cannot expect a thoroughbred from a degenerate horse. I curse the Envers, for I don't want heroism from a swindler [madrabaz]. And my eyes are sick of the Cemals. I do not miss the gallows and executioners'.[37]

In the absence of fear and restraint, representatives in the Chamber of Deputies were just as forceful in voicing their own indignation towards the wartime regime. Multiple parliamentary sessions grew raucous as Greek and Armenian members laid out detailed charges against CUP officials. At least a million Armenians, one parliamentarian declared, were 'massacred and exterminated'. Hundreds of thousands of Greek Orthodox Christians were killed or displaced and their homes taken from them.[38] A handful of Muslim representatives joined their Christian colleagues in demanding justice for those who were killed. Ahmet Rıza, the estranged founder of the Young Turk movement, rose and condemned his former colleagues. 'The atrocities', he told the chamber, 'were not simply done to Arabs, Armenians and Greeks. They were done to Kurds, [immigrant] Albanians and Roma as well. Even Turks are [victims] among them. I am saying all of them are Ottomans and I am demanding justice for each of them'.[39] Such calls tended to receive qualified majority support at best. Several representatives, including former Young Turks, agreed that crimes had been committed during the war, but that these were less extensive or severe than Armenian and Greek members claimed. Everyone knew, one former Unionist countered, 'that in the last four years we have endured terrible, truly harmful currents that have clouded our country, turning it upside down'. And yet, he added, 'however much the Greek, Armenian or Arab peoples have suffered, I assure you that the Turkish people have suffered in the same way and probably have suffered much more'.[40] Several representatives were far less charitable. Some dismissed claims of mass killings or the unlawful appropriation of property, countering instead that Armenians and Greeks were responsible for massacres and acts of brigandage during the war. In the minutes of these last parliamentary sessions, Greek and Armenian representatives were regularly jeered or interrupted when calling for restitution or justice. Yet, remarkably, the Chamber of Deputies eventually did find some common ground for establishing a legal inquiry into the conduct of the wartime regime. Among its proposed initial goals was the investigation of the country's 'baseless and premature entrance into the war', the state-imposed regime of censorship and the CUP's role in promoting corruption and larceny, as well as the government's rejection of peace overtures at multiple junctures in the conflict.[41]

The grand vezir's own partiality, however, looked increasingly suspect in light of Enver's and Talat's escape from the country. Ahmet İzzet consequently resigned from his post, leading his successor – another aging general, named Tevfik Pasha – to begin the formation of an official tribunal. By December, the first such commission was formed in order to gather evidence of criminal infractions committed by provincial officials. The scope of these investigations expanded considerably into the new year. By the end of January 1919, several former high-ranking CUP members were arrested in connection with the deportation and massacre of Armenians. A far fiercer blow was struck weeks later, when many more former senior officials were indicted for their roles in the wartime government. By March, the authorities had indicted twenty-three former CUP ministers and members of the party's central committee. While some, such as Talat, Enver and Cemal, were tried *in absentia*, the majority of wartime officials were rounded up and put on trial between April and June 1919.[42]

This repudiation of the Young Turk government was only partially the result of a sincere pursuit of justice. The partisan motivations for holding wartime officials accountable appeared increasingly clear before 1919 opened. In December 1918, Mehmed Vahideddin told a British journalist that it 'was a great sorrow' to hear of the violence 'certain political committees in Turkey instigated against the Armenians'.[43] His demand for justice echoed earlier calls of a hitherto peripheral member of the imperial senate, Damad Ferid. Fighting on the eastern, Syrian and Iraqi fronts, Ferid declared in November, was grossly mismanaged. The welfare of both the army and the general population had been neglected, leading to starvation and outbreaks of typhus. Both soldiers and civilians were exposed to penalties that were 'contrary to personal law or military principles, such as deportation and execution without trial'.[44]

Ferid's personal relationship with the sultan added weight to his pleas for an inquest. In the years before the Great War, he had cemented his reputation as a staunch foe of the Young Turk order. Educated at the Sorbonne, and possessing a unique affection for the culture and liberal politics of Western Europe, Ferid married into the Ottoman royal family, making him a brother-in-law (or *damad* in Turkish) of Mehmed Vahideddin. In 1911, he ranked among the founders of the only political party ever to challenge the authority of the CUP, the Freedom and Accord Party (*Hürriyet ve İtilaf Fırkası*). His fortunes, however, turned sour after the establishment of the Young Turk dictatorship in 1913.

With his party effectively banned, and many of his former comrades either executed or exiled, Ferid lived out the war quietly in his seaside mansion. Vahideddin's coronation, followed by the CUP's fall, allowed him the chance to reassert himself under the protection of the newly empowered sultan. As one of the leading voices demanding the prosecution of former Unionist officials, Ferid helped reconstitute his old party. By March 1919, the sultan granted him his ultimate wish and appointed him grand vezir in a government comprising cabinet members drawn from Freedom and Accord. Damad Ferid's rise to power appeared to finalize trends that were evident from the closing days of the war. In taking over the reins of government, Ferid, with the sultan's blessing, aimed to finish off the CUP once and for all.

The mass trials of Unionist leaders, by and large, achieved their desired result. Over the course of many weeks, prosecutors presented reams of internal documents. Collectively, the balance of evidence painted a damning picture of the CUP state. Central to the case against the indicted was the role each played in authorizing or carrying out the violence committed against Armenians through the war. In reaching their decision, the judges in the matter issued a sweeping condemnation of the Young Turk dictatorship. The CUP, according to one verdict, 'subjected [the country] to enormous disasters by taking the overall power of the state . . . and through unlawful actions such as participation in the World War, profiteering, deportations, massacres, banishments and expulsions of persons, and the like'. 'The Ottoman Realms', the judges concluded, 'were thereby afflicted, internally, with the greatest degree of privation and all manner of calamity and externally, by the subverting of the power and prestige of the state'.[45] For their crimes, Talat, Enver and Cemal were sentenced to death *in absentia*. Other fugitives from the court received lengthy prison sentences and had their assets seized. The majority of the defendants were remanded to British custody and dispatched to the island of Malta to serve out their time. Ottoman authorities justified this transfer of custody on security grounds. Relinquishing them to foreign hands, however, underscored an uncomfortable truth. Britain and the rest of the Allies had cheered the mass arrests. London's eagerness to play the role of jailer led many to assume that the sultan's government was happy to serve the interests of the Allies.

Collaboration with Britain and France was a strategy many in Istanbul believed was the only way forward. Fears of reigniting the conflict had led senior officials to allow Britain to seize Mosul and land troops in Istanbul uncontested. With much of the empire facing the threat of partition, many elite opinion-makers placed all their hopes in the United States. Wilson's early assurances that he supported 'secured sovereignty' in Turkish portions of the Ottoman Empire were embraced with enthusiasm.[46] Istanbul dailies printed commentaries assuring readers that Washington would support official Ottoman claims in areas where Muslims predominated. The capital, one newspaper promised, was bound to stay under imperial control since Muslims outnumbered resident Christians 603,919 to 361,808. After all, 'if the Wilson[ian] principles are to be in command, it means that the pleas of the [native] Greeks will not be considered'.[47] One paper went so far as to publish a warm account of the life of George Washington on his birthday.[48] Arguably the more active advocate for American intervention was the Wilsonian Principles Society, founded in Istanbul in January 1919. Among the noted journalists, bureaucrats and activists who joined the association was the empire's most prominent female writer, Halide Edip Adıvar. As a prominent member of the Turkish Hearth, and a woman with strong ties to the CUP, she addressed a letter to Wilson himself asking specifically for American aid in re-establishing a strong and united empire. An American-run administration, she proposed, was likely to endure for 'a minimum of 15 or a maximum of 25 years'. Under this system, there would be no need for partition or the granting of autonomy to Armenians or Greeks, since Muslims held majorities in every part of the empire.[49]

Precisely how the sultan or his loyalists in the government went about planning for negotiations with the Allies remains somewhat unclear. Through early 1919, leading politicians were willing to grant some concessions, such as allowing free navigation of the Turkish Straits or perhaps ceding some territory to Armenia. Any new regime in the Arab lands, however, would have to be maintained 'in friendship with the Ottoman government'.[50] Damad Ferid's appointment reinforced his more narrow approach to diplomacy. His primary governing impulse, as Ahmet İzzet remembered it, was to 'destroy the

Unionists, or more correctly [his party's] enemies and rivals, and after that, if there is time, look to the country'.[51] It was during the height of Ferid's drive to prosecute senior CUP leaders that the talks in Paris focused on the status of Izmir. By April 1919, Greece's unwavering demands for Ottoman territory became a more acute source of tensions among the Allies. Italy was also promised territory along Anatolia's Mediterranean and Aegean coasts, building on its colonial holdings in the Dodecanese Islands. Prime Minister Vittorio Orlando, Rome's representative at Versailles, continued to insist upon Italian claims to Izmir. Fortunately for Athens, other disputes ultimately put Italy on the defensive. In late April, Wilson came out against Rome's plan to seize the Dalmatian coast from the newly formed state of Yugoslavia. Orlando responded with indignation, ushering the entire Italian delegation home in early May. It was at this moment that Venizelos, backed by Lloyd George, pressed for and received the Allies' blessing to land troops in Izmir. Even though news of Greece's intentions had circulated for weeks in advance, many officials in Istanbul were caught off guard by the developments. The palace's response to the invasion was particularly labored. Initial drafts of the sultan's statement were carefully revised to include language that was believed to be more Wilsonian in tone. Editors accentuated Mehmed VI's status as Islam's caliph, as well as Ottoman sultan, and made careful reference to the government's 'absolute protection of the nation' as well as the 'rule of law' (hukuk-u devlet).[52]

Greece's seizure of Izmir left Damad Ferid reeling politically. He submitted his resignation as grand vezir to the sultan, only to be retained by Mehmed VI. With local Ottoman units struggling to resist the Greek advance, and the public crying out for stronger action, Ferid chaired a grand council comprising activists and representatives from throughout what remained of the Ottoman-held territories. This attempt at demonstrating unity and deference to the popular will, however, largely came at the grand vezir's expense. A number of the sultan's attendants demanded the government do more to counter Greece's invasion. Questions were also raised as to public security in the country as a whole and the viability of diplomacy in light of the Allies' approval of Greece's actions. Woodrow Wilson, Ferid was reminded, had promised that areas with Turkish majorities would remain under Ottoman control. 'Is this principle', he was asked, 'still the basis of negotiations today? If not, has this principle been abandoned?'[53] To these and other questions, Damad Ferid offered no immediate response. Within days, however, he was able to offer a more complete rendering of the government's position. In early June, two weeks after the fall of Izmir, Istanbul was invited to participate in the discussions in Paris. Ferid himself led the delegation along with Tevfik Pasha, the previous grand vezir. When his day before the council of Allies finally came, he presented what was by then an aspirational vision of the empire's future. It was Istanbul's desire, he argued, for a complete return to the 'status quo ante bellum' with respect to Ottoman sovereignty. All areas of Anatolia, including those recently occupied by Greece, should remain Ottoman. Critical to this line of reasoning was Istanbul's assertion that all of the empire's provinces possessed Muslim majorities. Even with their Arabic-speaking populations, the Levant and Mesopotamia were 'indissolubly linked with Constantinople by feelings which are deeper than the principle of nationality'. Severing the Arab lands from the Ottoman whole, Ferid warned, would lead to greater upheaval in the region. Even if Arab independence was approved by popular referendum, maintaining Ottoman sovereignty over the Arab lands was in 'the supreme interests of more than three hundred million Moslems', a global body which formed 'an important fraction of the whole of the human race'.[54]

The scorn Wilson and Lloyd George heaped upon Damad Ferid was not the only indignation endured by the Ottoman delegation. It left Paris without any agreement, or any indication of when the Allies planned to settle. Negotiations over a final treaty would not begin again until the spring of 1920. In the meantime, affairs at home could not be described as anything but disastrous.

'THE GAME OF JACKALS': OTTOMAN SOCIETY AFTER THE ARMISTICE

In the spring of 1916, there was still cause for optimism within elite circles in Istanbul. British and French troops had retreated from Gallipoli by early January. In April, a dramatic victory was scored in Kut, in central Iraq, after the surrender of an entire British division. A stalemate had settled over the lines in eastern Anatolia and there was no sign of a British advance across the Sinai. In this climate, at least some in the capital dared to ponder the future. It was time, as one commentator from the Turkish Hearth put it, for the government and intellectuals to pay greater attention to the home front. The one region in need of greater care was Anatolia. 'Anatolian peasants, Anatolian producers, Anatolian traders and artisans' received the least attention from those at the head of government. 'The greatest burdens of the state and country are loaded upon them [and] we never thought that we should have any obligations towards them'. This pattern of neglect also extended to what was termed the 'speech, needs and moral character' of Asia Minor. Recognizing Anatolia's economic and cultural denigration was simply the first step in national renewal. Improving the region's economic output was a matter of both public investment and social change. A state-led reform program aimed at simplifying the imperial language, thus bringing it closer to the speech of everyday Anatolian peasants, would bring about a revolution in education and cultural awareness. Such reforms, the commentator concluded, would make the native *volk* of Asia Minor 'the most lively and exalted of the country'.[55]

The force of these convictions did not diminish as the empire's fortunes faded into the following year. With the battle lines in the Levant and Mesopotamia creeping northward, intellectuals and activists in the capital increasingly turned their attention to events in Russia and to the eastern front. The tsar's overthrow in March 1917, followed by the Bolshevik seizure of power in November, led to the complete collapse of Russian forces in Anatolia. For many senior CUP leaders, Lenin's decision to pursue a separate peace with Istanbul was greeted as more than vindicating the Ottoman war effort. With the struggle in the east virtually over, members of the Turkish Hearth intensified their calls for greater government attention to affairs in Anatolia. It was time, in the words of one pundit, for a more populist approach towards the people of the region. Anatolia, 'with its virginal, innocent, hearty and hardworking *volk*', expected and deserved nothing less.[56] Consternation within the Turkish Hearth rose, however, with an Ottoman invasion of the Caucasus in late spring 1918. Some members cheered the move, heralding the advance as an effort to aid Muslim freedom fighters in Azerbaijan and Dagestan. Others decried the offensive as a wasteful distraction. 'Our house', Halide Edip exclaimed, 'namely Turkey, is in utter chaos and in the midst of catastrophe'. It was more important for the government to take care of the welfare of citizens in Anatolia than to send doctors and teachers to help the empire's Muslim brothers in the Caucasus. 'Young Turkey requires the service and affection of all of its youth'. To do otherwise would 'forfeit claims to their own people's home'.[57]

One German academic who visited the empire in 1916 took note of these debates concerning the home front. Economic advancement and national unity were undoubtedly of critical importance. 'Right now', he observed, 'all of the efforts in this direction are chimeric. Every idea that has been directed towards this is a waste that cannot be afforded'.[58] Other observers reporting from within the German government were more pointed in expressing their fears. Young Turk policies, both within and beyond the war itself, had taken a terrible toll on the population. The general mobilization of 1914 had stripped much of the country of workers. Labor shortages assumed graver proportions as a result of the mass removal and murder of Christians. 'The Armenians were exterminated', one German official reported back, 'and left – it was harvest season – the entire crop to rot in the fields'. The dire repercussions the deportations held for the country's food supply were only the beginning. By the spring of 1916, rumors of mass starvation and disease were rife. It was said, but not confirmed, that malnourishment was taking the lives of 400 people a day in the country. Istanbul itself was subsumed by such hardships. In addition to commodity shortages, typhus, smallpox and cholera were rampant. Large numbers of citizens were compelled to drink unsanitary water. Evidence of price gouging and self-dealing led to open talk of conspiracies. One frequent explanation heard for the shortages was that the Young Turks were all 'apostates' or, more specifically, *dönme* (that is, Muslims who descended from converted Jewish families). Rumor had it, according to German sources, that even senior officials believed 'the Young Turk government was a toy for the "Grand Orient"', France's oldest network of Freemasons.[59]

These observations bore only a faint resemblance to the hardships most citizens in the country endured. As early as 1915, starvation as well as mass flight had already begun to depopulate large portions of the empire. By the war's end, whole villages and towns, particularly in the east, were almost completely emptied of people. Elsewhere, mass displacement was creating new challenges for peasants and city dwellers. While much of Istanbul's literati blinded themselves to the plight of non-Muslims and non-Turkish speakers, citizens throughout the country were confronted with a variety of issues that cut across sectarian or ethnic lines. When activists like Halide Edip wrote of Anatolia before the end of 1918, it was naturally assumed the empire would survive the war. The Arab lands, it was presumed, would abide within the empire as the government worked to transform Asia Minor into the bedrock of the state and nation. By the spring of 1919, this vision was in complete disarray. As the shadow of foreign occupation loomed, citizens throughout Anatolia – both Muslims and Christians – were losing faith in the empire and its leaders.

It does not appear that Ottoman officials undertook any general survey of the physical devastation wrought by the Great War. Much of what is known about the scale of carnage comes by way of anecdotes or through projections made well after the fact. The reports that do exist, however, offer grim insights into the plight of those who lived in the towns and villages. In the east of Anatolia, the shifting battle lines, as well as the mass deportations, appear to have extracted an especially heavy toll. In Trabzon, on the Black Sea, American missionaries found homes stripped bare or destroyed after a two-year Russian occupation. 'The city itself', it was reported, 'was terribly unsanitary because of filth accumulated during the terrible days of the Russian revolution. Dozens of skeletons of horses strewed the streets; cemeteries were desecrated; water mains broken, and filth indescribable was on every hand'.[60] The damage done to basic infrastructure generally reflected the losses incurred among Ottoman civilians. According to the governor of Van, bordering Iran in the east, almost 95 percent of the province's prewar residents had died, taken flight or were internally exiled.[61] By 1933, local officials estimated that Erzurum possessed only 27,000 inhabitants, or perhaps no more than 20 percent of its prewar population.[62]

For those who managed to retain their homes and survive the war, multiple hardships marked the passage of daily life. As in the rest of the empire, the scarcity of food was among the first miseries villagers and townspeople endured. Mass conscription of local men – as well as of draft animals – forced women, children and the elderly to take their place at work. Communities went without teachers, doctors, farm laborers, administrators or gendarmes for months or years at a time. Adding to the scale of the suffering was the spread of disease. Areas that faced endemic threats to public health, such as marshy regions of the interior, were soon forced to come to grips with a variety of illnesses. It was in the summer of 1918 that Istanbul newspapers reported the first cases of the era's gravest pandemic, the Spanish flu. Although a full accounting remains elusive, the Ottoman press reported as many as 11,000 fatalities in the capital by the end of 1920.[63] Such losses, taken together with those caused directly by the fighting on the various fronts, exacted a terrible toll on many families. 'I was thirteen or fourteen years old at the time of mobilization', one native from Izmir remembered. 'In my family two of my uncles died, martyred in Russia. We encountered many troubles, a great deal of hunger. On the one side locusts came and on the other side plague. In a day, three or four people would die'.[64]

Mass flight added further complications to the problems of health, housing and safety. By the war's end, the number of refugees residing within the empire's borders was immense. In addition to the hundreds of thousands of native Greeks, Armenians and other Christians forced from their homes in 1915, an equally large pool of people – perhaps as many as 900,000 – populated the ranks of those displaced by the conflict.[65] A significant proportion of these refugees were themselves subject to many of the same policies that had been geared towards Ottoman Christians. Kurds fleeing the fighting in the east arguably bore the brunt of these government resettlement efforts. By 1916, regional officials were instructed to assess the number of Kurdish refugees living within their districts and determine whether they isolated themselves from local Turks and so were still 'preserving their customs and language'.[66] Those identified as doing so were forcibly relocated elsewhere, this time in the hopes of assimilating them into Turkish-speaking communities. As with displaced Armenians, specific instructions guided the relocation of Kurdish refugees. It was mandated that communities of resettled Kurds not exceed 5 percent of local villages or towns – a safe-guard, administrators were told, that would lead them to abandon their language and 'tribal' customs. Without adequate supplies or housing, it is likely that thousands of Kurdish citizens died en route to their assigned places of settlement.

The empire's looming defeat in late 1918 helped to partially reverse government settlement policies. Shortly before the armistice, Ahmet İzzet Pasha issued a formal proclamation allowing deportees the right to return home from exile. The grand vezir's decision to restore ban-ished Armenians, Greeks, Kurds and Arabs to their homes came amid promises meant to appeal to the sympathies of the Allies. In Izmir, for example, the local governor declared before a crowd that the govern-ment would henceforth uphold the 'future rights of the nationalities' in accordance with Woodrow Wilson's Fourteen Points.[67] These reas-surances, however, did not produce an immediate return to the prewar status quo. All available sources suggest that a mere fraction of the wartime deportees returned home over the course of the following months. According to figures released to the Ottoman press, the government estimated that only 335,000 Greeks and Armenians had returned to their homes by February 1920. Equally few Muslims dis-placed by the war proved able or willing to return to their points of origin. Out of the estimated 800,000 people displaced by the fighting in eastern Anatolia, just over half had made it back to their home-towns by the winter of 1920. The overall size of this refugee population remained enormous after the signing of the armistice. According to the same sources, more than 1.4 million refugees from the Russian Civil War passed through the Ottoman lands by 1920. In addition to the 147,000 people displaced by the Greek invasion of Anatolia, offi-cials estimated that the government was still tracking another 443,000 refugees who had fled from the Balkans between 1912 and 1920.[68] In many parts of the country, wartime refugees continued to linger, or were still searching for a way home, months after the armistice was signed. One British officer who toured the central Anatolian towns between Eskişehir and Konya in the spring of 1919 found an incred-ible host of displaced and banished peoples: Turks from Thrace, Greeks from the Black Sea, Kurds from Bitlis and even Arabs exiled from Medina, thousands of kilometers to the south.[69]

Istanbul's overtures towards the displaced only partially mitigated the harm done by the war. For most localities, the damage proved irreparable. The district of Adapazarı, the adopted home of Hüseyin Fehmi, possessed several thriving Armenian neighborhoods and villages in 1914. Five years later, the fighting and attendant deportations and massacres had cut a swath through the whole of the province. Of the 16,000 Armenians who lived in Adapazarı in 1914, only an estimated 3,000–4,000 survived their banishment in 1915.[70] The Aegean port town of Ayvalık similarly boasted a robust community of native Greeks, with as many as 23,000 Orthodox Christians residing in the area at the outbreak of the war. The CUP's deportation policies, as well as outmigration to Greece during the war, reduced the community to only 8,000 by the war's end.[71] The implications of the war bore a different set of consequences for the district of Antep, in Cilicia, north of Aleppo. At the start of the war, Antep possessed a considerable Armenian community, ranging from 15,000 to 40,000. A far larger population of 90,000 Muslims, comprising Turkish, Kurdish and Arabic speakers, represented the region's majority.[72] Although the area was no less affected by the fighting, the town became a magnet for Armenian refugees dispatched to the deportation camps of greater Syria. As a consequence, Antep's Armenian population grew rapidly in 1919, thus shrinking, or in some estimates overtaking, the area's historic Muslim majority.[73] Radical population swings affected Muslim communities around Antep and other districts as well. Conscription, not to mention disease, starvation and other hazards, also contributed to similar declines, even in otherwise peaceable areas of the empire. Another British officer, who toured villages in the central region of Yozgat, estimated that 50 percent of Muslim men had died fighting along the various fronts. 'In one village', he claimed, '120 men went to the war, and of these 80 are dead'.[74]

In light of the armistice, these wild demographic shifts held stark consequences for the prospects of peace in the Ottoman lands. According to imperial census data, relatively few provincial districts in Anatolia possessed demonstrable Armenian or Greek majorities before 1914. Greek and Armenian campaigners rejected Ottoman population figures and presented their own statistics in their place. In presenting his case before his fellow Allies, Venizelos provided surveys compiled by the Greek Patriarchate showing Greek majorities in various portions of what remained of the empire. Bursa, just south of the capital, was cited as possessing an Orthodox population of 278,000 inhabitants (almost four times the number recorded by Ottoman census-takers in 1914).[75] For Greece's Prime Minister, the depredations endured by Ottoman Greeks during the CUP era gave Athens more than enough reason for Anatolia's partition. 'The mere reinstating of the survivors [of deportation] in their homes and on their confiscated lands', he argued, 'presupposes necessarily the abolition of Turkish sovereignty'.[76]

Issues of property and financial restitution added still graver strains to postwar Ottoman society. Shortly before his resignation as grand vezir, Ahmet İzzet endorsed plans to oversee the return of – or payment of compensation for – lost homes and businesses to all of the 'fatherland's children who were subject to such great misery'.[77] To speed the process forward, the government formed dozens of 'mixed commissions' tasked with overseeing and directing the restitution of lost property in the provinces. A variety of difficulties harried the restoration of confiscated lands and homes. For those stripped of their businesses, warehouses and factories, obtaining full compensation for lost revenue and capital was a daunting task. In Izmir, one returnee took three of the wealthiest merchants to court, claiming they had unlawfully seized his textile mills. The judge in the case ruled in favor of the plaintiff, but awarded him less than a third of his stated losses of 1.4 million lira.[78] Most deportees were nowhere near as lucky. In many instances, returnees found their homes ransacked beyond repair. Lost valuables, such as jewelry, furniture and carpets, were often impossible to recover. Questions of ownership and inheritance added further complications. In some cases, relatives sued for lost homes and businesses in the place of loved ones either deceased or still missing. Some properties were sold without ever ascertaining if the original owner was dead or alive. In many more cases, returning Armenians and Greeks were forced to contend with defiant occupants. Mixed commissions possessed the authority to remove such inhabitants but were directed to find proper accommodation for the evicted. The fact that most Armenian and Greek homes had been given to poor Muslim refugees from the Balkans or eastern Anatolia often made such transfers difficult or very volatile. Provincial officials added to these tensions. When a series of refugees from Kosovo and Macedonia refused to vacate the homes they occupied, the governor of the northern town of Bafra advised returning Greeks to instead 'go and live with the Albanians and become their servants'.[79]

Other issues plagued the restoration of shattered communities. In addition to supervising the return of properties, commissioners also faced the challenge of finding and returning abducted women and children to their families. Throughout Anatolia and the Levant, tens of thousands of young women, boys and girls had been forcibly kidnapped or deposited in orphanages, a process that often entailed their forced conversion to Islam. Talat Pasha's Interior Ministry did much to hasten this agenda, going so far as to mandate that banished young Armenians found to be 'unattended' (*kimsiz*) or 'parentless' be relocated to Muslim villages and forcibly 'adjusted to local customs'.[80] Amid the chaos of the post-armistice months, a number of perils made it difficult for deportees to be released. Untold numbers of young Christian women and children remained in their assigned homes and orphanages on account of official resistance and, in some cases, the refusal of the abductees themselves to depart.

The war did not leave Muslims completely divided from their Christian neighbors. If anything united communities across the empire, it was their shared anxieties over personal safety. From the earliest stages of the war, brigandage, extortion and other banal acts of crime became endemic in provinces throughout the country. This breakdown in law and order, which was in part brought on by the initial strains of mobilization, grew worse as Ottoman armies retreated into the empire's interior. Overwhelmed gendarmes often found themselves helpless. One local gendarme described his recruits from late in the war as 'bearded men advanced in age with grandchildren, who were not conscripted, who couldn't run and did not know how to shoot a gun'.[81] Disorder in the countryside grew especially acute as desertion rates swelled. With as many as 500,000 soldiers abandoning the army in the war's last year, many districts became inundated with bands of armed, desperate troops. An air of intransigence and of disrespect for authority hung over many towns. One regional governor perceived a general 'removal of fear of the government and of the law among the people'.[82]

As the fighting drew to a close, officials in Istanbul, as well as the sultan himself, grew more desperate to restore order in the countryside. In August and again in November 1918, the government issued two general amnesties for all citizens charged with desertion and banditry. Rather than encouraging criminals to renounce the lawless life, the amnesties were seized upon by gangs which then strengthened their hold over captive communities. Broad swaths of Thrace and Anatolia, including districts lying just outside the capital, became the virtual fiefdoms of bandit leaders. In some areas, brigands and warlords exacted tribute and enforced their own rule of law with the tacit approval of local elites and state bureaucrats.

For many citizens, the precipitous rise in theft and violent crime was symptomatic of a deeper rot affecting both state and society. In spite of the suffering witnessed across the country, it was clear that the war created opportunities for a select few to grow rich. Profiteering assumed epidemic proportions as basic goods and commodities grew scarce. In both small villages and large towns, consumers vented their rage against retailers and merchants as prices soared. As the war approached its tragic end, popular anger towards wartime profiteers knew few bounds. 'Behind their safes and behind their desks', one prominent editor inveighed, 'they applauded the war's continuation and saw peace as a black cloud'.[83] Among all of those who profited from the war, land dealers, government inspectors and local officials arguably garnered the worst reputations. In the wake of the 1915 deportations, government agents took possession of an immense fortune in abandoned property and unclaimed businesses. To regularize their redistribution, Talat Pasha's Interior Ministry created state-run commissions to seize and auction forsaken lands and goods. Local agents widely ignored statutes directing the distribution of property to the highest bidders or to poor Muslim refugees. By the war's end, popular opinion had generally come to believe that the greatest recipients of non-Muslim lands and goods were large estate owners, rich entrepreneurs and corrupt officials. Public prosecution of such cases of corruption, however, was rarely if ever pursued.

The rampant nature of all these transgressions corroded popular faith in the government and the CUP. Over time, correspondence between officials in the capital and the provinces became rife with talk of public discontent, a phenomenon which at times bordered upon open defiance. During the CUP's annual congress in 1917, members were forced to openly address rumors that the party profited from hoarding and short selling goods. The war, one senior Young Turk countered, had produced 'a commercial and economic awakening in the country'. It was for this reason, he argued, that the 'war's wealthy' should be celebrated and not vilified.[84] The government's decision to sue for peace one year later invalidated such claims. With the lifting of public censorship, few within the press dared defend the CUP's management of state affairs. Anecdotal evidence broadly suggests that the public shared the enmity that inspired the rise of Damad Ferid and other enemies of the party. For some, feelings of rage towards the Young Turks were not simply grounded in the nation's defeat or the hardship suffered at home. Social conservatives decried the CUP as a moral blight. The increased visibility of women in society proved particularly divisive for critics of the government. As in other combatant states, the war provided new outlets for both elite and impoverished women to find work outside the home. Services and industries aimed at meeting the military's needs (such as hospitals, textile mills and administrative jobs) allowed women broader economic and social opportunities. By the war's end, government ministers approved a law allowing women to be trained and to work as doctors, dentists, pharmacists and urban constables.[85] Desperate conditions compelled equally large numbers of women into prostitution and sexual exploitation. Forced either by hunger or by abandonment (a plight particularly suffered by displaced Armenians), women by the tens of thousands were drawn into prostitution during the war years. Alarm over public hygiene and the outbreak of disease led CUP functionaries to impose greater regulation on the opening and running of brothels. By the close of the war, the CUP sanctioned the licensing of brothels throughout the country (with Istanbul claiming 175 self-identified houses of prostitution for itself).[86] For these and other reasons, many would remember the end of the CUP era as a time in which 'the foundation of our national morality was shaken'.[87]

In the immediate term, the horrors that had befallen the empire spurred on lingering conspiratorial suspicions towards the Young Turks. Since the days of the 1908 revolution, rumors had persisted among the party's opponents that the CUP's leaders were either Free-masons, Jews or both. Driving these suspicions was the fact that the party had been established in the Macedonian city of Salonika, the home of a unique community of Muslims who descended from a messianic Jewish sect. News that senior party leaders, including Talat Pasha, were members of one of Salonika's fraternal lodges led to wide-scale speculation that the CUP itself was a Masonic institution. These associations made between Freemasonry, the CUP and Saloni-ka's 'crypto-Jews' also affected the ways in which many foreign observers perceived politics in the Ottoman capital. Conjecture that the party was 'seriously influenced by Jewish and atheistic political Freemasonry', as one British ambassador asserted, sharpened feelings of alienation found in the capital and the provinces.[88]

As conditions worsened throughout the country, the economic cleavages that plagued towns and villages appeared to grow ever wider. The spoils garnered during the war, such as abandoned prop-erty or state contracts, were mostly enjoyed by those with ties to Istanbul, or those who were themselves Young Turks. The divide between the haves and have-nots appeared even more glaring given the social origins of many within the CUP. To the end, the Young Turks were overwhelmingly urbanites, men who were well educated and upwardly mobile. A considerable portion of the party's member-ship also came from the Balkans, a fact that appeared particularly glaring to many inhabitants of provincial Anatolia and the Arab lands. Amid all of the country's misfortunes, the CUP's elitism, as well as its supposed 'alien' origins, assumed new significance. For many, the country lost the war not because of mismanagement or folly, but precisely because it had been ruled by religious deviants, foreigners and the morally corrupt. The CUP's collapse, in this light, was an act of deliverance.

However common these impressions might have been, it remains difficult to say how ordinary citizens perceived the future of the empire at the war's end. Efforts to glean popular opinion were generally spotty and slanted during the post-armistice era. British intelligence officers, for example, tended to survey the attitudes of more well-off townspeople, as opposed to the impoverished or those living in villages. The responses interviewers often received were generally conciliatory towards the imposition of a British or American mandate in the region. While lacking resources to probe the question beyond the capital, Germany's ambassador largely agreed that the empire's population would accept some form of foreign tutelage. 'All Turks are unanimous in rejecting the dismemberment of Turkey', he asserted, since it naturally would result in the terminal breakup of the empire. 'The greatest portion of Turks', however, favored 'the assignment of a mandate for an undivided Turkey with the granting of extensive autonomy to the eastern provinces', historically the most restive part of the country. Of all the prospective occupiers, the United States tended to receive the greatest support from Ottoman citizens.[89]

Abstract acceptance of foreign rule faded as the realities of an Allied occupation came into view. The first significant signs of public consternation became evident with the appearance of Allied ships off Istanbul's shoreline in mid-November 1918. As the fleet lay at anchor in sight of the city's heights, the streets of Pera, Galata and other cosmopolitan neighborhoods erupted in scenes of elation. Local Armenians and Greeks mobbed British and French troops coming ashore, demonstrations that quickly degenerated into wild processions of exultation. For many Muslim residents, the sight of these expressions of joy was absolute proof of their worst suspicions. 'In every part, flags were waving', one Ottoman officer wrote in his diary, 'especially the Greek rags as well'. As the days passed, Christian supporters of the occupation hurled insults at passing Muslim officials and grew more provocative in expressing their pleasure. With the British dreadnought *Superb* moored quayside, an officer watched as 'the drunkenness of the deceiving Greek rascals [*palikarya*]' reached its full majesty, 'insane with giddiness and joy', upon the docks.[90] The local press went further still in fanning the outrage. 'If six or seven hundred thousand Armenians died', one editor declared, 'another two to three million Turks passed on [during the war]. But the day of justice, the day of reckoning, has come today, has it not? A grisly and fatal Europe has brought the offenses of the Armenians and Greeks to light'.[91] Harassment of Ottoman officials eventually subsided (in part due to a British decree threatening to treat any 'lack of proper' respect towards local police and soldiers as an attack on the Allies).[92] Though the winter of 1918–19 passed quietly, the divisions created by the Allied presence remained.

An even more combustible climate reigned further south, along the frontier districts of the armistice line. Since the cessation of hostilities in October, Ottoman negotiators initially believed that they had prevented the fall of Cilicia, the vital flatlands straddling the periphery of northern Syria. By December, however, British and French forces utilized a key provision of the armistice to push beyond the front lines north of Aleppo. There was little denying that French interests lay at the heart of this appropriation of authority. With its rich history dating back to antiquity, Cilicia captured the imagination of several noted French imperialists. But it was particularly French sympathies towards Armenians that guided their desire to occupy Cilicia. Leading French officers foresaw a 'moral conquest' of the region, one that would not only restore Armenians to their homes but also pave the way for an Armenian state.[93] Local reaction to the change in regime, at least initially, was relatively muted. British and French troops met no resistance in assuming defensive positions in each of Cilicia's major towns. Provincial Ottoman authorities, which remained nominally in charge of the region, worked in tandem with Allied officers despite a mutual amount of distrust. Even the initial return of Armenian refugees did not necessarily upset public order. Some old neighbors, one survivor later testified, welcomed the deportees home as they walked through the central market of Urfa. For returning natives, emotions tended to waver between sadness and joy. In taking in the state of Urfa's old Armenian quarter, many residents 'could not withhold tears upon seeing everything in ruins, with the bones of beloved martyrs strewn here and there'. 'Nevertheless', one survivor observed, 'putting their thoughts to the future, they were happy to find some survivors and eager to rebuild'.[94]

The fragility of this initial peace became more exposed as 1919 progressed. As in other parts of Anatolia, the rights to abandoned property were a source of unending personal and legal disputes between their displaced Armenian owners and their Muslim custodians. Despite their responsibilities, Ottoman officials were inconsistent in mediating or enforcing agreements between parties. The inaction or overzealousness of British and French authorities further aggravated

1. Kalusd Sürmenyan
(*seated on the left*).

2. Hüseyin Fehmi.

3. A procession in Merzifon, northern Anatolia, to celebrate the opening of the Ottoman parliament in December 1908.

4. Izmir/Smyrna, *c*.1922.

5. Galata Bridge in central Istanbul, October 1922.

6. Interior Minister Talat Pasha (*center*) delivering a celebratory address on Ottoman Independence Day.

7. Sultan Mehmed VI Vahideddin.

8. Ships of the Allied fleet firing a salute in the Bosphorus.

9. Damad Ferid Pasha (*front row, fourth from the right*) leading the Ottoman peace delegation in Paris, 1919. Tevfik Pasha, in the white waistcoat, stands beside him.

10. Local Armenians and French African troops welcome General Henri Gouraud to Mersin.

11. British troops marching through the streets of Istanbul.

12. A protest meeting in Sultanahmet Square, central Istanbul, 1919.

13. Mustafa Kemal in the study of his Ankara home in 1921.

14. An open session of the Grand National Assembly of Turkey, February 1921.

15. A view of Ankara, late 1922.

these and other strains. Signs of violent unrest cast an even graver pall over the occupation. In February, a crowd attacked a camp of returning Armenians outside Aleppo. By the time British and local troops intervened, more than a hundred refugees, as well fifty of their assailants, had died in the course of a two-hour struggle.[95] Armenians were not the sole targets of indiscriminate violence. To augment France's presence in the region, French authorities employed thousands of Armenian refugees as gendarmes and soldiers in the occupation. The most feared of these detachments was a force comprising thousands of recruited deportees, the Legion d'Orient. In towns across Cilicia, the Legion acquired a bitter reputation as Muslims fell victim to incidents of murder and physical abuse. 'Many of these Armenian soldiers frankly avowed that they come to this country for revenge', as one visitor saw it. 'In Adana every night Armenian soldiers were shot by Turks, and Turks by Armenian soldiers'.[96] Even so, French and British authorities attempted to remain conciliatory towards both sides, leaving many to wonder with whom they actually sympathized. 'My people were bitter', one veteran Legionnaire later professed; 'they had received what they thought were inviolable promises. I was bitter but not surprised because I knew the treachery of diplomacy'. 'War', he concluded, 'made beasts, vicious, often heroic beasts of men in battle; diplomacy was the game of jackals'.[97]

As unease gripped towns and villages across Cilicia, most of the country's attention remained transfixed on the fate of the Aegean coast. Rising trepidation over the future of Izmir and surrounding districts was only partially driven by Greece's well-publicized influence at Versailles. Many saw the burgeoning crisis as the continuation of long-simmering internal and international tensions. Much like the Cilician towns of Adana, Antep and Urfa, Izmir and its counterparts on the Aegean were the beneficiaries of unprecedented economic growth in the decades leading up to the Great War. The fruits of the Aegean's prosperity, however, tended to be unequally distributed in both town and country, with Anatolian Greeks often enjoying the lion's share of the gains. As with Cilicia, commentators and activists, particularly in the CUP, interpreted the growing economic divide in the Aegean as an outgrowth of foreign influence and irredentism in the region. In the wake of the Balkan Wars, Greece appeared to be setting its sights on Izmir, Ayvalık and other coastal communities. While it was by no means clear when a Greek takeover would happen, one Austrian diplomat prophesied in 1913 that it was 'almost certain' that 'Greece will assert its political claims to the Anatolian coast'.[98] These suspicions, together with the agitation of nationalist ideologues inside the CUP, helped spur much of the violence that wracked the Greek communities of the Aegean interior in the years that followed 1914. After the declaration of the armistice, foreign observers readily concluded that native Greeks supported the region's annexation. 'The attitude of the Greek population at Smyrna and of the Greek officers who have come in is almost one of proprietorship', an American consular official noted. It was an attitude that was due 'in part to their majority in the city and to the firm conviction that the Smyrna region will be given to Greece'.[99]

Other signs, many of them less noticed by outside observers, complicate this picture of the Aegean in the spring of 1919. To some extent, enthusiasm for Greece's annexation of the region extended well beyond the provincial borders of Izmir. Public demonstrations in support of Venizelos were staged in Bursa, in Gallipoli and in Greek communities much further afield. In Manisa, just northeast of Smyrna, community leaders organized a plebiscite in favor of Greek rule. And yet significant elements of Izmir's non-Muslim population tended to oppose partition altogether. In addition to among Jews, who comprised 10 percent of the city's population, anti-annexation sentiments were strongly associated with Smyrna's community of Levantines (a group of some 20,000 Christians whose heritage spanned the Mediterranean world and Europe).[100] In more remote or rural districts, areas where Orthodox Christians were far fewer in number, relations were often less strained by confessional differences. 'They [Muslims and Christians] got on well with one another; it was like that in Kemalpaşa', an aging Turkish gentleman remembered of his village. 'Near us here there were not a lot of Greeks. But I want to say, native Greeks [*yerli Rumlar*] said they felt uneasy about the Greeks coming to Turkey'.[101]

Events eventually rendered such expressions of fraternity moot. Well into the spring, Allied diplomats, intelligence officers and private citizens living in the Aegean warned of a coming disaster if Greece invaded. Grisly incidents of sectarian violence foretold of bitter fighting ahead if Athens was to have its way. Reports of Ottoman gendarmes and Muslims attacked by disgruntled local Greeks, as well as the murder and mutilation of Christian villagers, were readily cited as evidence of what was to come. 'This is the sort of thing that is going on all over the country', one British resident of Izmir wrote, 'and is, in my opinion, largely due to Greek propaganda which has irritated the Turkish population ...' It was for this reason, he told a newspaper proprietor in London, 'it would be a terrible mistake to give this country, or any part of it, to the Greeks at the present time'.[102] These and other appeals for restraint ultimately mattered very little. For Britain, Greece, the United States, France and Italy, far greater concerns were at play in deciding the future of the Ottoman Empire: national pride, strategic ambitions, as well as – to various degrees – economic interests.

The violence that ultimately overtook the remnants of the empire was not purely an outgrowth of imperial competition. Harsh local realities provided much of the tinder. By the spring of 1919, very few communities enjoyed any respite from the hardships of the war. Some conditions, such as hunger, disease and displacement, remained unaddressed for months to come. It is against this backdrop that many regions confronted the repercussions of the wartime massacres and expulsions. The return of Armenians and Greeks did more than just compel communities to deal with guilt, stolen property and lost loved ones. Even more fundamental were issues of power and authority. All of the empire's citizens, including those now living under foreign occupation, understood Woodrow Wilson's principle of self-determination in a majoritarian light. Minorities, at best, were to be tolerated. Yet given the country's inherent diversity, as well as the chaos and dislocation brought on by the war, the question of who was in the majority could not always be easily answered. In communities along the Aegean coast, those who favored annexation relied heavily upon the presumption of a Greek majority in the environs of Smyrna. Opponents of Greece's acquisition of Anatolian territory often countered with figures showing a far larger Muslim majority in the wider countryside. In Cilicia, a region that had once been home to the medieval kingdom of Lesser Armenia, Armenians were historically outnumbered in both town and country. In the aftermath of the genocide, France's stated plans to back an Armenian state, and resettle the region with up to 100,000 refugees, promised to change these imbalances permanently.[103] Then there were the lands further east in Anatolia. By 1918, fighting, deportations and massacres had thoroughly emptied several provinces of both Muslim and Christian residents. The arguments over self-determination that raged thereafter in Erzurum and Van were thus predicated on communities that by and large no longer existed.

3

The War Resumes

The Origins and Implications
of a Resurgent Ottoman Empire

On 13 May 1919, the vanguard of a Greek expeditionary force set sail for Anatolia. Soldiers aboard the steamer *Patris*, as well as on other vessels, remained unaware of their true destination well into the trip. Their original orders had commanded them to sail for Ukraine to take part in the broader Allied effort against the Bolsheviks. Once at sea, senior commanders informed them that they would soon disembark at the port of Smyrna. The reason for the subterfuge was both political and tactical. Days earlier, Wilson, Clemenceau and Lloyd George privately granted Venizelos final approval of Greece's plans to seize the town and its surrounding districts. With Italy still hoping to occupy the whole of Anatolia's Aegean coast, Greece's Prime Minister ordered his troops to move surreptitiously for fear of an open confrontation with Rome. Intelligence sources in Smyrna also encouraged Greek troops to make haste. It was widely believed that local Ottoman troops and civilians were beginning to gather arms and were intent upon resisting any Greek landing. While stressing the solemnity of their task, commanding officers aboard the *Patris* and other ships bade their men to remain disciplined and vigilant. 'Wherever we may go', one colonel declared, 'we must know that we are going to liberate our brethren under alien rule. The enthusiasm filling our hearts is fully justified but any improper manifestation of this enthusiasm will be entirely out of place'. With that, the men were reminded that Muslims, Jews and Christians from throughout the Mediterranean resided in Smyrna. No harm was to come to them. 'In a little while', the colonel closed, 'they will become our brothers as if they were true Greeks'.[1]

In legal terms, the Greek troops deploying to Izmir possessed only a probationary mandate. The city's final territorial status, like the rest of the Ottoman Empire, remained a matter of debate as peace negotiations in Paris continued. The invasion was instead sanctioned under a provision of the armistice allowing for the seizure of Ottoman land on the grounds of maintaining security (the same rationale employed in the British and French occupation of Cilicia). Representatives of each of the major Allied Powers were also to partake in the landing to ensure a peaceful transfer. From the outset, however, Greece's commitment to secrecy and ambiguity created confusion. Greek officers excluded their British, American and French counterparts in planning their arrival in the port. There was no communication or coordination between the Greeks and Ottoman authorities in Izmir proper. News of the invasion, however, spread through the town on the eve of the flotilla's arrival. When the *Patris* docked on the early morning of 15 May, a huge crowd lined the shore to greet the soldiers as they disembarked. The atmosphere was euphoric as local Greeks danced and embraced the troops as they assumed ranks. Upon entering the city center, advancing units received a far more hostile welcome. As one detachment passed the central government offices, the first shots were fired. By the end of the day, pandemonium descended on the city as Greek forces found themselves enveloped by Ottoman soldiers and civilians. After the armed resisters barricaded within the government offices had been subdued, a wave of attacks targeting Muslim residents and local businesses swept through the town. Following the restoration of order, local officials estimated that forty Ottoman officers and officials were killed in the fighting, with another sixty left wounded.[2] An investigation led by a commission of Allied officers later found that up 400 Muslims and sixty Ottoman Greeks died as a result of mob violence that day.[3]

It did not take long for citizens across the empire to register a strong response to the events in Izmir. Over the following days, newspapers and government offices received waves of telegrams from protest meetings and civic organizations based in towns throughout the country. Speaking on behalf of a crowd of a thousand protesters gathered in the town of Sivas, a committee of prominent citizens wired the capital that the nation would not tolerate Izmir's loss. 'It is said with one voice', they declared, 'that Izmir's occupation by the Greeks is contrary to the principles of justice and humanity. This right is clear and the preservation of our law is correct'.[4] Istanbul also seethed with activity. In the days that followed the landing, spontaneous demonstrations and public forums drew tens of thousands as details of the occupation filtered through the press. The stoutest displays of indignation were saved for the first Friday after the bloody events of 15 May. Leaflets circulating through the city called upon citizens to convene in Sultanahmet Square after the close of prayers. 'Think of the nation', one notice read. 'Learn about the atrocities at Izmir. Anatolia is waiting for your decision'.[5] By midday between 100,000 and 200,000 people had assembled between the two great mosques of Sultanahmet and Aya Sofia. Each of the speakers, many of them noted CUP ideologues, decried the Greek attack and implored the crowd to rally to the nation's defense. 'This Ottoman country', one speaker roared, 'is historically, civilizationally, religiously and racially Turkish and Muslim and it will always remain Turkish and Muslim'.[6]

The government, by contrast, displayed few signs of resolve. Rather than move decisively, the sultan dissolved the cabinet, allowing only Damad Ferid to stay on as grand vezir. The Freedom and Accord Party, which had held sway as the most powerful faction in the cabinet, offered only a brief statement of support to the protesters. Ministers and regional officials, however, issued more hesitant guidance to officials in the provinces. Izmir's governor assured the press that Athens stood prepared to offer 'every kind of help and ease' in seeing Izmir's government restored as it had been before. Together, he hoped, Greeks and Ottomans 'would be able to properly look after the interests of the Muslim people'.[7] Allies of Damad Ferid's in the press offered a broader defense for the state's inaction. By virtue of the armistice, one editor reasoned, Istanbul had conferred upon the Allies the right of occupation. Greece, as one of the victors, was within its legal right to send an 'assisting force' to assume control of Izmir. Editors assured their readers that British, French and American officials were aware that Athens was 'not known as a just or qualified government' capable of fair administration. 'The Allied states certainly have a much better appreciation of what will or will not be acceptable for Izmir'.[8]

Few public servants readily accepted such dull justifications for

Istanbul's inaction. For many officers and officials, there was simply no reason to tolerate Greece's seizure of the Aegean coast. This was certainly the case of Eyüp Durukan, a thirty-seven-year-old staff officer based in Istanbul. As a veteran of the Balkan Wars and the Gallipoli front, he committed to his diary a daily account of the humiliations he saw and heard in the weeks that followed the armistice. On more than one occasion, he watched with indignity the wild exuberance of Istanbul's Greeks during the arrival of Allied troops. He regularly kept tabs on rumors, news reports and government circulars, particularly those related to signs of Christian insurrection. As the threat of an Allied takeover of Izmir approached, the administration of Damad Ferid vexed him that much more. For Eyüp, the state's eager prosecution of the CUP's former leaders revealed the true nature of the postwar regime 'The government's work', he wrote that April, 'and [practic-ally] the only thing it pursues, consists of treacherous acts that torment the true sons of the fatherland and divide the nation into two and thus [they] put oil on the bread of our enemies'.[9] Izmir's fall, and the news of massacred Muslim innocents, were the last straw. Five days after the Greek landing, Eyüp met privately with other officers assigned to the Ottoman general staff. All of them believed that the government was unwilling to counter the invasion and that there was little time to lose. The best solution, they agreed, was to take 'collective and indi-vidual steps to counter these invaders'.[10] It would be weeks before Eyüp and his colleagues could gather weapons, ammunition and other supplies for Ottoman forces defending the Aegean hinterland. In the meantime, news soon circulated among the general staff that Mustafa Kemal, once rumored to be Minister of War, was 'going into action' on Anatolia's north coast. 'This news strengthened my hopes', Eyüp wrote in his diary. 'My courage rose'.

May 1919 occupies a very important place within the collective memory of Turks today. It is on 19 May that Turkish citizens remem-ber what is characterized as a key moment in the making of the Turkish Republic: Mustafa Kemal Atatürk's arrival in the Black Sea port of Samsun. Symbolically, his landing on Anatolia's north coast marked the launch of a national resistance aimed at liberating the empire from foreign occupation. Almost a decade later, Kemal memo-rialized this time in his life as the start of his own rise to national prominence. Yet Turkey's founder was by no means a household name in May 1919. More importantly, virtually nothing about Atatürk's future appeared fated from the perspective of that spring. He came to Samsun with nothing more than orders to maintain peace in the Anatolian countryside. As a senior Ottoman officer, he had no political experience and no stated desire to challenge the fundamental order governing the empire.

The story of how he and officers like Eyüp resumed the war against the Allies, and eventually overthrew the sultan, is by no means a simple one. Mustafa Kemal's political odyssey is a tale largely defined by opportunism, contingency and pure chance. There were, however, important threads of continuity that spanned his spectacular emergence onto the global stage. Atatürk and the majority of those who followed him were products of the Young Turk era. The suffering they endured during the Great War, and their desire to reverse the war's consequences, bound them together. Ideologically, Mustafa Kemal and his closest supporters were nationalists in the mold of Talat, Enver and other senior CUP leaders. In taking up arms against the Allies, they accepted the consequences of the party's policies of deportation and social re-engineering. To that end, many who supported Atatürk's leadership envisioned a restoration of the CUP state once the new war was won.

The sultan and his supporters looked upon the resistance as a movement driven by something other than patriotism. With hundreds of wartime officers, bureaucrats and civic leaders flocking to Mustafa Kemal's side, many in the capital interpreted the resistance's efforts as a vehicle for the CUP's resurgence. Large numbers of common citizens arrived at the same conclusion. While many in the countryside felt duty-bound to defend the empire, significant segments of the population were too tired or too embittered to take up arms so soon after the Great War. A deep loathing of the Young Turks prevented many citizens from throwing in their lot with Kemal's fighters. Mehmed VI and his closest retainers seized upon these expressions of opposition to the CUP and exploited them for their own benefit. By the beginning of 1920, these political divisions created new fault lines in what remained of the empire. It was no longer simply a question of what lands would remain part of the Ottoman state. Who truly ruled the country, and what it meant to be a loyal citizen, became issues of profound contention.

Mustafa Kemal acknowledged these fissures only in part. At first, he and others around him tended to ignore signs of the sultan's displeasure. Indications of popular discontent were similarly eschewed as symptoms of 'reaction' or foreign meddling. Yet as the fighting against the Allies intensified, and with negotiations in Paris at a standstill, Kemal's self-proclaimed Nationalists slowly conceived of a very different vision of the country and its future. By the spring of 1920, the first true signs of the empire's dissolution came into view.

'WE WILL FIGHT LIKE RAMS':
THE ORIGINS OF
THE NATIONAL MOVEMENT

It was not until 1952 that Ahmet Şükrü Oğuz decided to commit his memoirs to paper. At the age of seventy-one, he had never been one to draw the public's attention. His silence, it is largely assumed, was on account of events a quarter of a century earlier. In 1926, both he and his younger brother, Nail, had been put on trial for attempting to overthrow Mustafa Kemal, then president of the young Turkish Republic. He, along with several other of the indicted, also stood accused of hoping to reinstate the CUP as the governing party. Though Şükrü was acquitted on all charges, his brother was not so lucky. Nail was convicted and sentenced to hang. Şükrü escaped this fate and lived the rest of his life in obscurity.

The former Ottoman officer revealed very little of himself in the opening pages of his memoirs. This inattention to his early life has resulted in some uncertainty as to his background and his early experiences. It appears clear that he was born in Istanbul in the neighborhood of Yenibahçe (it is for this reason he was known for most of his life as 'Yenibahçeli Şükrü', or 'Şükrü of Yenibahçe'). At the end of his life, it was reported that his family had descended from Turkic tribes from Anatolia's western coast. Others would later claim that his family was not Turkish at all but had arrived as immigrants from the North Caucasus (a group most often referred to as 'Circassians'). Be that as it may, Şükrü graduated from the Harbiye in 1903, just a year after Mustafa Kemal. He spent the early part of his career fighting nationalist rebels in the southern Balkans. The bitterness of this experience, coupled with his exposure to like-minded officers, apparently brought him into the CUP fold. By the time of the Young Turk Revolution, both he and his brother Nail possessed reputations as *fedai*, or radical members willing to kill for the party. The outbreak of war in 1914 catapulted him further up the ranks of the military. As a skilled marksman and promising officer, he was dispatched to Germany to receive special training in the hopes of establishing an elite unit of Ottoman storm troopers. His men, he later boasted, formed an 'excellently drilled and disciplined' force despite the war's hardships.[11]

Like others still serving in uniform, Şükrü was rendered disillusioned and angry by news of the empire's capitulation. He initially rejected orders for his unit's demobilization, arguing to senior officials that he should move his command to the interior of the country instead and fight on. 'With which soldiers and with which arms?' responded the army's chief inspector. 'Against what imagined attack? Have you not read Wilson's principles? The war is over for the whole world'.[12] This admonition did little to deter or discourage him. He soon began to meet in secret with long-time comrades in the hopes of finding some other means of continuing the war. 'We will fight like rams', proposed one old friend, a doctor by the name of Fahri Can. To strike with the greatest force, he explained, rams typically withdrew backwards, gaining space and time. 'We will move to the east', Fahri continued. 'We'll pull ourselves together and launch [ourselves] when we get our full speed'.[13] As early as December 1918, Şükrü and his companions claimed to have joined a secret organization, dubbed 'Karakol', aimed at restarting the war.

For a Turkish reader in the early 1950s, such assertions may have come across as somewhat heretical. By then, textbooks and public proclamations celebrated Atatürk as the spark that began the so-called National Struggle. Şükrü, to some extent, acknowledged this belief while still affirming his own role in reigniting the war. Resistance, he declared, was what 'anyone with a sane head was thinking'.[14] In highlighting this historical contradiction, Şükrü's memoirs bring forth one of the murkiest elements of the empire's end. His version of events tells of a chaotic set of circumstances that led to the renewed fighting in 1919. These recollections, as well as those of others, also reveal a broad, initially disjointed, effort by the CUP's remnants to counter the Allies and forestall the empire's partition. Atatürk's place in the early makings of this resistance movement remains somewhat difficult to pin down. By extension, his eventual rise as the nation's savior appears less than predestined.

Şükrü tells us next to nothing of his activities within the CUP. He is equally silent as to his thoughts about the party and its disgraceful dissolution. A host of other sources, however, suggest that he was intimately tied to the CUP's tumultuous final years in power. By 1916, rifts over matters of politics and personality were beginning to tear at the party's inner sanctum. The most pressing issue, the conduct of the war, proved especially polarizing. In the fall of that year, senior leaders narrowly averted a coup attempt by officers hoping to seek a separate peace with the Allies. The leader of the plot, a notorious *fedai* named Yakup Cemil, was one of several toughs who gravitated to the empire's two most prominent figures, Enver and Talat. Tensions between the Minister of War and the Minister of the Interior simmered into 1918, their respective factions each fearing the prospect of assassination or a coup. As someone personally close to Enver, Şükrü Oğuz was intimately involved in this internal struggle.

The impending threat of defeat, it appears, helped to heal relations between the two ministers and their entourages. By the fall of 1918, both men began to talk of contingency plans in the event of Istanbul's surrender. Multiple sources suggest that Enver counseled several devotees to prepare for some kind of resistance effort in the event of the country's occupation. The plan, to the extent that there was one, counted on an offensive led by Ottoman troops stationed in the Caucasus (with troops commanded by Enver's uncle, Halil, taking the lead). The organization of this initiative continued after both Enver and Talat fled the country in early November 1918. It was during this stage of the preparations that Şükrü Oğuz was brought into the Karakol organization. His selection was not accidental. Of the personalities linked to this conspiracy, most were close friends and admirers of Enver Pasha. Taken as a whole, the cast of characters who populated Karakol resembled a who's who of the CUP's most violent supporters.

This effort, according to Şükrü's reckoning, planted the seed of what became Mustafa Kemal's army of liberation, the National Forces (*Kuva-yı Milliye*). 'No matter what anyone says', he asserted, 'in the National Forces there was a Unionist [CUP] spirit'.

It is also likely that a Turkish reader in the early 1950s would have found this claim somewhat blasphemous. By then, it had become state dogma that the Young Turks had sought to undermine Atatürk from the beginning of his rise to power. More to the point, Şükrü's assertions would have struck many as an attempt at restoring his own good name and that of his former comrades. Indeed, there is little doubt that he sought some degree of vindication in writing his memoirs. Şükrü Oğuz, however, was just one of many veterans who stressed the CUP's role in launching the National Struggle. To understand this contradiction, as well as appreciate the broader factors that fueled this movement, one must first grapple with the internal politics of the CUP after the armistice. More precisely, one ultimately must confront both the realities and the mythos that surround the emergence of Mustafa Kemal.

At the moment of Enver and Talat's departure from the empire, the CUP, as a party, was a shadow of its former self. In spite of its rebranding as the Renovation Party, very few of the remaining stalwarts commanded the loyalty and respect enjoyed by those who fled. Many formerly influential figures drifted to the margins of imperial politics as anti-CUP sentiment took hold of the press and the sitting parliament. Among the few to benefit were former Young Turks known for their independence or dissent. Some, such as the party's founder, Ahmet Rıza, sought a place in the government despite the ascendancy of the CUP's opponents. 'I am against the *komiteci* mentality', one former CUP minister avowed. 'If Union and Progress resume their position in power it should be with new personalities. Henceforth, those with a *komiteci* mentality will not be allowed a place'.[15] The CUP's political decline accelerated following the mass arrest of members associated with the Armenian massacres and deportations. Among those taken into custody were senior members of Şükrü Oğuz's clandestine group. Rather than face imprisonment, he and a small cohort of organizers left Istanbul with orders to re-establish themselves in the Anatolian interior.

Despite the eviction of would-be resisters like Şükrü Oğuz from the capital, several factors helped galvanize their focus and energies.

Perhaps the most immediate catalyst was the fear of a Christian rebellion. In the wake of the armistice, loyal Unionists, as well as less partisan citizens, were dismayed at the joy expressed by Greeks and Armenians at the prospect of an Allied occupation. Amid the scenes of triumph witnessed in Istanbul's predominately Christian quarters, news reports and rumors of more violent demonstrations began to circulate. Soon after the empire's capitulation, for example, Şükrü had ordered his men to take defensive positions around Istanbul's Aya Sofia mosque for fear local vandals would hoist Greek flags from its minarets. In March 1919, newspapers broke news of an attack by a gang of some dozen Greeks in Bostancı, an affluent Istanbul suburb. The alleged details of the assault proved particularly shocking. After breaking into one seaside villa, the robbers 'bound the hands of servants and workers' and brutally murdered the home's principal resident, an official working for the Foreign Ministry.[16] The crime, as well as others attributed to Greek and Armenian bands operating outside the capital, was interpreted as a political act. Şükrü and his comrade Fahri Can especially dedicated themselves to combating what was likened to a broad campaign to 'destroy the Turks'.[17] Once the pair had settled in Gebze, a town on the main coastal road leading from Istanbul into the Anatolian interior, they helped arm and direct the activities of local Muslim paramilitaries. Şükrü's men, who largely comprised poor immigrants from the Caucasus and Balkans, preyed upon suspected Christian militants as well as hapless civilians. Two of their random victims, local Greek merchants from the nearby town of Pendik, were accordingly seized and their faces mutilated. After their ears were ripped off, the perpetrators told them to take their severed parts 'to your friends the English, whom you cheered so loudly the other day. Perhaps they will help you'.[18]

Further enabling Şükrü Oğuz's activities was the CUP's network of provincial offices. During the prewar years, the party had amassed a diverse body of supporters rooted in rural and urban communities throughout the empire. In some regions, the power exerted by local CUP clubs augmented or exceeded the influence of its imperial administration. Though weakened, the integrity of the party's provincial base largely survived the CUP's formal dissolution. As Karakol agents dispersed to the provinces, they found willing supporters among a large cast of local figures: policemen, mayors, bureaucrats, educators, journalists, merchants, landowners and, in many cases, bandits. Adding further strength to Karakol's operations were men who had also served as wartime provocateurs, assassins and paramilitaries in the Ottoman secret service, the Special Organization (*Teşkilat-ı Mahsusa*). Long before Şükrü took up residence in Gebze, his brother Nail, himself a Special Organization veteran, was dispatched to rally CUP loyalists in Anatolia's eastern provinces. This effort, by all accounts, immediately found willing participants. For Karakol agents, establishing a base of operations on the Black Sea was crucial to the state's survival. Both the Republic of Armenia, as well as Greek irredentists, eyed Anatolia's north and east for annexation. Yet, from the early days of the armistice, cutthroats and outlaws proved as much a threat to public order as any political conspiracy. One of the most notorious figures to haunt the Black Sea hinterland was a former merchant-turned-paramilitary named Topal Osman (or 'Osman the Lame'). During the war, Osman had accrued a vicious reputation as a killer under the command of the Ottoman Special Organization. With the cessation of hostilities, he and his loyal band sacked local Greek villages at will. Being a man known for killing '10–15 Orthodox Christians a day', as one Ottoman administrator remembered him, did not disqualify him in the eyes of local resisters. His fierceness, as well as his willingness to share the proceeds from his raids, ultimately made him a revered commander within the National Forces.[19]

A very different set of conditions shaped the beginnings of resistance efforts in Izmir. There, a separate cohort of Young Turks, one largely independent of Karakol's activities, struck out on their own in the hopes of forestalling an Allied occupation. Within a month of the armistice, a small circle of CUP stalwarts, several of them noted members of the Turkish Hearth, formed an organization dubbed the 'Committee for the Defense of Ottoman Rights'. With the aid of local officials, the group worked through the spring of 1919 in the hopes of rousing popular opposition to any Allied landing. Officers from the regular army intermingled with and conspired alongside the committee's leading members. On the eve of the Greek invasion, commanders of several local infantry units, men who also possessed strong Unionist credentials, coordinated with the committee in anticipation of the fighting that was sure to come.

There were still other former Young Turks who laid their own plans to initiate resistance efforts against the Allies. Among the most prominent of these officers was a corps commander and early CUP devotee called Kazım Karabekir. As perhaps the most prolific memoirist of the early Turkish Republic, Karabekir's writings depict his activities in Istanbul as uniquely pivotal in initiating the National Struggle. After he departed from his command in eastern Anatolia in late November 1918, his diaries testify to his early efforts to convince fellow officers to join him in resuming the war. These initial appeals, by his own account, met with little success. Yet, as he settled into life in the capital, he drew closer to a circle of officers who eventually came to form the core leadership of the National Forces. Among his earliest collaborators was a colonel newly arrived from the Syrian front, his friend – and the future Turkish president – İsmet İnönü. A second officer in his circle of companions was Rauf Orbay, former Minister of the Navy and leader of the Ottoman delegation at Mondros. Then there was Mustafa Kemal, whom he had known for more than a decade. As winter turned to spring, Karabekir and his colleagues debated at length what steps should be taken in the wake of the armistice. Karabekir remained vocal in his desire to return to Anatolia to fight off Greek and Armenian encroachments in the north and east. Mustafa Kemal, who was ailing, was not opposed to such plans but possessed different priorities. He preferred to stay in Istanbul and 'take any kind of assignment in the sultan's government'.[20] Karabekir left anyway, arriving in eastern Anatolia in late April 1919. In the weeks before Greece's seizure of Izmir, he commiserated with local Anatolian leaders and gathered intelligence on British, Greek and Armenian activities in the Caucasus and along the Black Sea. Years later, Karabekir claimed that it was he who 'determined the political and military plans' that began Turkey's War of Independence.[21]

It was not until the 1960s that Turks were allowed to read Kazım Karabekir's full account. Like Ahmet Şükrü, Karabekir's later acquittal on charges of treason resulted in his banishment from public life until after Atatürk's death in 1938. The first iterations of his memoirs were deemed so scandalous that most of the original drafts were seized and burned on government orders. Why his account would provoke such harsh acts of suppression only partially stemmed from his indictment and prosecution in 1926. His version of events, if even partially true, underscores a challenge that still confronts historians today: if Mustafa Kemal was but one of several men who helped lead the National Struggle, how did he ascend so far? What exactly made him the movement's eventual leader?

Mustafa Kemal first addressed these questions just as the war with Greece was approaching its climax. In 1922, he arranged to meet with a prominent Istanbul journalist and offered an expansive retelling of his life. He was raised in Salonika, the son of a provincial bureaucrat and a religiously conservative mother. His second name, Kemal, meaning 'perfection' in Arabic, was awarded to him by a teacher in school. As a gifted student, he acceded to the Harbiye. Like many young cadets of his generation, his time in the academy bred both a fierce patriotism and a fiery loathing for Sultan Abdülhamid II. After falling foul of the authorities, for which he was briefly imprisoned, he was allowed to graduate and was posted to Ottoman Syria. There he established himself as a dissident and activist, forming a secret society dedicated to restoring the constitution. Shortly before the 1908 revolution, his organization merged with the CUP. From the outset, Mustafa Kemal claimed he did not readily fit in among his fellow revolutionaries. 'I found their personal displays ugly', he explained in 1922. 'I saw the actions of some of the comrades as worthy of criticism and did not refrain from criticizing [them]'.[22] Even though he took issue with the CUP's politicization of the army and clashed with senior officers, he remained in the party till its dissolution. With the empire's entry into the war in 1914, he came to serve as a regimental commander. He made no mention in his interview of his heroics at the Battle of Gallipoli, during which he was both wounded and decorated. He focused instead upon his record as a critic of the war and its management. At the war's end, he asserted, he lobbied officials in Istanbul to be named a minister in the aftermath of Ahmet İzzet's resignation. With no appointment forthcoming, he returned to Istanbul to carry on his lobbying in person. 'The [only] thing I was thinking at the time', he stated in 1922, 'was [how] a strong footing for the defense of the country could be established while pleasing every [political] faction'.[23] Finding consensus among Istanbul's various ideological camps, however, proved too daunting. It was primarily for this reason that Mustafa Kemal 'made the decision to leave Istanbul and go to the nation and work among them'. The government, seemingly by chance, then offered him a position in Anatolia which he took 'after consulting with friends'.[24] It was by mere coincidence that he departed the capital a day after the Greeks entered Izmir.

The contention that the National Struggle began under his solitary initiative was a subject Atatürk embellished upon as the years passed. During his famed 1927 Nutuk, or 'Speech', he again placed himself at the center of the story and made no direct mention of the months he spent in Istanbul conspiring with Kazım Karabekir or other officers. The weight of this narrative grew as Mustafa Kemal garnered greater power and international renown. Even before his death, the mythos of his arrival in Anatolia in May 1919 became singularly associated with the legitimacy of his rule. European and American authors were especially important in legitimizing Atatürk's singular relationship with the National Struggle. He alone comprehended that the empire had died the day the Greeks invaded, as one French biographer told readers in 1937. He alone, Kemal explained, understood 'there was still time to save what remained, which would constitute the real heritage of the Turks, and form the nucleous of a State exclusively Turk'.[25] Atatürk's rendition of history, in this regard, was his mandate to establish the Turkish Republic. To challenge this version of events was to question in principle the revolutionary reforms he eventually imposed upon the whole of the country.

Some who knew Mustafa Kemal during those days sustained elements of his account. Rauf Orbay, for example, depicted him as active among officers hoping to resist the Allies. However, both he and others implied Kemal was hesitant to leave the capital. Ample evidence suggests that he continued to angle for a cabinet position as late as the end of March. Precisely why he received an appointment to oversee an army inspectorate headquartered in Erzurum is even less clear. In his Nutuk, Mustafa Kemal claimed the position granted him the jurisdictional authority he needed to commence resistance operations. Other sources, such as the diary of one senior general, suggest that his superiors planned to send him away before Damad Ferid had him arrested for his 'intrigues'.[26] Complicating this matter further still is the conflicting evidence of Mustafa Kemal's relationship with conspirators in the Karakol organization. In 1927, Atatürk claimed he learned of the organization's existence only after he came to Anatolia. Upon learning that it was a 'secret and frightful gang [komite]', he ordered the group to cease its activities.[27] Testimonials published after his death in 1938 contradict this assertion entirely. Ahmet Şükrü Oğuz went so far as to swear that Karakol sought Kemal's support and hoped that he would take a leading role in the resistance forming in the east. It was through the intercession of a mutual friend, Oğuz avowed, that Karakol sympathizers introduced the idea to both Atatürk and the Minister of War. All agreed that his record as an able commander was not his only qualification. He was, as one friend of Kemal's put it, a 'frightful enemy' of the CUP, someone who would drown Enver Pasha 'in a teaspoon of water' if he ever laid his hands on him.[28]

The contradictions that envelop Mustafa Kemal during this time are no accident of history. As early as 1922, Atatürk worked to shape the historical record in his favor. Guiding him in this pursuit was his desire to undermine or marginalize political rivals. Show trials, like those that targeted Karabekir and Şükrü Oğuz, were one manifestation of this effort. Erasing or minimizing the roles they played in the National Forces served as another. Censorship efforts both during and after Atatürk's reign limited the publication of contradictory accounts. As a result, there are still remarkably few sources in the mold of Karabekir's personal journal (which was only published in 2009). The effects of this campaign are also evident in testimonials that only partially challenge Atatürk's formal retelling of the National Struggle. Throughout their memoirs, both Rauf Orbay and Şükrü Oğuz are careful to emphasize their loyalty to Mustafa Kemal despite having been prosecuted and driven from politics.

The inconsistencies that mire aspects of Mustafa Kemal's life do not obscure all aspects of his evolution as a historical figure. The documentary record makes it clear that the CUP did lay much of the foundation for the National Struggle. Multiple accounts affirm that there were several centers of Young Turk activity geared towards building a resistance movement. The party's organizational capacity, and the enthusiasm of its members, helped it overcome many of its weaknesses after its formal dissolution in 1918. That said, Mustafa Kemal's ultimate ascendancy suggests that members were conscious of the party's unpopularity following the empire's defeat. Many commentators perceived Kemal's reputation as a naysayer within the Young Turk camp as a potential asset. He was also among the highest-ranking officers known for supporting a resumption of the war. However, it was only later that supporters associated his heroics at Gallipoli with the legitimacy of his leadership (an impression, ironically, that grew after European and Australian writers identified him as one of the more impressive officers on the Gallipoli front). With the start of heavy fighting outside Izmir in May 1919, all of these elements helped instill resistance forces with an air of legitimacy and coherence in the weeks and months ahead.

'SUBJECT TO THE NATIONAL WILL':[29] THE FIGHTING BEGINS

Ali Çetinkaya first went to war in 1902. As a first lieutenant fresh from the Harbiye, he spent the next seven years of his life fighting guerrillas in the mountains of Macedonia and Albania. The experience drove him, like so many of his generation, into the arms of the CUP. By his own account, he became a feared *fedai*, or, as he put it, 'one of the most trusted agents' of the party.[30] Between 1911 and 1918, he served as a front-line commander across the Ottoman landscape: Benghazi in Libya, Kut in Iraq, Van in eastern Anatolia and then finally in the Balkans alongside German and Austrian troops. After the signing of the armistice, witnesses state he was among the first to join the Karakol organization. Kel Ali – or 'Bald Ali' – as he was known to his friends, does not mention this in his memoirs. He admits instead that he actively corresponded with other officers and activists linked to Izmir's Committee for the Defense of Ottoman Rights ahead of the city's fall. In the weeks that followed Greece's invasion, the resumption of armed conflict arrived on his doorstep.

In early 1919, Çetinkaya was assigned to a unit stationed in Ayvalık on the Aegean coast. The town, according to those who visited that winter, was still slow to recover from the war. One British officer who passed through found many of the houses intact 'though denuded of their contents' following the wartime deportations of native Greeks. 'The inhabitants', he observed, 'well known for their energy and thrift, now walk about aimlessly till sunset', with only vague thoughts of tending their fields in the spring.[31] Çetinkaya, as a garrison commander, saw it differently. He and his men found themselves alone among Ayvalık's Greek inhabitants, who were 'filled with feelings of animosity and seditious aspirations'.[32] His deepest fears were realized when a riot broke out in town the day after Greek troops arrived at Izmir. Order was quickly reimposed, but a far greater danger appeared increasingly imminent. Within the week that followed Izmir's fall, the first Greek detachments began to probe towns and villages closer to Ayvalık. Accompanying these Greek regulars were contingents of local Christian volunteers. One such force, around 800 strong, attacked and burned villages as it went.[33] In anticipation of a Greek attack on Ayvalık, Çetinkaya and other Ottoman officers mustered their own auxiliaries to augment imperial troops along the north Aegean. Among the peasants and reservists recruited into these 'national units' were cohorts of Bosnian immigrants. Their recruitment alone was of value, Çetinkaya reasoned, since local Greeks tended to fear Balkan refugees due to their association with crime and violence. Such preparations, however, proved insufficient. Under the cover of darkness on the morning of 29 May, Greek troops and irregulars disembarked from ships off Ayvalık's coast and headed into town. Having lost the high ground, Çetinkaya withdrew eastward and linked up with other officers determined to hold the Greeks back. At a time when Damad Ferid's government was still rounding up 'enlightened and pure young men' for their association with the CUP, their actions received little support from Istanbul.[34] At that point, Çetinkaya and his comrades were largely on their own.

News of Ayvalık's fall aggravated what was already a heightened state of public outrage. The week that followed the Greek seizure of Izmir was one of near-constant excitement and direct action. Waves of popular protest shook central Istanbul as students, teachers, politicians and activists assembled in the name of the nation's defense. Members of the Turkish Hearth assumed an especially visible role in articulating the demands of protesters taking to the streets. Those who spoke before the protesters repeatedly intoned a single point: the empire's remaining Muslim majority was united in opposing both partition and foreign occupation. Proclamations and letters of protest issued by gatherings and local congresses equally denounced Greece's invasion as an attack on all Muslims. Regular officers aided these efforts, often without the express permission of their superiors. As Greek detachments slowly expanded their beachhead from Izmir deeper into the western province of Aydın, nearby garrisons and police stations distributed arms and ammunition to citizens willing to fight. Early reports of the massacre of Muslim civilians in Izmir proved an especially potent tool in mobilizing civilians to take up arms. For even the most war-weary, fear of Greek rule and Christian insurrection drove many into action. The country, as one CUP activist reminded a crowd, was 'on the operating table', ready to be cut to pieces.[35]

The spontaneity and rage seen in the capital and towns throughout the country soon gave way to a more concerted campaign of mobilization. As Damad Ferid's government dithered over the reshuffling of the cabinet and the peace talks in Paris, officers and bureaucrats coordinated among themselves to meet the advancing Greeks. Men drawn from the middle ranks of the imperial administration, such as Eyüp Durukan, were at the forefront of this first wave of mobilization. One of the most influential organizers to emerge after Izmir's fall was the former Minister of the Navy, Rauf Orbay. After departing from the capital on 24 May, Orbay toured towns inland from the northern and western Aegean coastline. Along the way, he met with local garrison commanders who were beginning to deploy against the advancing Greeks. He also reached out to acquaintances and old friends whom he deemed especially vital. Rauf's background and service record aided him considerably at this critical juncture. As a stalwart Young Turk and veteran of the Ottoman secret service, he was familiar with a number of families and communities known for their loyalty to the party and their service as fighters and paramilitaries during the Great War. Orbay was also the son of Circassian immigrants. As a decorated officer and former cabinet minister, his status as one of the empire's most commanding personalities allowed him entrée among the tightly knit Circassian communities of western Anatolia. By June, he and other officers secured the recruitment of hundreds, if not thousands, of fellow immigrants into the 'National Forces'. While serving alongside more conventional volunteers (such as former gendarmes, army veterans and military reservists), the Circassians that Orbay helped induct into the National Forces lent this nascent army an air of danger and ruthlessness. One individual who helped cement the National Forces' notoriety as a ferocious, and at times pitiless, insurgent army was Orbay's most notorious recruit, Çerkes Ethem (or Ethem 'the Circassian'). Both before and after the war, Ethem made his mark as both a CUP *fedai* and the leader of a private army of Circassian raiders and bandits. During the Great War, he acquired an especially rough reputation as a paramilitary commander in the Anatolian east. Ethem was a killer and the National Forces needed men willing to fight to the end for the sake of the nation.

Clashes between Greek troops and elements of the National Forces erupted piecemeal as May came to a close. After initially ceding ground, the Nationalists established stable lines of battle outside the towns of Ayvalık, Soma and Alaşehir. Fighting to the south and east of Izmir proved especially vicious. An estimated 3,000 civilians were massacred when the town of Aydın changed hands in early July and another 25,000 displaced. Greek and Nationalist guerrilla units burned and sacked dozens of villages, emptying large swaths of the Aegean hinterland of their inhabitants. Meanwhile, British and French officials were left in the lurch as they implored Greece to limit the scope of their occupation. In the wake of Izmir's capture, Allied officials conducted multiple formal inquiries into the conduct of the Greek forces. The findings of these internal investigations ultimately cast grave doubts on the viability of Athens's attempted annexation of the Anatolian coast. 'Apart from the abstract principle of right and wrong, and of self-determination, it would be exceedingly costly for a Greek government to hold permanently any large Turkish area', one British intelligence officer confided. It was not unsafe to assume, he concluded, that the Greeks would remain beleaguered by both the National Forces to the east and a hostile Muslim population to the rear (unless, of course, the Greeks 'exterminated or expelled the latter').[36]

After completing his tour of the Aegean interior, Rauf Orbay departed for the east. On 19 June, he arrived in Amasya, a quaint provincial town in the central highlands south of the Black Sea. It was there that he was reunited with Mustafa Kemal, who had taken up his duties as commander of the Ottoman 9th Inspectorate. Kemal had moved cautiously inland after disembarking at Samsun. During his travels, he had written to other officers and stated his belief that the Ottoman government was in a 'captive and helpless state'. His solution, as he described it to one corps commander, was to unite all of the local committees and organizations geared towards the nation's defense. In doing so, he planned to invite representatives of all resistance groups to a general congress in Sivas, to the southeast. 'If necessary, a steering committee could be formed' from its members, one that would act in the place of the government in Istanbul.[37] Once in the company of Rauf Orbay, Kemal wired a general bulletin to provincial administrators informing them of his intentions. Senior officials in the capital issued a mixed response to this circular. The Interior Minister, an ally of Damad Ferid, denounced it and called upon the imperial bureaucracy to desist from aiding regional groups that supported the National Forces. Mustafa Kemal's authority as an inspector was then officially curtailed, thus denying him legal authority to issue orders to civilian administrators. Facing the threat of recall or dismissal, he resigned his commission as brigadier general.

At the time of his resignation, Kemal had moved his base of operations to Erzurum. The town, which had been Kazım Karabekir's headquarters since April, was to be the scene of a congress of Nationalist supporters from across the east. In his diary, Karabekir griped that it was he who was to be in charge of the meeting so as to 'assign to Mustafa Kemal his course of operation'.[38] Now devoid of any rank or government authority, Kemal instead was elected chairman of the congress. The meeting lasted over ten days. At times, the attendees, who comprised landowners, former officials, Islamic jurists and professionals, proved fractious. Many who came were former CUP members, a fact that vexed some who took part. Out of fear that factionalism would doom the congress, one provincial administrator called upon his colleagues to let the past go. 'From now on', he asserted, 'Unionism or what-have-you does not exist. We all stand for the defense of our land and the integrity of the fatherland'.[39] Other disagreements were more philosophical. A cleric who attended the proceedings objected to an official statement which proclaimed that the nation celebrated its 'modernizing' efforts. The term 'modern' alone was cause for concern, one clerk wrote, since it was associated with activists in the Turkish Hearth, 'who were not interested in religion or faith'.[40] By its conclusion, the Erzurum congress did arrive at a consensus around several key issues. There was to be no compromise with the Allies. Each member agreed to rally the nation and liberate the empire from foreign occupation.

A second congress in Sivas ratified most of the decisions passed by Mustafa Kemal's steering committee in Erzurum. With the close of the meeting in Sivas in early September, a new organization, calling itself the 'Anatolia and Rumeli Defense of Rights Association', came into being. Its steering committee, again headed by Kemal, assumed the authority to speak for all groups and fighters aligned with the National Forces. Its fundamental goal was simple: 'The Ottoman lands' – which were defined as all the territory left under Istanbul's control at the time of the armistice – were to be respected as an 'indivisible whole'. Within these lands, a 'decisive Muslim majority' reigned. The association rejected all Greek and Armenian claims to Anatolia and Thrace. It further affirmed that the sultan would continue to preside as monarch and caliph. However, his office was bound by what the steering committee determined was the 'national will'. It was now imperative for the sovereign to reconvene the Chamber of Deputies, thus allowing 'the nation to engage with the future of the country'.[41]

The creation of a unified Defense of Rights Association posed a direct challenge to administrators in the capital. Since Damad Ferid's return from Paris in June, the imperial government appeared terminally indecisive in the face of Greece's invasion. Between May and October 1919, the grand vezir reshuffled his cabinet twice in the hopes of signaling a willingness to address the state's needs. Privately, in spite of his failure at the peace conference, he remained faithful to his belief that Britain would back Istanbul's demands if a final settlement was reached. When Lloyd George announced that the Ottoman Empire's survival was a 'life and death issue for England', Ferid rejoiced before members of the sultan's court. The sultan's chief clerk, however, cautioned the grand vezir that such a reading was perhaps too optimistic. The Prime Minister's sentiments could also mean that

Britain would simply 'prevent Turkey from being thrust into the arms of other states'.[42] Whether Ferid's complacency reflected a broader consensus within the halls of power is not clear. It is likely that many within the middle ranks of the imperial bureaucracy saw the consolidation of what was alternatively called the 'National Movement' (*Hareket-i Milliye*) as rejuvenating. From his perch in Istanbul, Eyüp Durukan felt unmitigated joy on reading Mustafa Kemal's proclamation from Sivas. It was, as he confided to his diary, a beacon that 'shows the right way ahead, illuminating it with hope'.[43]

With the empire looking ever more set against itself, the sultan agreed to take action. In accordance with the counsel of his advisors, Vahideddin appointed a new grand vezir, Ali Rıza. Rıza, a sturdy fifty-nine-year-old statesman whose career predated the Young Turk Revolution, was tasked with obtaining 'a compromise and rapprochement' with the Nationalists in Anatolia.[44] In early October, representatives from the new government conceded to the demands of the Defense of Rights Association and called for elections to be held that winter. Privately, Ali Rıza's negotiators made it clear that elections would proceed only if the association was found 'not to possess any connections to Unionism'.[45] Despite its repudiation of the wartime government, the organization's obvious links with the CUP made the 1919 election a polarizing affair. Throughout the country, members of Ferid's Freedom and Accord Party, as well as the majority of non-Muslim citizens, boycotted the polls altogether. The shattered state of security in the country led prominent newspapers in the capital to admit they did not know how 'the election activities in the provinces were occurring'.[46] By all accounts, the conduct of the election was deplorable. In Samsun, Nationalist troops under their feared commander Topal Osman forced two opposition candidates, a judge and the provincial governor, to flee for their lives. A mayor of one village near Bursa stuffed the ballot box with pro-Nationalist votes after 410 out of 500 residents failed to show up at the polls. In another western town, resident Armenians were threatened with violence if they abstained from voting for the local candidate, a former CUP member who had helped carry out the 1915 deportations in the region.[47] When the imperial parliament was finally seated, British intelligence reported that at least 24 of the 164 representatives elected to the body had played some role in the deportation or massacre of Armenians during the Great War.[48]

The last session of the Ottoman Chamber of Deputies opened its proceedings on 12 January 1920. A little more than a year earlier, representatives from Baghdad and Yemen still sat within the chamber. Now, in the wake of the 1919 elections, the composition of the body was smaller and more uniform. Those who gathered in Istanbul that winter represented only districts within the borders of the 1918 armistice line (except for British-occupied Mosul). In contrast to the previous parliament, which possessed representatives who were Greek and Armenian, all but one of the men who took their seats in 1920 were Muslim.[49] These dramatic changes to the body's configuration did not blunt the outlook of its members. 'We are passing', the Chamber's leader declared, 'the most important and most critical period in Ottoman history'. The empire had thankfully avoided the 'nightmarish calamity' that had brought down the Russian tsar. The Chamber of Deputies now needed to commit itself to upholding the state's sovereignty and to ensuring its survival. No one, he vowed, would 'consent to the trampling of the laws that recognize the Turkish nation [among] all the nations and peoples in today's day. And the country shall not be broken into pieces'.[50]

Within a month of its first meetings, the Chamber of Deputies formally submitted its own proposal for a peace settlement. Labeled the 'National Pact' (*Ahd-ı Milli* or *Misak-i Milli*), it echoed core principles advocated by the Defense of Rights Association. To start with, it reiterated the demand that all territories found within the armistice lines of November 1918 be considered a single, indivisible country. Within these lands, an 'Ottoman Islamic majority' held sway. Outside these borders, in those parts of the Ottoman state 'with an entirely Arab majority', the chamber proposed that local peoples should decide their future on their own. A similar recommendation was submitted for two other territories, both with large Turkish-speaking populations: western Thrace (demanded by Greece) and the provinces of Batum, Kars and Ardahan (coveted by Georgia and Armenia). The Chamber of Deputies was more unequivocal when it came to the sovereignty of the capital, the Straits and the Sea of Marmara. The 'seat of the caliphate of Islam, the exalted sultanate and the Ottoman government' was to remain fully in national hands. As for the 'minorities' of the country, the parliament agreed to observe their rights so long as 'Muslim people in neighboring states also securely utilize the same law'.[51]

After approving the National Pact to roars of applause, the Chamber of Deputies moved on to old business. Left unsettled was the wording of a statement to be submitted to the sultan. Days earlier, the body was presented with a proclamation by the grand vezir on behalf of Mehmed VI. The declaration was brief, frilly and anodyne. It called upon the Chamber and the government as a whole for unity in light of the ongoing peace negotiations in Paris. Only brief reference was made to the 'painful events similar to the sudden occupation of Izmir and its environs by the Greeks'.[52] Several of the members within the audience reacted to the grand vezir's proclamation with indignation. Why, it was asked, did the vezir fail to mention other regions occupied by the Allies? Were not territories such as Mosul, Urfa, Ayvalık, Thrace and Adana under occupation? And what of the atrocities suffered by Muslims? And what of the nation? Several speakers, including noted members of the Turkish Hearth, insisted upon official recognition of the suffering and rights of the Turks. For the dissatisfied, the parliament's rules allowed for some degree of redress. By right, members of the Chamber of Deputies were obliged to craft a formal reply to the grand vezir. A day before the announcement of the National Pact, committee members presented a draft of the Chamber's response. The proposed reply, which appealed for recognition of the nation's suffering since the time of the Balkan Wars, made no mention of Turks, Muslims or even Ottomans. Moreover, as several members pointed out, the language was too opaque. It was better, several suggested, that the statement be written in 'plain Turkish', devoid of elaborate expressions deriving from Arabic or Farsi. Doing so, one reasoned, was important so that 'the people and the whole nation would be able to understand'.[53] Most of the advised changes, however, were not approved by the body. A number of representatives were loath to challenge the sultan outright. Many more were opposed to diluting or dumbing down the language of the Ottoman state. If there was a nationalist spirit that guided the elected parliament, it was one rooted in imperial traditions.

Leading figures in the capital could all agree, however, that the empire's future was on a knife edge. Even Damad Ferid, who remained a representative in the imperial senate, agreed that the country 'faced colossal events akin to the collapse and destruction of the Roman Empire'.[54] Amid these trying times, even bitter partisans were united in their desire to preserve the Ottoman state. There were no calls for altering the empire's system of government. No one of note in Istanbul clamored for Mehmed VI's overthrow. Superficially, at least, Mustafa Kemal was no less devoted to the sultanate's survival. Despite later claims that he had kept his desire to establish a republic a secret, nothing in his behavior as head of the Defense of Rights Association betrayed any such intention.

What devotion to the Ottoman state meant at the start of 1920, however, had changed significantly. From their first meetings in Erzurum and Sivas, Mustafa Kemal's Nationalists were most adamant in retaining only those territories held by Ottoman troops at the time of the armistice. What made these territories integral to the empire's sovereignty was supposed Muslim majorities residing within them. This assertion of majoritarian rights, a position grounded in Woodrow Wilson's peace terms, was one also shared by the likes of Damad Ferid. All the lands where Turkish was the dominant language, Ferid declared, should remain under the sultan's rule. Such lands included not only territories lost during the Great War, but also regions ceded beforehand (such as western Thrace, as well as Kars and Batum). On the surface, there were also signs that leaders in the Chamber of Deputies were unwilling to completely abandon the Arab lands. In principle, the National Pact's call for a plebiscite among Arab citizens left the door open to some sort of reunification with the empire. That winter, even pro-Nationalist newspapers still asserted 'Arab and Turkish allegiance to the caliphate and sultanate [was] eternal'.[55]

The rhetoric of this critical time, however, betrayed some degree of ambiguity. While senior leaders were unanimous in their belief that a Muslim majority prevailed in the empire, few were consistent in how they referred to this population. By early 1920, a variety of terms were frequently used. To some, Anatolia was fundamentally a 'Muslim land', or perhaps a 'Muslim and Turkish' land. At times, the empire's majority was qualified as being 'Ottoman Muslim' or 'Ottoman

Turkish'. A similar lack of consistency also plagued references to the empire's name. In formal matters, government officials and Nationalist representatives tended to speak of the 'Ottoman state' or 'Ottoman lands' as the proper name for the country. 'Turkey', however, remained a commonly used synonym for the empire and its government. In some respects, these linguistic trends stood in continuity with the past. However, at least some contemporary observers began to notice a subtle change. One Istanbul newspaper editor took specific note of the shift that January. Fellow journalists had recently decided to change their guild's name from the 'Ottoman Press Society' to the 'Turkish Press Society'. The decision, he believed, was fundamentally political and an indicator of a broader change in opinion. Ottomanism, a construct born nearly a century earlier, appeared to be failing. As he saw it, this was due to the disloyalty of native Greeks and Armenians. 'There is no obvious reason', he argued, 'to believe that these two nations will remain loyal to the Ottoman community'. Moreover, there were Muslims – be they Albanians, Arabs or Kurds – who had also proven untrustworthy. These trends, he concluded, validated those who identified with Turkishness.[56]

Impressions such as these, however, were beset by certain paradoxes. While it was possible that 'pensive and intellectual Turks' saw a distinct difference between Ottomanism and Turkishness, it was still commonplace for people to speak of 'Turkish' and 'Ottoman' things interchangeably.[57] Not every individual who spoke Turkish saw themselves exclusively as a Turk. Among supporters of the Defense of Rights Association, many who saw themselves as Turks also identified themselves as Circassian, Albanian, Bosnian or Kurdish. Such individuals were often integral to the growth and potency of the National Movement. These contradictions remained difficult to reconcile. As it had been at the height of the CUP's power, what Ottoman identity truly meant remained unclear. Was being a Turk just another way of saying one was Ottoman? And if 'Turks and Muslims' formed the political and demographic core of the empire, where did that leave Muslim Arabs or Armenian Christians? Did they legitimately have a place within the empire's future?

Then there was the issue of strategy. Before leaving Istanbul in July 1919, Germany's ambassador stated that the imperial elite was hopelessly divided over how to approach the Paris peace talks. None in the Ottoman capital, of course, wished to see the empire partitioned, although some were willing to contemplate 'increased autonomy of the eastern provinces'. Accepting a foreign overlord, in the form of a mandate, was largely seen as an inevitability. A majority, the ambassador suggested, were willing to accept American governance, although influential circles in Istanbul were willing to entertain rule by the British or French as well. Only a minority, a group 'principally composed of Young Turk extremists', demanded nothing short of 'absolute independence in consultation with and with the support of a great power'.[58] Six months on, opinions in the capital were clearly beginning to turn. The Nationalist ascendancy largely silenced talk of a foreign mandate over the whole of the empire. With the Greeks hemmed in along the Aegean, as well as the opening of a Nationalist offensive against French forces in the south, the imposition of mandate rule over the whole of the empire appeared unlikely. Conservatives, however, tended to offer little support for armed resistance. Representatives in the imperial senate, who received their positions by appointment from the palace, continued to put their hopes in a diplomatic solution. For the last 150 years, Damad Ferid told his colleagues, Britain and France had 'defended the existence of the Ottoman state'. This, he believed, was a reason to have faith in a peaceful solution.[59]

Vulgar politics, more than anything, informed these views. For many in the capital, there was nothing patriotic or selfless in the Nationalists' cause. Their sudden rise, crowned with their victory in the 1919 elections, represented nothing short of a CUP resurgence. Fundamentally, as one conservative described it, the National Forces were a 'hearth' movement (a reference to the Turkish Hearth) and therefore driven by Unionist ideologues. Despite their stated interests in saving the state, what they truly desired was to turn back the clock despite the crimes committed by the wartime government.[60] These sentiments, broadly speaking, were not limited to loyalists close to the sultan's palace. Within weeks of the first battles along the Aegean coast, popular dissent against the National Movement began to rear itself. Before the close of 1919, Nationalist detachments found themselves fighting rebellious peasants alongside Greek and French troops. This surge in local opposition heartened and emboldened opponents of the Defense of Rights Association in the capital. By the spring of 1920, it became increasingly clear that stalwarts of the Ottoman establishment, including the sultan himself, aimed to crush the National Movement by force. This drive, ultimately, proved decisive in undermining the integrity and the legitimacy of Ottoman dynastic rule.

'FAITH IN MY BREAST, THE KORAN ON MY TONGUE AND A DECREE IN MY HAND':[61] THE RISE OF THE ANTI-NATIONALIST OPPOSITION

Like so many officials, Hacim Muhittin spent the weeks immediately following Izmir's fall in a state of frenzy. As a provincial bureaucrat with years of experience, he was among the hundreds of administrators in Istanbul who worked feverishly to rally friends and citizens to the country's defense. Like many others who rose to the fore of the National Movement, he was a man with close ties to senior members of the old Committee of Union and Progress. After consulting with friends and raising money for the Nationalist cause, he met with one of the founders of Karakol at the end of May. It is likely that it was upon his advice that Hacim elected to leave Istanbul for the Anatolian interior. In the second week of June 1919, he arrived in the port of Bandırma on the Sea of Marmara. As a railhead for lines serving the Aegean countryside, Bandırma was teeming with Nationalist officers and sympathizers. Hacim was familiar with the area. Having been a regional administrator in several local townships, he knew many of the prominent landowners, religious leaders and officials. His knowledge of the provincial landscape, it was presumed, would aid him in helping Nationalist leaders recruit fighters from outlying villages. However, from the outset, the task still proved difficult. Both he and his companions were threatened after locals accused him of promoting 'Union and Progress propaganda and enterprises'.[62] Volunteers failed to muster despite the promises of local leaders. In one case, only thirty-eight out of an expected contingent of 200 riders joined the National Forces.[63] Worse still, many of the men who offered their services possessed awful reputations. One cohort of ten to fifteen recruits came from a local gendarmerie unit infamous for raiding villages.[64]

Despite the fighting that raged just to the southwest, many communities Hacim visited were engrossed in their own bitter conflicts. For years, districts to the south of the Sea of Marmara had grown synonymous with violence. Though lawlessness was not unusual in provincial Anatolia, the region's proximity to the capital imbued the communal fighting with unique political dimensions. Several coastal and inlying districts, such as Bandırma, Gönen, Manyas, Biga, Karacabey and Çanakkale, were heavily populated with migrants. Though the region's migrant settlements reflected the Ottoman world's full diversity, Circassian refugees from the North Caucasus were most often identified with the region's worst traits. Rough men like Çerkes Ethem – Rauf Orbay's prized recruit – lorded over the countryside. His power, like that of many others in that area, derived from multiple sources. Ethem commanded the loyalties of hundreds of young, violent men cast in his mold. His father, a wealthy landowner, and his brother Reşit, an early CUP activist, were both well acquainted with powerful individuals in Istanbul. Ethem, however, was merely one of many Circassians who wielded such influence. Throughout the war years, Circassian gangs clashed with rival groups – of migrant Albanians in particular – over the right to raid and extort ransoms from villages and towns. The intensity of this competition drew in elements of the provincial bureaucracy, including mayors, gendarmes, governors and representatives of the CUP. Anxieties grew to such an extent that wartime officials contemplated exiling Circassians en masse to inner Anatolia. Talat Pasha, however, resisted such calls. It is likely that military considerations weighed upon his decision. Large numbers of the region's Circassians, including the likes of Çerkes Ethem, were serving in the empire's armies. Many, including Ethem, had played pivotal roles in the deportation and massacre of non-Muslims.

The rule of law continued to deteriorate along the shores of the Sea of Marmara in the wake of the armistice. The region's close proximity to the capital had spared few of its communities many of the war's worst hardships. Food shortages and disease remained rampant. The mass expulsion of tens of thousands of Greeks and Armenians had emptied villages and towns, leaving shops bare, homes ransacked and fields unplanted. Thousands of young men had failed to return from the front. Those who had gained the most from the war years tended to come from the political establishment. In addition to officials and landlords tied to the CUP, militia leaders like Çerkes Ethem had grown stronger. With the announcement in late 1918 of a general amnesty for all accused of banditry, fighting between rival gangs further intensified. By the spring, the imperial administration all but broke down in large parts of northwestern Anatolia as provincial officials either threw in their lot with rival warlords or just gave up. Many prominent Circassians refused to join the National Forces until their rivals, including elements of the local government, announced a truce.

Personal animus, however, was not the only thing that made many wary of the Nationalist call to arms. As time passed, fears of a different kind undermined the confidence of many Circassians. By the end of 1919, prominent Circassian citizens voiced their concerns that the Defense of Rights Association would seek to deport and destroy them 'like the Armenians'.[65] Though it is difficult to trace the exact origins of this anxiety, a certain logic likely led to such suspicions. Armenians were long deemed a troublesome, rebellious population. Regional administrators, as well as officials in the capital, often saw Circassian immigrants in a similar light. The sight of local Armenians and Greeks sent away – and at times murdered – was still a fresh memory. Many young men, as one British officer put it, were known to have served in the 'CUP's murder gangs' on the eastern front.[66] For Circassian residents in the Marmara region, there was an acute awareness of the potential penalties that befell communities deemed disloyal or recalcitrant.

Nationalist organizers and field commanders were incredulous at such apprehensions. Circassians, after all, could be found at all ranks of the National Forces. More importantly, the movement was unequivocally one that sought to defend the rights of Muslims. The Defense of Rights Association, according to its own bylaws, asserted that all Muslims were its natural members. Within this context, refusing to join the National Movement meant placing oneself in the same category as non-Muslims or perhaps foreigners. At this hour of absolute need, why would some Muslims turn their back upon the nation?

This lack of public support was often less about politics than it was about survival. Throughout the empire, the war had drained communities of the will and the means to fight on. Calls for citizens to volunteer often yielded limited results in areas where there were now few men capable of bearing arms. As the Defense of Rights Association asserted greater unified control over the operations of the National Forces, demands for food, animals and money fell heavily upon struggling villagers and farmers. Those who refused were often met with stern discipline. In many cases, the line between the requisitioning of supplies and outright acts of banditry completely dissolved. Along the Aegean front, Çerkes Ethem's men earned shameful reputations through acts of theft and rapine. In Geyve and Adapazarı, fellow Nationalists accused Ahmet Şükrü Oğuz of looting state banks of more than 150,000 lira during his time as a Karakol commander.[67] While neither rejecting nor confirming the charge, Şükrü himself agreed that many looked down upon the Nationalist fighters as 'brigands, adventurers and tobacco smugglers'. Those who did reap spoils from the war – such as abandoned homes and property – were often stripped of their booty once the war was over. This was unjust according to Şükrü. Those same men who 'did battle for years and years in blood and fire while sacrificing everything that belonged to them' deserved whatever treasure that fell into their possession.[68]

Senior figures within the National Movement attempted to compensate for these difficulties and blemishes as best they could. In laying out the parameters for the enlistment of local militias, recruiters were expressly warned not to accept those who committed acts of brigandage or who engaged in blood feuds. After a wave of gang violence swept northwestern Anatolia in the fall of 1919, Nationalist generals, including men of Caucasian descent, assured their superiors that warring Circassian chieftains were still supporters of the National Forces. Conditions in the east of the country, however, left Nationalist commanders more visibly unsettled. Since the armistice, Kurdish interests had gained greater international attention. Unlike Circassian immigrants in the west, Muslim Kurds comprised large majorities in various areas east of the Euphrates River. The potential redrawing of the Ottoman map left open the possibility that Kurds would be vital to the empire's territorial survival. Yet for many in the National Movement, Kurdish loyalties could not easily be counted upon.

Nationalist misgivings towards Kurds derived from their interpretation of recent imperial history. For many senior officials, Kurds embodied a savagery that seemed particularly medieval. Since the beginning of the state reform movement in the early nineteenth century, Kurdish lords were persistent in their opposition to Istanbul's expanding reach and power. Many provinces in the east constituted fiefdoms under the influence of reigning Kurdish families and clans. Government efforts to break the influence of their patriarchs often proved bloody. When rebel leaders barricaded themselves inside Diyarbakir's ancient city walls in 1819, imperial troops stormed the town and massacred up to a third of its inhabitants.[69] In spite of such losses, Kurdish-led insurrections continued unabated through the nineteenth century. Decades of failure ultimately led Istanbul to modify its approach. Under the direction of Abdülhamid II, officials leveraged the state's influence and largesse to forge closer alliances with numerous Kurdish tribes. In exchange for their loyalty and services, influential patriarchs were offered money, titles, military commissions, and schooling for their sons. By the First World War, the Ottoman army had amassed a standing force of Kurdish militias. Their contribution to the war effort proved important in both fighting the Russians and implementing the Armenian Genocide.

In spite of these inroads, some Kurdish communities never reconciled themselves to direct rule from Istanbul. One prominent family, the Bedirhans, stood out as among the most vocal and active in defying government authority. In 1914, one scion of this line, Abdürrezak, threw in his lot with St Petersburg in the hopes of establishing an independent Kurdish state. Resistance also came in the form of broader patterns of provincial defiance. Dersim, a region located at the heart of eastern Anatolia, ranked as the most troublesome pocket of Kurdish recalcitrance. Mountainous, remote and sparsely populated with close-knit communities, Dersim set itself apart both culturally and linguistically. Alongside their Armenian neighbors, many Kurdish villages in Dersim actively resisted government intrusion well into the twentieth century. This shared will to defy Istanbul led to broad acts of opposition to the 1915 deportation orders. One local leader estimated that up to 36,000 Armenians in Dersim were saved from exile and massacre by local Kurds.[70]

The signing of the armistice in 1918 added new complications to Kurdish politics. Until the Young Turk Revolution, Kurdish nationalism was at best a liminal force within the empire. Its leading advocates, mostly men from elite families, played marginal roles in political circles and in society at large. The rise of the CUP offered some an opportunity for advancement, one that several Kurdish intellectuals embraced heartily. The very first nationalist organization, the Kurdish Mutual Aid and Progress Society (*Kürt Teavün ve Terakki Cemiyeti*), began its work in 1908 as a pro-government group dedicated to a modest program of education and national awareness. After the CUP's fierce turn towards authoritarianism, the society's founders soured towards the party, leading to the organization's dissolution within a year of its establishment. The brutality of the war, particularly the government's efforts to disperse and suppress Kurdish refugees, inflamed the opinions of Kurdish nationalists. With the announcement of Woodrow Wilson's Fourteen Points, the former founders reunited and set themselves to work with a far more ambitious agenda. This new organization, dubbed the 'Society for the Advancement of Kurdistan' (*Kürdistan Teali Cemiyeti*), called for international recognition of the rights of Kurds in the Ottoman Empire. At Paris, an aging former diplomat, Şerif Pasha, presented the peace conference with a memorandum outlining the society's demands. It disputed Armenian territorial claims, arguing instead that Kurds held absolute majorities in all districts along Anatolia's eastern border (save for areas around Lake Van). Independence, the memorandum insisted, was a Kurdish birthright, one that would put them on the 'road of progress and civilization' and allow them to live in peace with their neighbors.[71] With that in mind, the Allies were beseeched to establish a commission aimed at settling the territorial and political future of the Ottoman Empire's Kurds.

Şerif Pasha's appearance before negotiators in Paris was the source of considerable angst within the Nationalist camp. Kazım Karabekir consistently raised the danger of 'Kurdish propaganda' among his peers in the months before the Greek landing in Izmir. Kurdish claims made before the peace conference were not so much expressions of local dissent as they were linked to larger foreign conspiracies. 'Our enemies', he cautioned one officer, 'are working to create a greater Armenia. Our Kurdish brothers mostly reside there. Those who are working in the name of Kurdish independence are our enemies. Their goal is to create an Armenia after they separate the Kurds from us'.[72] He wagered, however, that Kurds collectively feared an Armenian takeover of eastern Anatolia. Kurds were Muslims, making them 'true brothers' in faith with the Turks. Upon his arrival in Anatolia, Mustafa Kemal also hammered home this point. An independent Kurdistan was unimaginable given the deep religious ties Turks and Kurds shared. If there were problems of rights or of recognition, such concerns, as he put it, were best worked out 'within the family'.[73] He did concede, however, that a change in regional administration might be in order. 'I am in [favor] of granting all manner of rights and privileges in order to ensure the attachment and the prosperity and progress of our Kurdish brothers', he declared to one notable from Diyarbakir. His sole condition was that the Ottoman state should not be divided.[74] Yet at Erzurum, and then later at Sivas, no specific reference was made to Kurds or the issue of Kurdish self-rule.

Nationalist engagement with Kurdish leaders produced somewhat ambiguous results. The Defense of Rights Association welcomed only a handful of Kurdish representatives into its midst. None would assume leading roles in the organization itself. Though Mustafa Kemal received telegrams of support from various tribal heads through the fall and winter of 1919, none offered to volunteer in the fight against the Greeks. Moreover, much of the support Nationalists received from the east came from urbanites who did not necessarily identify themselves as Kurds. Whether one could actually count this encouragement as representative of Kurdish politics was a matter of some debate. In many areas, the divide between Kurds and Turks was hardly neat. 'In these lands', as notables from Erzurum put it, 'Turkishness and Kurdishness are like the difference between town and country . . . While only some of the townspeople who are considered to be Turkish know Kurdish, a great many Kurds speak the Turkish language'.[75]

These incongruities did not change the fact that at least some Kurds favored the demands of Şerif Pasha and other Kurdish nationalists. The Society for the Advancement of Kurdistan remained active throughout 1919, opening offices in Dersim, Diyarbakir and Mardin. The visibility of the organization aroused the attention of British officials in both Istanbul and Iraq. During the summer, the intelligence officer Edward Noel toured much of Kurdistan in the hopes of gauging popular attitudes towards independence. He, too, found a mixed set of opinions on matters of politics and loyalty. Some locals he met affirmed that calls for Kurdish independence played into the hands of British and Armenian interests. Others, while supportive of greater autonomy, looked suspiciously upon the leaders of the Society for the Advancement of Kurdistan, believing them to be out of touch with provincial politics. As Noel passed from town to town, it became clear that there were genuine limits to the extent to which outsiders could distill the public's mood. Any European, he admitted, who did not know the local languages had to rely upon others for information. The fact that most individuals willing to host foreign visitors or translate on their behalf were either Armenians, CUP sympathizers or American missionaries added still more uncertainty. In the end, he concluded, 'what can such a traveller know of the Kurds?'[76]

Conservatives in the capital generally disapproved of the activities of the Society for the Advancement of Kurdistan. When Şerif Pasha announced that he had sealed a prospective border agreement with Armenian representatives in Paris, Damad Ferid and others close to the palace denounced him as a traitor. Kurds, one senator declared, were 'eternally devoted to the high caliphate and exalted sultanate' and would never clamor for independence.[77] Said Nursi, one of the most prominent Islamic scholars of the day, heartily agreed. As a Kurd from a village outside Bitlis, he insisted that Şerif and other separatists were merely tools of Armenian expansionism. 'Kurds', he proclaimed, 'would rather die than accept autonomy under foreign protection'. If Kurds desired independence, only the Ottoman state could grant it to them.[78] Belief that Kurds were supremely loyal to the Ottoman state nourished hope among opponents of the National Forces. In September 1919, the Ministers of War and the Interior enlisted a governor from the region of Dersim to help undermine the Defense of Rights Association in Sivas. The sultan, the governor told Edward Noel, personally directed him to 'liquidate the Unionist organization' and place Mustafa Kemal under arrest. With the support of Noel and leading members of the Society for the Advancement of Kurdistan, a force of 100–200 Kurdish riders was ultimately assembled to carry out the order. Yet, when the moment of truth arrived, the attack was called off. Upon further reflection, the governor feared the assault would shift a worrying amount of power into the hands of local Kurds. Provincial tribal heads, according to Noel, were also relieved when violence was averted. The war, he explained, had taught them 'a very healthy respect for the power and the long arm of the CUP'.[79]

This failure to strangle the Defense of Rights Association in its cradle underscored key limitations that confronted the likes of Damad Ferid and other Nationalist opponents. Mustafa Kemal's sudden ascendancy compromised much of the imperial bureaucracy and armed forces. Beyond the capital, palace loyalists possessed few natural allies. The patriotic stance assumed by the Nationalist leadership provided yet another hurdle. Delegitimizing a movement claiming to defend the state from foreign foes and Christian traitors proved fundamentally daunting. Despite these disadvantages, anti-Nationalist figures in the capital remained undeterred. The sultan at various times had voiced his displeasure with the National Forces. The weight of Mehmed VI's office, as both emperor and steward of the Islamic faithful, endowed these critiques with legitimacy. In this vein, newspapers friendly to Damad Ferid's Freedom and Accord Party insisted that the empire's citizens were being deceived. The National Forces, from the top down, comprised former Young Turks. What drove the Defense of Rights Association was not a desire to save the state but to recapture the government. Sympathetic officials and provincial elites reiterated this message, stoking pockets of rage in various portions of Anatolia. Beginning in the fall of 1919, this rage gave way to open acts of defiance. Over the next two years, popular opposition ate at the interior lines of the National Forces. Though derided as reactionaries and foreign patsies, anti-Nationalist agitators harnessed a genuine groundswell of anger and revenge. Those who answered these rallying calls reflected the full range of groups victimized by the CUP: Muslims, Christians, natives and immigrants alike.

Beginning in late October 1919, a long-retired officer toured villages south of the Sea of Marmara at the head of a small body of cavalry. Ahmet Anzavur, the leader of this band, was very much a relic of the past. He had come to the region in the mid-1800s as a refugee from the North Caucasus, placing him among the first generation of Circassian immigrants to settle there. Anzavur's new life in the empire, like that of countless Circassians before him, was shaped by the Ottoman institution of slavery. His sister, it was said, was sold to the royal family as a concubine. As a consort of Abdülhamid II, she helped Anzavur secure an appointment to the gendarmerie as a captain. The position earned him both wealth and status (at some point, the sultan presented him with a gilded sword as a personal gift). Though he served in the war in the secretive Special Organization, he was well known for his hatred of the CUP, a likely result of a 1909 decision to force officers close to the palace to retire. A man with ties to both Mehmed VI and Damad Ferid's Freedom and Accord Party, he toured the Marmara region in the fall of 1919 with an imperial edict calling upon him to lead the fight against the Greeks. To follow Mustafa Kemal, Anzavur declared, was to commit an act of treason. The Nationalists, he argued, possessed no other goal 'than [to bring about] the collapse of this state' and overthrow the royal family.[80] He pledged to put a stop to the taxes imposed by Nationalist activists and reimpose rule from Istanbul. In destroying the Defense of Rights Association, his 'Army of Muhammad' would redeem all those wronged by the Nationalists and by the Young Turks before them. 'I and the notables and lords who are with me', he avowed, 'are under the command of the Sultan and we say that we will remove these men and send them to prison'.[81]

Ahmet Anzavur's activities left Nationalist commanders groping for an appropriate response. Initial efforts to negotiate his peaceful withdrawal from the region proved fruitless. Reflexively, senior leaders branded him as nothing more than a bandit in the pay of Damad Ferid and the British. Others saw him as a harbinger of more Circassian troublemaking in a region vital to the supply and organization of the National Forces. Circassian generals sought to defuse the crisis by appealing to prominent Circassian citizens to disavow Anzavur as a demonstration of their true loyalties. One colonel beseeched his kin to be 'grateful to the Ottomans' who graciously accepted them after abandoning the Caucasus 'in the name of religion and all things sacred'. To do otherwise was 'not becoming of Circassian national history'. Though some heeded these pleas, other Caucasian notables believed the rumor that, as the colonel put it, 'the National Forces will deport the Circassians'.[82] The National Movement's unwillingness to counter these suspicions only fed the vibrancy of this move against them. Meanwhile, Anzavur's tirades grew more pointed. It was 'the wicked Unionists and Freemasons', he told one rival militia leader, who 'are the ones who have brought forth the marauding and banditry to this Islamic government for the last ten years'. The Nationalists were the same men who sent the nation's youth off to war in 1914 while profiting from the seizure of abandoned homes. While families starved, 'the young Freemasons', as he called them, gave licenses to 'a hundred thousand Muslim women and girls in Istanbul and made them into prostitutes'. Anzavur, as a genuine and righteous Muslim, promised to punish the Nationalists for such wrongs. 'I shall be a protector of the government', he vowed, 'and a slave according to the just decrees of our Shariah [Islamic law]'.[83]

The violence Ahmet Anzavur unleashed reverberated throughout western Anatolia for months. His guerrillas surged towards Nationalist strongholds at various points between late 1919 and the summer of 1920. Fortunately for the Defense of Rights Association, most of the men who joined him were unruly, untrained and undersupplied. Yet, by taking to the field, Anzavur's forces inflicted deep wounds on the National Movement. At its full strength, his army comprised thousands of sympathetic Circassian immigrants. Other disaffected groups, such as Muslim refugees from Bulgaria, native Turkish Shiites, wartime deserters and local Greeks, joined in the campaign. For critics loyal to the palace, Anzavur's offensive gave credence to those who argued that the National Movement was neither popular nor truly representative of a Muslim consensus. 'We are obliged to accept that Ahmet Anzavur is struggling only with the Union[ists]', one loyalist newspaper declared. His death at the hands of the Nationalists would mean the loss to the country of 'a brave coreligionist during these tragic days'.[84] Upon resuming the post of grand vezir in April 1920, Damad Ferid threw the government's full weight behind Anzavur, establishing a parallel 'disciplinary army' tasked with 'doing away with the organization carrying the name the National Forces'.[85]

Other regions plagued the Nationalist cause through the early part of 1920. Unlike the Marmara basin, these troubled spots were not historic centers of restless migrants and refugees. The province of Konya, in the heart of Anatolia's dusty southern flatlands, was overwhelmingly inhabited by Muslims and Turkish speakers. Yet when officers worked to extend Nationalist control over several districts, locals resisted. As in the case of the Marmara region, the Defense of Rights Association's leadership blamed popular opposition on the machinations of antagonistic officials and provincial notables. Konya's governor, it was said, not only despised the CUP but also was openly sympathetic towards local Armenians (critics deridingly called him 'Artin', a common Armenian first name).[86] Popular resentment also extended east to Yozgat, a region that possessed an unmistakably large Muslim Turkish population. A long-established prominent family there, the Çapanoğlus, played an early role in rousing anti-Nationalist sentiments. Disgruntled locals, however, possessed their own motives for defying the Defense of Rights Association. When one town outside Yozgat rose up, looters ransacked homes and businesses belonging 'to people who were long-time Unionists and the wealthy', acts rooted in anger dating back to the Great War.[87] There, too, many peasants believed the National Forces to be the work of 'crypto-Jews from Salonika and infidel Freemasons'.[88]

Nationalist troops put down each of these waves of discontent with much brutality. The man most responsible for bringing Ahmet Anzavur to heel was Çerkes Ethem. Though both men came from immigrant Circassian families, Ethem eagerly denounced Anzavur and his Circassian supporters as traitors to the nation and their ethnicity. Circassians, he told a local newspaper, sought refuge in the empire after suffering oppression at the hands of unbelieving Christian enemies. Since their arrival from the Caucasus, Circassians had 'performed truly renowned acts of service in exaltation and preservation of the Ottoman fatherland'. The National Forces, as he understood it, were now the true protectors of that fatherland.[89] In reasserting Nationalist control over the Marmara region, Ethem exercised little restraint in punishing those he believed guilty of treason. He freely ordered the burning of villages and homes and put to death dozens accused of rebellion. In some cases, personal vendettas inspired Ethem's wrath. In Düzce, a mountain town lying on the main road between Istanbul and the Anatolian interior, some fifty men were lynched for various crimes. Among the executed was a local notable who had helped secure the freedom of a captured Nationalist officer. He was put to death, one local later asserted, because he had married

Ethem's former girlfriend.[90] Other punitive expeditions were no less merciless. In Bozkır, south of Konya, Nationalist efforts to regain ground exacted a similar toll despite meeting little resistance. One column of cavalry, according to the Armenian patriarch, 'levied incredible devastation wherever they have entered, sparing neither Muslims nor Christians'.[91]

The ease with which Nationalist troops put down these acts of defiance seemed to reveal the movement's genuine strength. As the early months of 1920 came to a close, Nationalists were making key gains against French and Armenian forces in Anatolia's south. Anzavur's successes in February and March did little to weaken the resolve of the Nationalist detachments that hemmed in the Greeks along the Aegean. To at least some outsiders, events over the previous year appeared to reveal an Ottoman military that had come a long way since its defeat in 1918. Regular units serving under Nationalist commanders that winter 'were well armed, well fed, and in most cases – at least until recently – were regularly paid for the first time on record', according to British intelligence estimates.[92]

All of these successes did little to soften a clear divide that split the imperial elite in two. In mid-April, the Ministry of Education issued a general order to all students, teachers and administrators in what remained of the empire. The directive forbade all students from engaging in 'religious disputes' and from participating in any kind of political activity both in school and off campus. 'Our state', the decree read, 'was founded as the Ottoman state. Our nation is the Ottoman nation. Students need to be raised as both loyal and attached to their sultan, their religion and their beliefs'. Ideas such as Turanism – or pan-Turkish nationalism more generally – were now forbidden in the classroom.[93] Anyone who read this announcement would have understood the underlying stakes at play. By denouncing any act of political activism, the government declared itself at odds with the tens of thousands of citizens who had joined the Nationalist cause. Expressly forbidding any promotion of Turanism, an ideology long associated with the Turkish Hearth, suggested that the ministry was concerned about the CUP's return. Thus, to remind students that they were Ottomans who served the sultan took on a specifically partisan connotation. Declaring yourself an Ottoman and someone loyal to the sultan-caliph was to remain devoted to Mehmed VI and the government of Damad Ferid. To do otherwise meant choosing to side with Mustafa Kemal.

The circulation of these new guidelines generally proved fruitless. The successes achieved by the National Forces allowed their leaders to elude the potential challenges posed by such decrees. Mustafa Kemal was doing more than the sultan or Damad Ferid to secure the state's independence. And yet no one in Ankara explicitly repudiated the sultan or rejected the notion of Ottoman identity or citizenship. What proved more difficult to ignore were the political ramifications of any Nationalist victory. If Mustafa Kemal was to emerge victorious, all those who had denounced him – as well as those who persecuted the CUP's leaders – ran the risk of retribution. The same could also be said of the empire's core institutions. Would triumphant Nationalists have mercy upon the offices that had attempted to destroy them?

The Ministry of Education's circular that spring also alluded to a more fundamental divide within society. Most Ottoman citizens, both Muslims and Christians, tended to perceive their nationality in connection with their religion, language, geography and bloodlines. The sentimental appeal of the empire or royal family was increasingly fading. In the grand scheme of things, world events reinforced these trends. The apparent vibrancy of the new republics of Eastern Europe continued to draw a strong contrast with the Ottoman sultanate. Revolution was transforming Russia. Successor states like Poland, Czechoslovakia and Lithuania moved forward, albeit painfully, in the aftermath of rule under the Romanovs, Habsburgs and Hohenzollerns. It is true that none within the Ottoman press necessarily dared to question the future of the royal family in the spring of 1920. Yet the Allied occupation of the capital, coupled with what appeared to be the sultan's indifference or complicity, was a fact that many could not ignore. In looking to the future, it became increasingly clear, particularly to those in the camp of the Defense of Rights Association, that the nation was no longer willing to restore the country to what it once was.

4

Towards a Sovereign State

The Politics of Reconsolidation in the Ottoman Lands

In late 1919, Cilicia still beckoned Armenians seeking a place to begin again. For tens of thousands banished to towns, villages and desert camps in greater Syria, there often was little choice but to resettle there. This was the case for Karnig Panian, who was not yet nine years old when the war ended. After losing his mother during their journey south from Anatolia, he spent the bulk of the war in a state-run orphanage in Antoura, just north of Beirut. His internment in the Lebanese foothills brought him little solace. As inmates of an institution chiefly designed to Turkify its residents, he and other orphans were regularly subject to beatings and other cruelties for not speaking Turkish or for not answering to their new Muslim names. After briefly running away, he returned to the orphanage to find its teachers and administrators gone. The arrival of new staff, all Armenians, was just the beginning of what he hoped was his deliverance. One Sunday, during a festival featuring the visit of several hundred Armenian soldiers, it was announced that the children 'would all go to Cilicia and rebuild Armenia'. The news, Karnig recalled, elicited an outpouring of emotion and excitement among the boys. While only some were native to the region, all embraced the hope and adventure that came with returning to some semblance of home. Teachers fanned these expectations with promises of a brighter future. 'You now have your own government, which will take care of you', one adult announced. 'You will go to school, and when you're done you will go to university to study. You will become doctors, chemists, and engineers'. Some of the orphans, Karnig later remembered, were not satisfied with such prospects. Some dreamed of being soldiers in the hopes of exacting what they believed was their just revenge. 'Once we get to Cilicia', one boy crowed, 'we won't leave a single Turk alive!'[1]

At some point in 1919, Karnig was transferred alongside hundreds of other boys to an orphanage in Antep. His new life in Cilicia, as he remembered it, began wonderfully. He ate well, he went to school and he enjoyed many of the basic pleasures of being a child. It was only later that he realized he was spared many of the realities of life in town. For most Armenians, salvaging what had been their lives before the war was more difficult. Unlike Karnig, Father Der Nerses Babayan was born and raised in Antep. Before 1915, he was a schoolmaster in a village east of town, close to the Euphrates River. Having survived exile in a high desert village in what is now Jordan, he was among the tens of thousands rescued after British troops marched into Palestine. His opportunity to return home came after months of living in an Egyptian refugee camp. Before his departure, a British official told him to remain hopeful but wary. 'It is true that the war concluded with an Allied victory. Turkey and the nations it allied with were defeated, but the destiny of Cilicia and the Near Eastern states is not yet certain. Black clouds swirl above this region'.[2] More personal challenges troubled Father Babayan after his arrival in Antep. On returning to his village, he discovered his church in ruins. Only eleven of the 110 or 120 individuals of his former flock survived their deportation to the Syrian desert.[3] Having lost much of his own family, he elected to resettle in Antep proper. There he fared better after taking up work as the head of an aid committee that cared for 200 destitute families. By November 1919, however, the political situation was growing worse. Tensions in the countryside were forcing large numbers of rural families to relocate to Antep. The growing fear that fighting was imminent led fellow Armenian leaders to gather arms and organize a militia. 'Afterwards', he later admitted, 'the inevitable happened'.[4]

It was in Marash, Antep's slightly smaller neighbor to the northwest, that Cilicia's slow drift towards bedlam commenced. The first rumors of insurrection came from outlying districts during the early winter months. By January 1920, outright rebellion gripped the town's Muslim quarters. French authorities in Marash quickly found themselves besieged as Nationalist detachments took command of the main road leading to the south. After three weeks of intense combat, hundreds of French colonial troops led an exodus of fearful Armenian civilians to the safety of Islahiye, some seventy kilometers away. The first column of survivors arrived starving and frostbitten after braving a three-day march through 'a Russian cold' of snow and ice, as one French officer remembered it. Others were not so lucky. Days later, a second retreating contingent of some 2,000 Armenians was massacred by Nationalist troops.[5]

News of France's bloody withdrawal from Marash reverberated in the international arena. It had been over a year since the first negotiations were held in Paris and still there was no sign that the Allied Powers were any closer to settling the territorial future of the Ottoman lands. This lack of progress did little to dull French aspirations in the Levant. After British troops relinquished direct control over Syria and Cilicia in late 1919, French authorities assumed that the territories had been pacified. The Nationalist offensive against Marash shattered this presumption. By the spring of 1920, French forces found themselves on the defensive throughout Cilicia. French journalists warned that 'all of the periphery of Cilicia' save for Adana – the largest town in the region – was now in a state of agitation.[6] Matters were visibly worse further south. In early March, defiant Arab nationalists crowned Sharif Hussein's son king of an independent Syria. Paris saw the coronation as an unmistakable rebuff. Military force, it increasingly appeared, was the only means of ensuring France's grip over Syria as a whole.

Similar apprehensions plagued British observers as well. Through the previous fall and winter, intelligence reports suggested that nationalists in the Arab lands were seeking to coordinate with Mustafa Kemal's fighters. Before spring was out, British officials also would contend with violent outbursts in Palestine and Iraq. Public opinion both at home and in the colonies was cause for still more concern among British and French officials. From North Africa to India, Muslim critics warned of a groundswell of popular indignation if France or Britain impinged upon the authority of Mehmed Vahideddin, caliph of the Islamic world. All Muslims, as one Algerian editor put it, feared the beginnings of a 'new crusade', one specifically 'aimed at the annihilation of Turkey or the restriction of its sovereign rights'.[7]

These anxieties, for the time being, did little to impede the resumption of peace talks in Europe. On 12 February, two days after French troops abandoned their positions in Marash, Allied negotiators reconvened in London to finalize the terms of the treaty that they intended to deliver to the Ottoman Empire. The resumption of discussions featured a dramatic set of changes among the presiding heads of state. In October 1919, a stroke had incapacitated Woodrow Wilson. With the president bedridden, efforts to approve the Versailles treaty languished in the United States Senate. In the absence of Wilson's more moderate American presence, France's new premier, Alexandre Millerand, enjoyed greater leverage. Arguably David Lloyd George remained the most forceful voice among the Allies, even though his own cabinet was as divided as ever. Within a month of the first meetings, a general outline for peace was sketched out. Istanbul would remain in Ottoman hands but much of the western interior, including the whole of Thrace, would be annexed by Greece. An international commission made up of the war's premier victors would oversee the Turkish Straits, an agreement that fundamentally demilitarized one of the most strategic passageways in the world. Greek troops, however, would remain in western Anatolia, although Izmir and the rest of the Aegean coastline would remain under nominal Ottoman authority. While Italy and France would retain spheres of influence in the south of Anatolia, the Allies agreed to transfer several provinces to the Armenian Republic (although, even then, there was faint hope that such provisions could ever be enforced). As for the rest of what had been the empire in 1914, all Ottoman claims to the Levant and Mesopotamia were officially nullified. The future of these lands was decided without the involvement of the sultan, Mustafa Kemal, Faisal or local nationalists.

From the perspective of many who attended the talks in London, there was good reason to believe that they were finally laying the issue of a Turkish peace to rest. The terms they agreed upon followed the logic that had guided negotiations at Versailles: Istanbul had lost the war and therefore had to be held accountable. The partitioning of the empire, by their reckoning, was in line with the conditions pressed upon Berlin and Vienna. The Habsburg Empire, after all, was dismantled with little fanfare. Recognizing the national rights of Armenians and Greeks was fundamentally no different than making the concessions that allowed for the establishment of an independent Poland or a greater Romania. Allied negotiators believed, however, that it was vital to preserve at least some semblance of the Ottoman order. Strategic interests, as well as domestic pressures among the Allied states, demanded the conservation of Mehmed VI's offices as sultan and caliph. Otherwise, Allied heads of state were confident that any resistance to the treaty could be dispatched with ease. When the Secretary of State for War Winston Churchill publicly questioned the feasibility of the treaty, stating that the Allies lacked the manpower to enforce the agreement in the Ottoman interior, Lloyd George overruled him. Allied troops outnumbered Mustafa Kemal's forces by two to one, the Prime Minister assured him. If two Allied soldiers 'could not defeat one Turk', the Allies should go no further and simply 'ask the Turk upon what terms he would condescend to make peace'.[8]

Affairs on the ground ultimately proved Lloyd George frightfully wrong. Other reversals quickly followed France's retreat from Marash. By the year's end, Nationalist counterstrokes in Cilicia and eastern Anatolia rendered large portions of the Allied peace plan moot. Growing international attention magnified the gravity and significance of these gains. Yet for the time being, certain pretenses endured. Mehmed VI continued to rule as sultan and caliph. Nationalists, with Mustafa Kemal in the lead, continued to avow their loyalty to their ruling sovereign. Yet in communities in the south and east of the country, these political formalities were increasingly irrelevant. As the fighting continued, it eventually became clear that the empire could not be fully restored. Warring factions devastated towns and villages across what remained of the old Ottoman periphery. The intensity of this year of fighting rarely spared either Muslim or Christian civilians. However, Nationalist victories in both the south and east resulted in several common conclusions. Mustafa Kemal's forces were now the arbiters of the empire's future. What shape the borders of the empire would take depended upon his movement's successes on the battlefield. For those who opposed them, there was little room for compromise. For the tens of thousands like Karnig Panian and Father Babayan, returning to some semblance of their lives before the war became an impossibility.

'WE HAVE NO NEED OF THEIR CIVILIZATION': THE NATIONAL MOVEMENT GOES ON THE OFFENSIVE

The last full session of the Ottoman Chamber of Deputies began in a state of indignation. Almost two weeks earlier, Greek forces had seized a series of villages near Ödemiş, roughly 75 kilometers east of Izmir. The assault, according to a telegram read before the Chamber, drove thousands of Muslims from their homes, leaving behind a fortune in property and livestock. The nearby towns of Alaşehir and Uşak were filled with miserable refugees. For four straight days, the roads had been 'tied up with the excruciating passage of wretched, hungry and abject convoys' looking for relief. The news provoked one representative, Mahmud Celal, to inveigh at length against the horrors wrought by Greece and the Allies. Celal, who later served as president of the Turkish Republic, was native to the region. During the First World War, he had helped oversee the mass expulsion of Orthodox Christians from the environs of Izmir. Now, he claimed, the whole of the Aegean interior was being cleansed of Muslims. 'Within an area of sixty kilometers from Urla to Izmir', Celal reckoned, a traveler would not see 'a single Muslim today'. From the hour the first Greek soldiers set foot in the country, 100,000 Muslims had fled 'torture and attacks'. All of these transgressions occurred before the very eyes of the European nations. 'I ask you', Celal pleaded before his colleagues, 'is this the civilization Europeans are bringing us?' One of the Chamber's oldest members, Tunalı Hilmi, offered the most obvious response. 'We have no need of their civilization', he replied. 'We are civilized'.[9]

Three days later, British and French troops fanned out across Istanbul. By the afternoon, leading members of the Chamber of Deputies were placed under arrest. With the assistance of British troops, many of them Muslims from South Asia, key ministries were stormed and occupied. In the days preceding the takeover, the Allies had given no public hint of this coup. Yet in moving against each of the principal arms of government, British and French forces brazenly asserted that Istanbul now fell under their authority. Events, they contended, warranted such a move. Ever since the fall of Marash, none of the imperial

ministries had sought to curb the behavior of soldiers or civilians supporting the Nationalist offensive in Cilicia. Nationalist representatives
cheered the French defeat and decried what they considered were the
'attacks and various calamities and tragedies' inflicted by 'Armenians
found to be in the service of foreign forces'.[10] Worse still, known leaders of the National Movement freely walked the streets of the capital
without fear of apprehension or reprisal. Placing Istanbul formally
under Allied control put a firm halt to these perceived provocations.
In making their presence felt, British officials arrested eleven of the
most outspoken Nationalists in the capital, including Rauf Orbay and
Kara Vasif, co-founder of the Karakol organization. All were then
deported to Malta for internment.

Mustafa Kemal responded to Istanbul's seizure with predictable
fury. In a statement dictated to both military and civilian leaders
aligned with the National Movement, he denounced Ferid and the
various steps taken to undermine the National Forces. Up until recently,
efforts to suppress the 'determination and will of the Ottoman nation'
had come to naught. However, in Kemal's estimate, the occupation of
Istanbul represented a critical juncture. By virtue of the capital's seizure, seven centuries of Ottoman rule 'were put to an end'. 'In other
words', he continued, 'today the Turkish nation has been invited to
defend its civil prerogatives, its right to life and independence, and its
entire future'. Years later, as president of Turkey, Mustafa Kemal would
point to this pronouncement as the precise moment when the empire
was deemed dead and dissolved. However, others within the Nationalist camp continued to hedge regarding the empire's survival. When
Kemal's statement was printed in the official newspaper of the Defense
of Rights Association, the wording was subtly changed. There were
those, it read, who 'desired to bring about the end to the Ottoman
Empire'. Contrary to Mustafa Kemal's original claim, the Ottoman
state endured despite the dangers that threatened its existence.[11]

How the sultan greeted the occupation of his capital is not clear.
Mehmed VI, according to British intelligence sources, was delighted
at the apprehension of so many prominent Nationalists. The Allied
seizure of power likely saved the sultan from attempting 'a similar
"soft" coup with inferior forces and considerable risk of failure'.[12]
With the remaining members of the Chamber of Deputies refusing to

reopen parliament, and the resignation of yet another grand vezir, Mehmed VI reappointed his brother-in-law, Damad Ferid, to head the government. Confidants in the palace, however, were wary of the consequences of such a decision. A new government under his stewardship, one official advised, might help glean greater British support or leniency. And yet, if Ferid failed, his tenure likely would 'have a very bad effect upon the country'. In hindsight, given what was to come, another attendant was left to wonder whether the change of government amounted to an over-elaborate plot. 'Did the English deceive Ferid or Ferid deceive the sultan or the sultan deceive us [all]?'[13]

After taking the reins of government for the second time in two years, Ferid had an audience with Sir John Michael de Robeck, British high commissioner in Istanbul. Ferid arrived at the embassy full of confidence. With his reinstatement as grand vezir, he possessed a comprehensive plan aimed at suppressing the National Movement once and for all. As the two men spoke, the government was planning to send a 'disciplinary' force that would crush the Nationalists. Ahmet Anzavur, meanwhile, remained active south of the Sea of Marmara. Ferid asserted that Anzavur's successes could be reproduced in other parts of the country as well, such as Trabzon, Konya and Harput, or far off in Kurdistan. He also explained that the government was seeking a ruling, or fatwa, from the empire's highest jurist, the şeyhülislam Dürrizade Abdullah, which would condemn the Nationalists. The weight of such a decree, coupled with the sultan's own endorsement, would do much to sap the legitimacy of the National Movement, both at home and abroad. Indian Muslims, he explained, had been misled in believing that the likes of Talat and Enver were 'champions of Islam'. It was hoped the commissioner would agree that Ottoman affairs should be shown 'in a true light, and that India should know the views of the Caliph, for whom Indian Moslems had so much respect'. All Ferid desired was British moral and material support in seeing the campaign through.[14]

It did not take long for most of these proposals to misfire or fail outright. By the end of May, Çerkes Ethem and other components of the National Forces had dispatched both Anzavur and Ferid's 'disciplinary army'. The rebellion under the leadership of the Çapanoğlu family met a similar fate one month later in Yozgat. Countering the government's fatwa, however, required a bit more diplomatic skill. As the empire's highest jurist, Dürrizade Abdullah was fully within his rights to render an informed opinion upon matters pertaining to state and society. In early April, he exercised this prerogative, condemning Mustafa Kemal and his National Forces rebels to death for apostasy. History, as well as contemporary politics, cast suspicion upon Dürrizade's fatwa from the outset. For centuries, the *şeyhülislam* had possessed little political autonomy. Be it condemning dissidents, or perhaps overthrowing sultans, partisanship often trumped theology during the crafting of important rulings. Dürrizade's 1920 fatwa appeared no different. Nationalists readily suspected that it was actually his predecessor, Mustafa Sabri, who had authored his decision. Ever since the days of the 1908 revolution, Sabri had been a well-known opponent of the CUP and was the doyen of conservative clerics in the capital. As a former *şeyhülislam*, he had decried the National Movement as nothing more than a group of 'Unionist bandits' who had taken flight to Anatolia.[15] A committee of Nationalist leaders responded almost immediately to the *şeyhülislam*'s decree. Headed by Ankara's local Islamic jurist (who was also a member of the Defense of Rights Association), the body disputed the authenticity of Dürrizade's words, claiming that he, as well as the sultan, were hostages living under Allied occupation. It was instead the legal and moral duty of all Muslims to liberate the caliph from his captivity. The weight of this counter-decree was augmented by the expressed support of 153 fellow jurists living throughout Ottoman Anatolia.

The speed and resolve with which Nationalists responded to the Istanbul fatwa were a testament to the administration forming around Mustafa Kemal. In December 1919, Kemal re-established himself in Ankara, some 400 kilometers east of the capital. As a railhead linking much of central Anatolia to the south and west of the country, Ankara possessed strategic advantages as a base of communication and command. In the nineteenth century, the textile trade, as well as the possibility of greater economic growth, contributed to a population boom and increased prosperity. The empire's entrance into the war, however, reversed many of the city's gains. Much of Ankara's old core burned down in a fire in 1917. Despite possessing a modest population of 84,000 in 1914, hunger and disease, as well as the government's banishment of local Christians, devastated the population and crippled its economy.[16] The marshy landscape surrounding the town made malaria a challenge for residents, including newly resettled Nationalists. Nevertheless, its central location and dry, rugged terrain afforded Ankara defensive advantages other towns lacked. With the Allies at a safe enough distance, Mustafa Kemal and his staff worked diligently through the winter to make Ankara a thriving center for the movement. By January 1920, his aides established a newspaper, *National Sovereignty* (*Hakimiyet-i Milliye*), which endured as his government's semi-official organ for the next fourteen years.

The launching of the paper, to some extent, also reflected Ankara's relative isolation. Through the winter, Kemal remained dependent upon surrogates like Rauf Orbay to maintain avenues of communication with government officials in Istanbul. Discontent came to a head in January when Nationalist representatives in the Chamber of Deputies reorganized themselves and decided to formally discard their affiliation with the Defense of Rights Association. In founding a new, more inclusive party, they adopted what they believed was a more congenial name, the National Salvation Group. The move, as one of Mustafa Kemal's followers later put it, was indicative of individuals who believed 'they could achieve great goals by groveling to the sultan, while indulging foreigners and behaving tenderly and kindly'. For this reason, he quipped, it was better if members dub themselves 'the peasants of the fatherland' (*fellah-ı vatan*), as opposed to a group devoted to 'national salvation' (*felah-ı vatan*).[17]

Ankara's emergence as the seat of Nationalist power in the country was beset by other substantial risks. For opponents of the movement, the establishment of a permanent Nationalist presence in Ankara provided fodder for claims that the National Forces hoped to overthrow the sultan. Kemal's overt influence over the broader military and bureaucracy further sustained these suspicions. Ironically, it was the Allied decision to appropriate *de jure* control of Istanbul that helped dispel these contradictions. The arrest of Rauf Orbay and other senior leaders forced an exodus of Nationalist supporters from the capital. Mustafa Kemal, who may have possessed some foreknowledge of the Allied coup, eagerly presented his base in Ankara as a place of refuge for officials fleeing the capital. On 19 March, just four days after the Allied takeover, Kemal's steering committee called upon local governors and military commanders to hold snap elections in their provinces. All those elected, they declared, would then be welcome to take a seat in a parliament to be convened in Ankara. Though presented as a means of continuing the Chamber of Deputies' work free from foreign interference, the Ankara parliament assumed a new name, the Grand National Assembly of Turkey. This attempt at rebranding the imperial Chamber of Deputies constituted the first instance in which Turkey was formally adopted as the name of the country. To this day, the Grand National Assembly has endured as Turkey's primary electoral body.

The first session of the Grand National Assembly occurred in the last week of April. It began with a procession which culminated in prayers and the ritual sacrifice of sheep. Members then took their seats within what had been the official meeting hall of the CUP's provincial chapter. On the following day, Mustafa Kemal took the role of the body's president and addressed the representatives at great length. To some extent, the content of his inaugural address provided the basis for his famous 1927 Nutuk. Much of Kemal's attention focused on his interpretation of events since Izmir's fall one year earlier. He condemned the Allies as faithless and brutal. He denounced those politicians who consorted with foreign occupiers, particularly Damad Ferid. Official correspondence between members of the Defense of Rights Association was entered into the record. Many of these telegrams and cables explicitly professed devotion to the sultan. In the afternoon, Kemal discussed in detail the convening of the Erzurum and Sivas congresses and the dangers he and his followers were forced to brave. All of these events brought him to the implications of the Allied occupation of Istanbul and what he believed was Ankara's inherent legitimacy as a new seat of power. There was now a need 'to fix the legal conditions that brought about the events in Istanbul' in order to preserve the nation's independence.[18] The National Assembly's mandate, he insisted, was in keeping with Islamic law and history. 'We, your deputies', Kemal later declared, 'swear in the name of God and the Prophet that the claim that we are rebels against the sultan and caliph is a lie. All we want is to save our country from sharing the fate of India and Egypt'.[19]

Before the end of the first day, the National Assembly closed its doors and met in private. Mustafa Kemal again took the floor, this time to address the immediate goals and concerns of the National Movement. Like his remarks earlier in the day, the subject of his speech varied widely. He particularly took time to address the situation in Cilicia. He reported that he had met with a French diplomat in the fall of 1919 to discuss the future of the region. He admitted that the French offered to relinquish their territorial claim to Cilicia so long as they could maintain their economic and security interests there. No such deal, he vowed, was in the offing. The French had 'agitated all of Europe and all of America' with charges of massacres and violence. It was the French, and most notably their local Armenian allies, who were responsible for the carnage in Marash. Muslim acts of retaliation against the French were now taking a toll on occupying forces. 'All of these reprisals have resulted in the French retreat and recently it can be said that French forces are only found in Adana, Taurus and Mersin'. What remained of Cilicia was in the hands of 'the Muslim *volk*'.[20]

The circumstances under which the National Forces achieved this rapid success remain very much in dispute. Nationalist sources, particularly accounts produced after the war, overwhelmingly emphasize the experiences and perspectives of Muslims. Among the first published Turkish accounts dealing with the fighting in Cilicia was that of Mustafa Nureddin, a munitions officer native to the town of Antep. Released in 1924, Mustafa's memoir described the arrival of British troops as the beginning of months of oppression and insults. The arrest of local notables accused of crimes against Armenians was the first act that broke the public's spirit. The torture and insults suffered by those apprehended was, in Nureddin's estimation, deserving of 'an entirely separate book'.[21] As 1919 progressed, British officials undertook a widespread campaign aimed at disarming the population. The transfer of power from Britain to France in October 1919 did not ease the humiliation felt by Antep's Muslims. As in other towns in Cilicia, French officials ordered the removal of the Ottoman flag from official flagposts, an act that was considered a grave insult. Like they had under the British, local Armenians delighted in the suffering of Antep's Muslims. From the moment many Armenians returned from exile, they 'insulted and defamed Turks' and 'smiled under their mustaches' when troops searched their homes.[22]

Many aided in the round up of arms from peaceable citizens, with one contingent of Armenian militiamen laying siege to a village outside the town. Events came to a head in January 1920, when Armenian auxiliaries assaulted a Muslim woman in the street. Neither the French authorities nor the Ottoman constables proved willing or effective in reining in Armenian abuses. Even more inexcusable was the inaction of what Mustafa called many of Antep's 'foolish and ignorant' Muslim elites. Several prominent citizens continued to work in the city's administrative offices under French supervision. The town's true patriots, the ones who refused to collaborate and who resisted, 'were made up of the people and righteous clerics'.[23]

Mustafa Nureddin's recollections resonate with those of the handful of other soldiers who published early accounts of the struggle in Cilicia. Ali Saib, who commanded Nationalist troops in Urfa, similarly emphasized the flagrant behavior of British and French occupation authorities. Yet it was Armenian transgressions, particularly stories of assaults upon women, that inspired the greatest indignation. 'These [attacks]', Ali Saib later argued, 'were done in such a vile and disgraceful manner that it is impossible to correctly describe them'. Armenian auxiliaries, 'who, like monsters, were vile, wretched and free of any constraints or responsibility', were specifically accused of forcing Muslim women to become Christians as a way of intimidating all Turks.[24] The complete documentary record, however, leaves many unanswered questions. Most accounts, including those of Ottoman officials, rely heavily upon second-hand information. The divisions created by the occupation, as well as events beforehand, clearly amplify the hardened partisan prejudices of Turkish, Armenian and Western observers. These two factors make some charges, such as the supposed forced Christianization of Muslim women, problematic or difficult to verify. It is possible the charge stemmed from searches conducted by Allied officials for Armenian women who were abducted during the 1915 deportations. This effort to reunite abducted women and children led Nationalists to accuse Armenians of attempting to 'Christianize' converted Muslim women, thus elevating their population statistics.[25] In accounts left by Nureddin and others, the testimony or experiences of the women and children themselves are not considered.

Be that as it may, there is good reason to believe that the tensions dividing Cilicia's Muslims and Christians were not insurmountable. There is ample evidence, for example, that Armenians and Muslims continued to live in mixed neighborhoods in each of the region's major cities before the start of the Nationalist campaign in early 1920. Moreover, it is clear Muslims served alongside Armenians in the French administration. These enduring signs of coexistence and cooperation do not take away from the seriousness of accusations levied by Ali Saib and others. They do suggest, however, that at least some segments of Cilician society were willing to accommodate one another.

Resistance efforts were slow to take root. As in other portions of Anatolia, committees demanding the restoration of Ottoman sovereignty formed in Cilicia soon after the armistice. Momentum towards a more sustained resistance was halted by the spring of 1919 with the arrest of local leaders involved in the 1915 deportations. It was not until the late fall that organized resistance efforts again got underway, this time under the direct authority of Mustafa Kemal's Defense of Rights Association. Overall command of operations in Cilicia was awarded to Kılıç Ali, a native of Antep and a veteran of the 1918 Ottoman offensive in the Caucasus. At the local level, Defense of Rights operatives, many of them officers and petty bureaucrats, worked in secret to mobilize neighborhoods and villages for the coming conflict. In appealing for all to serve 'their religion, fatherland and nation', officers trained and armed villagers and townspeople through the winter for what many expected would be a general uprising.[26] Fighting in the region began in January 1920 when French troops and Armenian auxiliaries quartered themselves in a village between Antep and Marash. When news spread that Armenians had plundered and set fire to homes in search of food, Nationalist militias attacked, inflicting heavy casualties on the Allied detachment. The threat of ambush compelled French garrisons to further fortify their position in the region's key town, thus isolating themselves from the countryside as a whole. All modes of communication and travel between Marash and the outside world were severed by the time the Nationalists began their assault on the town in late January. The situation grew desperate as Armenian civilians and foreign aid workers sought shelter in hospitals and government buildings. 'We are besieged by an invisible army', one American wrote in his diary. 'There are few enemy soldiers in sight, and these are seen through our glasses, running for cover, or hurrying out of their trenches, or stealing over the mountains in little groups to reach the city'.[27] Short of food and devoid of news, the outnumbered French inside Marash lashed out violently. As the full weight of Kılıç Ali's units bore down on their positions, French defenders responded indiscriminately with artillery and machine-gun fire. Between the shelling and deliberate acts of arson, whole sections of Marash were laid waste. By early February, all of the town's nine churches were in ruins.[28] It remains far more difficult to calculate the human toll from the Nationalist siege. American aid workers attested to the deliberate execution of hundreds of unarmed Armenians in the course of the fighting, with many killed in the most gruesome of ways. One woman who fled to the American compound told of days of hiding in a cellar before Nationalist fighters forced them to surrender. Despite promises of mercy, dozens of survivors were slain, including her husband. 'He was shot immediately in the doorway by one of their own Turkish neighbours whom she knew', one American confided to his diary, 'and who was a gendarme in the service of the Government. After the men had been taken out [of the cellar] there was a scene of indescribable horror as the Turks came in with axes and knives and began their murderous work'.[29]

France's hold over Cilicia weakened rapidly in the weeks that followed the fall of Marash. In early February, Nationalist detachments surrounded the city of Urfa. When the French garrison refused to retreat, Muslim supporters rose up in support of Ali Saib's troops. As in Marash, French forces quickly found themselves outgunned and short of supplies. Weeks into the siege, Ali Saib issued an ultimatum to the town's Armenians, requesting that they cease any collaboration with the French and 'remain tied to the fatherland and to the Turks'.[30] Many Armenian fighters indeed were wary of the French presence and fearful of inciting Muslim anger. Nearly five years earlier, in the midst of the deportations, Ottoman troops had stormed the neighborhood after residents resisted their removal, killing hundreds. 'Our strength next to that of the Turks was nothing. We could have held out hardly one or two days in case of attack, once again to die honorably', one survivor remembered. 'The Turks were glad we did not join the French'.[31] The French surrendered Urfa in early April. Despite promises of safe passage, retreating French troops were ambushed a few hours' march from town. Of the estimated 450 soldiers allowed to depart, only fifty to a hundred were reported to have been spared.[32]

The mass killing of French troops and Armenian civilians weighed heavily on the mind of Father Babayan as the Nationalist siege of Antep began. When the first shots were fired in early April, he and other local leaders rallied resident Armenians to prepare to fight. 'Everyone felt the coming danger', he professed. 'Our fierce enemy had decided to murder the Armenians who survived the 1915 genocide in order to take full control of Antep'.[33] Yet, like his comrades outside Urfa, Kılıç Ali declared that his quarrel was not with the town's Armenians but with the French. 'You have lived together with us for six hundred years', he decreed in a letter to local Armenians, 'and you can be sure that you will live like this again'. Rather than accept the terms, Armenian fighters responded to the Nationalist commander that, for them, the choice was 'either Armenia or the graveyard'.[34] The end of negotiations led to intense fighting for much of April and May. France's unbridled use of artillery, as well as attacks by aircraft, inflicted a heavy toll on Antep's residential quarters. For Karnig Panian and his fellow orphans, the siege of the city reprised many of the worst horrors they had experienced during the war. Amid heavy shelling and house-to-house fighting, the American administrators of his orphanage took on the added responsibility of feeding large numbers of other desperate Armenians. When supplies ran low, refugees in the compound resorted to raiding the adjacent Muslim neighborhood, looting and setting fire to homes and shops as they went. The growing intensity of the battle ultimately forced his teachers to evacuate the orphans to a cave beneath a nearby school. The days that passed thereafter were marked by profound stress and uncertainty. 'Every morning, there was utter chaos – the cries and complaints of the infants, the exhortations of the mothers, the laughter and games of the orphans'.[35] Karnig remained in the cave into the early summer, suffering through intense heat and fearing the threat of stray shells. It was only with the announcement of the French withdrawal from Antep that he and his fellow orphans were finally allowed to emerge.

Nationalist advances across Cilicia came as disorder gripped the whole of French-occupied Syria. Faisal's coronation as King of Syria brought Paris into direct contention with both local nationalists as well as their British allies. While trying to assuage Lloyd George from objecting to a French mandate in the Levant, Premier Alexandre Millerand was forced to contend with intense criticism of his foreign policy from both leftist and rightist members of parliament. Ongoing attempts at negotiating an accord with Mustafa Kemal's representatives proved even more daunting. From the Nationalist perspective, an agreed-upon truce in late May seemed to suggest that the French were losing their appetite for further bloodshed. Meanwhile, across the region, Armenians interpreted French reversals as an indication of impending doom. As early as April, thousands of Armenians began fleeing their towns and villages in the hope of seeking passage abroad. One American aid worker in Adana warned that French indifference was leading to a stampede of hopeless refugees to the coast, particularly to the port of Mersin. 'They are going wherever they can go', he exclaimed. 'As the realization of the fact that they can expect no protection grows stronger with them, they are going in larger numbers'.[36] The outflow of refugees continued to intensify after Antep's surrender in June. After weeks of hiding below ground, Karnig Panian was told that he and the rest of the children would again be on the move. Under French guard, administrators placed him and his classmates on trucks that took them south into French-held Syria. The boys of Karnig's school were eventually settled outside Beirut. Life eventually established a new routine of learning and comfort. Memories of Antoura and Antep, however, still lingered. 'We often spoke of the past', he later admitted. 'The previous five years had been imprinted indelibly onto our souls. But we had to keep looking to the future'.[37]

Father Babayan, however, chose to stay on in Antep. Though he cursed the French withdrawal as nothing short of betrayal, he and other remaining civic leaders came to terms with Nationalist representatives upon their seizure of the town. For a time, there were signs that life was returning to normal. 'Armenians', he wrote in mid-June, 'continue to go about their work in the Arasa Bazaar and Turks have begun visiting districts where we [Armenians] live'.[38] Elsewhere in Cilicia, communal tensions boiled over. In Adana, piecemeal clashes between Muslim and Armenian neighbors escalated into generalized violence. On 10 July, 'a wind of panic' overtook the city. 'Everyone', a French commander remembered, 'Christian or Muslim, took his gun and began to shoot from his window. Posts [manned] by Christian volunteers opened fire with no specific objective'. Further attacks by Armenian auxiliaries, coupled with rumors that the city was to be shelled or bombed, led to a mass exodus of an estimated 40,000 Muslim residents. Looters and arsonists then proceeded to ransack Adana's Muslim quarter, plundering goods and torching homes.[39] By late July, hostilities in Antep also resumed. After overthrowing Faisal's government in Damascus, French troops reassembled before Antep, hammering it with artillery fire and aircraft. Fearing for their lives, the town's dwindling community of Armenians declared their neutrality rather than risk the fury of their Muslim neighbors. The siege continued into the next year, reducing much of the city's historic center to rubble. By the winter of 1920–21 Nationalist fighters and Muslim civilians were in a desperate state. 'Our misfortune and calamities deepened in response to our efforts and ardor', Mustafa Nureddin recalled. 'We found a solution for ammunition, but what could we do for bread? Just as a ship needs coal to set sail, people need food to act'.[40] Finally, in late February, the Nationalist garrison surrendered. The resumption of French control featured a return of many of the trappings of the early months of the occupation. Muslim administrators and gendarmes, including those possessing known anti-CUP and anti-Nationalist credentials, were appointed to keep the peace. Aid work among local Armenians began again. However, Armenians and Muslims were forbidden from entering each other's quarter of the town. Much of Antep itself continued to lie in ruins for months to come.

A lasting Nationalist victory over the French came by way of diplomacy. In March 1921, Nationalist negotiators opened direct talks with the Allies in London. Then and there, Ankara and France agreed that a resolution of the tensions in Cilicia was in reach. After months of diplomatic discussion, Nationalist control over Cilicia was formally recognized with the signing of the Treaty of Ankara in October 1921. Mustafa Kemal's representatives, however, paid for this victory with certain concessions. Some of the Cilician territory claimed under the auspices of the National Pact was abandoned, most notably the districts of Antakya and Alexandretta. For fighters like Mustafa Nureddin, it was the overall cost of this victory that made Cilicia's conquest bittersweet. 'For eleven months, we struggled continuously with the enemy on the one side, with the lack of provisions on the other, and then finally with hunger, and we lost', he wrote in 1924. France's cruelty in subduing Antep's defenders, however, absolved any Nationalist guilt at surrendering. 'The enemy was disgraced by their victory at Antep. We do not feel and we will never feel humiliated as a result of our defeat'.[41]

By the time Cilicia was in Ankara's grasp, Nationalist troops had also secured a fixed border in eastern Anatolia. Yet the story of how Mustafa Kemal recaptured the empire's east differs in many respects from the campaign in Cilicia. Unlike in the towns of Antep and Adana, few foreign officials and aid workers witnessed the events that unfolded. There is also a substantial absence of first-hand accounts by soldiers, junior officers or civilians who were present in the region at the time of the Nationalist offensive. Much of what has been written about the fighting instead comes from foreign intelligence reports as well as the accounts of senior generals in the field. The political dynamics of the struggle over eastern Anatolia were also more complex and chaotic. In reasserting Ottoman control over the country's historic eastern frontier, Nationalist troops were confronted with the politics of four young states, Georgia, Armenia, Azerbaijan and Soviet Russia. Playing lesser roles in the conflict were the leaders and fighters representing other ethnic groups in the Caucasus, such as Ajaris, Dagestanis, Circassians, Abkhazians and Kurds. The struggle to determine eastern Anatolia's fate was, lastly, far shorter and, in some ways, more decisive. The extent to which it was as violent or destructive as the fighting in Cilicia, however, is more difficult to say.

The origins of the Nationalist campaign in the east date back to the last months of the First World War. The signing of the Treaty of Brest-Litovsk in March 1918 marked the Soviet government's formal recognition of its defeat at the hands of the Central Powers. In signing the agreement, Istanbul won the right to reclaim three provinces, Batum, Kars and Ardahan, which had been lost to Russia in the nineteenth century. This victory, however, was offset by counterclaims raised by various peoples in the region. In the wake of the October Revolution, Georgian, Armenian and Azerbaijani leaders had formed a new state, the short-lived Transcaucasian Republic, which disputed the borders laid out at Brest-Litovsk. An even more potent source of resistance was the remnants of Armenian forces that had supported the Russian occupation of eastern Anatolia. Led by fierce revolutionary leaders like Andranik Ozanian, the last of these troops held out in the hopes of claiming the Ottoman east as part of an independent Armenian state. Among the officers tasked with asserting Istanbul's claim to the 'three provinces' (elviye-i selase) was Kazım Karabekir, then a corps commander on the eastern front. With orders in early March to press eastward, Karabekir's men advanced against a force of only a few thousand Armenian irregulars. In his diary, he took steady note of the carnage he encountered along the way, including grisly scenes of women and children bayoneted to death and set on fire. He, as well as journalists and officers who followed him, were particularly shocked at the scale of destruction left behind in Erzurum after the Armenian retreat. According to his estimate, at least 1,700 Muslims were massacred in the days before the town fell to Ottoman forces.[42] Karabekir continued to advance, eventually taking the fortress town of Kars in mid-April. The restoration of Ottoman rule over the region came with promises of protection and the rule of law for all remaining Armenians. While Enver Pasha declared that Istanbul would uphold 'their security, property and freedom', Talat floated a plan to offer native Armenians a general amnesty from prosecution. For those who had lost property, they would be able to choose monetary compensation or perhaps restitution of their lands so far as it was possible.[43]

The ease with which the Ottoman troops took hold of the three provinces did not lay to rest Istanbul's ambitions. As German and Austrian armies advanced into territories ceded by the Bolsheviks in Eastern Europe, Ottoman forces pressed further into the Caucasus. By then, the Transcaucasian Republic had divided itself into the three states of Georgia, Armenia and Azerbaijan. Affairs in the region also drew the attention of Germany and Great Britain, with each power anticipating a scramble for control over the rich petroleum trade emanating from the ports of Baku and Batum. Amid this uncertainty, leading Young Turks saw the opportunity to transform the Caucasian map to their benefit. Since the start of the war, CUP operatives had cultivated strong relations with dissidents and rebels in various parts of the Russian Empire. In supporting independence movements in

Ukraine, Dagestan and Azerbaijan, planners saw a chance of dulling any future invasion from the Russian north. For some, including perhaps Enver, the war offered Istanbul the prospect of cementing a claim to portions of Central Asia, the mythic cradle of Turkic civilization. Turanists, as these romantics referred to themselves, did not necessarily dominate the thinking of the Ottoman high command. When Enver offered Kazım Karabekir an opportunity to take part in an invasion of the Caucasus, he brusquely turned him down. An old friend known for his Turanist leanings accosted Karabekir in his camp, skewering him for his decision. 'While we are on our way to the fantasy land called Turan', Karabekir needled back, 'the Germans will be taking up residence on the Bosphorus'. The joke, he confided to his diary, made his friend turn pale.[44]

Enver's summer campaign threw much of the Caucasus into turmoil. Border territories belonging to Georgia were seized, in some cases at the invitation of local Muslim communities. In June, Ottoman troops marched imperiously through Tabriz in northern Iran – an act, one commander explained, meant to 'show the grandeur of the Turkish Army to the Persians, who are infatuated with showiness and force'.[45] The main thrust of the campaign passed through Azerbaijan, a state wracked by upheaval since it declared its independence in late May 1918. The unfolding revolution in Russia, as well as the repercussions from the wartime massacres in Anatolia, created a groundswell of anxieties among intermixed communities of Muslims and Armenians throughout Azerbaijan. In March, Bolshevik troops, backed by Armenian nationalists, fought fierce street battles with local Azeri militias, a struggle that eventually led to an anti-Muslim pogrom that cost the lives of 12,000 innocent people.[46] In an effort to back the nascent Azerbaijani government, Ottoman troops set their sights on Baku, promising to restore the town to the young republic. Heading this expedition was Enver Pasha's uncle, Halil, as well as Enver's half-brother Nuri. It was under Nuri's command that a motley force calling itself the 'Army of Islam' seized Baku in September 1918. A campaign of revenge followed the town's capture as bands of local Muslims, including many displaced by the massacres that spring, set upon Baku's Armenian community. In an interview with British officials in 1920, Nuri Pasha took no responsibility for the killings, which may have resulted in the death of up to 9,000 Armenian civilians. 'I did my duty; I did everything in my power', he later exclaimed. 'A tiny spark can set a prairie on fire, but scores of acres will be laid waste before the burning flames are choked'.[47]

These advances, as well as others made to the north into Dagestan, were short-lived. With Bulgaria's surrender opening the way for French, Serbian and British troops to threaten Istanbul, Ottoman operations in the Caucasus ground to a halt. The signing of the armistice at the end of October compelled Istanbul to pull back its forces and relinquish all gains made since the spring. The surrendered territories included the three provinces won at Brest-Litovsk, Batum, Ardahan and Kars. For provincial leaders residing in Kars, the likelihood of Armenian rule moved them to immediate action. With the help of the imperial secret service, local notables declared the establishment of a Southwestern Caucasian Republic in November 1918. As a body willing to submit itself to the authority of the Ottoman state, the republic's government included representatives from lands inside Georgia as well as portions of Nakhchivan in Azerbaijan. Warnings of renewed intercommunal fighting (a 'second Macedonia', as the Kars government put it) helped persuade thousands of demobilized soldiers and officers to refuse to return home.[48] A British intelligence report from late 1919 estimated that more than 25,000 Ottoman troops remained in Azerbaijan, with nearly another thousand operating in Dagestan.[49] While these numbers may have been exaggerated, the presence of thousands of Ottoman volunteers in the region spoke to the continued importance of the Caucasus within imperial affairs. Before departing for exile, Enver Pasha reputedly ordered Nuri and Halil to prepare their forces to lead the fight against any Allied occupation of Anatolia. Despite their capture by British troops after the armistice, the two men remained committed to Enver's plan. After miraculously escaping from captivity, Nuri and Halil returned to Azerbaijan to serve as volunteer officers. As they assisted Baku in its bitter border disputes with Armenia, both men continued to see the Caucasian struggle as linked to the emerging National Movement. 'Turkey is as my mother', Nuri Pasha told a British officer, 'the Mussulmans are my brothers. I want to help the Mussulman. I wanted to see an independent Azerbaijan'.[50]

Meanwhile, affairs just inside the empire's eastern border remained relatively static. For much of 1919, pro-Nationalist officers were slow to implement a coherent plan to reassert Ottoman authority over the territories lost with the armistice. As commander of the bulk of imperial forces in Erzurum, Kazım Karabekir clashed with Halil Pasha over strategy and tactics. Though Halil had been his senior officer during the Great War, Karabekir scolded him and his brother Nuri for their insular focus on Caucasian affairs, warning them that their failure to coordinate would be a disaster for 'both the Azeri people and [their] true nation', the Ottoman Empire.[51] Intervening between the three generals was Mustafa Kemal, who dispatched Halil as an envoy to the Soviet government. With Lenin embroiled in his own war against the Allies and anti-Communist forces, Kemal viewed the Bolsheviks as a potential partner and patron. After months of negotiation, Halil Pasha succeeded in winning a bonanza in Soviet aid. The prospect of receiving financial and material support from Moscow, however, came at the expense of any immediate attempt to recover lands lost as a result of the Great War. While Karabekir awaited orders to move forward, he kept an account of the fighting between Armenian and Azeri forces. By the early summer, large numbers of Muslim refugees had fled Armenian advances in the regions of Erivan, Nakhchivan, Karabagh and Zangezur. Though he directed units to assist Azeri and Ottoman troops across the border, the political situation did not allow Karabekir to advance. In early spring 1920, conditions began to change. Anti-Bolshevik forces holding Ukraine and the lower Don River collapsed, paving the way for the Red Army to march on the Caucasus. For officials in Ankara, the Russian push southward represented a potential lifeline that would allow direct aid to reach the National Forces from Moscow. Lenin's government, however, initially resisted sending any of the promised support until after the Red Army compelled the Caucasian republics to accept Soviet rule. While many former Ottoman officers accepted the necessity of such a concession, Nuri Pasha initially refused to abandon his commitment to an independent Azerbaijan. In May, he led Azeri forces in a last stand against the Red Army in the contested region of Karabagh, close to the Ottoman border. When Nuri pleaded for reinforcements, Karabekir issued a stern command. Nuri was to leave Azerbaijan, or his actions would be counted as 'committing treason with our enemies and no one would save him from his crime'. 'Stop this childishness', the order ended.[52]

Karabekir's lack of concern for Azerbaijan was tempered by his loathing for Armenia. Since the founding of an Armenian Republic in the spring of 1918, officials in Erivan labored to assert control over the mountainous lands within the state's declared borders. Virtually every district of the country comprised Muslim communities that refused to be governed by Armenians. According to the 1914 census, more than a third of the population within the province of Erivan was made up of Muslims.[53] Armenia's demographic complexity laid the groundwork for a heated contest with Azerbaijan over various mixed districts. The intense fighting that wracked areas such as Zangezur and Karabagh added to the climate of crisis that hovered over the republic. In the year after Erivan declared independence, almost 300,000 Armenian refugees had taken up residence inside the country's borders.[54] The bulk of them came from the Ottoman east as survivors of the deportations and massacres. At birth, the state of Armenia was bankrupt and riven by factionalism. With up to a third of its food supply historically coming from Russia, scarcity and disorder left a terrible toll. By the summer of 1919, up to 200,000 people, some 20 percent of the republic's population, died as a result of hunger.[55] Nevertheless, with the Allies poised to award Armenia lands inside the Ottoman Empire, leaders in Erivan pressed forward with attempts at consolidating control over the disputed territories of Kars, Ardahan and Artvin. Tasked with achieving this effort was an army that grew weaker as weapons and money became scarce. To offset these shortcomings, Armenians in Istanbul and other parts of Anatolia furiously raised funds to pay their 'blood debts' to those fighting for independence.[56] Armenia's fragility grew even more apparent as the Red Army threatened to march on the Caucasus in the spring of 1920. When a British representative asked Kazım Karabekir if he would give fleeing Armenians sanctuary from the advancing Bolsheviks, the general refused. 'Public opinion in this region', he countered, 'would not accept even one of the Armenians within our borders under any circumstance'. How could they, after all, given the news of 'every kind of atrocity and outrage against Muslims' in Cilicia, not to mention the 'cries and howls' of Muslims living under Armenian rule?[57]

Karabekir's long-awaited offensive against Armenia began in late September 1920. Over the next two months, Nationalist regulars, supported by local Kurdish militias, pushed the harried defenders back towards the border established by the Treaty of Brest-Litovsk, inflicting devastating losses. According to Karabekir's records, the fall of Kars at the end of October cost the Armenian army at least a thousand dead and more than a thousand captured (the Nationalists, by contrast, suffered only nine killed in taking the town).[58] The fighting continued after Nationalist troops surged eastward. As Karabekir's men threatened Erivan proper, territories in their path were left devastated. The bodies of almost 12,000 people – 90 percent of them purportedly women and children – were later collected and buried by Soviet authorities in Armenia in the year that followed the Nationalist invasion.[59] Hostilities came to an abrupt end at the beginning of December. By then, Soviet agents had taken hold of Erivan and declared the establishment of a socialist republic. A lopsided peace was soon signed between Nationalist and Armenian negotiators in the town of Alexandropol. All Armenian claims to Ottoman lands were thereafter abandoned.

The final contours of Anatolia's eastern border were not finalized until the spring of 1921. By then, Soviet troops had seized control of Georgia, an act that prompted Nationalist troops to retake the province of Batum on the Black Sea coast. This brief Nationalist offensive added to what was already a tense series of negotiations between Ankara and Moscow. When a treaty of friendship was signed in late March 1921, both governments were forced to make concessions. In return for the recognition of Ankara as the country's true seat of power, the Nationalists relinquished rights to Batum and its port. Ankara, however, insisted that provincial autonomy be granted to Batum on behalf of the region's Muslim majority, the Ajaris. Negotiators also demanded local authorities receive similar powers in the region of Nakhchivan, adjacent to the border. Not only would the majority Muslim province attain local rule, but the region was also deemed an exclave belonging to Azerbaijan, not its neighbor Armenia. No such arrangements were granted within Ottoman territory.

Lenin's pact with Mustafa Kemal effectively brought all hope for a completely independent Armenian state to an end. For many survivors who sought refuge under Erivan's protection, life under the new 'Sovietized' government brought fresh hardships. This was especially the case for nationalists and soldiers like Kalusd Sürmenyan. Immediately after the 1918 armistice, he had moved to Batum, still hoping to reunite with his family and start his life anew. It was there that a representative from Erivan offered him a commission to lead a unit of men comprising other Ottoman Armenians like himself. Kalusd, along with his family, jumped at the opportunity. 'An Armenian army, Armenian ministers, on all sides Armenians. One goes crazy from the human elation', he later explained. 'Two years earlier we were in a Turkish hell, hopeless and desperate. Today we are in our fatherland'.[60] Yet in serving this new state, he and his family again nearly paid the ultimate price. Beginning in 1919, he and his men found themselves engaged in a seemingly endless fight with enemies from both within and without. After clashing with Kurdish tribes and helping put down a Bolshevik-inspired revolt, Sürmenyan was captured by Karabekir's forces during the defense of Kars. Though he was released and returned to Erivan, the Soviet takeover of the government landed him in even greater trouble. The new Bolshevik regime sentenced him and other officers loyal to the republic to exile. Those who failed to go were shot. Rather than submit to an uncertain term of banishment, Kalusd managed to escape, fleeing with members of his family to Iran. From there, he hoped to journey on to America and gather his family there. Disease, however, struck him down along the way, marooning him and other loved ones in Baghdad. Necessity forced him to stay in Iraq, where he made a living first as a teacher and then as a merchant. At the close of his memoirs, twenty-three years after his arrival in Baghdad, he was still living, as he put it, 'with the deep belief of one day seeing my homeland again, and with the permanent memory of our country'.[61]

The Red Army's oppression of Armenian nationalists and suspected dissidents forced thousands of people like Kalusd Sürmenyan to flee abroad. Within Anatolia, a different sort of politics resulted in an even larger, more devastating exodus. After 1921, the likelihood of a Nationalist victory made it harder for Armenians in Cilicia and other portions of the interior to remain. Father Babayan, for one, stayed on in Antep months after the French agreed to abandon the town. For a time, after the fighting ended, a quiet unease settled over his daily affairs. Armenians whom he knew resumed their shopping in Muslim districts, where they were often met with everyday courtesies. 'Can Turks genuinely be kind?' he pondered in his diary. 'Is it possible to be so naïve as to use a polite word and believe it? If the Turks were given the chance tomorrow, they would tear us to pieces'.[62] Nevertheless, Babayan remained, continuing his work aiding the poor and displaced while others chose to abandon the town. His decision to resettle in Aleppo came only after French troops formally laid plans to hand Antep over to the Nationalists in the fall of 1921. After several months of preparation, he joined a convoy of sixty Armenians which made its way across the Syrian border in August 1922. By January 1923, French officials estimated that Antep's Christian population had dwindled to a mere eighty residents.[63] The near-complete disappearance of Armenians in Antep mirrored much of Cilicia. American missionaries watched in despair as shop owners and residents sold valuables for a pittance in order to pay for their passage abroad. In the port of Mersin, Armenians slept in the street awaiting overcrowded ships to take them to Syria. 'It seems to be the custom', it was observed, 'as each family left the house for the last time, to throw the water jar into the street, breaking it into thousands of pieces, a symbol of a broken home'.[64]

Similar patterns were witnessed in towns and villages beyond France's former occupation zone. Between 1918 and 1922, thousands of deported Armenians, Assyrians and other Christians had managed to return to their homes in places like Diyarbakir, Harput and Malatya. All of these regions were spared the sort of violence and destruction witnessed in Cilicia. However, as the fighting elsewhere drew to a close in 1922, local officials – including those complicit in the massacres and expulsions of 1915 – forced thousands of Christians to leave Turkey's east. The overall effect of this final campaign virtually extinguished the presence of non-Muslims in eastern Anatolia. In Diyarbakir, for example, the 1914 Ottoman census recorded 20,263 residents who were Armenian, Assyrian or Chaldean (of whom, more than 13,000 were Armenian).[65] In April 1924, French officials estimated that 5,400 remained in the town. Nine months later, it was presumed only 545 were left.[66]

The treaty signed with the Soviets, coupled with the settlement reached with France, lent Mustafa Kemal's government a needed air of legitimacy and vibrancy in the spring of 1921. In the year that had passed since the opening of the National Assembly, it had become clear that Ankara represented the country's political future. Attaining peace with France and friendship with the Bolsheviks also marked important moments that determined the physical shape the country would assume once the fighting was truly over. Acts of war and diplomacy, however, were not the only forces that helped define what became the borders of the Turkish Republic. Just as essential were evolving perceptions of what constituted the natural frontiers of the Ottoman (and eventually Turkish) nation. The pact reached with the Soviets was a statement, however reluctant, of an incontrovertible fact: the lands east of Kars constituted separate and distinct nations. It was clear, as Mustafa Kemal put it, that the Circassians and other peoples in the North Caucasus were 'closely connected to the salvation, existence and independence of Turkey'.[67] However, their struggle for survival, as well as the challenges facing Azeris and other Caucasian Muslims, was not to be amalgamated with the goals of the National Movement. Some Nationalist officers, such as Nuri Pasha, never fully accepted this reality. Twenty years later, he continued to work towards the goal of forming a united confederation encompassing Turkey, the Caucasus and the peoples of Central Asia. His enthusiasm for what had been a dream shared with his half-brother Enver moved him to volunteer his services to the Nazis, going so far as to offer to raise a battalion of Soviet Muslim prisoners of war for the Waffen SS during the Second World War.

A different set of complications framed the way Nationalists viewed the country's southern border. Unlike the Caucasus, the Arab lands possessed a long, storied history as a portion of the Ottoman Empire. The pain of losing these territories was still fresh in the memories of the soldiers and civilians who joined the National Movement. Dulling this sense of anguish, however, were debates over the loyalties and national sympathies of the peoples living in the Arab lands. Though there was no denying the humiliation of the retreat from Syria, Iraq and Arabia, many perceived the loss of these provinces as blessings in disguise. The state and nation, they reasoned, were stronger and more secure without Arabs in them. With noted exceptions, civic leaders in the Levant and Mesopotamia largely agreed they were better off on their own. The shared threat of British or French rule, however, helped forge close contacts between Ankara and Arab resistance fighters. In the two years that followed the armistice, rebels in Iraq and Syria drew support and inspiration from Mustafa Kemal's National Forces. A shared rhetoric rooted in national sovereignty and Islamic unity added to the potency of this alliance. However, despite glimmers of reconciliation, a commitment to reunification of the prewar empire remained elusive. The wounds were too deep and the political realities were too daunting.

'BRIGHTEST JEWELS IN THE OTTOMAN CROWN': THE NATIONAL MOVEMENT AND THE FATE OF THE ARAB LANDS

In Damascus today, a wide boulevard known as an-Nasr runs west from the foot of the city's ancient citadel. On either side of the street lie two of the most important landmarks left in Syria's largest city by the Ottoman Empire. Just north of the street is Martyrs' Square, which served as the administrative epicenter of Damascus after the late nineteenth century. To the south, at the far west end of the street, sits a disused railway station which once connected Damascus to Istanbul and to the holy cities of Mecca and Medina. When it was first built, the boulevard was named after the military governor who oversaw its construction, Cemal Pasha. As commander of the imperial Fourth Army during the Great War, Cemal Pasha endorsed a series of infrastructure and renovation initiatives throughout the Levant. He constructed intercity highways and urban streets, widened roads, and beautified thoroughfares with trees and walkways. He supervised the opening of primary and secondary schools as well as mosques and religious endowments. With German help, he lent government support to the excavation and restoration of the region's antiquities. Expanding the protection of ancient sites, he declared, was critical, so that 'no Ottoman patriot could fail to respect the artistic achievements of past civilizations'.[68]

One of Cemal's wartime aides, Ali Fuad, did not necessarily see the governor's dedication to public works in altruistic terms. The paving of

Cemal Pasha Boulevard clearly served no military purpose. The same could be said for other efforts he endorsed, such as the building of parks, clubs and casinos in Beirut and other cities and towns. Such ventures, as Fuad put it, were 'decorative symbols of civilization' suitable only in peacetime.[69] More than anything, they distracted from the perilous state of Cemal's beleaguered administration. After a failed offensive against British-held Egypt, the Ottoman Fourth Army contended with the constant threat of Allied invasion from the coast. Famine devastated much of the countryside within the war's first year. Conditions in Beirut were so hopeless, as another aide to Cemal Pasha put it, that the city's streets echoed with 'the moans of those in their death throes from hunger'.[70] Then there was the threat of popular insurrection, an anxiety that plagued senior officials through much of the war. By his own account, Cemal 'felt perfectly sure of the civil population', never once sensing the need to question the loyalty of the Arab soldiers who defended the Levantine coast.[71] His subordinates, however, later testified that this was not the case. By the closing stages of the war, Cemal and his staff saw to it that they were guarded by units comprising Sufi dervishes from Anatolia and volunteers from the Balkans, not Arabs. Their headquarters, in the words of Ali Fuad, was 'like an isolated island in a sea of revolt'.[72]

The sentiments and actions of Cemal Pasha and his staff epitomize a paradox at the heart of the empire's final years. As senior officers, they shared deep-seated convictions about the unity and integrity of the Ottoman state. Though Cemal, his staff and the majority of his field commanders did not come from the Arab lands, they approached Syria, and its defense, as a task in the service of the Ottoman fatherland. For most of the war, at least, there was good reason to believe that Arab citizens were no less dedicated than other Muslims to the empire. Arab recruits, including volunteers, made up 25–37 percent of the military.[73] Units comprising Arab soldiers were found on virtually every front. There is no evidence to suggest that Arab troops were poorer soldiers or less reliable than conscripts from anywhere else in the country. To a large extent, the dedication of Arabs serving at the front was indicative of the strength and popular appeal of Ottoman patriotism. As in other parts of the country, devotion to the empire was a value most often learned in school. Arab graduates of institutions like the Harbiye often remained Ottoman patriots to the very end. A good number refused to leave the Ottoman military even after the armistice. Of the 431 officers to die in the service of the National Movement, thirty-three have been identified as of Arab origin. More remarkably, fourteen of this number were from Libya, a province Istanbul effectively relinquished in 1912.[74]

The roads and schools built by Cemal Pasha were often conceived of as the embodiment of this shared allegiance to the state and nation. In the decades leading up to the First World War, generations of Ottoman officials dedicated themselves to similar enterprises throughout the empire's predominately Arab territories. Aleppo, Jerusalem, Beirut and Mosul were each the beneficiaries of state-backed projects aimed at improving education, transport, health and security. The services that came with these investments made cities such as Baghdad, Jeddah and Sanaa less remote and more integrated into the imperial whole. But it was not simply the practical benefits that motivated officials to provide greater government services to majority Arab districts. With the loss of Algeria, Egypt and Tunisia during the first part of the nineteenth century, many feared that Istanbul's hold over its remaining Arab territories was slipping. The future of the empire rested upon the state's willingness and capacity to govern even the most distant outposts of the country. In building schools, roads and barracks, officials hoped to inspire loyalty and demonstrate the durability of Ottoman rule. Even after the war, Cemal Pasha saw no irony in declaring the Arab lands the 'brightest jewels in the Ottoman crown'.[75]

Construction projects and appeals to patriotism, however, proved only so effective. Past precedents, some centuries old, mired the politics of the Arab lands. For much of their history in the empire, the inhabitants of North Africa, Mesopotamia and the Levant possessed a somewhat detached relationship with Istanbul. Unlike the Balkans and western Anatolia, which were thoroughly transformed under Ottoman rule, pre-Ottoman patterns endured well into the nineteenth century. Powerful provincial families, and not appointed officials, tended to hold sway over regional politics. Conversely, few Arabs ascended to the heights of power within the capital. It was far more common to find Albanians than Syrians among senior bureaucrats and general officers as late as the First World War. The nineteenth century brought with it other complications. After the rulers of Egypt won their autonomy in 1840, Cairo challenged Istanbul's monopoly over Ottoman political thought and reform. After the establishment of Lebanon as an autonomous province in 1861, Arab intellectuals assumed an even more visible role in imperial society. For the remainder of the century, activists based in Beirut, Cairo and Damascus commanded greater influence over political debate in the Arab lands. Though few rejected Istanbul's legitimacy, elites in the Levant grew more assertive in demanding more control over provincial affairs. Why was it, many asked, that local offices and schools were so often staffed by Turkish-speaking appointees? One parliamentarian wondered aloud why no one from Syria had 'attained in the last six hundred years the office of the grand vizier, *şeyhülislam*, or minister of finance'.[76] After his coronation, Abdülhamid II sought to counter these grievances with appeals for unity under the aegis of Islam. For Young Turk leaders such as Cemal Pasha, expressions of Arab national identity were acceptable so long as they remained grounded in religious solidarity and loyalty to the empire. He, for one, saw nothing harmful or wrong in Arabs and Turks securing 'their unity while remaining separate nations'. What was demanded of all citizens, however, was fidelity to the sultan-caliph.[77]

Undermining these declarations of fraternity were sentiments rarely expressed in the public record. Among themselves, officials appointed from outside the Arab provinces often held locals in low esteem. Bedouin were regularly demeaned as barbaric nomads incompatible with civilized society. Arabs were broadly stereotyped and derided for having darker skin and curly hair. In his memoirs, Cemal Pasha claimed to have been rebuked by a well-known Arab nationalist who regularly heard disparaging comments towards Arabs. In Istanbul, he claimed, dogs were referred to as Arabs while anything obscure and incomprehensible was likened to 'the hair of an Arab'. Cemal rejected such aspersions, stating that these were merely 'a few popular expressions' which did not represent the views of 'Turks, and particularly Anatolian Turks'.[78] With the outbreak of war in 1914, cultural and social differences were magnified with the conscription of tens of thousands of Arab citizens. The lack of Arabic-speaking officers, as well as charges of mistreatment and physical abuse, created rifts within many units.

After the war, officers who came from outside the region avowed that Arabs possessed their own bigotries towards them. 'In that vast land from Aleppo to Aden please do not think that there is an Arab Question', one of Cemal's aides wrote. 'All the Arab Question consists of is *hatred for the Turks*. Remove this feeling and the affairs of Syria and Arabia will become like the hair of the Arab (*Arap saçı*), so tangled and twisted that you cannot make sense of it'.[79]

The resentment found in these impressions, however, cannot be separated from the raw feelings the Great War would invoke. On the one hand, there were signs before 1914 that relations between Istanbul and the Arab lands were improving. The 1911 invasion of Libya had roused thousands of citizens, including prominent Young Turks, to volunteer in the defense of the region. A shared sense of Ottoman patriotism, undergirded by a strong belief in Muslim camaraderie, bolstered the spirits of many who partook in the fighting outside Benghazi, Derna and Tripoli. And yet, with the crushing loss of the Balkans in 1913, much of this enthusiasm evaporated. With the empire's long-term future in the balance, a collection of prominent Arab nationalists publicly lobbied for a general reorganization of the state. At a much-touted 'Arab Congress' held in Paris, representatives advocated the formation of a dual Turkish–Arab empire akin to Austria–Hungary. The CUP acknowledged these calls. At its 1913 convention, the party agreed to promote an 'expansion of responsibilities and distribution of obligations' in the provinces, a phrase interpreted as the beginnings of a more decentralized approach towards provincial Arab administration.[80] Expressions of Young Turk support for this position obscured deeper apprehensions among the party's most senior leaders. French sympathy for Arab demands, coupled with French commercial penetration of the Levant, carried with it an implicit threat of invasion and partition. Moreover, past calls for decentralization and autonomy in the Balkans did little to forestall insurrection and conflict.

When the war finally came in 1914, a number of events confirmed many people's worst fears. Shortages in essential goods, brought on by mobilization and an Allied blockade, shattered public confidence in the CUP regime. The execution of leading intellectuals in Damascus and Beirut, coupled with the mass deportation of tens of thousands from Iraq, western Arabia and greater Syria, heightened popular outrage that much further. Many officers and officials found confirmation of their own biases in the prosecution of suspected Arab nationalists and dissidents. Though Talat Pasha assailed Faisal's self-styled 'Arab revolt' as 'provoked by the gold and the promises of the English', officials at various levels of the Ottoman administration suspected that Arab support for the war was at best half-hearted.[81] With the conclusion of the armistice, public opinion was of two minds when it came to the future. Defeat at the hands of the Anglo-French alliance was perceived as a major disaster. The prospect of partition and European rule constituted even graver dangers to both the state and Islam. The armistice, however, was also received as a blessing for both administrators and everyday citizens in the Arab lands. For many Arab residents, Allied soldiers had liberated them from a government that had starved and oppressed them. The departure of Syria, Iraq and Arabia was similarly significant for many who remained under Ottoman rule. For those who saw Arabs as traitors and miscreants, their parting made Istanbul stronger, not weaker.

The months and years following the armistice in the Arab lands cannot be condensed into one story. How local elites and populations perceived this change varied widely, reflecting the inherent diversity of the territories as a whole. A closer inspection of this time also reveals the degree to which local actors toyed with the retention of some kind of relationship with the Ottoman state. For some, re-establishing a connection with what remained of the empire was a tactical decision, one brought on by common enemies and anxieties. For others, a shared sense of belonging roused fleeting hopes for some sort of reunion. Practical realities, as well as deeply felt animosities, ultimately rendered any return to the old order moot.

Geography played an outsized role in permanently severing Istanbul's connections with the Arabian Peninsula. Through the nineteenth century, Ottoman officials labored mightily to establish more direct control over the regions of the Hijaz, Asir and Yemen. As in other portions of the empire, the building of barracks, schools, courts and telegraph offices lent Ottoman rule an air of authenticity in these more distant provinces. Istanbul's efforts at expanding the 'lights of civilization', however, proved bitterly contentious.[82] Guerrilla warfare raged in Yemen through the turn of the century, leaving thousands of

Ottoman conscripts dead before a final peace was signed in 1911. In reaching an agreement, the CUP-led government granted Imam Yahya, leader of the rebels north of Sanaa, de facto rule over the province. Yahya reciprocated with pledges of fealty to the sultan and permitted Ottoman troops to remain in the region. Ottoman authorities were far less successful in reining in the lands along the coastal stretches of Asir. There, local tribes under Muhammad ibn Ali al-Idrisi remained at odds with Istanbul, establishing close relations with Italian colonial authorities across the Red Sea in Eritrea. Al-Idrisi's ties with Rome assumed greater significance with the outbreak of war in 1914. For the next four years, Ottoman authorities found themselves squeezed between al-Idrisi in the north and British-controlled Aden in the south. Yemen's defenders, however, proved themselves more than a match for the Allies. Under the command of the imperial governor, Mahmud Nedim, the province's 1,800-man garrison hurled back incursions from British troops, seizing a critical market town outside Aden in the summer 1916.[83] Despite losing direct contact with Istanbul midway through the war, Nedim's men held out until the armistice forced them to surrender. Like his counterparts in the Caucasus, Nedim, who had spent twenty years as an official in Yemen, refused to leave. Together he and other officers, including several from Iraq and Syria, stayed on as personal advisors to Imam Yahya.[84] Under the legal opinion that 'no part of the Ottoman Empire can be considered abandoned and detached', more than a hundred Ottoman civil servants remained at their posts in Sanaa, with many continuing to receive salaries from Istanbul as late as October 1922.[85] For Nedim, preserving Yahya's rule was a duty in harmony with the spirit of Muslim unity and Ottoman patriotism. Muslims were beginning to rally, he declared in 1919, and were now realizing 'the deceit and designs of the Western states'. They now knew that 'there was no survival and life without [forging an] alliance under the banner of the Islamic Ottoman state'.[86] Mahmud Nedim's service in defense of Yemen came to an end soon after Mustafa Kemal's victory over Greece in 1922. The last holdouts of the old Ottoman bureaucracy, which included 111 petty judges, inspectors, scribes, gendarmes and soldiers, finally left Yemen for Turkey in 1926.[87]

Ottoman rule came to a more abrupt close further north, in the

Hijaz. As late as the first year of the Great War, the region's three principal cities, Mecca, Medina and Jeddah, remained very much under imperial control. While local inhabitants sent troops and camels to the front, Medina's most influential magistrate, Sharif Hussein, father to Faisal, spoke openly in support of the war. His fealty, however, was only skin-deep. The CUP's desire to cement its control over the provinces was the cause of considerable worry, leading to suspicions that it planned to eventually depose him. In the year before the war, Hussein reached out to British representatives in the hopes of finding a lasting guarantor for his position in Mecca. London slowly warmed to his overtures. As the fighting began, Hussein's support for the Allies was deemed beneficial both for the war and for Britain's standing among Muslims worldwide. Before Hussein and Faisal declared their independence from Istanbul in the summer of 1916, neither professed any commitment to Arab nationalism.

Successive strikes against Mecca and Jeddah left most of the region in Hussein's hands before 1916 was through. Medina's garrison, however, refused to submit. The inflexibility of the Ottoman forces there is largely credited to the town's military commander, Fahreddin Pasha. His dedication to Medina's defense, according to subordinates, was grounded in his solemn belief that the town, the burial place of the Prophet Muhammad, was to remain in the care of the Ottoman state. While Fahreddin's lieutenants remembered him as a man of strict religious and patriotic devotion, locals reviled him as the man who 'exterminated Medinian society', due to his decision to expel almost all native residents in 1917.[88] Before the general finally surrendered his command in January 1919, one witness claimed that he had made plans to set alight the garrison's ammunition depot and blow himself up, along with the rest of his command, in an act of defiance. He was instead apprehended by junior officers and remanded to the custody of rebels outside the town.

Sharif Hussein's ambitions met with greater difficulties once the war was over. Although he declared himself 'King of the Hijaz', he labored to consolidate his rule even before peace negotiations commenced in Paris. With Faisal's government facing its own challenges in Damascus, Hussein's rule in Mecca was contested by his rivals to the east. Ibn Saud, lord of the oasis communities of the Nejd, scored a number of victories against Hussein's forces in 1919. A dramatic decline in British material support unsettled the 'King of the Hijaz'. To what degree these misfortunes were linked to affairs in Anatolia, however, is not clear. According to British intelligence, a Nationalist representative with a 'considerable sum in gold' journeyed to Arabia in February 1920 in the hopes of forging an alliance with Ibn Saud.[89] Hussein is also said to have sent similar delegations north to Anatolia, although it appears that neither he nor Ibn Saud attained decisive support. What continued to interest him most in Ottoman politics was the title of caliph. With Sultan Mehmed VI's power clearly waning, Hussein undertook a noisy campaign aimed at usurping his status as shepherd of the world's Muslims. In an interview with the *Times* of London, Abdullah, Hussein's younger son, argued that the Ottoman royal family lacked the requisite traits for holding the caliphate in the first place. 'The power of the sword', he told the paper, was the sole reason the Ottoman sultans reigned as the caliphs of Islam. Now was time for his family, as natives of the Hijaz and direct descendants of the Prophet Muhammad, to claim what was properly theirs.[90] As the fighting shifted in Mustafa Kemal's favor after 1921, Hussein placed his hopes on Ankara's willingness to cede him the office in Mehmed VI's stead. No such deal would ever be made.

Iraq's divorce from the Ottoman Empire forms a number of sharp contrasts with other portions of the Arab lands. Like the Hijaz and Yemen, the Mesopotamian provinces differed from one another in political and social terms. Mosul, Baghdad and Basra each hosted large nomadic populations but varied in terms of the sectarian and ethnic make-up of their permanent inhabitants. Local elites often reflected this regional diversity. Heads of tribes, members of the clergy (particularly among Shiites) and influential urban families tended to dominate local politics, often at Istanbul's expense. An important exception to this trend was found in the environs of Baghdad, an area home to large numbers of local Sunnis who sought service in the state bureaucracy and military. With the arrival of the First World War, the vast majority of provincial leaders answered the government's call to mobilize. Thousands of recruits, including levies from local tribes, numbered among the first defenders to clash with advancing British and Indian troops. Yet after the fall of Basra in November 1914, the character of local politics began to change. The Ottoman army's failure to hold the British back led to open displays of indignation by members of the Shia clergy. After popular revolts in Najaf and Hillah, Ottoman authorities responded with mass public hangings and the deportation of thousands to Diyarbakir. In Baghdad, heavy flooding and the outbreak of disease heaped severe hardships on residents as early as 1915. Local opinion soured towards CUP administrators after a series of heavy-handed policies. While resident Christians and Jews became regular targets of extortion, government officials made little secret of their suspicions towards their local counterparts. Arab nationalism, as one officer from Anatolia saw it, grew in appeal among Baghdadi administrators after openly suffering such slurs as 'dirty Arab' or 'Arab ass'.[91]

Heavy fighting raged on after the fall of Baghdad in March 1917. By the time of the armistice, large swaths of central and upper Mesopotamia were left desolate. When British troops entered Kifri, a small town lying between Kirkuk and Baghdad, they found local imperial offices empty and their records destroyed or taken away. 'The population of the town consisted almost exclusively of women and children', it was reported, 'the men having been taken for military service or run away to avoid it. These women and children were starving: many had had nothing but grass to eat for weeks, and deaths were occurring every day'.[92] By then, life in larger towns, such as Baghdad and Basra, was beginning to recover. What remained thoroughly unresolved, however, was the region's political status. By the time of the Paris peace conference in 1919, urban and rural elites found themselves divided over their collective futures. British rule, for some, brought needed relief and hopeful signs for the future. Merchants in Basra, for example, had long enjoyed strong trade relations with clients based in India (a fact that led many Ottoman officials to refer to the town as 'an open door to England').[93] Far larger numbers of local leaders looked upon the occupation with disdain. For many Shia and Sunni clerics, rule under British Christian authorities was an abomination. A number of large tribes similarly rejected the occupation as well as British efforts to raise taxes and keep order. Urban notables, including a number of former Ottoman officers, broadly embraced calls for the creation of a sovereign Arab government. Who was to lead such an administration, as well as whether Iraq should merge with other Arab territories in the Levant, remained widely debated questions. Relatively few, it appears, contemplated reunification with the Ottoman Empire. Most imperial administrators in Iraq fled northward as British troops advanced. Initially, many fled no further than Mosul, where they entertained hopes of going back after an Ottoman victory. Some, it appears, returned to Baghdad despite the empire's defeat. 'We found the public offices choked with [former] salaried persons having no visible duties', one British administrator later claimed; 'unemployed, and to a great extent unemployable, they returned to Baghdad and formed a nucleus of discontent and hostility'.[94]

Mustafa Kemal's National Movement was well formed and active by the time Iraq erupted in full revolt. As with resistance efforts in Anatolia, popular rage and elite activism against the occupation provided the kindling. The goal of most of Iraq's rebels in what became known as the 1920 Revolution, however, was limited to achieving their own liberation. Among the few prominent Arabs to declare themselves in direct alliance with Anatolia's National Forces was the powerful tribal leader (or shaykh) Ujaymi al-Sadun. As the head of the Muntafik confederation, his influence had spanned much of Basra's provincial landscape. Having murdered more than fifteen rival shaykhs in an inter-tribal dispute, al-Sadun had attained an unenviable reputation for violence before the war. Yet his loyalty to Istanbul, and specifically to the CUP, earned him the distinction of being the region's *şeyhülmeşayihi*, or 'shaykh of all shaykhs', a title that had been bestowed on him by Sultan Mehmed V. When British and Indian troops landed outside Fao, on the Persian Gulf, in late 1914, he was among the first local leaders to organize volunteers in defense of Basra. Though he briefly flirted with deserting to the British, his fealty to the sultan, as caliph of Islam, as well as perhaps his fear of ceding all claims to his family's lands, anchored him to the Ottoman side. If the Ottoman government continued to 'be a protection to the purity of Islam', he declared during the war, 'it is my helper and the helper of my tribes'.[95] It is likely his service late in the war under Mustafa Kemal's command brought him into the Nationalist fold. In a letter addressed to Ujaymi in June 1919, Kemal called upon him to continue to fight for the 'freedom and the independence of the *ummah*', or the community of Muslims. 'The separation of the Turkish and Arab nations', Kemal averred, 'which are the two pupils in [the eyes of] the whole world of Islam, caused weaknesses on both sides'.[96] With this instruction, Ujaymi and members of the Muntafik confederation joined the National Forces in their campaign in Cilicia against the French. In doing so, he appeared to have convinced other Iraqi tribal leaders to throw in their lot with the Ankara government, too. In January 1920, elements of the Shammar, a large confederation with roots in Arabia, western Iraq and northern Syria, declared its intention of marching 'from Mosul to Baghdad' in defiance of the British. 'The leaders of the Shammar', one Nationalist newspaper reported, 'would never submit to the British and were completely and eternally tied to the Ottoman government'.[97]

Just how receptive the Nationalist high command was to such pledges of solidarity is not clear. One National Forces commander later claimed that a committee comprising rebels from Najaf communicated in 1920 a desire to link arms with Ankara. Should the two insurrections succeed, the committee purportedly stood ready to establish 'an Islamic Iraqi government, with an Ottoman prince at its head, formed in connection with the Ottoman government'.[98] Though negotiations were broken off following Britain's suppression of the 1920 revolt, Ankara had retained some hope that portions of Iraq would return to the Ottoman fold. This was especially the case with Mosul, Iraq's northernmost province, where Nationalists believed they were well within their legal rights to assert Ottoman claims to the region. At the end of the Great War, Ottoman defenders had retained their grip over the bulk of Mosul despite dwindling supplies and steady British pressure. With the decision to surrender in October 1918, the local commander capitulated to British forces believing that Istanbul's control over the province was secure. British officials, however, ignored the terms of the armistice and laid claim to Mosul as a whole. By January 1919, British troops seized each of Mosul's major administrative centers, compelling what remained of the Ottoman army to withdraw. As in other parts of the empire, Ottoman officers refused to fully demobilize their forces or surrender their weapons. Rather than 'await the circumstances', the departing commander of the Mosul front issued orders to distribute guns and ammunition in the hopes of forming 'volunteer defense units from the local people'.[99] Armed resistance to the British occupation materialized soon thereafter. Signs of trouble first appeared on the horizon in April 1919, when a British officer was murdered in a village near Zakho, close to the contemporary Turkish–Iraqi border. Despite the threat of air assault, open acts of defiance towards the British escalated. Ten days after Greek troops landed at Izmir, a 600-man contingent of British troops was ambushed and routed on the main road between Kirkuk and Sulaymaniyah.[100] Long before Mustafa Kemal consolidated his grip over the National Forces, Ottoman officials noted that Mosul's regional leaders, most of them clerics or heads of Kurdish tribes, appeared eager to coordinate their endeavors and fight on. To do so, however, they required help. Kurdish fealty towards Istanbul, one observer believed, remained intact, 'since they were convinced that they would not be able to protect themselves against foreign and Armenian invasion without relying on the material and spiritual strength of the Sublime [Ottoman] State'.[101]

A full-blown insurgence raged along Mosul's mountainous periphery by the time Mustafa Kemal was ensconced in Ankara. With the opening of 1920, tribes in the north and east of the province, in areas such as Rowanduz and Arbil, had staged attacks on British personnel. Though these predominantly Kurdish uprisings were still largely detached from the fighting taking place in Cilicia and the Aegean, Nationalists welcomed them as indications of Ankara's growing strength. Attacks across Mosul, as one editor insisted, demonstrated that National Forces were consolidating 'in every part of Kurdistan'. What drove this fight was not a desire for Kurdish independence but 'feelings of attachment to Ottoman society'.[102] The true basis of Kurdish antagonism towards the British, however, was far more complicated. Generalized hostility to foreign, Christian rule was sharpened by growing British demands for taxes and regularized government. In doing so, officials in Baghdad made enemies out of several Kurdish leaders otherwise willing to accept the occupation. This was the case for Shaykh Mahmud, an influential patriarch of the Barzan family and a Sufi cleric from Sulaymaniyah. In the waning days of the war, Mahmud declared his support for the advancing British. Personal ambition likely shaped his decision to abandon his allegiance to the Ottoman Empire. Since the late nineteenth century, the Barzan family had struggled with both Istanbul and competing tribes for influence over eastern portions of Mosul. In reconciling himself to British authority in 1918, he gleaned in return the title of *hükümdar* (governor) of southern Kurdistan. This arrangement, however, hardly lasted a year. By the spring of 1919, he declared himself opposed to foreign rule, leading to open clashes with the British authorities. Though Nationalist newspapers cheered each success scored by Mahmud and his allies, Ottoman officials turned down private appeals for arms and ammunition.

Barzan's arrest and deportation to India in late 1919 resulted in a brief pause in the violence that wracked Mosul. Following the French surrender in Cilicia, the Nationalist high command assumed a more direct role in Mosul's affairs. In August 1921, Nationalist officers began organizing guerrilla units among Turkmen communities living in the far north of the province. Ankara escalated its involvement a year later with the appointment of an Egyptian-born officer, Ali Şefik Özdemir, to oversee a more concerted campaign to oust the British completely from Mosul. As a veteran of the Ottoman Special Organization, Özdemir built an impressive alliance made up of various Kurdish tribes eager to reclaim local control from Baghdad. The tribes of Mosul, one officer told the National Assembly, would accept nothing 'other than to enter the community of the Ottoman government'.[103] Stemming this progress, however, was the re-emergence of Shaykh Mahmud. Facing the collapse of their administration in Kurdistan, British officials returned him to Sulaymaniyah as head of an independent Kurdish government. As he had in 1919, Mahmud utilized his stature – now as the self-declared 'King of Kurdistan' – to play British interests off against those of the National government. Late in 1922, he stated his willingness to serve Ankara as Sulaymaniyah's governor or as its representative in the National Assembly.[104] Meanwhile, he pledged his loyalty to Baghdad and privately denounced Özdemir's campaign to the British. Özdemir, it appears, possessed no illusions when it came to Shaykh Mahmud or his attempts at establishing an independent Kurdistan. Captured correspondence between Mahmud and Özdemir revealed the Nationalist commander to be evasive on whether Ankara truly supported Kurdish autonomy. For the Nationalists, the Kurdish leader was used 'merely as a pawn' in the struggle to recapture the province of Mosul.[105]

Ankara continued to contemplate an extensive campaign to retake

Mosul late into the war. Bedeviling these ambitions was the lack of resources. When Özdemir took charge of the Mosul front in the spring of 1922, local Nationalist officers decried his paltry forces as nothing more than 'randomly collected men, career officers and volunteer officers'. Among Özdemir's troops were seventy-five Algerians who had deserted the French army in Syria. These, as well as the rest of the men under his command, were later declared useless, leading to further delays.[106] By December, an internal memo declared that a force of more than 7,000 infantry and cavalry was now ready to invade Iraq pending the accumulation of supplies.[107] No offensive, however, would materialize. By the close of 1922, peace talks with the Allies were well underway in Switzerland. Later in the spring of 1923, negotiators agreed to allow the recently established League of Nations to settle the question of Mosul's future status. Officials in Ankara, meanwhile, ceased to refer to Ottoman sovereignty or Islamic unity. The province, Turkish negotiators insisted, was both historically and racially tied to Turkey. Kurds and Turks, they explained to League officials, not only formed the province's majority, but also constituted a single people devolved from the same bloodline. Even the name 'Kurd', it was said, was of ancient Turkic origin.

Gauging elite or popular views of these efforts to reclaim Mosul remains a murky proposition. On the one hand, it is clear that the region's Christians, who included tens of thousands of displaced Armenians and Christian Nestorians, were virulently opposed to the resumption of Ottoman rule. Of the 40,000 Nestorians that British authorities resettled in the town of Baquba, many were recruited to serve in militias comprising other disaffected peoples.[108] On the other hand, groups with long-standing ties to the Ottoman state, such as Turkmen and portions of the Shammar confederacy, saw their salvation in a Nationalist takeover. Pinpointing a general Arab or Kurdish consensus in Iraq remains daunting. Despite the disappointing collapse of the 1920 revolt, a number of insurrectionary leaders threw their support behind British-backed plans to form a semi-independent 'Arab' government in Baghdad. The list of those who supported the crowning of Emir Faisal as King of Iraq included officers who were known to retain pro-Ottoman sympathies up until 1920. Similarly, Britain's overthrow of Shaykh Mahmud in 1924 solidified broader

Kurdish support for an independent Kurdistan. Almost a century later, members of Mahmud's extended family continue to stand at the forefront of this movement.

An even greater amount of convolution marked greater Syria's separation from the empire. For many who witnessed the war's final months there, the collapse of Ottoman authority had the appearance of a final, bitter divorce. Feelings of joy and retribution washed over the region following the army's retreat from Palestine in late September 1918. There was dancing and celebrations in the streets of Damascus after Allied soldiers entered the city. Local civilians aided Emir Faisal's Arab army as they attacked retreating Ottoman troops. For many of the soldiers who fought on to the armistice at the end of October, the depredations of this final month left lasting feelings of resentment. The general belief that Arabs delighted in the army's defeat defined how many veterans came to see the nature of the empire's end in Syria. Among the earliest accounts to echo such accusations of 'Arab treason' can be found the memoirs of a demobilized infantry lieutenant named Vecihi. Published in Istanbul in 1921, his recollections repeatedly underscore his belief that it was Turks, specifically conscripts and officers from Anatolia, who were responsible for defending the empire's Levantine provinces. The Arabs, he argued, 'did not want us. They helped the enemy in part in the open, in part secretly. We, conversely, worked to defend Arabia from the enemy and the Arabs'.[109]

An even more diverse body of evidence suggests that equally caustic feelings prevailed in Syria after the war's end. Among his first acts as head of an Arab government in Damascus, Emir Faisal hosted a ceremony commemorating the 'martyrdom' of Arab nationalists at the hands of the CUP government. It was in this spirit that 'Cemal Pasha Boulevard' was eventually stripped of its name and became 'an-Nasr'. The central plazas of Damascus and Beirut, the sites of Cemal Pasha's brutal executions during the war, each came to be known as 'Martyrs' Square'. While the renaming of these locations occurred well after the armistice, it was under Faisal that the denunciation of CUP rule became the norm. Reviling the reign of Cemal 'the Bloodshedder', however, ultimately constituted something more than a call for justice. For many nationalists in Syria, as well as Iraq, the Young Turk administration embodied a 'Turkish yoke' that had always exploited and oppressed Arabs. Istanbul's defeat at the hands of the Allies served as proof that the empire had failed as a state and a nation. For Faisal, as well as others hoping to build an independent Arab state in the Levant, contemplating any return to the old order was inconceivable. The Arab nation, Faisal told a crowd in 1919, 'was eager for a revival of its past history and hoping for an escape from the snares of its enemy'.[110]

These denunciations of Ottoman rule largely followed the departure or marginalization of those still loyal to Istanbul. As in the case of Iraq, large numbers of appointed officials destroyed their records and fled northward in the wake of the army's withdrawal. Others, such as the families and associates of departed bureaucrats, waited until the fighting was over before heading north. This exodus, however, did not leave greater Syria completely empty of pro-Ottoman sympathizers. Established families, particularly those with historic ties to the capital, tended to stay on in the hope of finding a place within the emerging order. This was especially the case in Aleppo, which possessed close links to Cilicia and other territories north of the armistice line. In December 1918, local newspapers demanded the expulsion of all imperial civil servants from the town. However, it was agreed that anyone married to an Arab, who had entered into business with Arabs or who were 'Turks' born in Aleppo had the right to stay.[111] For at least some observers in Istanbul, Faisal's ascendancy, as well as the broader prospect of losing all of the Arab lands, brought mixed feelings. An editor of the daily *İkdam* acknowledged that many in the capital saw no loss in Arab secession. 'We had always been foreigners in the Arab provinces', was one common lament heard in the capital. 'What value are we to them or they to us . . . it is almost now like we have been liberated'. Yet before declaring 'well done' to the CUP, the editor reminded readers of what the empire was indeed about to lose. After all, the peoples of Beirut, Damascus and Lebanon suffered greatly during the war. If the empire did relinquish control over territories to the south of Diyarbakir and Mosul, the state would be abandoning many thousands of Kurds and Turks, as well as Arabs. For these reasons, the editor believed it was important to assert Istanbul's claims to the Levant under both the Wilsonian principles and 'Ottoman law'. If Arabs did pursue a 'special administration', it was still possible to develop relations for the 'benefit of the two sides' economic preservation and growth'.[112]

Greater Syria's fate appeared even more uncertain following Faisal's return from Versailles. As Britain appeared ever more likely to cede the region to the French, factions in Damascus grew more desperate to chart a new course. By the summer of 1919, committed nationalists and fearful local leaders began to organize volunteer militias in anticipation of a French takeover. Among the leaders of this effort was Yasin al-Hashimi, a Baghdadi colonel who fought with Ottoman forces until his capture in late 1918. Though never close to Faisal, he proved himself an able administrator alongside other Iraqi officers serving the nascent Arab government. By the fall of 1919, he took the initiative in forming militias dedicated to protecting Damascus from a French takeover. British observers believed, however, that his motives had more to do with his personal ambitions as well as lingering Ottoman loyalties. Belief that al-Hashimi was aiming to 're-establish Turkish rule in Syria' eventually stirred the Allies to arrest him, a step that further weakened local independence forces.[113] Nominally, Faisal continued to place his hopes in brokering some sort of accord between Britain and France well into 1920. Yet it was during this tenuous period that the emir first made contact with Mustafa Kemal. As early as August 1919, rumors circulated in British intelligence circles that Kemal's and Faisal's representatives agreed in principle upon forging an alliance. Although the documentary record has yet to conclusively confirm this development, other pieces of evidence suggest that efforts to unite the two sides continued through late 1919. According to Talat Pasha, then living in exile in Germany, emissaries from Damascus had approached him with plans to reunite Syria with the rest of what remained of the empire. Even ardent Arab nationalists, Talat was told, 'would prefer to unite with the Turks like old Germany or Austria-Hungary and cooperate [with the Turks] to hinder the occupation by the Allies'. Mustafa Kemal informed Talat that he too had been approached with such a proposal but remained wary. 'The thought and the possibility that Fayşal might be following a secret policy on behalf of the French makes us proceed cautiously'.[114]

The beginning of the Nationalist campaign in Cilicia breathed new life into a possible Syrian–Anatolian alliance. In December 1919, a force of some 2,000 Bedouin riders attacked British positions in Deyr Zor in the eastern Syrian desert. Although the assault was staged independently of Mustafa Kemal's forces, pro-Nationalist newspapers credited the town's capture to the activities of 'the Arab National Forces' (*Arap Kuva-yı Milliyesi*). As Nationalist detachments laid siege to Marash, Antep and other towns in Cilicia, newspapers close to the Defense of Rights Association cheered similar strikes staged against French forces south of the armistice line. For some observers, the rise of the anti-French resistance in Syria was testament to the empire's indissolubility. The Arab seizure of Deyr Zor, as one provincial newspaper put it, compelled Lloyd George to accept that 'Istanbul is to remain Turkish and the realization of the Ottoman [Empire's] territorial wholeness is demanded'.[115] In speaking before the National Assembly, Mustafa Kemal privately speculated that some kind of restoration of imperial control over Syria was in the making. The Arabs, he admitted, did collaborate with the enemy during the war in order to 'follow their objective of being independent'. Times had now changed and it was possible to establish a 'federate or confederate structure' in conjunction with the Arabs of Syria.[116] Not every Nationalist, however, was willing to let the past rest. 'The current condition of Arabs', as one Sivas newspaper put it, 'who opposed their coreligionists and caliphs with promises of sovereignty and independence is indeed pitiful'. The Arabs now understood that they had 'wasted their blood spilled in getting rid of the Turkish yoke'.[117]

In truth, things were far more chaotic and fluid than many Nationalists perceived them to be. Many in Faisal's government wanted nothing to do with either the French or Mustafa Kemal's forces. Despite his stature, Faisal found himself on the defensive in the face of local demands to assert Syria's independence. In the fall of 1919, Syrians and Palestinians went to the polls to elect a congress to oversee what many hoped was a genuinely independent government. By the spring, the congress voted to crown Faisal king of the Syrian Arab state. His coronation day, 8 March 1920, was dubbed the 'day of resurrection' in light of the country's many centuries under Ottoman rule. Realizing Syria's 'ancient glory and flowering civilization', one celebrant declared, meant not only to be liberated from Istanbul's authority but also 'to demand full independence and a free life as a nation'.[118] The collapse of Faisal's government following the French invasion in July 1920, however, did not put an end to Nationalist interests in Syria. In Aleppo, the region's wartime governor, who was an established CUP loyalist, continued to wage a guerrilla campaign in conjunction with the National Forces. In the northwest, French troops contended with attacks staged by bands made up of local Alawi fighters. As adherents to a unique sect related to Shiism, Alawi communities in portions of Latakia and Antioch had initially welcomed the French, believing they would be protected as a regional minority. Yet amid waves of attacks by Armenian paramilitaries, Alawi bands embraced the Nationalists as their defenders and patrons. One Alawi militant leader continued to coordinate with Nationalists active in Cilicia well into 1921. 'There is no doubt', he wrote to Ankara, 'that the Turkish and Arab nations will continue to walk hand in hand in fighting the foreigners' aggression, until the liberation of our homeland'.[119] Before the end of 1921, however, Nationalist commanders abruptly severed their material and financial support for Syria's rebels. After making peace with France in October, talk of a confederation with Syria largely ceased.

As in the case of Mosul, it is difficult to say how the public conceived the potential reunification of greater Syria with the rest of the empire. The Levant's diversity, like that of Iraq, lent itself to a wide range of opinions and desires. It is likely, for example, that many in Lebanon opposed any return to Ottoman rule. During the war, the CUP government annulled Lebanon's provincial administration, which allowed for local autonomy under a Christian governor. Lebanon's intellectuals and civic leaders played pivotal roles in advocating independence from the empire (though were less enthusiastic about inclusion in Faisal's kingdom). While Palestinian observers tended to revere Mustafa Kemal as a potential savior, demonstrators in Amman were heard offering praise for both Faisal and the sultan in November 1920.[120] The National Assembly, for its part, briefly entertained issuing a demand for the creation of an Ottoman mandate administration in Palestine. The possibility of such an endeavor, which was raised by a committee comprising prominent Jews from Istanbul, appears to have been dismissed, given the physical and political complications it would have involved. The issue of the country's relationship to Palestine was revisited two months after the empire's formal dissolution. While some members of the National Assembly agreed that the state still had an interest in Palestine given the lengths to which the empire had gone in defending the territory during the Great War, others derided the prospect of intervening in the affairs of Jews and foreigners. The issue appears to have been laid to rest after one member questioned the genuine feasibility of any Turkish involvement in the region. 'Without anyone knowing the state of affairs that the matter will take tomorrow, who is the majority there [in Palestine], what are they, based on what kind of right do they advise us to try to take Palestine into our endeavors? Well, it is an entangled thing'.[121]

It is also difficult to assess how serious Nationalist leaders were about recovering other parts of greater Syria. Over a decade after taking power, Atatürk professed his regret for not advancing further to liberate Turks residing under the French. When he personally toured the border in 1923, Kemal claimed to have been brought to tears by a group of 'beautiful sobbing girls' who pleaded with him to liberate their families in Alexandretta.[122] The anecdote eventually became a part of popular Turkish lore after Ankara secured Antioch's annexation in 1939. On more than one occasion after 1923, Turkish newspapers presented readers with evidence that residents in Aleppo also still hoped to be absorbed into Turkey proper.

Politics, more than anything, appears to have prevented the National Forces from further campaigning in Syria. By the spring of 1921, both France and the Soviet government were on the cusp of recognizing the legitimacy of the Ankara government. Peace with both of these states represented an end to combat in the south and east, as well as the potential arrival of needed aid and materiel. Superficially, Nationalists in Ankara still spoke of reincorporating portions of Syria and Iraq. In agreeing upon the National Pact, assembly members had left the door open to some sort of reunification (by way of plebiscite, however, not conquest). The rhetoric of this period also suggests that senior Nationalists were mindful not to define too distinctly who truly belonged or deserved to be liberated. In May 1920, a casual debate in the Grand National Assembly brought this point sharply into focus. When a member discussing issues pertaining to public health declared that 'the health of Turkishness' was at stake, a

Circassian from the region of Sivas objected. 'We did not gather here in the name of Turkishness', he pleaded. 'I request that it is sufficient to say "Muslims", even "Ottomans", not only "Turks"'. At this point, Mustafa Kemal intervened to assert his own feelings on the matter. It was true, he argued, that the National Assembly was a body made up of more than just Turks, since Kurds, Circassians and other Muslims were present. More to the point, the National Pact made clear that they were all fighting for the liberation of the lands from Alexandretta in the west to Sulaymaniyah and Kirkuk in the east. The unity they hoped to forge, Kemal contended, was grounded in Islam.[123]

Attitudes, however, changed rather dramatically in the space of a few years. In September 1923, the National Assembly took up the issue of whether Ottoman officials automatically qualified for Turkish citizenship. There were former imperial officers, for example, still in Yemen waiting to be repatriated. While some were likely 'Turkish in race', one representative contended that there were likely others who were 'Albanian, Arab or Syrian'. The question was whether these latter sorts of officials deserved citizenship. Another member speculated that a Damascus-born officer could be granted citizenship if he had served the empire honorably. When other assembly members objected, it was agreed that greater restrictions were needed. Arabs, as well as other groups whose 'eyes looked abroad' at their own peoples, had to be forbidden from entering the country. Anyone granted Turkish citizenship had to believe that 'our country is Turkish'. 'From now on', a third member proclaimed, 'our country and our army must survive [as] Turkish'.[124]

Why the National Assembly eventually excluded former Arab citizens from obtaining Turkish citizenship was the product of many forces. Many who voiced an aversion towards Arabs may have long harbored personal prejudices against them and others perceived to have been Ottoman 'minorities'. Memories from the war – be it Faisal's rebellion or the supposed poor conduct of Arab conscripts – may have reinforced such ill feelings. It is likely that more immediate events also shaped their feelings of who did and did not belong. By 1923, Faisal reigned over an Iraqi kingdom that, within a decade, would become independent from Britain. France was in full control over Syria and had willed a separate Lebanon into existence. Other former imperial territories, such as Egypt and the Hijaz, had clearly moved on from any sense of Ottoman solidarity. The choice, as one parliamentarian put it, seemed simple. '[If] one is Syrian, their eyes are on Syria. We don't want to restrain this by force. They should go to Syria'.[125]

These changes in attitude also reflect important shifts that occurred in Ankara after 1920. There was a growing consciousness within Nationalist circles that their struggle mirrored those of other nations. Prominent Afghanis, Indians, Algerians and Egyptians voiced support for Kemal's fighters and decried what many believed was the Ottoman caliph's captivity under Western occupation. In truth, following Mehmed VI's decision to endorse the Allied peace plan, ties between Ankara and Istanbul were becoming frayed beyond repair. The signing of this formal treaty of peace in August 1920 came as the National Forces suffered devastating setbacks at the hands of Greece. As Nationalist troops reeled eastward, Ankara's legitimacy was further tested along the Black Sea coast and in Kurdistan. Mustafa Kemal's own position came under increased strain from personal rivals. All of these conditions facilitated a hardening of the political rhetoric and outlook in the Nationalist camp. It is in this period that notions of Ottoman identity and legitimacy entered their final death throes.

5

'Beyond the Reach of Scorn'

A Fateful Year of Protests, Atrocities and Combat

If all had gone to plan, assassins would have taken the life of Damad Ferid in early June 1920. The plot was to have unfolded either while the grand vezir was in transit from his seaside mansion or while he was scaling the steps of the Ministry of War. An absurd turn of events, however, revealed the conspiracy. According to local press accounts, the lead assassin, Dramalı Rıza, fell out with his accomplices and denounced them to the police. As a result, both he and a host of other Nationalist agents were taken into custody. For conservatives in the capital, news of the attempt on the grand vezir's life confirmed their worst impressions of 'Ankara's rogues'.[1] It was no secret that Rıza had fought for the National Forces. Earlier in his life, he had possessed a reputation as a killer and *fedai* loyal to the CUP. Mustafa Kemal, by association, appeared to possess the same murderous proclivities as the Young Turks. When the day of Rıza's execution came, local police stood guard for fear of Nationalist reprisals. The fact that Ferid's government 'was terrified of the Unionists being cut down from their gallows and spirited away' struck one of Ferid's aides as sadly ironic. 'During the days of the CUP terror, the party's security personnel would erect scaffolds in the middle of the night on every corner of Galata Bridge and Aya Sofia Square and would hang clusters of men'. 'Never', he remembered, 'did you see the slightest fuss or commotion'.[2] The plot might have failed, but Istanbul appeared within Ankara's reach.

However, far weightier issues overshadowed Dramalı Rıza's execution. In late May 1920, Allied representatives officially informed the Ottoman government of their final peace terms. Though there had never been a lack of speculation over the possible contents of the agreement, the moment of decision had finally arrived. Confronting the Ottoman state was a dramatic reduction in the size and sovereignty of the empire. With the Arab lands gone, France and Italy formally laid claim to Anatolia's south as 'zones of influence'. Much of Erzurum, Trabzon and other eastern provinces was to be ceded to the Republic of Armenia. The Dardanelles and the Bosphorus would come under an impartial international regime and virtually all of eastern Thrace was awarded to Athens. Greece would continue to occupy Izmir and its surrounding districts. Although Izmir remained nominally under the empire's suzerainty, many assumed that this was only temporary. Meanwhile, the Allies were to take control over many of the state's financial levers in order to recover outstanding debts.

The challenge that remained was whether the treaty would be validated. In addition to an official signature from a government representative, Ottoman law demanded the imperial legislature ratify the terms. For the Allies, the first obstacle proved daunting enough. Grand Vezir Damad Ferid accepted the treaty in principle but asked for more time for deliberation. The terms of the treaty in its present form, he argued, placed the sultan and his government 'in a most embarrassing position'. Allowing for key revisions, such as the retention of Thrace and Izmir, would do much to soothe public concerns. When the British ambassador countered that Istanbul was obliged to accept 'a treaty of the most rigorous description', Ferid was bemused. A treaty that lopped off the empire's arms and legs was 'rigorous enough in all conscience'. Depriving the country of Thrace and Izmir 'struck at vital parts of the head and trunk as well'. That, he explained, was 'something more than rigorous. It meant the annihilation of Turkey'.[3] Citizens in the capital tended to agree. In May, a crowd of between 10,000 and 20,000 spilled into the square before Sultanahmet with the release of the treaty's details. Speakers that day echoed the demands made at past demonstrations, with many calling for the independence of all 'Ottoman land that was Turkish and Muslim'.[4]

One thing the Allies and senior figures in the Ottoman government could agree upon was the trouble caused by Mustafa Kemal. Although Mehmed Vahideddin purportedly loathed the treaty and cryptically stated he 'would support his people' in the event it was forced upon them, neither he nor Damad Ferid showed any inclination to endorse the Nationalist cause.[5] Ferid continued to beg for Allied material support to combat the National Forces as the summer of 1920 began. Defeating them, he promised, would allow Istanbul to reassert proper control over the country and would ensure a smoother transition towards peace. Allied representatives tended to agree, but there were fissures among the war's victors as well. Italy never forgave Britain for awarding Smyrna to Greece. By the end of 1920, Italian occupation authorities were openly collaborating with Nationalist representatives in Antalya and selling them arms. France also showed signs of breaking ranks as affairs in Cilicia and Syria became more desperate. Britain was willing to commit some troops to aid Ferid's government, but military resources were stretched thin as they battled disturbances elsewhere in the British Empire. There were also lingering doubts within Lloyd George's government over the efficacy of the proposed peace. The agreement with the Ottoman Empire, as one senior diplomat confessed ruefully, was talked about as a thing 'beyond the reach of scorn, intact though dead, whole though unratified'.[6] Winston Churchill, then Minister of War, as well as Foreign Secretary Lord Curzon, bluntly believed that the treaty was liable to make affairs in Anatolia more untenable. Of all the Allies, Greece appeared the most willing to see Mustafa Kemal's fighters crushed. Venizelos's eagerness to drive towards Ankara appealed to Lloyd George as a ready solution to a collective problem. 'It was indispensable', he told France's Prime Minister Millerand, 'to show that the Allies meant business'.[7]

After weeks of secret negotiations, Greek troops positioned along the Aegean coast struck eastward on 22 June. The offensive made quick work of the Nationalist detachments that encircled Izmir. After months of fighting restive peasants throughout northwestern Anatolia, thousands of Nationalist troops surrendered or abandoned their posts. In little more than a few weeks, Greek units captured several major Anatolian towns, including Balıkesir, Bursa, Akhisar and Bandırma. As Nationalist troops retreated east, local officials who chose to remain faced an uncertain future. The prospect of a wider Greek occupation, coupled with the animosity wrought by Anzavur's campaign against the Defense of Rights Association, transformed villages into veritable tinderboxes. Still, hundreds of Ottoman officials remained at their post in spite of the dangers posed to them. 'There was no doubt', one former gendarme explained, 'that if news spread of our retreat the prisons would open up and all kinds of evil-spirited people, be they Pomaks [Muslim Bulgarians], Circassians or Turks, would bring about a widespread rebellion in the land'.[8] The ease with which Greece conquered much of western Anatolia was complemented by its near-bloodless seizure of eastern Thrace. Despite months to prepare the defense of the empire's last European province, Nationalist units posted there offered Greek troops virtually no resistance.

By the end of July, a deep depression settled over the Istanbul press. Amid the sorrow brought on by the Allied peace treaty, Greece's rapid advance was more than many could take. What the Greek offensive appeared to reveal, as one editor put it, was how irreconcilable native Muslims and Christians had become. Istanbul again bore witness to scenes of joy among local Greeks, a humiliation that echoed the arrival of the Allied fleet in November 1918. It was enough to know that residents in Athens were lighting candles 'to the glory of Venizelos'. To deal again with displays of elation by residents of the capital was the last straw. 'Let us speak plainly', the editor concluded: 'because of our painful situation, we Turks do not cease to attach great importance to small things. We do not hesitate to value at their true worth the demonstrations which in these days distinguish our friends from our foes. Will we forget them, or not? Time will tell'.[9]

Damad Ferid registered his own disapproval of the Greek advance. The spark which ignited Izmir, he told Europe's powers, 'had [now] left Anatolia entirely in flames'.[10] Greece's offensive, however, brought a benefit he was reluctant to admit. The withdrawal of Nationalist troops made Mustafa Kemal weaker and the sultan's government potentially stronger. Accepting the terms of the Allied peace, he told Mehmed VI's imperial council, now stood as the only viable path forward. It was, he said, the difference between 'living for better or for worse' and being 'completely erased from the world map'. Despite a few objections, most members of the council agreed with the grand vezir's appraisal. When the time came for Mehmed VI to render his decision, 'he became pale like the dead', as one attendant remembered. Standing up, Mehmed simply requested all those who supported signing the treaty to rise to their feet. 'At this request the sultan's council immediately jumped and rose as one mass'.[11] With the sultan's approval in hand, Ferid hoped that Ottoman goodwill would help persuade the Allies to relax some of their demands. Allied assistance, after all, was essential if the treaty was to be fully implemented.

Ottoman delegates signed the treaty in Sèvres, outside Paris, on 10 August 1920. When news of the empire's official acquiescence trickled into the country days later, public outrage again engulfed the capital. Muslim shop owners closed their doors and flags were furled from view. At one o'clock on 12 August, boats, streetcars and other vehicles came to a halt in recognition of the tragedy that had befallen in the empire. To the east, in Ankara, attitudes wavered between stoicism and defiance. 'We have shattered the Treaty of Sèvres', Mustafa Kemal declared to the National Assembly. 'We said that our confidence is increasing day to day and there is nothing that will be done about it'.[12] His certainty, even at this stage, was well warranted. Istanbul's capitulation was mostly symbolic. There was no chance anyone in Ankara would accept the terms of the treaty. And despite serious setbacks on the battlefield, neither Mustafa Kemal nor his National Forces appeared close to defeat.

Events outside of the Ottoman Empire soon overshadowed Istanbul's acceptance of the Treaty of Sèvres. Late that summer, Soviet troops were advancing through Poland. The Bolshevik offensive appeared to signal Communism's resilience in spite of the Allies' best efforts. Poland's dramatic victory outside of Warsaw in August 1920 only partially soothed Western European nerves. Other points of crisis demanded attention. Atrocities and fierce fighting embroiled British security forces in Ireland. Hungary continued to heave with violence in the aftermath of a brief Communist revolution. Civil insurrection plagued Germany and the newly formed Yugoslavia. Further off, in India, nationalists under Mohandas Gandhi pressed British authorities for independence. The Treaty of Sèvres, Gandhi declared, was yet another of the many grave injustices wrought by London.

Damad Ferid's endorsement of the Allied peace treaty ultimately proved his undoing. Rumors circulated that many in the cabinet, the bureaucracy and the palace loathed his imperious character. Even the sultan, it was said, tired of his brother-in-law's insistence that collaboration in exchange for British patronage was key to saving the nation. Two months after the signing of the treaty at Sèvres, Ferid resigned, citing poor health. The post of grand vezir fell once more to one of its former occupants, Tevfik Pasha, whose reappointment was interpreted as an olive branch to Nationalists as well as less partisan interests in the capital. With the future of the country hanging in the balance, Mehmed VI grew even more isolated. Factions previously close to the sultan turned on one another as the balance of power shifted towards the Nationalists. The clearest indication of what the future held came in January 1921. In spite of the peril of Greece's continued offensive, the National Assembly enacted a new constitution. In it, the prerogatives of neither the sultan nor the caliph were mentioned. A more subtle, but no less profound, statement was made with the official redesignation of the country. From 1921 onward, the National Assembly spoke for the government of Turkey, not the Ottoman Empire.

Those who approved of the 1921 constitution, however, equivocated as to the significance of these changes. In revising the original constitution of 1876, Mustafa Kemal explicitly defended the sovereign's place as the head of state. 'We accept the offices of the sultan and caliph in principle', he told the National Assembly. Ideally, the head of the Ottoman royal family would receive 'extensive rights and authority'. However, he and the National Assembly agreed that there would be no discussion of these things at present.[13] Mehmed VI, Kemal privately declared in September 1920, was a traitor.[14] Fortunately for the Nationalists, current events allowed them to skirt the issue of whether the sultan should be deposed. International disapproval of the Treaty of Sèvres, particularly among Muslim activists in the wider colonial world, was often contingent upon Mustafa Kemal's promise to liberate the Ottoman sultan-caliph from foreign rule. Pushing the issue of Mehmed VI's treason also came with the potential danger of popular reaction at home. The editor of the middle-of-the-road Istanbul daily *İkdam* saw no problem in debating whether Ankara represented the true seat of government. Discussion of potential changes in 'the location of administration came and went', given Istanbul's geographic and strategic vulnerabilities on the Bosphorus. What everyone wanted, however, was a system with the sultan at its center.[15]

Other threats harried the Defense of Rights Association. Over the course of 1920 and 1921, dozens of former luminaries of the CUP plotted their return to Anatolia. Many presumed they were as qualified as Mustafa Kemal to lead the National Movement. With the National Forces struggling to hold their ground against the Greeks, Kemal's authority appeared vulnerable. Offsetting these internal challenges were more clear-cut risks. Reports of abuse and acts of mass violence in Greek-occupied areas of Anatolia fomented anger and intolerance within Nationalist circles. The knowledge that Muslims collaborated with Greece or resisted Ankara's authority added to the movement's growing inflexibility. By the end of 1921, certain ambiguities that had defined the Nationalist cause began to dissipate. Rather than resorting to some version of the prewar order, representatives in Ankara spoke more definitively of a 'new Turkey'. The phrase 'new Turkey' itself seeped into European parlance during the period, a development which reflected iconoclastic attitudes becoming more visible in Ankara. Though the empire was not officially dead, it was clear that many Nationalists were ready to move on. To talk explicitly of the Ottoman Empire increasingly came with reference to its flaws. The empire had been defeated. It embodied a nation that was weak, corrupt and unruly.

'THE DANGER OF ASIA':[16]
THE GLOBAL POLITICS OF THE
OTTOMAN EMPIRE'S FINAL YEARS

After his capture in Iraq in March 1918, Hüseyin Fehmi spent nearly three years as a prisoner in India. His life there, for the most part, dragged on endlessly. Aside from brief excursions from his camp at the fortress in Bellary, newspapers were his lone inlet to the world. What he read, at least according to his diary, nourished both hopes and anguish. News from home was rarely good. He grew particularly jaded towards the rule of Mehmed VI after stories circulated of the sultan's admiration for Great Britain and his condemnation of the Armenian deportations. Reports from elsewhere offered more encouraging signs. In his account of his time in Bellary, Hüseyin filled his diary with references to events in Egypt, Ireland, Russia, Afghanistan and India. In each of these places, fighters were resisting Western imperialism. Mohandas Gandhi's efforts at leading a general strike against the British authorities in India in the spring of 1919 was not something he

personally witnessed. As with millions of others, it was through newspapers that Hüseyin came to comprehend what was at stake. India's
'complete enslavement' was painfully obvious. 'For example', he wrote,
'an Indian who sees an Englishman strolling through a market or
bazaar will fall silent, as will everyone else'.[17] His growing consciousness of world affairs further heightened his political awareness as well
his sensitivity to his duties as a Muslim. The diversity of the prisoners
around him helped to sustain his renewed faith. With the few rupees
he and other prisoners collected every week, they pooled their money
to allow imams a reprieve from their chores. The extra time and
resources enabled these teachers and prayer leaders to run a café and
open a school. 'Here', Hüseyin explained, '[the importance of] being a
Muslim greatly increased. Everyone began to honor Islam and no one
missed prayers or offerings'.[18]

Hüseyin Fehmi's captivity came to an end in the summer of 1921.
Soon after arriving home in Adapazarı, he enlisted in the army once
again, this time as a telephone operator. His diary entries during this
period, like those from his time in Bellary, are largely a digest of things
he read in newspapers. He took particular interest in diplomatic chat-
ter late in the war as a negotiated peace seemed more likely. From his
standpoint, the world had finally taken note of what the Nationalists
were achieving. It was from the press that he learned that representatives from Iran, Afghanistan, Azerbaijan, the Crimea and Central Asia
had taken up residence in Ankara. These signs of Muslim solidarity
appeared to pressure the West into dealing directly with Mustafa
Kemal. A year earlier, he wrote, 'Europeans said we would never condescend to reach an armistice or sit at the peace table with the head of
the bandit gang [in Ankara]'. The possibility that Britain felt obliged
to join France and other Allies in pursuing a peaceful resolution to the
conflict was indeed 'a blessing from God to us Turks'.[19]

How Hüseyin Fehmi perceived himself and the National Movement
was certainly shaped by his experiences as a soldier and a prisoner.
What his diary also suggests is the extent to which he, as well as others,
came to reimagine the Ottoman Empire as the result of news from
abroad. The complexity of events in Europe and Asia was an issue of
profound interest in the popular press after the 1918 armistice. Despite the deluge of news closer to home, even provincial papers in the

empire kept an eye trained on foreign affairs. Newspapers drew heavily from international wire services, translating telegrams, essays and interviews on a daily basis. Readers of the Turkish-language press, as well as publications in Armenian, Greek and French, could easily stay abreast of rumors and developments from outside the empire. Interestingly, editors did not draw regular connections between Ottoman affairs and significant developments in Europe, particularly among the Allies. Yet, depending on the context, the local ramifications of events abroad appeared clear enough. As peace talks turned more serious in 1922, a newspaper editor in Giresun, on the Black Sea, assured readers that discontent in Britain was rife. An economic crisis, he warned, wracked the United Kingdom and its empire. 'Bankruptcies are following one after the other. In Ireland and India, the squabbles are worse than before. No one is content with the arrangements in Egypt'. 'All of these events', the paper suggested, 'have exhausted public opinion after turning against Lloyd George'.[20] The implication of these trends was clear: London's bargaining position was weakening.

The broader contrasts between events in Europe and Asia were especially glaring. In the immediate aftermath of the war, Ottoman newspapers carefully tracked the fall of the Habsburg and Hohenzollern monarchies. The sudden breakup of these two empires introduced Ottoman readers to new political realities. Austria and Hungary now formed two distinct 'nation-states' (*milli devletler*), each without a ruling monarch.[21] Editors and commentators do not appear to have pondered what the dissolution of the Habsburg Empire meant for the sultan, the government or the future of the Ottoman nation. Yet as representatives met in Versailles, the politics of Central Europe's shifting borders appeared to diverge sharply from what seemed to await other parts of the world. No outside power forced Austria and Hungary to part ways. Though the process was indeed fraught with chaos and violence, leaders in these and other Habsburg successor states readily agreed to separate. This was less the case outside Europe. In greater Asia and in Africa, the Allies were dead set upon determining how the map was to be redrawn and who was to benefit most. 'Muslims and Turks', as one Nationalist noted in late 1919, were not the only peoples to suffer such injustices. Iran, China and India were all lands subject to foreign rule. As the West 'tore off pieces of their soul with each passing day', Asians were searching 'with hopeful hearts' for a savior to rescue them. Local heroes certainly were answering the call and helping to deliver their own people from Western imperialism. The National Forces, he believed, embodied this global struggle. The spilling of Muslim blood before Izmir had 'given life to three hundred million Muslims living in Asia and Africa'. Muslims across India and other parts of Asia were now praying for a Nationalist victory. Success in Anatolia, he concluded, would lead to 'a better world tomorrow' for all those who endured injustices at the hands of the West.[22]

Sentiments such as these were not merely expressions of bravado. Empathy and a sense of unanimity with Muslims outside the empire were long prominent traits of Ottoman politics. For centuries, the sultan used his status as caliph of Islam to bolster his image both at home and abroad. At various turns, Ottoman officials interpreted this claim as a mandate to contest the growth of European empires well beyond the country's borders. Under Abdülhamid II, intellectuals and statesmen came to see the empire as uniquely qualified to lead and represent Muslims worldwide. Though hard pressed by European imperialism, the Ottoman state remained independent while Muslim lands in Asia and Africa fully succumbed to colonialism. Ottoman activists took pride in their newfound culture of reform, a characteristic, they believed, that set the Ottoman state further apart from the wider *ummah*. In this regard, Japan in the east served as an especially inspirational model. Tokyo's uncompromising commitment to material and social reform, coupled with its conquests in Asia at the expense of China and Russia, appeared to blaze a path for Istanbul to follow. 'A Turkish world', one member of the Turkish Hearth prophesied, 'will arise between the world of the white and yellow races. And in this middle world, the Ottoman state would assume the task that Japan now wants to do in the world of the yellow race'.[23]

CUP leaders seized upon the First World War as an opportunity to lead such a revolution. With the formation of the Ottoman clandestine service, the Special Organization, Istanbul dispatched agents to various parts of the Muslim world. The focus of this campaign was areas deemed ripe for colonial rebellion: British India, the French Maghrib and Russian Central Asia. The exact details of many of these secret ventures remain fuzzy. Substantive results, however, appeared to have been limited. An early Ottoman offensive against British-held Egypt partly counted upon the ability of the Special Organization to foment instability behind enemy lines. When Ottoman troops finally attacked the Suez Canal in early 1915, hopes for local Egyptian assistance quickly faded. Planners, one former agent later admitted, grossly misread the nature of Egyptian discontent. While it was likely that citizens in Egypt and other colonies loathed British rule, such feelings did not translate into an explicit 'affection for the Ottoman Empire'.[24]

Allied officials were aware of these Ottoman efforts abroad. More significantly, leading figures in London and Paris understood such acts of subversion as attempts at exploiting a source of imperial fragility. Beginning in the late nineteenth century, British and French officials acquired an acute fear of Muslim activism. Berlin was equally conscious of this anxiety and actively monitored events in British India as well as other parts of the French and British empires. In advance of the First World War, German officials made no secret of their willingness to fan Muslim discontent. In this light, the sultan's declaration of a global jihad against the Allies in November 1914 appeared to many as a holy war prepackaged in Germany. The fear that colonial Muslims would respond to the Ottoman pronouncement led London to take preventative steps. To inoculate the empire against the threat of what was so often termed 'pan-Islam', British agents anxiously cultivated the sympathies of friendly Muslim leaders. Yet the support British and French troops gleaned from the likes of Sharif Hussein and Emir Faisal did not set Allied nerves at ease. Signs of Muslim discontent were ubiquitous in the colonized world well after the war was over. The start of fighting in Anatolia appeared to beg a broader reassessment of the inherent danger of pan-Islamist activism. 'The war has turned Islam upside down', editors at *Le Temps* argued, 'and after this great upheaval we cannot practice politics with folded arms'.[25]

Inside the British government, officials actively debated the relationship between Muslims at large and the defeat of the Ottoman Empire. Among the sharpest voices within imperial circles was the chief interpreter (or dragoman) at Britain's embassy in Istanbul, Andrew Ryan. Ryan had lived many years in the empire. More than a mere functionary, he prided himself as being the eyes and ears of the high commissioner. His rich years of experience, as well as his many contacts inside Istanbul, lent him an air of credibility that others in Britain's military and civil services lacked. By 1919, Ryan had urged senior officials to see the future of the Ottoman Empire against a global backdrop. Pan-Islamism, as he explained it, was shaping up to be 'one of the world-forces of the new era'. At its heart was not simply discontent with the governance of European empires but rather the principle that Muslims should not be subjects of Christian states. 'That is why', he proffered, 'in the conditions in the modern world, there must always be at least some potential for conflict between Islam and the West'. Britain's challenge was to prevent other powers from influencing mass opinion among the world's Muslims. For this reason, he believed, London had no choice but to take more direct control of Istanbul. A robust British presence in the capital, he reasoned, would go far in reining in the authority of the sultan-caliph. Future sultans who were more amenable to British interests, at the very least, would not incite Muslim rage in the colonies. It was possible, he admitted, that such an arrangement would offend some Muslims. But, in Ryan's estimation, the short-term risks posed by the Nationalists and others were outweighed by the long-term benefits of exerting direct influence over the sultan. What would inevitably result was a 'knock-out blow for political pan-Islamism'.[26]

Men of greater weight ultimately discarded Andrew Ryan's prescriptions. As Allied negotiators finalized the details of the Ottoman peace plan, Edwin Montagu, Secretary of State for India, railed against any thought of a permanent occupation of Istanbul. The full dismemberment of the empire, let alone stripping the Ottomans of their capital, would likely leave Britain without a 'single friend from Constantinople to China'.[27] Montagu's insistence, backed by the Secretary of State for War, Winston Churchill, helped persuade the Allies to leave Istanbul and the offices of sultan and caliph in Ottoman hands. Yet the damage ultimately rendered by the Treaty of Sèvres would prove severe. From India to Afghanistan to Egypt, Muslims mobilized in large numbers to protest London's actions against the Ottoman caliph. Muslims in the French colonial world, as well as former Ottoman subjects in the Balkans, also rallied in defense of the sultan's sovereign rights. Such calls to save the Ottoman caliph also, in turn, amplified the strength of local movements demanding self-rule and national recognition.

The Ottoman Empire's uncertain future arguably registered most strongly in India. That this issue came to affect so many Muslims in the subcontinent was in large measure a product of deep historic ties. For generations, merchants from South Asia had traded and settled in port towns around the Persian Gulf and Red Sea. Over the course of centuries, pilgrims journeying to Mecca and Medina stayed on as residents in various parts of the Ottoman Empire. The personal nature of these connections had grown more profound by the late nineteenth century. As debates over national identity and political sovereignty intensified, Muslims in British India drew heavily upon the Ottoman Empire for inspiration. Intellectuals celebrated the Young Turk Revolution as a movement that brought parliamentary rule and civil equality to a predominately Muslim land. Indian Muslims organized relief campaigns in the wake of the Libyan and Balkan Wars. Above all, both liberals and conservatives identified with Abdülhamid II's drive to unite Muslims under his spiritual leadership. There were limits, however, to how far many Indian Muslims were willing to act on the Ottoman Empire's behalf. When war broke out in 1914, prominent Muslim leaders lobbied Istanbul to remain neutral. The conflict, activists declared, was a struggle between greedy European empires. Worse still, any open support for the Ottomans against the British would likely split India into rival camps, thus jeopardizing the subcontinent's chances for independence. With hundreds of thousands of Indians serving in the British colonial army in 1914, such fears appeared real. This did not prevent many from secretly wishing for Istanbul's success. 'There is not a Musalman [*sic*]', one leader later swore, 'who in [his] heart does not pray for the victory of the Caliph and the defeat and destruction of his enemies, including Britain'.[28]

With the end of the war, popular anger with British governance came to the fore in Indian politics. Wartime hardships debilitated the economy. Economic distress sharpened public disappointment with British reforms regarding voting and provincial assemblies. Food remained scarce in various parts of India, a situation brought on by government requisitioning. Meanwhile, colonial authorities retained the harsh Rowlatt Act, which allowed for indefinite detention without trial, for fear of public disorder. It was at this time that news of the Allied peace plans for the Ottoman Empire began to circulate. Less than a year before the armistice, David Lloyd George assured Parliament that Britain would uphold Ottoman sovereignty over Istanbul, a gesture specifically meant to ease fears in India. Greece's invasion in the spring of 1919, coupled with Britain's likely seizure of the Turkish Straits, led many in India to conclude that the Prime Minister had lied. Fearing that London sought to dissolve the Ottoman state altogether, the Muslim League – the largest Muslim nationalist organization in India – issued its first appeals for the preservation and independence of the Ottoman caliphate. By the beginning of 1919, rallies and press articles carried the League's campaign throughout India, leading to a groundswell of popular support. Even conservative and otherwise apolitical groups, including diverse elements of India's Islamic clergy, readily took to what came to be called the 'Khilafat movement'.

Mohandas Gandhi's rise to prominence in India occurred amid this brewing political storm. Having cut his teeth as an activist in South Africa, he too took advantage of the postwar political climate in the hopes it would contribute to the cause of India's independence. His campaign of passive resistance to the Rowlatt Act commenced as the Khilafat movement grew in appeal. Gandhi was no stranger to the importance of the Ottoman caliphate. Before 1919, he had publicly voiced his support for more lenient treatment of the Ottoman Empire in the event of peace talks. Tactical considerations led him to take an even greater interest in aiding the Muslim League. For decades, an 'all India' alliance, one that equally drew upon Hindu and Muslim support, had eluded pro-independence nationalists. In an early display of his political shrewdness, Gandhi identified the Khilafat struggle as a vehicle for weaving his movement into the broader pro-independence cause. While Muslim representatives lobbied Lloyd George and other officials on Istanbul's behalf, Gandhi wrote letters and spoke at length about the sovereign rights of the Ottoman Empire. No Muslim soldier, he declared in 1920, would ever have fought on Britain's behalf if they knew London intended to nullify Istanbul's territorial sovereignty. As for the rights of non-Muslims in the Ottoman lands, he took the Ottoman government at its word that it would uphold their civil and religious liberties. 'I do not know how far the conditions of Armenia and Syria may be considered as anarchy', he stated in 1920, 'and how far the Turkish Government may be held responsible for

16. Nationalist fighters in Antep.

17. Armenian women identified
as pro-Greek guerrillas in Kirmasti
(modern Mustafakemalpaşa),
near Bursa.

18. Muslim Indian migrants (or *muhajirun*) marching towards Afghanistan in protest at British treatment of the Ottoman caliph.

19. Ahmet Anzavur.

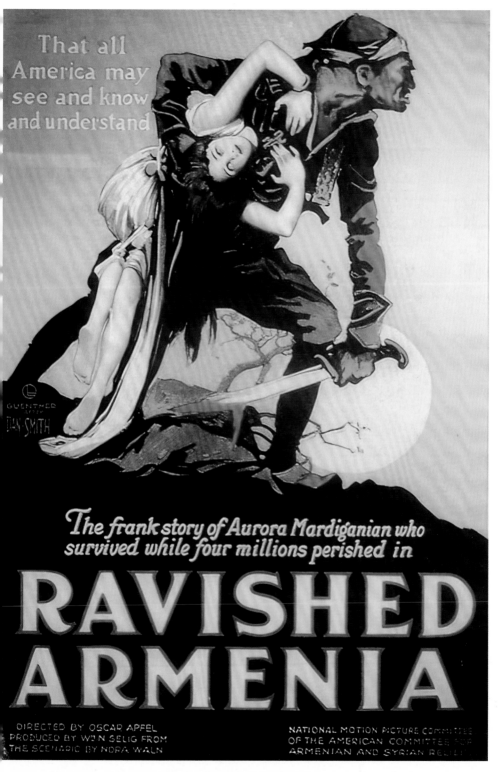

20. An advertisement for the American film *Ravished Armenia* (1919). Based on the memoir of a survivor from eastern Anatolia, the film was never released and all copies have since been lost.

21. A village in flames during the Greek rout from western Anatolia, September 1922.

22. Masses of refugees fleeing a burning Smyrna, September 1922.

23. Refugees from western Anatolia aided by the American Red Cross.

24. Women inspecting the ruins of the Cihanoğlu mosque in Aydın.

25. Nationalist troops parade through Istanbul, November 1922.

26. Abdülmecid II proceeds to the ceremony to install him as caliph, November 1922.

27. Mehmed VI arrives in exile in Malta, November 1922.

28. The celebration of the fourth anniversary of the liberation of Izmir, September 1926.

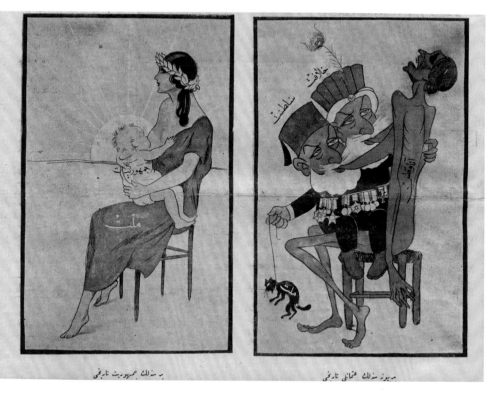

29. A cartoon from the satirical Turkish newspaper *Akbaba*, 30 October 1924. On the left, the infant Turkish Republic suckles on the breast of the nation. On the right, the Ottoman sultan-caliph strangles a cat symbolizing the Turkish nation as he drains his mother Anatolia dry.

30. Desire (*Emel*) bears the coat of arms of the Ottoman royal family as she brandishes the scarlet flag which has served as the standard of both the Ottoman Empire and the Republic of Turkey.

it'.[29] What mattered most was that Lloyd George had promised Muslims that the caliph would continue to reign. To threaten to dissolve the Ottoman caliphate, he charged, was to attack Islam itself. Both Muslims and Hindus were rightfully outraged that the Prime Minister broke that promise.

Gandhi's support for the Khilafat cause did little to pre-empt the signing of the Treaty of Sèvres. Nonetheless, his decision to align himself with the interests of the Muslim League transformed the campaign for India's national sovereignty. His calls for a national non-cooperation effort targeting the colonial administration and economy drew large numbers of young Muslim nationalists to Gandhi's camp. This budding alliance between Muslim and Hindu activists helped mobilize millions of Indians, laying the foundation for greater popular agitation for independence in the years ahead. Yet for some leaders, particularly more senior members of the Muslim League, Hindu support for the Khilafat movement came at too great a cost. Neither non-violent resistance, nor Gandhi's leadership, appeared likely to save the Ottoman Empire from dismemberment. For many conservative activists, London's punitive approach towards Istanbul was symptomatic of a government eager to destroy Islam. This perception prompted thousands of Indians to choose another, more radical solution: migration. Spurred on by various agitators, including established members of the Muslim League, thousands of Indian Muslims declared their intention of leaving 'infidel India' altogether. 'When a land is not safe for Islam', two prominent activists declared, 'a Muslim has only two alternatives, *Jehad* [holy war] or *Hijrat* [flight] ... In view of our weak condition, migration is the only alternative for us'.[30] Up to 60,000 people, many of them desperately poor, set out for Afghanistan in 1920, seeking refuge in what was heralded as a land where Muslims and Islam were genuinely safe.[31] This impression was fanned by Afghanistan's new ruler, Amanullah Khan. In the spring of 1919, he had led a series of attacks across the border into British India in the hopes of freeing his country from Delhi's influence. From Amanullah's perspective, Indian calls for migration north gave him further leverage in dealing with the British after concluding a treaty with London in August 1919.

For those who supported Kemal's National Forces, both the Khilafat movement and the flight of Muslims to Afghanistan also inspired the belief that Indians and Afghans could be moved to rise up on their behalf. The potential appeared real enough. Pro-Khilafat activists were gathering large amounts of money for the Nationalist war effort. Muslim mobs in the subcontinent, driven on by Khilafat calls for action, had attacked colonial offices and police stations, killing dozens. Among those who were eager to capitalize upon tensions in South Asia were exiled members of the former CUP government. In the summer of 1920, Talat Pasha, the former Interior Minister, met with a Khilafat representative in Switzerland. There, the two men discussed plans for an uprising in India, perhaps one reinforced by an Afghan invasion from the north. Around the same time, Cemal Pasha, the infamous former governor of Syria, relocated to Afghanistan. With the backing of the Bolshevik government, he arrived in Kabul with offers to reform and lead Amanullah's national army. Promises of Soviet and Ottoman military aid, however, came with expectations that the Afghans would resume their attacks against British India. Nationalists in Anatolia augmented Cemal's effort through more direct appeals to Kabul. In April 1921, an Afghan delegation was fêted as representing a 'fraternal Islamic nation' and the first state to establish a formal embassy in Ankara.[32] Such expressions of affinity, however welcome, clearly came with risks some Afghans were not willing to bear. Many suspected that lurking behind Cemal Pasha's patronage was Soviet Russia and a possible Communist takeover. This reality, coupled with Ankara's apparent self-interest, had compelled others in Central Asia to be wary of Ottoman overtures. What many Ottoman officers wanted, one revolutionary noted, was 'to continue the [First World] war which they had lost in the West against the Allies'.[33] Fears of a pro-Kemalist offensive subsided after Cemal Pasha departed Afghanistan in late 1921. The potential for a mass uprising in India also waned in India by early 1922. Gandhi's decision to abandon popular protests after demonstrators killed nearly two dozen policemen deflated the Khilafat movement's own organizational efforts. By 1922, Muslim League leaders fell under suspicion of embezzlement and mismanagement after the movement was declared financially bankrupt.

In North Africa, subjects living under British and French colonial rule gave their own interpretations of events in the Ottoman Empire. With the convening of the Paris peace conference, local agitators from throughout the Maghrib demanded seats at the negotiating table. After all, tens of thousands of Egyptians, Algerians, Tunisians and Moroccans had served the Allied cause as imperial troops and laborers. Few in either London or Paris readily entertained such demands. When British authorities arrested an Egyptian delegation intent upon traveling to Versailles, Cairo and other cities along the Nile exploded. The Egyptian uprising in the spring of 1919 immediately set Lloyd George's government on its heels. As London groped for a potential solution to the crisis in Egypt, British officials tended to see the insurrection as at least a partial outgrowth of affairs in Anatolia. The belief that Ottoman agents helped to fan the flames of Egyptian nationalism was partly grounded in reality. British officials correctly surmised that elements of the Special Organization remained active in the protectorate. As in India, sympathizers raised money on behalf of the National Forces. Mustafa Kemal's successes likewise drew the admiration of Egyptians who otherwise disagreed profoundly with one another on issues of religion and reform. Nevertheless, Ottoman politics remained largely separate from the question of Egypt's future. Egypt had begun to develop its own separate state institutions within the Ottoman Empire beginning in the early nineteenth century. After it became a British protectorate in 1882, few in Egypt contemplated any return to rule under Istanbul. Pro-Ottoman discussions among educated Egyptians, as one British observer put it, were 'frequent' but 'rarely passionate'.[34]

Observers from French North Africa had even more reason to stand aloof from what was happening in Anatolia. Morocco, for one, had never been part of the Ottoman Empire. In Algeria and Tunisia, rule from Paris had replaced Ottoman governance decades before Britain seized Egypt. French rule, however, proved far more invasive than anything British officials had ever conceived of for their territories in North Africa. For the tens of thousands of colonials who served in France's army, the Great War exposed many to French colonialism's worst traits. Racial abuse and other forms of unequal treatment disillusioned many who fought at the front or toiled as laborers in France. With the war's end, Wilson's Fourteen Points appeared to offer an opportunity for redress for these and other parts of France's empire. French unwillingness to accommodate appeals from North African activists lent new significance to the region's ties to the Ottoman lands. Pro-independence activists in Algeria found ready parallels between the plight of Muslims in Anatolia and the injustices suffered by *indigène* residents. France, one Algerian editor believed, possessed a historical and moral obligation to defend the sovereign interests of Ottoman Muslims. It was France, beginning in the sixteenth century, which was the first great European state to forge strong ties with Istanbul. Now, as an empire possessing 25 million Muslims 'living under its laws', it was in the country's interest to be in the 'forefront of defenders of the integrity of Turkey'.[35] Mustafa Kemal's emergence as the face of the National Movement had an especially strong influence upon the aspirations of North African Muslims. Kemal's photos, as one young activist remembered, were 'like talismans' among Algerians living in Paris.[36] Yet, as in Egypt, there were limits to which North Africans identified with Ottoman causes. Tunisia's history of constitutional self-rule, as opposed to Ankara's example, inspired activists to form the country's first pro-independence party in 1920. In Morocco, insurgents struggling against French and Spanish rule took only a partial interest in what was occurring at the other end of the Mediterranean. Moroccans, like Muslims elsewhere, tended to cheer Mustafa Kemal's victories, but drew more inspiration from their own institutions. Morocco had its own sultan whose sovereignty and legitimacy were threatened. Ethno-national antagonisms also fostered disinterest among many Moroccans. As one newspaper put it, Mehmed VI, as 'caliph of Istanbul, [was] a usurper, since [he was] of non-Arab descent'.[37]

The politics of Ottoman sovereignty possessed a rather more oblique – but no less significant – resonance in Libya. After the territory was ceded to Rome in 1912, both local fighters and Ottoman agents continued their struggle against Italian troops over the next several years. The willingness of some Libyan leaders to aid Istanbul in its fight against Great Britain drew further Ottoman attention in the early stages of the Great War. One of the most prominent figures to answer the empire's call for support was Ahmed al-Sharif al-Sanusi. As the head of one of the largest Islamic fraternal orders in Libya, al-Sanusi organized and led detachments of his followers in attacks against British positions in western Egypt. His decision to join the Ottoman war effort ultimately proved disastrous. When his cousin agreed to come to terms with both the British and Italians, al-Sanusi found himself on the run, with little hope of returning to power. The signing of the armistice, however, allowed him an opportunity to escape to Istanbul. While in exile, he cultivated close relations with both the sultan's representatives and the National Forces. His fame as a redoubtable warrior and cleric added to his visibility as a defender of Ottoman and Libyan independence. Upon al-Sanusi's arrival in Ankara in 1920, Mustafa Kemal personally hailed him as a patriot who had remained loyal since the days Italy 'attacked and assaulted our Ottoman Africa like a bandit'. His decision to 'strengthen the state of Turkey [*Türkiya devlet*]', Kemal declared, reinforced the country's place as 'the fulcrum of the Islamic world'.[38] In lieu of any return to Libya, al-Sanusi threw himself behind Nationalist efforts in Syria and Iraq. Together with a small band of devotees, he resettled in eastern Anatolia, raising troops and promoting propaganda campaigns aimed at boosting Arab support for Ankara's war against the Allies. In 1921, pro-Nationalist agitators led efforts in Iraq to rally local support for al-Sanusi's candidacy as its founding king. His increasingly global celebrity as an Islamic leader and nationalist, however, failed to earn him any lasting place of authority. After Ankara came to terms with the Allies in 1923, al-Sanusi left Turkey and wandered the Levant and Arabia in the intent of either returning home or securing some new position of power. Until his death in relative obscurity in 1933, he continued to embody the hopes of Muslim activists and rebels eager to form a united front against Western imperialism.

Interest in Ottoman affairs also permeated the Balkans. In the years since the end of the Balkan Wars, large numbers of Yugoslav, Bulgarian and Greek Muslims retained close ties with the empire. It was not uncommon for individuals and families to visit, do business with or resettle in the Ottoman lands despite the ongoing fighting in the region since 1912. As in other portions of the former empire, Balkan Muslims generally sympathized with Mustafa Kemal and the National Forces. One Muslim representative in Greece's parliament, for example, saw no contradiction in believing 'Mustafa Kemal's [movement] would succeed and the Greeks and the Allies would be cast into the sea'.[39] For local elites, however, the future of the Ottoman state was not an immediate concern. After the flight of hundreds of thousands after the Balkan Wars, Muslims who remained in their native towns and villages often worked diligently to adapt to life in their new states. This was especially the case in the newly formed Kingdom of Yugoslavia. In the territories that became Kosovo and Northern Macedonia, many local Muslim leaders invested themselves in the country's emerging party politics. From the perspective of *Hak* (*The Right*), Skopje's Turkish-language newspaper, the war in Anatolia was no different from any other item of foreign news. What was of primary concern, in the minds of many civic leaders, were matters of health, education and security for local Turkish-, Albanian- and Slavic-speaking Muslims. However, as the fighting between the Nationalists and the Greeks drew to a close, old wounds were suddenly reopened. In late 1922, news spread that thousands in Kosovo and Macedonia were preparing to abandon Yugoslavia in the hopes of finding refuge in Anatolia. Poverty, as well as ongoing acts of oppression at the hands of local authorities, was compelling many to leave home. Editors at *Hak*, however, denounced the very principle of Muslims ever abandoning Yugoslavia. While most local Turks and Albanians 'appreciate the tragedy of Muslim migration, they also feel the pain of changing their fatherland [*vatan*], [and] so they do not desire to drag themselves and their families back into misery'.[40] Tens of thousands ultimately ignored such appeals. From 1923 to 1939, 115,000 Yugoslav Muslims elected to emigrate to Turkey. They joined close to 300,000 Bulgarian and Romanian Muslims who fled to Anatolia in the fifteen years that followed the war against the Allies.[41]

It is more difficult to find outspoken supporters of Mustafa Kemal and Ottoman independence in Western Europe. Animus from the First World War, particularly over Istanbul's treatment of its Christian citizens, continued to color how many viewed the empire. This aversion to the plight of the Ottoman Empire also extended to nationalist dissidents. Irish insurgents, for example, never went as far as to make common cause with the National Movement in Anatolia. Activists in Ankara, however, did take a keen interest in Ireland's struggle for independence. 'In the east', one Nationalist editor declared, 'those who suffer under oppression see the sacred struggle of the Irish as a natural ally in the struggle for revenge against injustice. However, the Turks in particular – Sinn Féin's real comrade in arms – see ourselves as the brothers of Ireland's heroic manhood'.[42] Among the few Europeans to present Ottoman affairs in a more positive light were journalists and

artists. Arguably the most noted of these supporters was the French
novelist Pierre Loti. Before the Great War, Loti had made a name for
himself as the author of exotic love stories set in Asia. His affection
for Istanbul and the Ottoman Empire was consummated with his first
book, *Ayizadé*, a torrid novel of taboos and forbidden desire. In the
wake of the Great War, Loti wrote a number of essays unabashedly
denouncing the Allied occupation of the Ottoman lands. He categorically condemned the machinations of Ottoman Christians, whom
he characterized as the true villains residing within the empire. He
decried what he called 'the mad exaggeration in the complaints of
these Armenians, who for centuries have been so vilely cheating on
their neighbors the Turks', and who had played 'on their title of
"Christians" in order to stir up Western fanaticism against Turkey'.[43]
Newspapers in Anatolia delighted in reprinting his articles and reciprocated his affection. The country owed Loti its eternal gratitude,
Mustafa Kemal told him, for he was 'a friend who has not lost his
trust in us for a moment'.[44]

American attitudes towards the Ottoman Empire stiffened considerably in the aftermath of the Great War. Woodrow Wilson's desire to see
the empire's 'Turkish portions' retain their sovereignty had helped give
life and legitimacy to the National Movement. Yet, from the outset of
the Paris peace talks, neither Wilson nor members of his administration stood prepared to aid Ottoman efforts in this endeavor. To the
contrary, events on the ground inflamed American opinion against the
National Forces. Well before the war's end, hundreds of Americans
journeyed to the region to aid in relief work among Armenian refugees. 'We had very little sympathy with the sick man of Europe . . .',
one missionary doctor remembered, 'but we went on to serve wherever
the need seemed greatest'.[45] Groups such as Near East Relief continued
this work in Syria and the Caucasus well after the signing of the armistice. The horrors witnessed by many of these workers, particularly the
fighting in Cilicia, fortified both popular and elite antipathy towards
Turkish Muslims. When an American fact-finding delegation journeyed to Istanbul on behalf of the Allies in 1919, its leaders devoted
little attention to Muslim concerns. Among the most pressing questions raised by the commission were whether the government would
'help restore Armenians (or other deported populations) to their home

and property', and whether 'the safety and rights of Armenians' could be assured in the future.[46] Early signs of American hostility towards the Ottoman government did not lay to rest the issue of whether Washington was willing to act as a guarantor of the empire's sovereignty. As late as the fall of 1919, even Mustafa Kemal privately expressed hope that an American mandate state would be created in Anatolia. The National Forces, he told an American journalist, 'will accept with thanks any conditions the United States chooses [to] suggest but some of those conditions should be disguised because of [the] excited state [of the] Turkish mind . . .'[47] Washington's inaction rendered Kemal's public denunciation of an American mandate moot. In the wake of the severe stroke in October 1919 which left Wilson partially paralyzed, American senators rejected ratification of the Treaty of Versailles. A distinctly anti-Turkish climate continued to hover over Congress well after the fighting in Anatolia ended. In 1927, senators again rejected ratification of a peace with Turkey. No Congress, one senator insisted, would ever accept any treaty with the Turks while 'nearly a million Armenian refugees and exiles' remained without a country.[48]

Nationalists in Anatolia found far sturdier friends in Moscow. In the wake of the armistice, Lenin and other Bolshevik leaders saw the Allied occupation of Anatolia as a threat to their revolution. With Athens – backed by Britain – poised to annex the Turkish Straits, Russia's outlet to the Mediterranean and the wider world was in jeopardy. Early signs of goodwill among Nationalist leaders helped soothe these fears. In August 1919, the former CUP leaders Talat and Enver visited the Soviet government's foreign minister while he was imprisoned in Berlin. Even though the two pashas were living in exile, they insisted that they spoke for both the National Forces and the Islamic world. 'The Moslem east', Talat and Enver explained, 'could free itself from slavery' only through the direct support of the Soviet government.[49] Many in Ankara, however, remained leery of Soviet aid. In February 1920, editors at *National Sovereignty*, the National Movement's principal newspaper, denounced Bolshevism as a threat to the independence and freedom of Muslim lands in Asia, as well as to Europe as a whole.[50] Privately, Mustafa Kemal voiced similar suspicions. Pursuing relations with Moscow likely left the country open to Communist subversion, something he was not willing to risk. Yet as 1920 progressed, conditions on the ground compelled

Moscow and Ankara to draw closer. The Red Army's victory over anti-Communist forces in the south of Russia made it more likely that the Caucasus too would fall back under Moscow's control. With Nationalist leaders eager to seize territory claimed by Armenia in eastern Anatolia, Kemal dispatched Enver Pasha's uncle, Halil, to reach an understanding with the Soviets. By the end of summer 1920, Bolshevik representatives began transferring generous amounts of financial assistance to Nationalist emissaries. Before the year was out, senior leaders in Ankara softened their tone towards both the Soviet government and the benefits of Communism. Turks and Bolsheviks, declared *National Sovereignty*, were 'nations of the same cast'. After years of living under the 'same absolutism and bureaucracy' both 'new Russia and new Turkey were leaders of the movement which will save the world from the tyranny of imperialism'.[51] Mustafa Kemal also grew more deferential with time. Communism was admittedly a 'distant and foreign concept to an Anatolian government', he told one local activist. But to receive aid from Moscow, it was necessary for the country to open 'its doors to Communist views'.[52]

Kemal's change in attitude reflected a calculated strategic gambit. Beyond the material benefits of a Soviet alliance, Ankara's pro-Bolshevik posturing clearly alarmed the Allies. As the tide of the Russian Civil War turned in the Red Army's favor, many across Europe and America feared Communism's growth closer to home. Soviet-inspired uprisings had wracked Germany, Hungary and other Central European countries. Bolshevik agitation appeared to build within the French left. By 1920, a 'red scare' had swept over the United States, leading to the arrest and deportation of hundreds. For British and French observers, Mustafa Kemal's apparent turn towards Communism appeared in lockstep with these trends. British intelligence officials were among the most vocal in speculating that a broad Young Turk–Bolshevik conspiracy was at work from Egypt to India. To some extent, material fact fanned these apprehensions. Former Ottoman officials were indeed visibly active in Central Asia, Iran, the Caucasus and other areas closely linked to Soviet interests. In 1920, Enver Pasha relocated to Soviet Russia. His arrival as a guest of the Bolshevik government coincided with the convening of what was dubbed the 'Congress of the Peoples of the East' in Baku. There he joined close to 1,900 delegates dedicated to raising rebellion throughout the Islamic world.[53] Soviet newspapers and representatives conspicuously highlighted the congress's relevance to Ankara's struggle against the Allies. As ominous as these threats appeared, at least some European observers saw Kemal's relationship with Moscow in a more subtle light. The Soviets clearly hoped 'to be able to put pressure upon the Entente Powers through [Ankara]', one *Times* correspondent supposed. The Nationalists were also clearly in need of munitions, security guarantees on their eastern border and the 'moral support of a great Power'.[54]

For whatever benefits the National Movement derived from its ties with the Soviet government, Mustafa Kemal understood that Moscow's friendship carried serious risks. By 1920, local Communist activists, including some with direct ties to the Bolsheviks, clamored for greater influence within the National Movement. Kemal attempted to pacify native activists with the formation of an official Communist party, one that remained firmly under his thumb. Lenin's eager embrace of Enver Pasha posed an even greater danger. In the year following his flight from the empire, Enver and other CUP leaders had touted themselves as agents of the National Movement. Many, including both Enver and Talat, corresponded directly with Mustafa Kemal during the movement's formative months. Though they were willing to serve in Ankara's interests, all of them voiced a sincere desire to return home. For Kemal, Enver's revived fortunes opened the door to a potential power struggle. Though the CUP still bore a stigma as the party of war and defeat, former Young Turks populated much of the Defense of Rights Association. And there was no denying that Enver Pasha remained particularly beloved within many quarters of the National Movement. Whether Enver was backed by the Soviets or not, Mustafa Kemal had every reason to fear his return.

Kemal's skills as a politician, as well as a good bit of luck, prevented an immediate reckoning with the CUP's old guard. Though he entertained their insights and recommendations, Kemal forbade the return of the party's former luminaries. As Enver understood it, the message was clear: 'You may not come in but you may work abroad'.[55] This did not prevent him from at least trying. In the summer of 1921, he journeyed to Batum, just across the border from Ottoman territory on the Black Sea coast. There he negotiated with local Nationalist officers and plotted his dramatic return to domestic politics. His moment never came. Wary of Enver's ambitions, Mustafa Kemal arrested officers sympathetic to the former War Minister. With the fighting against Greece turning in Kemal's favor, Enver left after months of waiting. Thereafter, his celebrity brought him little solace. After falling out with the Bolsheviks, he died leading pro-independence rebels in Tajikistan in August 1922. His death occurred after a wave of assassinations took the lives of multiple CUP leaders. Talat Pasha was shot dead in Berlin in March 1921. Cemal was gunned down more than a year later in July 1922 in Tbilisi. Both Talat and Cemal, as well as several other noted Young Turks, were the victims of a concerted campaign of revenge carried out by Armenian nationalists. Of the surviving senior leaders of the CUP, none would return home until after the war with Greece was over.

The problem posed by Enver's resurgence encapsulated much of the uncertainty that hovered over Ankara. After the Greek offensive in the summer of 1920, there was plenty of reason to believe that the Nationalist cause might yet fail. Successes in Cilicia and in the east could not offset continued Greek gains in western Anatolia. More-over, there were still signs of factionalism and dissent elsewhere in Anatolia. All of these pressures threatened to overwhelm Mustafa Kemal before the end of the summer of 1921. His ability to ride out this storm, and capitalize upon his moments of success, cemented his place as a national hero and as the country's true ruler.

THE FINAL TIDE: THE FIGHTING OF 1921

İzzettin Çalışlar had first watched the fighting in Anatolia from afar. As a lieutenant colonel assigned to the imperial army's personnel office, he resided securely in Istanbul during the eighteen months that followed the armistice. His decision to stay on at his post for so long is not clear. For much of his career he kept a regular diary, only to abandon it soon after the fighting in 1918 ended. His detailed records suggest that perhaps he had had enough of the front. He had served almost unremittingly in uniform between 1912 and 1918, bearing witness to campaigns in Macedonia, Gallipoli, eastern Anatolia and Syria. When he resumed his diary in the spring of 1920, it appears he had settled into a life of idle office work. The release in May of the peace terms by the Allies, however, appeared to jolt him from complacency. 'Today, along with the other department administrators, I was given command of the personnel office', he wrote that month. 'This matter had absolutely no effect on me. Given the state of the country, the uncertainty of its future lies before me'.[56] The opening of Greece's offensive in early summer prompted him into action. He left the comforts of Istanbul and eventually joined Nationalist troops east of Eskişehir. There he found many of the troops in a terrible state. 'Most of the men had bare feet, were devoid of any uniforms or clothes, no spirit, [leading] many to desert'. Among the things he particularly noted of those who remained in camp was the number of irregulars. Several units were made up of refugees and migrants, particularly Albanians and Circassians. As a whole, they garnered a reputation for their criminal proclivities and their lack of discipline. Among the worst of these offenders were the men loyal to Çerkes Ethem. Though he had proven himself indispensable in mopping up anti-Nationalist rebels in various parts of Anatolia, his troops robbed villagers at will and were quick to execute anyone they believed deserving of death. When İzzettin objected to the beating and killing of a fellow Nationalist officer by Ethem's brother, senior commanders intervened before tensions escalated further. Even Mustafa Kemal took note of the fracas. 'So, you stood up to Ethem?' he quipped. 'You did well, but time is on his side'. Kemal advised İzzettin to 'move gingerly and with care' around Ethem, for fear that he would murder him, too.[57]

Kemal's advice reflected his own experience by that point. By the fall of 1920, the Nationalist retreat from the Aegean and Marmara coasts had led to open displays of discord within the ranks. Junior officers decried the lack of resources and poor performance of volunteer units on the battlefield. Refugee detachments, such as those made up of Bosnians, Albanians or Circassians, appeared increasingly less serviceable. Senior commanders quibbled as to how to respond to the Greek offensive. Politics in Ankara added to the confusion. Among those who pressed for more aggressive action was Çerkes Ethem. As the leader of the most effective unit in the National Forces, Ethem also relied upon the influence of his brother, who was a member of the National Assembly and an early founder of the CUP. Furthermore, the brothers represented an avidly pro-Communist faction within the National Movement. For Mustafa Kemal, both men posed a direct threat to his management of affairs in both Ankara and the front. Ironically, it was the result of further setbacks against the Greeks that allowed Kemal to shunt the brothers aside. In late October, Nationalist troops staged a counterattack. The assault failed, largely due to the lack of coordination between Ethem and the front's senior commander. Mustafa Kemal seized upon the defeat as an opportunity to reassign both Ethem and his brother to Moscow as envoys on Ankara's behalf. Ethem refused and abandoned the Nationalist camp alongside his brothers and thousands of his soldiers. When a detachment of Nationalist regulars attacked his forces after their desertion in December, Ethem and hundreds of Circassian riders sought refuge behind the Greek front lines. Their defection allowed Kemal to paint the brothers as traitors of the worst sort. 'There is no doubt that they delivered a lot of secrets to the Greeks', he declared before the National Assembly.[58] Elsewhere, Nationalist commanders declared Ethem and his brothers apostates unworthy of Islam.

Kemal strengthened his hand over his army and nascent capital in the wake of Ethem's defection. In January, the age of enlistment was lengthened and the army reorganized. By the spring of 1921, irregular units like those mustered by Çerkes Ethem were replaced by new commands made up of conscripts and volunteers. The passage of the new constitution in January 1921 signaled an even more dramatic consolidation of power. In addition to nullifying the legal prerogatives of the sultan, the 'Law of Fundamental Organization', as it was called, provided a framework for new ministries and governing councils to be staffed in Ankara. On the surface, the necessities of the war appeared to warrant the temporary creation of an administration parallel to Istanbul's authority. Underneath, there were clear signs that many of these changes were permanent.

The most obvious indication of this shifting political climate was the increased visibility of the CUP's foremost ideologues. When Mustafa Kemal settled in Ankara in December 1919, most senior members of the Turkish Hearth remained in Istanbul or were living abroad. Several of its most influential activists were arrested in connection with the deportation and murder of Armenians. Events in 1920, however, allowed the Turkish Hearth to reconsolidate itself, this time under the protection of the National Forces. With the closure of the Chamber of Deputies in the spring, many of the most noted figures in the Turkish Hearth sought refuge in Ankara. There they were generally received with open arms by Mustafa Kemal. In the months that followed, individuals with strong ties to the Turkish Hearth took positions within the new National Assembly and at various levels of the Nationalist administration. Whether on the floor of parliament or within the fields of education or propaganda, rhetoric and ideas long associated with the Hearth became commonplace. As pro-Nationalist officials took over the management of schools in the countryside, Ankara's new Ministry of Education mandated the creation of 'museum rooms' which would introduce children to the country's Turkic past. One activist prophesied that Ankara would lead a renaissance in matters of learning and letters in Asia. 'As soon as peace is concluded', he told a French journalist, 'the schools of Asia Minor will be filled with young people from Central Asia. An awakening of consciousness is taking place among all of us, from here to the borders of China and Siberia'.[59] One of the most venerable of the Hearth's leaders to join the National Movement was Ziya Gökalp. As a prolific writer and polemicist, Gökalp had been influential in senior CUP circles and a member of the party's central committee. His reputation as an ideologue during the Great War landed him in prison for having aided in the deportation and murder of Armenians. Upon his release, Gökalp threw his weight behind the National Movement, which he praised as the culmination of all his efforts. 'The idea of Turkism', he wrote as the fighting in 1922 closed, was a concept that few initially appreciated. The Great War, as well as conflicts in Libya and the Balkans, had helped widen its appeal, but it was Mustafa Kemal 'alone who made the ideal official and who actually applied it'.[60]

Neither Gökalp nor others associated with the Turkish Hearth held a monopoly over the politics of ideas in Ankara. Staffing the Nationalist government were large numbers of people with less stringent views on matters pertaining to nationalism, language, culture or religion. A survey conducted in the summer of 1921 offered a clear indication of this diversity within the Nationalist camp. Under an initiative by one of the National Assembly's younger members, parliamentarians were asked an open-ended question: 'For our victorious national independence struggle to be successful and fruitful, what is this dependent on?' Some of the respondents were decidedly flippant in composing their answers. 'Money' was the only word one representative wrote on his questionnaire.[61] Of the 315 respondents, at least sixty-eight parliamentarians believed that the nation had to adhere to its religious principles. The National Assembly's struggle would succeed, one member wrote, when 'state officials, big or small, cling to the pure Islamic law and administer state laws with competent justice and integrity'. 'Because', he avowed, 'justice is a scale of righteousness that God has given to his slaves'.[62] The National Assembly included some who explicitly echoed the rhetoric of the Turkish Hearth. Mahmud Esad, one of the National Assembly's fieriest members, called for nothing less than a revolution. Ottoman Turks, as he put it, had never known a government that favored them. 'Turkey, and most importantly the Turkish people, were like flocks of slaves under the oppression of the pharaohs who built the pyramids'. To realize their national independence, as well as free themselves from despotism (assuming this was at the hands of the sultan), the Turkish people had to embrace a state that embodied modern economic and philosophical principles.[63] In contrast, a bold few voiced their belief that Kurds and Turks needed one another for the National Movement to succeed. 'Our new administration should focus on the problem of the common future of Turks and Kurds', one member from Diyarbakir declared. 'Kurds cannot live without Turks and a great amount of pride and honor will be reserved for the Kurds from the bright future that awaits the Turk in Asia'.[64]

This lack of agreement also extended to debates over other existential topics. In the wake of the signing of the Sèvres peace treaty in August 1920, lawmakers in Ankara got to work on crafting the new constitution. Among the issues discussed that September was the precise wording to be used to describe the state's core characteristics. In outlining the supreme prerogatives exercised by the National Assembly, representatives initially considered identifying the state as the 'People's Government of Turkey'. The phrase, however, was abandoned in favor of simpler language. 'The State of Turkey' ultimately represented the country's sovereign interests.[65] This subtle initial shift in rhetoric was by no means happenstance. In the months preceding discussions of the new constitution, elements of Ankara's intelligentsia pushed for what they termed a 'populist' campaign of reform. For many Nationalists, it was not simply the nation, but specifically the Anatolian peasantry, which stood upon the precipice. Western imperialism, as well as despotic landlords, were the forces that most imperiled Anatolia's *volk*. Only a 'people's government' (*halk hükümeti*) would be able to protect the nation from these two great dangers. Such opinions most often came from those who looked upon the Bolshevik Revolution sympathetically. But populism (*halkçılık*) also attracted members of the Turkish Hearth, who seized upon the idea as a warrant for a forceful nationalist agenda. Conservatives, however, tended to see populism as a stalking horse for Communism. 'The aim of the Bolsheviks is humanitarian and the purpose they pursue is known to us', one parliamentarian declared. 'But our religious principles already command us [to do these things]'.[66] Demands for a 'people's government' also raised even more obvious questions about the future of the Ottoman sultan-caliph. In asserting that sovereignty resided with the people, and not the sultan, calls for a popular state appeared nothing short of revolutionary. Mustafa Kemal, mindful of the repercussions, forbade extensive debate on the matter. Mehmed VI's acts of treason, he repeated time and again, did not necessarily mean that the National Movement aimed to dissolve the monarchy.

These innate tensions stirred below a surface of more frivolous matters. Shortly before the Great War, the government had decreed 31 December to be a national holiday in celebration of the country's independence. From 1913 onward, public ceremonies marking Ottoman Independence Day (*İstiklal-i Osmani Günü*) touted the virtues of patriotism and sacrifice. By 1920, most newspaper editors in Istanbul and Ankara were at ease connecting this occasion with contemporary affairs. As the day associated with the founding of the Ottoman state in the year 1299, Independence Day appeared especially important given the dangers afoot. 'Enemies, attacking from all sides, from inside and outside, have been trying to destroy the independence of the Turk ...' one Nationalist editor claimed. 'However, the Turk has been accustomed to living independently from such ancient times that the idea of losing [his independence] was enough to commemorate it with the deepest excitement'. Still another prominent Nationalist journalist believed that an independence day belittled the nation. 'There is no time in history when the Turk was recorded as a prisoner', he countered. 'It is absurd to assign a special independence day to the Turk, who has always lived independently after taking his place in the world'. For Nationalist readers that winter, the assumptions behind these arguments emphasized a somewhat uncomfortable reality. It was increasingly said that it was the Turkish nation – and less so the Ottoman state – whose independence appeared at stake. In this light, liberating the sultan-caliph from captivity was of secondary importance. Rejecting even the idea of an independence day further fell in line with the thinking of self-declared populists. The Anatolian *volk* had never known a need to celebrate their independence. By implication, celebrating the monarchy's founding in 1299 had no bearing upon Turkish freedom. Reading between the lines, one could say that the sultan's liberty was becoming irrelevant.[67]

Yet with the fighting still continuing, many of these ruminations were of lesser importance. Fortunately for the leaders of the Defense of Rights Association, the Greeks were confronting internal cleavages of their own. In October 1920, Greece's young monarch, Alexander, succumbed to a fatal infection after being bitten by his pet monkey. The question of who was to reign reopened bitter debates that had lingered since the latter stages of the Great War. Resentment remained rife within Greece ever since Constantine, the last king, was compelled to relinquish the crown. The extent of this rancor was revealed a month after Alexander's death when Greeks went to the polls. The election delivered Venizelos a crushing defeat, forcing him to resign. Within a month, voters again went to the polls, this time choosing to restore Constantine to the throne. This sudden change in government widened the political divides within the army and civilian administration. Hundreds of officers linked to Venizelos were purged or reassigned. This included all three corps commanders and most of the divisional commanders deployed to Anatolia.[68] As time passed, morale among soldiers and officers in the field ebbed as factions formed within the ranks. Greece's 'National Schism' added to the country's growing disenchantment with the costs of the conflict. Upon accepting the crown,

Constantine swore that he would end the war. Yet, as the new year opened, he recommitted Greece to the offensive.

At the behest of the new government, two Greek army corps pressed forward in January 1921. The northern column targeted Nationalist positions outside the hamlet of İnönü, west of Eskişehir. Entrenched Nationalist troops were dogged in defending their positions and after days of fighting the Greeks fell back. The stubbornness of the Nationalists at İnönü was tested again two months later. In March, a far larger Greek force attacked Nationalist defensive works outside İnönü in the hopes of breaking through to Eskişehir. Nationalist troops retreated at various points along the line but failed to break. The momentum shifted back and forth over the course of five days' hard fighting. Without further reserves to draw upon, Greek generals ordered their troops to withdraw west towards Bursa. The fighting at İnönü was costly for both Greek and Nationalist forces, with each side losing roughly 5,000 dead, wounded or missing.

Greece's second reversal outside İnönü was as damaging politically as it was militarily. The Nationalist victory, newspapers noted from abroad, appeared to confirm that Mustafa Kemal was far from finished. From an international perspective, Ankara's apparent buoyancy held critical implications for the diplomatic front. Earlier in January, the Allies had announced plans to hold supplemental talks around the imposition of the Treaty of Sèvres. There was now little sign of unanimity among the Great War's principal winners. Having initially been promised Smyrna before peace talks at Versailles, Italy's feelings of betrayal at the hands of Britain and Greece led Rome to openly abet Ankara's defiance. With Italian support, Mustafa Kemal dispatched a delegation to London to represent the interests of the Defense of Rights Association. As negotiations among the Allies progressed, Nationalist successes in eastern Anatolia and Cilicia compelled French diplomats to meet separately with Ankara's delegates. Lloyd George remained as committed as ever to Athens's claims, yet British resolve also appeared to fade. Despite Greece's setbacks at İnönü, London refused to offer actual material or financial support to the Greek offensive.

The Greek retreat, however, provided the Nationalist cause with even more reasons to appeal to international sympathies. As thousands of Greek troops took up positions outside of Bursa, news of a concerted campaign of arson and murder trickled out to the world. By the beginning of summer 1921, newspapers were reporting the displacement of more than 15,000 Muslims from villages north of Bursa.[69] As in the case of Greece's capture of Izmir in May 1919, the dramatic extent of the violence elicited an investigation by a commission formed by the Allied states. Its findings were categorical. 'The Mission', it declared, 'came to the conclusion that for the last two months elements of the Greek army of occupation have been employed in the extermination of the Moslem population of the [Yalova-Gemlik] peninsula. The facts established – burnings of villages, massacres, terror of the inhabitants, coincidences of place and date – leave no room for doubt in regard to this'.[70] Allied condemnation of Greece's actions did not put an end to the violence. Greek troops and locally recruited irregulars continued to wage a scorched-earth campaign throughout the summer, driving thousands away and killing scores. This new wave of attacks again brought Allied investigators to the region. This second investigation denounced earlier acts of barbarism committed by the National Forces, as well as Greece's policy of extermination north of Bursa. The atrocities committed by both warring factions, according to the Allied commission, were 'unworthy of a civilised Government'.[71]

For observers in Istanbul and Ankara, the destruction of villages and towns on the Sea of Marmara was shocking but not surprising. Reports of rapes, thefts, beatings, killings and other outrages by Greek troops often graced the pages of the Turkish-language press. By this stage in the war, both government officials and private citizens went out of their way to publicize evidence of Greece's depravity. Before 1921 was over, eleven books documenting the violence of the Greek occupation came into circulation within major Ottoman cities.[72] The sheer number of violent incidents, however, did more than stir outrage and stiffen resolve. From the perspective of most Turkish-language publishers, the atrocities of 1921 were a demonstration of what many considered a cardinal truth: resident Christians, in collusion with their foreign patrons, were the prime perpetrators of violence in the empire. It was the invading Greeks and their local allies, as one newspaper put it, who shattered the 'happy centuries and years under the faith and comfort of the sultan and caliph'.[73] Europe's willingness to investigate Greece's crimes was immaterial given that Allied forces had failed to halt attacks against Muslims living beside the Sea of Marmara. It seems likely that many readers, particularly in Nationalist circles, would have assessed the West's muted response to anti-Muslim violence in contrast to their reaction to the Armenian deportations. In 1918, the Allies had gone to great lengths to hold Ottoman leaders accountable for war crimes. Three years later, no European state called for the prosecution of Greek officials despite inquiries conducted by the Allies themselves. This hypocrisy likely reinforced the belief that Europe had falsely maligned all 'Muslims and Turks' while native Christians escaped any accountability.

The killings and mass expulsions seen outside Bursa were indicative of the broader impact the Greek occupation was having on society. When refugees from the Marmara coast testified to the troubles they had endured, many claimed to have personally known those who had attacked them. Arnold Toynbee, a young professor of Greek and Byzantine studies from the University of London, met with many of these victims while serving as a special correspondent for the *Manchester Guardian*. Some of the survivors, he later explained, vowed that they knew the perpetrators during happier times before the war. Many were shopkeepers, shepherds, factory owners and merchants from the area. 'They were, in fact, ordinary Greek civilians who, under the brutalising influence of the war and the encouragement of the Greek army of occupation', had taken up arms against their neighbors.[74] What Toynbee discovered in the summer of 1921 was part of a broader pattern of local collaboration. Nationalist sources often reported that thousands of Christian citizens, particularly native Greeks and Armenians, volunteered to serve the Greek army and civilian administration in Anatolia. Newspapers in Ankara and Istanbul, however, tended to ignore the degree to which the National Forces were complicit in the flight of local Christians. As the battle lines shifted from west to east and back again in 1921, Greek authorities in Bursa found themselves caring for more than 12,000 local Greeks and Armenians who had escaped from the fighting.[75] Athens also invested resources in resettling Ottoman Greeks expelled from their homes in Anatolia in the years preceding the armistice. According to statistics compiled in 1921, Greek occupation authorities resettled almost 144,000 Ottoman citizens who had fled to Greece during the CUP's anti-Greek campaigns of 1913–18.[76] Officials from Athens issued strict guidelines to local agents tasked with rehabilitating these refugees, with an eye towards not inciting Muslim opinion against the returning Christians. More often than not, fulfilling these orders was more easily said than done.

Native Armenians and Greeks were not the only residents to contribute to Greece's occupation of Ottoman lands. In the months enveloping the Greek offensive of June 1920, thousands of Muslims offered their services to the Allies. Many did so out of a sense of obligation to the Ottoman state. Since the Treaty of Sèvres assured Ottoman sovereignty over Greek areas of control, large numbers of gendarmes, judges and petty officials stayed on at their posts to oversee provincial affairs. Nationalist guerrillas often showed little mercy towards local Muslims accused of collaboration. In many cases, predominantly Muslims villages were subject to acts of arson, murder or theft for having lent support to the Greek authorities. Bowing to the demands of the occupying administration, as well as refusing to hand over cash or animals to Nationalist troops, was viewed as grounds for retribution. In an open decree posted in villages outside Balıkesir, one Nationalist guerrilla leader was candid in outlining his expectations of the region's inhabitants. 'To give animals to the enemy', he declared, 'is to take up arms against our army'. If local communities did have animals to spare, their choices were clear: hide them in the mountains or kill them. Those who handed their livestock over to Greeks, willingly or not, faced execution at his hands.[77]

What drew the greatest amount of Nationalist ire was Muslims who volunteered to serve as armed auxiliaries. On the heels of Ahmet Anzavur's failed campaign against the Nationalists in the summer of 1920, hundreds of Circassians flocked to join paramilitary bands sanctioned by the Greek authorities. Many of these former rebels seized this opportunity to exact revenge upon the National Forces. When Greek troops retreated west after the Battle of İnönü, Circassian militiamen were accused alongside local Greeks and Armenians of massacring Muslim civilians en masse. The most unsettling blow delivered by Anzavur's former supporters came in late 1921. In November, a congress comprising twenty-two Circassian representatives assembled under Greek protection in Izmir. The group, which called itself the

'Association for the Strengthening of Near Eastern Circassian Rights', issued a statement declaring it was the desire of all Ottoman Circassians 'to live as an element of peace under Greek protection'.[78] Esteemed members of Istanbul's Circassian aristocracy, as well as the Nationalist press, derided the declaration and swore that those 'who were tools of Greek designs' were representative of only a small handful of deviants.[79] The Izmir congress, nonetheless, forced Ankara again to publicly defend its contention that the Nationalists represented the popular will of all Muslims. The fact that some Muslims appealed to Greece for protection fundamentally undermined this claim.

Displays of defiance among Kurds during this time placed the Nationalist camp in an even greater bind. By 1921, Mustafa Kemal boasted the support of a number of Kurdish representatives in Ankara. However, in the countryside, he contended with tribes and local leaders who resisted rule from Ankara. One group that particularly troubled the Defense of Rights Association was the sizable Milli tribe. At the turn of the century, the Milli had lorded it over large portions of the flatlands between Urfa and Aleppo. The onset of Young Turk rule, however, broke their grip over the region, leading to lasting bitterness within the tribe. With the Allied occupation of their historic lands, several noted leaders of the Milli threw their lot in with the French and British. Shortly before the conclusion of peace between French and Nationalist fighters in 1921, Mustafa Kemal personally ordered local authorities to banish the Milli from the region altogether. Some members of the tribe were eventually exiled to Thrace and never allowed to return.

An even more profound display of Kurdish defiance occurred in Dersim. Unlike the case of the Milli, Dersim's lurch towards insurrection was rooted in an attempt to fan nationalist outrage among local Kurds. Since 1919, the Society for the Advancement of Kurdistan had continued to make inroads among leaders residing along Dersim's western fringe. As an area still recovering from Russia's occupation during the Great War, fear of foreign troops remained high. Agitators ingratiated themselves through appeals to local desires for greater political autonomy. In light of the Armenian deportations and massacres of 1915, the power and capriciousness of the Ottoman government loomed in the minds of many Kurds who supported calls for independence. At first,

Ankara hoped to counter such activism diplomatically, leading to the appointment of local tribal leaders to positions of official authority. Agitation for outright Kurdish statehood, however, persisted. In the spring of 1921, bands of armed men stormed the small town of Imranlı, killing a Nationalist cavalry commander. The attack prompted Ankara to respond punitively. Through the summer of 1921, a contingent of regular soldiers and provincial volunteers rampaged through Dersim. As with the Milli, the tribe most responsible for the unrest – the Koçgiri – was summarily exiled from its lands. Yet unlike the Nationalist crackdown outside Urfa, the conduct of the troops in Dersim drew the indignation of lawmakers in the National Assembly. Representatives from neighboring districts took to the floor to denounce the Nationalist commander, Nurettin Pasha, as a butcher. Innocent villagers, one speaker declared, had reported incidents of rape, as well as acts of murder, theft and arson, as a result of the offensive. Such behavior by Nurettin's men was, in his words, 'on a level not acceptable among the barbarians of Africa'.[80] Assembly members, however, shrugged at calls for an official investigation or reprimand. What the people of Dersim needed most, Ankara's Interior Ministry recommended, was bureaucratic and social reform.

Ankara's suppression of Kurdish rebels gleaned relatively little international attention. In Dersim and in Urfa, virtually no outside observers bore witness to acts of collective punishment endured by local Kurds. This was far less the case when it came to events along the Black Sea coast. Since the earliest days of the armistice, communities in the Black Sea interior were subject to intermittent bouts of fighting. Newspapers in Istanbul and Ankara regularly accused the region's native Greeks as the prime instigators of violence. One official study dedicated to 'internal uprisings' during the National Struggle later claimed that attacks by Greek militants in the area resulted in more than 1,600 Muslim deaths and the destruction of more than 3,700 homes.[81] As in other parts of Anatolia, Nationalists associated each atrocity with the broader threat of Greek irredentism. Local agitators, after all, had publicly lobbied for a separate Greek state extending along the Black Sea littoral. However, Greek Prime Minister Venizelos, as well as other Allied leaders, refused to back the establishment of a 'Republic of Pontus', insisting, among other things, that the region was too remote to be genuinely defensible. The signing of the Treaty of Sèvres, which made no reference to a potential Greek republic on the Black Sea, still did little to allay Ankara's fears. With Nationalist troops struggling to hold their ground in western Anatolia, commanders dispatched reinforcements north to crush the Pontic movement once and for all. In June 1921, the National Assembly sanctioned the use of mass deportation to punish all those guilty of insurrection. American missionaries throughout the region looked on in horror as thousands of men, women and children were expelled from villages and towns. Many who witnessed the 1921 deportations perceived similarities with what had happened in 1915. Men were separated from their families and shot, women and girls were raped, and homes were plundered or appropriated under the watchful eye of local officials. According to an American doctor who cared for refugees in Harput, local officials he spoke with 'were frank in their statements that it was the intention to have all the Greeks die'. In his opinion, the fact that Nationalist troops drove sick and starving refugees to poor, desolate places without any access to doctors 'seemed to fully bear this statement out'.[82]

By the end of 1921, Nationalist sources took pride in recording the heavy toll inflicted upon supposed rebels in the Black Sea region. One official study estimated that 3,400 Greek separatists were killed in clashes with Nationalist troops. More than 200 others were tried and condemned to death by hanging. According to Ankara, more than 64,000 civilians in total were forcibly removed and resettled in the Anatolian interior.[83] Reports printed in Western newspapers tended to paint an even bleaker picture. The commanders of the offensive, Nurettin Pasha and Topal Osman, became synonymous with wanton acts of murder and arson. The thievery and bloodlust of their men reinforced the belief that Ottoman Muslims were prone to such behavior. However, at least some in the Western press found cause to see the deportations in a more cynical light. There was no doubt, as one correspondent for the *Times* of London reported, that Topal Osman 'was given a free hand to deal with Greek and Armenian villages' and that his men had 'looted and massacred freely'. However, considering the region's separatist proclivities, it also appeared clear that 'the Greeks, both of the Pontus and of the Greek Kingdom', were in part to blame for what had befallen them.[84] The harshness of this judgment to a large extent reflected the extent to which foreign observers had grown disillusioned with Greece's adventurism in Anatolia. By early 1922, reports of Greek abuses in western Anatolia, particularly those around Bursa, had done irreparable harm to Athens's credibility.

In mid-July 1921, Greece again resumed the offensive. Having gathered more troops and supplies from the Greek mainland, Athens committed over 200,000 men for one massive push towards Ankara. This decision to attack, in hindsight, accompanied the recognition of Greece's tenuous standing. By then, the Allies had abandoned any pretense of unity on the question of Anatolia's future. No other state, not even Britain, stood prepared to intervene should Athens fail to land a decisive blow. As Greek troops moved forward, many in the press noted the physical challenges that beset any assault on the Nationalist stronghold. 'The fighting is carried on in difficult mountainous country', one editor observed, 'broken by occasional river valleys, large or small, which are almost the only means of communication'.[85] Nevertheless, Greece's July offensive bore almost immediate signs of success. Before the end of August, Greek forces took the towns of Eskişehir, Kütahya and Afyon. Having barely escaped encirclement, outnumbered Nationalist troops withdrew deeper into the interior. A long defensive line was eventually carved out along the eastern bank of the Sakarya River, less than 100 kilometers from Ankara. All signs suggested that Greek troops were beginning to envelop Nationalist positions and were laying plans for one last general assault.

It is possible that Mustafa Kemal failed to appreciate the dangers initially posed by the Greek offensive. In the midst of the Nationalist retreat from Kütahya and Eskişehir, he presided over a convention made up of provincial teachers drawn from throughout Anatolia. *National Sovereignty*, Ankara's foremost newspaper, held up the conference as evidence of the nation fighting two wars simultaneously. 'While the army of liberation and independence is fighting the Greeks on [different] fronts, the army of teachers in Ankara is preparing a defensive program against ignorance'.[86] In the last week of July, however, Mustafa Kemal assumed more direct control over military affairs. He ordered military authorities to mobilize greater swathes of the population and requisitioned huge reserves of food and livestock. Rather than re-establish the Nationalist government to the southeast in

Kayseri, he consented to keeping the National Assembly in Ankara as a sign of faith and defiance. The parliament reciprocated in early August, voting overwhelmingly in favor of proclaiming Kemal 'commander-in-chief' of the armed forces. In practical terms, the move allowed him greater latitude over taking command at the front (despite having resigned his commission two years earlier). Politically, however, it was yet another sign of the changing climate in Ankara. Under the old constitution, the sultan alone enjoyed the title of 'commander-in-chief'. Though legally only provisional, Kemal's newly assigned rank again underscored Istanbul's marginality at this crucial time.

The Battle of Sakarya, as it came to be known, raged for three long weeks. Despite the Greeks' superior numbers, they labored mightily in pressing forward. Amid rough terrain and sweltering heat, entrenched Nationalist troops withstood Greek advances at various points. In early September, however, Kemal's men were forced to abandon their positions along a crucial ridge at the very center of the Nationalist defenses. Kemal, according to many of his confidants, wavered between despair, indecision and bravado as conditions worsened. Kazım Karabekir, his staunchest critic, later suggested that Kemal's closest aides purposely delayed executing his plans for a general retreat. Regardless, Greek forces did not follow through on their important gains. After days of hard fighting, the assault was paused by Greek commanders to allow the men to rest. The tide of the battle soon shifted. The loss of momentum, as well as dwindling amounts of supplies and reserves, forced the Greeks to cede their hard-earned ground. By the middle of September, Greek troops pulled back entirely from the front and retreated westward from the Sakarya River. At the cost of 23,000 dead and wounded, the Nationalists held the field and prevented Ankara's fall. The Greeks suffered similarly heavy casualties; they would never stage another advance.[87]

Nationalists celebrated the victory at Sakarya with pomp and solemnity. Citizens in Ankara came out in droves to welcome Mustafa Kemal back to the city. After Friday prayers, prominent members of the National Assembly recited poetry and read speeches before the faithful. As the representative of the first state to recognize the Ankara government, Afghan Ambassador Ahmet Han spoke at length, declaring Sakarya a victory that 'illuminated the hearts of Muslims with the lights of joy'.[88] For his achievement, the National Assembly awarded Kemal with a rare honor: the title of *gazi*. Historically, *gazi* had been an appellation reserved for esteemed warriors who had fought to expand the territorial boundaries of Islam. In more recent times, the title had been bestowed on a very select few who had led the Ottoman Empire to victory. Mustafa Kemal accepted this distinction with grace and modesty. In a speech before the Assembly, he narrated the course of the battle that had transpired between İnönü and Sakarya. He paid homage to the fortitude and bravery of the army, attributing the victory to their heroism. In looking to the future, he emphasized that the war was not yet won. Earlier the government was forced to leave 'rich lands like Iraq and Syria'. The people of those lands were now 'repeatedly in a state of revolt' and desirous 'with all their hearts and conscience to be again under our administration'. The same could not be said of Christians, who 'showed ingratitude to the land that fed them and harmed and violated our national existence'. Through he swore that no harm would come to Christians living under Ottoman rule, he asserted that any end to the fighting depended upon Athens. It now appeared clear that the Greeks were giving way. Europe, he declared, had denounced Greece's atrocities, which he likened to the 'old invasionist barbarity' of the Crusaders. 'But, gentlemen', he avowed, 'God has helped us ... And the Greek army has turned back in the face of the Army of the Grand National Assembly of Turkey'.[89]

Kemal was certainly correct in one particular regard. Sakarya drained much of what remained of Europe's support for Greece. Normally bullish observers increasingly cast doubt upon a lasting Greek victory. With the fall of 1921, foreign interest in Ottoman affairs drifted away as the fighting died down. The likelihood of a revised settlement appeared imminent and there was little denying that Ankara would take the lead in securing a final peace. This realization slowly brought about a slight, but relatively profound, change in the way many commentators spoke about the crisis. The term 'new Turkey' had been part of European parlance since the early stages of the Young Turk Revolution. It was originally meant to convey a new spirit aimed at revitalizing the Ottoman Empire. By the beginning of 1922, foreign observers perceived a very different 'new Turkey' taking shape. As one French onlooker saw it, the National Pact, as it was declared in 1920, 'was the birth certificate of the new Turkey', signifying the complete reorganization of the country.[90] The Nationalist government abetted these impressions. Prominent activists, particularly those associated with the Turkish Hearth, nurtured the idea that Ankara embodied this spirit of change. The town, as one French journalist put it, 'powerfully synthesized [the Nationalist] state of mind'. Its unforgiving climate and stark beauty typified Anatolia's natural character. It also mirrored the discipline and urgency of the Nationalist cause. 'Here [there was] no indulgence, no loitering dilettantism: a hard, ruthless rule for everyone'.[91] After Sakarya, it seemed certain that Ankara represented the country's future.

Few close to Mustafa Kemal, however, spoke with certitude as to what precisely was to come. Yet as Nationalist troops laid preparations for a grand offensive to retake western Anatolia, some local commentators voiced opinions that were previously too taboo for print. 'The Sultan is a crown without a head', one Ankara newspaper declared, 'but Anatolia is a free country without a crown. In the lamp of the Grand Porte the oil is running out, but in Anatolia the new sun is rising'. A correspondent from Moscow's *Izvestia* was more blunt. 'Let us hope', he wrote, 'that the new Turkey will soon obtain the incarnation of its national desire, and, entering Constantinople, will crush, and annihilate, without the possibility of revival, the mummy of the Sultanate'.[92]

6

'A New Kind of Turk'

The Ottoman Empire's Final Days

As late as 1922, the pretense of Ottoman rule persisted in the city of Izmir. Istanbul had continued to exercise the right of appointing governors and other administrative posts. A local city council still ran many of the town's basic services. The education of Muslim children remained in the hands of Ottoman officials and local volunteers. Imperial law courts still heard cases dealing with inheritance or other personal claims. Few would deny, of course, that true power resided among the representatives sent from Greece. In most matters, their authority all but negated Istanbul's influence. The Greek high commissioner in Izmir ranked as the most powerful man in town and in the province at large. Many of the salaries paid to officials, including those of Ottoman functionaries, came from Athens. Above all, Greek officials held fast to the belief that Izmir's incorporation into a greater Greece was just a matter of time. Still, a façade of tolerance and shared prosperity masked much of the administration's work. In their day-to-day affairs, officials seldom spoke of annexation. Athens's attempts at soothing the fears of local Muslims often came at the price of angering prominent Greeks in the town. Smyrna's Orthodox archbishop, Chrysostomos, fell foul of local authorities after he was chided for his nationalist sermons. Greece's hold over the region, as one official put it, 'will depend on the impartiality of our administration and our strong defence of the rights of the minorities', assuming these to be Muslims. They had to resist their general inclination to 'avenge our suffering at the hands of the Turks for five centuries', since, he explained, 'we are carriers of a higher civilization'.[1]

Other facets of local life went on in spite of the political uncertainties on the horizon. Izmir remained a vibrant city dotted with coffee houses and theaters. Despite lingering hardships brought on by the war, the town still retained an impressive collection of cinemas and venues for live music. Late in the Greek occupation, filmgoers were still able to see movies imported from Italy, France or the United States. Contemporary politics did little to deter those who simply sought to stroll along the promenade by the harbor. Above all, Izmir remained a city where Muslims, Christians and Jews mingled together, albeit at times delicately.

Greek rule, however, did little to ease the hardships suffered by most citizens. Since the outbreak of war in 1914, trade into the city had slowed significantly. As the flow of goods into Smyrna's harbor continued to ebb, shortages of basic necessities plagued daily life. 'Before the war', one American observed in 1920, 'it is probable that few cities in the world were better supplied with food, and the food was sold at a low price. This is unhappily no longer true. Food is relatively scarce. Prices have advanced fifteen to thirty fold'.[2] Poverty and disease grew rampant as the city's economic prospects dampened. Those hit hardest were often found among the tens of thousands of refugees who lived in Izmir and its environs. Displaced Muslims and Christians tended to live in squalor, with multiple families packed into small, often ramshackle dwellings. By the end of 1921, one long-time British resident complained of a general collapse of good order and cleanliness. 'Since the Greek occupation the streets of Smyrna have reached a degree of dilapidation worse than at any time during the Turkish *régime*'. All the roads were bad, he observed, though some were made worse due to open drains. Even streetlights were no longer being lit due to the unwillingness of the Greek authorities to renew their agreement with the local gas company. 'The future of Smyrna under Greek rule', he concluded, 'does not look a rosy one'.[3]

Of course, no one in Ankara needed to be told of the Greek occupation and its many ills. To mark the third anniversary of Izmir's occupation, members of the Grand National Assembly issued a proclamation reiterating the country's sovereign right to the territory. 'There is not a Turk', it was declared, 'who accepts sacred Izmir's wailing under the usurpation and oppression of a brutal nation which has disgraced civilization like Greece'. One speaker went further in casting blame for the city's suffering. 'The debauched [*kahpe*] palace' – including, presumably, the sultan – was also responsible for the injustices wrought by the Greeks.[4] Members of the press tended to agree. The editor of *İkdam* falsely accused Damad Ferid, as well as Izmir's appointed governor, of having been forewarned of Greece's plans to take the city in May 1919.[5] Such accusations, however, were little debated in the Ankara or Istanbul press. After the Nationalist victory at Sakarya, it appeared to many that the Istanbul government had been on the wrong side of history.

Mustafa Kemal's triumph at Sakarya led to more visible doubts in Greece as well. A change in the command of the Greek forces in Anatolia did little to inspire enthusiasm for a renewed offensive. Internally, senior officers understood that the army's prospects were dim. Greece lacked the materiel and the means to maintain the deployment of troops over such rough and extensive terrain. Financially, the campaign was bankrupting the country, leading to widespread disillusionment among war-weary voters. Worse still, Greece's defeat at Sakarya widened political rifts in Athens. The persistent divide between supporters of the king and those of former Prime Minister Venizelos ate away at the government's legitimacy. Partisan tensions extended to the ranks of the military. As 1922 began, senior leaders confronted the possible splintering of the army, with rival factions supporting alternative plans for peace in Asia Minor. Even the election of a new Orthodox patriarch in December 1921 did little to heal the political divisions among Greeks in Anatolia or on the mainland. 'It is certain', Patriarch Meletios wrote in April, 'that all of us here [in Constantinople] and in Smyrna and in Athens are struggling in the dark and hitting out at friends and enemies without any definite aim any more'. All consensus appeared gone.[6]

Developments on the diplomatic front added to this shared sense of gloom. As Greece's sole champion among the Allies, Britain also wrestled with what appeared to be a losing struggle against the Nationalists. In the absence of a military solution, Lloyd George and his cabinet agreed that only diplomacy could salvage what remained of British and Greek interests in Anatolia. Discord at home, as well as pressures abroad, left London – like Athens – with few options. The signing of an agreement with Irish rebels in December 1921, followed by the declaration of Egyptian independence a few months later, signaled a broader exhaustion with the country's imperial woes. In March 1922, the Secretary of State for India, Edwin Montagu, was forced to resign due to his vocal opposition to the Treaty of Sèvres. Having long argued against the imposition of a harsh peace, Montagu publicly backed the criticism offered by Muslim Indian leaders in the Khilafat movement. 'Turkey was beaten [during the Great War] in the main by Indian soldiers', he told Parliament. India was therefore 'entitled to a predominant voice in the consideration of such questions'.[7]

The constraints facing Britain and Greece were fully exposed during a meeting of Allied Foreign Ministers in March 1922. With the Treaty of Sèvres appearing more dead than ever, virtually all in attendance agreed that a new compromise was needed if there was to be an end to the fighting. Yet unlike earlier gatherings, there was little doubt that it was Greece that needed to make the hardest concessions. Athens, it was proposed, would be allowed to retain some of the territory it had seized since 1919. Yet the powers agreed that the Greek army would eventually have to be withdrawn from Anatolia. This apparent display of Allied pessimism heartened Nationalist representatives and inspired them to bide their time. Ankara confidently rejected calls for an armistice, demanding instead that Greece vacate all occupied lands immediately.

With no resolution immediately in sight, leaders in both Greece and Smyrna grew desperate. In midsummer, news of Greek troop movements in Thrace sparked fears that Athens was planning to move on Istanbul. Tensions soared at the end of July when representatives from Athens openly declared their belief that a Greek takeover of the Ottoman capital was 'the only means of ending the war with Turkey'.[8] With Ankara threatening to counter Greece's provocations, British and French officials emphatically stated that they too stood prepared to meet any Greek offensive with force. As Greece demurred from pressing ahead with its attack, representatives in Smyrna took dramatic steps. For months, a group calling itself the 'Asia Minor Defense Organization' had declared its desire to defy Athens and form an autonomous state governed from the city. As a Greek military withdrawal from Anatolia appeared more likely, the government in Athens came to terms with Smyrna's elite and agreed upon a general reorganization of the territory. In late July, Greece's high commissioner in the city, Aristeides Stergiades, announced plans to designate the town and its surrounding provinces a separate state. Greece, he vowed, would never annex the territory. Instead, power would be shared among representatives of each of the region's diverse peoples. Stergiades' personal appeals were reciprocated by a handful of local Muslim leaders. The Muslim mayor of one nearby town issued his 'most profound thanks' to the Greek commissioner. Stergiades, he affirmed, 'did not deprive all the people and Muslims of his fatherly and compassionate grace and good deeds'. The new regime, he concluded, would eventually lead to a new era of freedom.[9]

All hope for a greater Greece in Asia Minor ended in August 1922. After months of amassing men and supplies, Nationalist troops launched their long-awaited counteroffensive against Greek positions east of Afyon. Advancing columns met with almost immediate success. Efforts at a controlled Greek withdrawal westward soon gave way to a general rout all along the front. By the first week of September, entire Greek divisions dissolved into mobs as they streamed towards the Aegean. In the chaos, fleeing troops ransacked and torched whole towns and villages. The devastation Nationalists discovered along the way shocked many of the most hardened officers. 'On the day of the occupation of Uşak', one remembered, 'some of our women were found nailed to the ground from various parts of their bodies after being raped, and, for a few days, Uşak's streets shook from the screams of the village women, who were severely deprived in the surrounding villages and exposed to all kinds of evils'.[10] Officials in Ankara never tabulated the final death toll wrought by the Greek retreat. The scale of the destruction, however, was unmistakable. Of the 286 buildings registered in İznik, a town built upon the ancient ruins of Nicaea, only thirty-three were reported as undamaged.[11] A host of other towns, as well as scores of villages, were leveled in the ensuing Greek flight. It would take years for many provinces to fully recover from the physical costs of the retreat.

Long before the Nationalist breakthrough, Allied observers expected that a Greek withdrawal from Anatolia would lead to a human catastrophe. In May 1922, the British high commissioner in Istanbul, Horace Rumbold, warned his superiors that the end of the

Greek occupation would likely result in a tidal wave of refugees. According to his calculations, at least 60,000 native Christians and Muslims had served the Greek administration. Given the precedent of France's withdrawal from Cilicia a year earlier, it was likely that they – as well as hundreds of thousands of others – would vacate their homes en masse at the first sign of a Nationalist breakthrough.[12] Rumbold's prediction proved correct. News of the Greek rout set off an immediate panic through western Anatolia. As Nationalist detachments inched towards the Aegean, tens of thousands took flight by all means available. Towns and villages became the scenes of bloody acts of retribution. When Nationalist detachments took the port of Foça, captured Greek troops were bayoneted or drowned before crowds of local onlookers. 'Oh son', one older woman called out, 'why are you doing this?' 'Do you know what they have done?' one Nationalist soldier replied. 'They killed our pregnant women in Manisa, ripped their bellies apart, bayoneted their children and played with their bodies'. Nothing like that, however, had happened in Foça.[13]

Senior Greek leaders had initially hoped to hold Smyrna at all costs. As the vanguard of Mustafa Kemal's army approached, Athens had dispatched ships carrying reinforcements to the city. Once they arrived, soldiers aboard revolted and refused to disembark. In the face of what they presumed was annihilation, the garrison – along with the Greek high commissioner – sailed off before Nationalist cavalry entered from the east. An orgy of violence and looting immediately ensued after Izmir's capture. Terror-stricken residents swarmed the harbor by the thousands as fears of a massacre gripped the town. Meanwhile, riotous soldiers and residents ransacked homes and businesses. Overseeing the bedlam was Nurettin Pasha, the same commander who had directed the bloody Nationalist campaigns in Dersim and along the Black Sea. As the newly appointed governor of the province, the general summoned the town's Orthodox archbishop, Chrysostomos, to appear before him. After berating the prelate for his acts of treason against the state, Nurettin handed him over to a mob. Chrysostomos was tortured, torn limb from limb and his remains dragged through the street.

Events in Izmir reached their bloody climax in the week that followed Chrysostomos' murder. On the night of 13 September, a fire broke out in the town's Armenian quarter. High winds and arsonists helped drive the conflagration towards other non-Muslim neighborhoods. The fire intensified the evacuation of local Christians and heaped even greater dangers upon fleeing refugees. 'That first night of the fire', one survivor remembered, 'the buildings along the shore, the luxurious cafés, the theater, were burning and the people were lined up, up and down the shore. The broken glass and the hot nails were bursting and scattered all around us, so we had to wet blankets in the water and put them on our shoulders to prevent us from burning'.[14] The blaze eventually consumed 75 percent of the city's core and left thousands dead.[15] Despite making no immediate effort to put out the fire, Nationalist administrators placed the blame squarely upon fleeing Greek soldiers and native Christians. A slew of local witnesses and foreign observers later professed to seeing Nationalist troops deliberately setting the blaze.

Much of what the fire destroyed would never be replaced or restored. In the decade that followed the Greek departure, the remnants of Izmir's old Armenian and Greek quarters were flattened and transformed into parkland. The monuments and landmarks of this new 'culture park' bore no reference to the past or its former non-Muslim residents. Those who rebuilt the city after 1922 instead hoped Izmir would embody the ethos of the young Turkish Republic. In principle, nostalgia for the Ottoman Empire was given little place in the revived city. For his part, Mustafa Kemal was purportedly ambivalent as to what was lost during the fire. At the start of the blaze, he had taken up residence in the city at the home of his future wife, Latife. During the first nights of the disaster, he asked if she stood to lose any property. Yes, she replied, but such a loss was acceptable. 'What is the value of property for people who see these happy days? The country has been saved. We will rebuild again and make it perfect'. Kemal was pleased with this response. 'Yes! Let it burn and crash down', he declared. 'The restoration of everything is possible'.[16]

More fundamental tensions influenced how others saw the legacy of the Izmir fire. After years of reflection, Kemal's stenographer, Falih Rıfkı, offered his own views. Turks, he argued, could no longer stomach the sight of the old city. Its 'waterfront mansions, hotels and restaurants' were the trappings of 'the minorities', as he put it, the

Greeks and Armenians. It was this aversion to their presence, and not some primal urge to destroy, that had also led to the Armenian deportations of 1915. 'A feeling of inferiority had a part in it', he argued. Nonetheless, Falih disapproved of the city's destruction and labeled Nurettin Pasha a 'fanatic and a rabble-rousing demagogue' for having inspired the violence that overcame the town.[17] Yet neither Falih nor others who established the Republic of Turkey lamented the cultural impact of Izmir's sacking. With the fire, the country came closer to becoming a nation that belonged solely to the Turks. He, along with Atatürk, would see to it that the diversity that had flourished under the sultans would be minimized or eradicated altogether.

For others who witnessed the events of 1922, it was hard not to see the fire that swept through Izmir as a defining point of rupture. The sheer extremity of the violence appeared to undermine any suggestion that the old order was worth preserving. In the near term, it gave credence to those who demanded that a genuinely 'new Turkey' take root. For many, moving forward meant more than simply disestablishing the Ottoman monarchy. The empire's culture, as well its history, was subject to repudiation and demolition. The times, in many ways, seemed to warrant such steps. A newer, more ideologically polarized age was taking shape in Europe and Asia. Reconstruction or modernization efforts across the world appeared to validate movements intent upon creating purer 'national' cultures grounded in race and ethnicity. Generally speaking, the global political climate tended to favor those who looked forward to a more utopian future. The fall of the Ottoman sultans only reinforced what many assumed was true in 1918: the era of time-honored dynasties was giving way to more popular, rational and authentic states and societies.

Expunging the last vestiges of the Ottoman Empire proved more difficult than many initially believed. Within Turkey, the regime of Mustafa Kemal struggled to do away with institutions associated with the old empire. Despite an official culture that tended to demean all things associated with the Ottoman past, admiration for imperial history proved resilient. Ironically, defining and enforcing a strict sense of Turkish national identity was often beset by ambiguities and resistance. In Turkey, as well as in other states, traits and identities born out of the Ottoman experience managed to survive among various communities. A century on, what the Ottoman Empire and its fall symbolize remains hotly contested.

'LET IT BURN AND CRASH DOWN': THE DISSOLUTION OF THE EMPIRE

Throughout his life, Ali Kemal wavered between principle and self-preservation. He prided himself on being an ardent liberal who was appreciative of European culture and ideas. He cultivated a particular affection for Britain, where he had lived during a period of exile. Though he was among the earliest to associate with the CUP, he grew to loathe the Young Turks and their politics. Ironically, his aversion towards the party's repressive inclinations led him to make common cause with the Ottoman royal family. Despite his earlier opposition to Abdül-hamid II, he eventually reconciled with the sultan and served as his ambassador to Belgium. His opponents accused him of hypocrisy and of acting as a paid informant on the behalf of the palace.

Like his compatriot Damad Ferid, Ali Kemal took full advantage of the changes that swept the Ottoman capital in late 1918. He quickly ingratiated himself with representatives from Great Britain, which he believed was the only power trustworthy enough to deliver an acceptable peace. The ascendancy of Damad Ferid and other former dissidents allowed him greater access to like-minded men in positions of authority. Above all, the collapse of the CUP rekindled Kemal's career as a journalist and provocateur. As the editor of *Peyam-ı Sabah* (or *News of the Morning*), he wrote frequent columns denouncing the many crimes of the Young Turk regime, including the Armenian deportations. He consistently defended the right of the sultan to rule as well as the continued importance of Ottomanism. Ottoman nationalism, he once wrote, was critical for 'fastening various elements', such as Arabs and Kurds, to the development and elevation of the nation.[18] Even after the apparent loss of much of Kurdistan and Arabia, he remained an advocate of Ottoman unity and identity.

Neither Greece's invasion, nor the rise of the National Forces, altered Ali Kemal's loyalties. In the wake of Izmir's capture in 1919, he accrued a reputation as the National Movement's most outspoken adversary. He regularly attacked Mustafa Kemal, calling him a brute and a rebel who had weakened the Ottoman state in the face of the Greek invasion. Ankara's defiance, he wrote, 'destroyed our relations with the Allies' and 'caused the terms of our peace agreements to be even heavier for us'.[19] Though his jabs aged poorly, he remained steadfast in his belief that the country could not afford a Nationalist victory. As late as August 1922, he continued to remind his readers of the crimes the CUP had committed during the Great War. 'The National Forces', he asserted, showed 'the same shortsightedness, the same negligence, with the same motives'.[20]

Those who were familiar with the political climate in Istanbul suggested that Ali Kemal's views resonated among elements of the imperial administration. Many former anti-CUP dissidents could not let go of the fact that Mustafa Kemal's movement was populated by former Young Turks. The many crimes of the Young Turks' regime, as well as the prospects of their revenge, outweighed any benefits that came with a Nationalist victory over the Greeks. It is difficult to say, however, how widespread such opinions were. It is very possible that the victory at Sakarya helped compensate for at least some of the sins associated with the National Forces. After all, the state's liberation appeared within reach and it had been a long time since the country stood on the threshold of winning a war. It therefore was hard to deny that the future belonged to Ankara. At least a handful of former CUP opponents were willing to embrace the likelihood of such a result. 'In the happiest time of the country', one long-time activist warned, 'we are coming out as if we were naked ... escaping from a fire because of these bastard [Nationalists]'.[21] Placing one's faith in Great Britain or the Allies was no longer wise or acceptable.

A different kind of soul-searching prevailed among commentators in Ankara. As Mustafa Kemal's army prepared for its grand assault, the Ankara press featured a stream of articles meditating upon the significance and implications of the impending triumph. One of the most prolific figures to write during this period was the young parliamentarian Mahmud Esad, who possessed deep links to the Turkish Hearth. In the months that followed Sakarya, many of his editorials pondered the National Movement's place in history. The approaching Nationalist offensive appeared to give further weight to his contention that the nation had reached a moment of transition akin to the French Revolution. What the world was witnessing in Anatolia, he argued, was a popular movement dedicated to both liberating the nation and ending the oppression of the Ottoman *ancien régime*. As in eighteenth-century France, the peasantry was the chief protagonist in this struggle. For Esad, the sultan had never ruled with Anatolia's interests at heart. Instead, through the centuries, the Ottoman state had exploited the labors and loyalties of Anatolia's peasantry while growing ever more corrupt and decrepit. The state's inherent backwardness, he reckoned, had long made the Anatolian peasant 'the saddest, most oppressed figure in Ottoman history'.[22] The horrors experienced since the 1918 armistice proved that the empire could neither be saved nor redeemed. Behind every tragic turn since the Great War, there was, in his words, 'a palace that smiles and cackles' at the disasters and mourning of the nation.[23]

Esad's harsh rendering of Ottoman history clashed markedly with earlier writings associated with the Turkish Hearth. Members of the group had long been critical of how Ottoman reformers went about attempting to save the empire. Ottoman nationalism, they generally agreed, was fatally flawed as a framework for citizenship and identity. The Ottoman state, however, was conceived of as a venerable institution, one that could be saved if it embraced its Turkic origins. The editorials Esad and other Nationalists published during this period marked a dramatic shift away from this consensus. While it is never stated explicitly, Sakarya gave Nationalists greater license to reimagine both the past and the future without deference to the sultan or the empire. There was no longer any incentive to celebrate the 600 years of Ottoman history as a testament to the empire's durability or legitimacy. After all, global trends seemed to suggest that a change of regime was overdue. 'Kicking out the putrid, murderous spirit of the Sublime Porte and the Palace', as another ideologue put it, would allow a more robust culture of reform to take flight.[24] The establishment of a genuinely 'new Turkey', in other words, was the realization of a country that was fundamentally closer to the Hearth's ideals.

Mustafa Kemal was not as forthright in expressing his views on current affairs. In the interviews he gave throughout much of 1922, he portrayed himself as someone who had always been out of step with both the CUP and the palace. Yes, he had been a loyal soldier, but he had not always agreed with the way the country was governed. He was now certain that 'populism' would be at the core of state policy. 'I believe that in the twentieth century', he told one French reporter, 'there is no longer a single man who can imagine that peoples are herds which some people drive before them with sticks'. Beyond that, both publicly and privately, he would say no more about what was to be done with the sultan. 'As to the future of Constantinople', he demurred, 'this is one of those purely internal questions and, like all the others of the same order, it will be settled by the government of the Grand National Assembly of Turkey'.[25]

How the broader public viewed the past, present and future of the empire remains far more elusive. After Sakarya, the possibility of radical political change did not yet lead to immediate shifts in day-to-day life. When one Ankara-appointed governor visited a school in rural Konya, young students were prompted to greet him with three cheers of 'long live the sultan'. This was one example, he later wrote, of the 'trouble we suffered internally because we were acting against the sultan'.[26] Meanwhile, activities around the palace retained an air of normalcy. Young princes and others close to the royal family still enjoyed 'a great many concerts and performances' during much of 1922.[27] Mehmed VI continued to impose himself upon matters of state, including issues of petty importance. In June, he went out of his way to wield his authority as caliph in rebuking women in Istanbul for tarnishing 'the reputation of the virtuous majority' by 'consorting with alien males in public and private places'.[28] If one had to pinpoint a more obvious shift in popular culture, it was that increasing numbers of people, particularly Muslims, no longer spoke of themselves as Ottomans. Print media, even outside Ankara, now almost uniformly referred to the country as Turkey. Journalists and editors, more often than not, referred to all Muslims as Turks, regardless of the language they spoke or their point of origin. To talk of one's identity with reference to the Ottoman royal family, let alone a 600-year-old empire, appeared ever more anachronistic.

Mustafa Kemal's looming presence both at home and internationally added to this growing sense of change and transformation. From the outset of the National Movement, he had not shied from the press.

His engagements with journalists were often self-conscious and performative. In welcoming a correspondent from Istanbul in the winter of 1922, he made a point of entertaining his guest at his hilltop manor in Ankara. Amid his marvelous collection of books and mementos, Kemal presented himself as an earnest character. 'The pasha immediately grasped the purpose of the questions with his deep understanding', the journalist remembered. 'He even read the questions that were on the tip of my tongue but were not well expressed on my face'.[29] It was during this interview that Kemal laid out the full extent of his life up to that point. He placed himself at the center of major events while emphasizing the degree to which he often parted company with the leaders of the Ottoman state. He subtly contrasted himself with Enver Pasha, who had led the empire to ruin. More importantly, he presented himself as the prime agent around whom the National Movement was conceived and constructed. The victories that had been won by 1922 were both his triumphs and also those of the men who had served under him.

Similar impressions of grandeur and destiny were made upon foreign observers as well. Sitting in the same drawing room decorated with swords and gifts from esteemed dignitaries, Kemal's controlled demeanor left one French correspondent enthralled. 'Everything in his attitude', the journalist noted, 'reflects strength, calm, self-confidence; no fuss, not a jerky, abrupt gesture ... He says exactly what he wants to say, but he says only that'.[30] With the culmination of Kemal's 1922 offensive, Western commentators tended to project his disposition upon the whole of Anatolian society. As an individual, he appeared to embody a dramatic change in the character and fortune of the country. From afar, even the editors at the conservative *Times* of London echoed the belief that Kemal represented 'a Turk of a new type', one that differed mightily from his predecessors. Unlike most personages of the Ottoman state, he was a young man honed by an 'extensive and hard education'. There was something impressive, even Arthurian, about the rise of this 'pauper of ignoble birth' to become the president of the Grand National Assembly. He did not suffer from 'the sloth of mind and body' that Westerners had long associated with Ottoman statesmen.[31] Kemal's emerging mythos as a man set apart from his peers and predecessors only grew stronger after 1922. Atatürk, as Winston Churchill later put it, was 'a Warrior Prince' born to rule.[32]

Within Ankara, however, his immediate political future remained an open question. After the Battle of Sakarya, rivals in the National Assembly labored to constrain him. Yet each effort to curtail the authority he derived from his status as the army's commander-in-chief failed miserably to garner a majority within the assembly. Nevertheless, Kemal was obliged to heed the guidance of a number of strong personalities. Power dynamics grew more complicated after Britain released several Nationalist leaders from their detention on the island of Malta. Many of these returnees, such as Kara Vasif and Rauf Orbay, ranked among the National Forces' earliest organizers. As newcomers to Ankara, they joined a sizable group of officials who were wary of Kemal's accumulation of power. For some, the reconstitution of the CUP – at least in some capacity – was preferable to the order taking shape in the Nationalist capital. One former minister was confident that there were still former Young Turks who were 'strong and honorable [and] who were free of any kind of stain' from the party's past.[33] That reckoning, however, would have to wait until the fighting was over.

For the time being, Izmir's fall in September 1922 left little doubt as to who commanded the day. In his very last editorial, even Ali Kemal applauded Mustafa Kemal's feat of arms and admitted that he had perhaps been mistaken in doubting Ankara's legitimacy. The war, however, was not completely done. British troops continued to occupy positions around the Dardanelles and the Greek army remained ensconced in eastern Thrace. There was also the question of Istanbul's status, the imperial capital having been under formal Allied control since 1920. Having succeeded in sweeping the Allies from the whole of Asia Minor, neither Mustafa Kemal nor his lieutenants stood ready to compromise. Through most of September, the specter of a wider conflict hovered over the region. Whitehall was adamant that Britain would not back down in the face of the Nationalist threat to Istanbul and the Dardanelles. Control over the waterway that divided Europe and Asia, in the words of Winston Churchill, was of 'great moral significance to the prestige of the Empire'.[34] Yet again, divisions within Lloyd George's cabinet and disagreements among the Allies undermined London's resolve. Having curried favor in Ankara, Paris feared that a joint Allied effort to hold the Turkish Straits would undermine France's relationship with Ankara. A fight over the Straits also carried the risk of igniting hostilities with the Bolsheviks, Ankara's ally. 'Moslem upheaval in Asia', the French Foreign Minister warned, also appeared likely if a peaceful resolution could not be found.[35] The British public, as well as leaders in the Dominion states, tended to agree. In the face of increased isolation and dissent, Lloyd George's government begrudgingly relented. The 'Chanak Affair', as it came to be called, ended with an agreement to begin discussions of a ceasefire. In exchange, London consented to a wider Allied withdrawal from the Straits, Istanbul and eastern Thrace.

The implications this reversal had for the British Empire and world politics were immediately overshadowed by the uncertainties that accompanied the transfer of these territories. While British, French and Italian representatives discussed the terms of an armistice with Nationalist negotiators, an officers' revolt overthrew Greece's King Constantine. The possibility of armed clashes lingered as both sides attempted to strike a hard bargain. Yet, after an early refusal to relinquish their nation's gains in Thrace, Greek representatives also succumbed to Nationalist pressures and signed up to the Allied armistice. The ceasefire reached at Mudanya on 11 October stirred a second mass exodus, this time from across Greek-occupied Thrace. As hundreds of thousands of Armenians and Greeks packed up what they could carry, residents in Istanbul waited anxiously upon the arrival of Nationalist troops. When Ankara dispatched a contingent of newly mustered gendarmes on 19 October, throngs of well-wishers lined the European shores of the capital. Unlike the masses who watched the Allied fleet sail into the harbor almost four years earlier, most who turned out that day were local Muslims. Whole families waving scarlet Ottoman flags thronged the streets as the Nationalist delegation toured the predominately Muslim quarters of the historic city center. Among the songs that rang out that day was the recently dubbed 'Izmir March', a tune originally penned in celebration of the 1918 Ottoman invasion of the Caucasus.[36] Senior members of the imperial government also turned out to greet the arrival of Refet Pasha, Ankara's chief representative. Their gesture of welcome, however, extracted little warmth. 'Our government', Refet scolded, 'is a democratic government which is administered completely by the people under national sovereignty'.[37] Neither the palace nor the offices of the Sublime Porte reigned over the country.

The elation that overcame Istanbul occurred as dramatic events were taking place in Europe. Lloyd George's reluctant retreat from the Turkish Straits wounded him politically at home. Having lost the support of his Conservative coalition partners, he resigned as Refet Pasha set foot in the Ottoman capital. Meanwhile, Italy heaved with excitement as Benito Mussolini gathered his supporters in a march on Rome. As the Fascists pressed forward with their revolution, Western opinion-makers weighed the prospects these and other occurrences would have upon a new set of peace talks. It was agreed soon after the Mudanya armistice that a revived peace conference would convene in the Swiss town of Lausanne. What remained unclear was which government would be negotiating with the Allies. The sitting grand vezir, Tevfik Pasha, declared his willingness to attend the talks in conjunction with representatives from Ankara. When a French reporter asked Mustafa Kemal his thoughts on the matter, his response was unyielding. The Ottoman government, he asserted, was 'old Turkey' and therefore a part of history. 'The government of the sultan and the sultan himself accepted, for example, the terms of the Treaty of Sèvres which ended Turkey's independence. We [therefore] can say that the sultan, and his government, have killed themselves'.[38]

Kemal's pronouncement reflected critical decisions unfolding in Ankara. At the end of October, the National Assembly took up a motion aimed at abolishing the office of the sultan. The legislation presented before the body formally described the empire as having already collapsed and that the 'new Turkey government' was taking its place. Through two days of debate, all who spoke agreed that Sultan Mehmed VI Vahideddin, as well as his brother-in-law Ferid, were guilty of gross acts of treason. Ranking first among their many crimes was the signing of the Treaty of Sèvres in 1920. Backers of the motion upheld the sultan's actions as evidence of a 'system of autocracy', one rooted in 'ignorance and debauchery'. Conservatives remained quiet while speakers disparaged the empire for having lasted six centuries. What was replacing it was a populist state that was 'young and vigorous'.[39] The final vote on the motion to dissolve the sultanate produced an overwhelming tally. Of the 140 members to cast their ballot, two voted against while another two chose to abstain. The rest agreed that the empire had indeed collapsed.[40]

Throughout the debate on the sultanate's status, it was clear that members hesitated when it came to doing away with the Ottoman royal family for good. A significant portion of the National Assembly insisted that an Ottoman prince should continue to reign as the caliph of Islam. This, many argued, was more than just a religious imperative. Muslims across the world, one member contended, recognized the caliphate as a Turkish institution, one for which a 'great many million Turkish sons' had fought and died. 'There is a creed which forges the unity of Islam and this nation knows it as a defender of the call of the book'.[41] Mustafa Kemal heartily agreed. Islamic history, he argued, made it clear that monarchies, as institutions, were in defiance of the will of God. Yet it was true that the 'state of Turkey', as he referred to the empire, had seized the office of the caliphate as a trophy of war in the sixteenth century. The Ottoman sultans had done so in the spirit of 'revitalizing and glorifying' the caliph's office.[42] Mehmed VI's traitorous reign now made it a necessity to abolish the sultanate. The caliphate, however, would live on as a purely spiritual office. Mustafa Kemal's reasoning left some of the assembly's more conservative members uneasy. When it was proposed to halt debate so that a separate committee could rule on whether the legislation was in accord with Islamic law, Kemal lashed out. 'Sovereignty', he told them, 'is acquired by force, by power and by violence. It was by violence that the sons of Osman acquired the power to rule over the Turkish nation and to maintain their rule for more than six centuries'. Should the assembly not act in accordance with his wishes, it was possible 'that some heads will be cut off!'[43]

Public expressions of sadness at the empire's passing were minimal. Newspaper headlines generally echoed Ankara's condemnation of Mehmed VI, the sultanate and the empire. In contrast to attitudes during the early days of the National Movement, the empire's six centuries of history were no longer a marker of pride. The sultanate's age instead was construed as an impediment or an anachronism that had suppressed the nation. How average citizens of 'new Turkey' fully absorbed the empire's dissolution is unclear. In Istanbul, large rallies celebrating the achievement of 'national sovereignty' were staged in various districts across the city. Many residing in the imperial capital also contended with the likely reality that their lives and livelihoods were about to change. For generations, the imperial bureaucracy had been the lifeblood of Istanbul's economy. Thousands of families depended upon the government and the palace for trade or public employment. With a new Nationalist government now fully in control of the country, hundreds of officials, attendants and prominent families were threatened with economic or personal ruin. How most of the rest of the country regarded events in the capital remains even more obscure. Between the destruction wrought by the Greek retreat, and the euphoria inspired by Mustafa Kemal's push westward, the public's reaction to the monarchy's dissolution may have been muted. The drama and overwhelming pace of events left little room for debate or wistfulness.

Fears of retribution also curtailed any outpouring of emotion. With the arrival of Refet Pasha in Istanbul, revelers smashed the windows of homes and businesses belonging to non-Muslims. Tensions continued to escalate over the coming weeks as angry protesters, many of them university students, vented their anger at the Allies and non-Muslims. Fearing that they would share the same fate as the Christian residents of Izmir, as many as 50,000 Greeks and Armenians elected to flee the old capital between October and December 1922.[44] Fear also prompted a smaller, but no less profound, exodus of palace loyalists. Damad Ferid's exit from Istanbul in late September had signaled the beginning of this wave of departures. Other former senior officials, such as the *şeyhülislam* Dürrizade Abdullah, who had condemned Mustafa Kemal to death, immediately followed him into exile. Ali Kemal remained, however, choosing instead to hole up in one of the city's more luxurious hotels. With Refet's entrance into the city, local Nationalists hinted at the fate that awaited him. In late October, the new editors of his old newspaper published a cartoon on the front page depicting his severed head upon a pike.[45] Ali Kemal dismissed such provocations and continued 'to keep up appearances' in the hopes that the courts and local opinion would prove him right.[46] In early November, men clad in black seized him while he sat in a barber's chair. Days later, news reports announced that his body was found hanging from a railroad trestle in the town of İzmit. Rumor had it that he was being brought to Ankara before he was interdicted by the feared general, Nurettin Pasha. As he had with the archbishop of Izmir, Nurettin urged a mob to beat him to death before stringing him up for all to see.

The sultan was similarly stubborn when it came to contemplating his immediate future. In the weeks that followed his dethronement, he did his utmost to adhere to the customs and protocols of his birthright. However, it became increasingly hard to ignore that he was an emperor without an empire. Newspapers regularly denounced him as a traitor and called for his arrest. During his last public audiences at the Yıldız mosque, just outside the palace, prayers were no longer offered in his name as sultan. After Ali Kemal's kidnapping, Mehmed VI's personal safety appeared even more precarious. The possibility that he too could be dragged away and murdered prompted many of his attendants to abandon the palace and flee. News that dozens of former palace loyalists had sought refuge in the embassy ultimately compelled British authorities to take drastic action. After a 'most painful' interview with Britain's high commissioner, Mehmed VI formally submitted a request for asylum.[47] Ironically, in acknowledgment of his demotion, Vahideddin signed his letter of petition as 'caliph of the Muslims'.[48]

The last sultan of the Ottoman Empire departed Istanbul in the early morning hours of 17 November 1922. Most of his family remained behind while he and his young son were secreted away aboard ambulances driven by British guards. The commander-in-chief of Allied forces, General Charles Harington, then escorted him to HMS *Malaya*, which awaited him offshore. Several hours elapsed before officials in the palace acknowledged that Mehmed VI had departed the city. The deposed sultan passed the ensuing weeks in pensive mood. He eventually settled in Italy in the resort town of San Remo. There he was welcomed by the country's new ruler, Benito Mussolini. Il Duce embraced Mehmed VI warmly, bidding 'the majestic Ottoman emperor' a pleasant stay as Italy's 'esteemed guest'.[49] He would never return home. In 1924, the Turkish National Assembly formally banned the royal family from ever setting foot in the country. Scores of others, such as Damad Ferid, were also declared traitors and stripped of their citizenship. Nevertheless, Mehmed's surviving attendants tried as much as they could to maintain the same decorum that he once knew in his palace in Istanbul. As guests and well-wishers came and went, he took to carrying a revolver for fear of assassination. He died absolutely penniless in 1926. His debts proved so substantial that Italian authorities initially confiscated his coffin until local accounts were settled. The passing of the last Ottoman sultan garnered fleeting international interest. It was common, as one French obituary noted, for death to be a salacious affair within the Ottoman royal family. Many former Ottoman princes had gone insane and died by their own hands. A good many others were strangled to prevent fratricide. Mehmed VI breathed his last 'having at least had the satisfaction of ending his days less tragically'.[50]

LESSONS LEARNED AND UNLEARNED: THE LONG SHADOW OF THE OTTOMAN EMPIRE

It would take months before a peace was agreed upon at Lausanne. Negotiations throughout were fraught with tensions, leading to periodic fears that the war would resume. By the time terms were finalized in the summer of 1923, all sides had been compelled to forgo at least some of their initial demands. Each of the Allies was obliged to recognize the existence of the independent state of Turkey. Mustafa Kemal's representatives secured most of the land claimed under the 1920 National Pact. Negotiators, however, failed to reach a final agreement on the old province of Mosul, which both Turkey and Iraq claimed in its entirety. It would take three more years, and an official League of Nation's inquiry, for Baghdad to secure its title over the oil-rich territory. Relinquishing Mosul, as well as other lands claimed to be fundamentally 'Turkish' in character, proved to be a bitter pill for some members of the Grand National Assembly. Most in Ankara, however, could still rejoice at the retention of all the gains that Nationalist troops had achieved through the force of arms. Moreover, Turkey was freed from having to repay a significant portion of the debts the Ottoman Empire owed to European creditors. Perhaps the most contentious component of the negotiations concerned what was termed an 'exchange of populations' between Greece and Turkey. Although Athens and Istanbul had agreed in principle to such an exchange in 1914, the violence of the intervening years made the discussions in Lausanne that much more volatile. Ankara, for example, desired the complete cleansing from Istanbul of its Greeks. Athens, in return, hoped to see all Muslims expelled from the border region of western Thrace. Both countries ultimately compromised and allowed these respective communities to remain. No other exemptions were extended. By the time the exchange was completed, approximately 400,000 Muslims had left Greece. Turkey expelled 1.2 million Orthodox Christians in return.

When lawmakers in Ankara ratified the agreement in August 1923, Mustafa Kemal had begun to lay out an expansive agenda for Turkey's future. In the spring, he had convened a grand 'economic congress' in Izmir. In opening the proceedings, he addressed what he believed were the causes of Turkey's economic weaknesses. The country's underdevelopment, by his reckoning, was a consequence of Ottoman history. Since the supposed 'golden ages' of the early sultans, state policy was driven by the 'feelings and desires' of the monarch. As a consequence, foreigners and non-Muslims lorded it over the economy at the expense of the peasantry. It was for this reason that the empire eventually went bankrupt, leaving the Turkish nation 'imprisoned among the Ottoman *volk*'. 'Gentlemen', Kemal decreed, 'if we look for the reasons for this sorrowful condition, this misery that afflicts the nation, we find it directly in the concept of the [Ottoman] state'.[51] It was in this spirit that he had earlier announced the establishment of a 'People's Party' that would take over the work of the Defense of Rights Association. By definition, it would be a populist party aimed at revolutionary reform.

After years of decrying the Nationalists as harbingers of Bolshevism and pan-Islamist insurrection, many of Ankara's fiercest critics slowly warmed to Turkey and the promise of Kemal's revolution. *The Times* of London, for one, received the overthrow of the sultan as potentially fortuitous. 'Old Turkey', with its 'curiously composite structure', 'Byzantine bureaucracy' and 'contemptuous tolerance for Christian peoples', had justifiably passed into history. Gone too were the ambiguities that defined the empire's national politics. Before Kemal, the country's leaders 'were still Ottomans, and not wholly Turks'. Now, with the sultan deposed, a more concrete sense of national belonging was taking shape in the country, a change that allowed a 'new kind of Turk' to blossom.[52] Mustafa Kemal's steady presence within the public eye reinforced this impression. While his representatives met with Allied negotiators in Lausanne, he busily toured western and southern Anatolia, giving speeches and visiting schools and social clubs. His oratory was consistently forward-looking, confident and reassuring. His exceptional willingness to appear before the public bolstered the credibility of his words. No Ottoman statesman, be it the sultan or the founders of the CUP, had ever traveled the countryside in order to consort with the people. The fact that Kemal's wife, Latife, often appeared at his side added to the impression that a more broad-minded era of leadership was dawning. A graduate of the Sorbonne, Latife spoke both English and French and was a staunch advocate of popular democracy and women's suffrage. The couple's combined vigor and authenticity heightened Western expectations of what appeared to be unfolding in 'new Turkey'. 'Turkey has been generally pictured as a "sick man,"' one *New York Times* correspondent wrote in the summer of 1923, 'but I think a better pictorial representation would be of a young woman who has just thrown aside her veil and is taking her first hopeful face-to-face view of the world'.[53]

To some extent, the prevailing mood in global politics encouraged Western commentators to see Turkey through kinder eyes. Allied negotiators arrived at Lausanne knowing that they had lost more than they had gained since 1918. Ankara's warm relations with France, Italy and the Soviet government added to Turkey's leverage. In the wake of Lloyd George's resignation, it was clear that Britain and Greece were bound to compromise on a variety of issues. Affairs beyond Europe, however, allowed the Allies to breathe a bit more easily. With civil war in the old Russian Empire winding down, fears of Soviet expansionism began to subside. Nationalist insurrections in the British and French empires also appeared on the wane. To the surprise of many, the overthrow of Mehmed VI did not result in an outpouring of Muslim rage. In India, several leaders of the Khilafat movement went so far as to defend Ankara's actions. 'Untrammelled powers in the hands of Caliphs and Sultans', one Indian dissident declared, 'just as much as in the hands of Czars and Kaisers, have been the cause of untold evils'. 'New Turkey', he concluded, therefore had every right to 'enter the comity of free nations' by virtue of its own actions.[54] Such assurances on the part of Indian Muslims fortified Ankara's claims that Turkey intended to become a more constructive and progressive state. Fatigue also bore upon the opinions of many global observers that winter. It had been four years since the end of the Great War. Throughout that time, many parts of the world had known little peace. Moreover, it was clear that the politics of nations and states had changed immensely since negotiators first arrived at Versailles. 'New Turkey' mirrored these political trends. Turkey's aspirations appeared in harmony with the youth and values of its new leader. Given what had happened, and the possibilities of what might come, there was little incentive to look back regretfully upon the Ottoman Empire. Its dissolution appeared a proper and natural outcome of history.

The mythos of 'new Turkey' grew even stronger over the following decades. By the outbreak of the Second World War, a political and cultural revolution had swept over the country. Following the declaration of a republic in October 1923, Mustafa Kemal sanctioned a raft of administrative and institutional reforms. Soon after, the Ottoman legal and educational systems were overturned and replaced. Reforms became more invasive, with the outright banning of the fez, turbans and the wearing of religious garments. Superficially, the introduction of these new restrictions was rationalized as an attempt at creating a more 'modern' society. As Kemal explained in 1925, 'sorrow and pain' had been the lot of the 'Turkish and Islamic world' since Muslims had failed to accede to the 'transformation and heights demanded by civilization'.[55] A similar logic helped to motivate an even more ambitious plan to reform the Ottoman language. In 1928, the government prohibited the use of the Arabic and Persian script associated with the Ottoman alphabet in favor of a new writing system based on Latin letters. Newspapers and book publishers were allowed only a few months to prepare before all publications were forced to adopt the 'Gazi's alphabet'. As the years passed, government efforts at language reform intensified, with the mandated use of newly contrived

'Turkicized' words meant to replace more common expressions deriving from Arabic or Farsi. Much of this new vocabulary had no basis in everyday speech, so much so that newspapers printed glossaries and word banks to aid readers. Nevertheless, 'New Turkish', as it was called, was heralded as a more organic language, one that genuinely reflected the history, culture and spirit of the Turkish nation. The Ottoman language, as one columnist put it, 'was as fabricated, artificial and forced as the Ottoman nation'.[56]

Western admiration for such reforms, as well as Atatürk's looming cult of personality, obscured many of the pains and realities that accompanied this revolution. From the first weeks following the abolition of the sultanate, an increasing number of commentators perceived a swelling trend towards authoritarianism in the country. What particularly concerned conservatives, as well as some loyal Nationalists, was Ankara's capricious use of power and its intolerance towards dissent. 'In a constitutional country, the Opposition is a legal instrument that furthers prosperity and perfection', one popular editor wrote in late 1922. Before the war, the CUP had mercilessly suppressed its opponents, a blunder, he added, that 'led us into catastrophe'.[57] Within a year of this column, Mustafa Kemal revealed he was just as prone to repression. Trouble first reared its head when several Istanbul newspapers printed a letter from two of the founders of India's Khilafat movement calling for the preservation of the caliphate. Authorities immediately placed several editors and columnists under arrest, charging them with treason. The letter itself was held to be evidence of a British plot to use the office of the caliph to undermine Turkish sovereignty.

The government's paranoia was not restricted to imaginary foreign plots. After unseating Mehmed VI, the National Assembly allowed his cousin Abdülmecid to assume the office of caliph. Abdülmecid II, as he was crowned, prided himself on being a scholar, with little interest in politics. Yet as dissidents in the National Assembly mulled plans to form an opposition party, Kemal's allies accused Abdülmecid of seeking to revive the power of the Ottoman royal family. As proof of these charges, critics pointed to his relationship with disaffected politicians. 'If at any time a Caliph takes it into his head to interfere with the destiny of this country', Prime Minister İsmet İnönü declared, 'we shall not fail to cut his head off'.[58] Hard upon this threat, the National Assembly voted to abolish the caliphate and expel the remaining members of the royal family from the country. Organized opposition to Kemal's rule soon met a similar fate. In 1925, authorities shuttered the country's sole opposition party on charges that it allied itself with reactionaries seeking to restore the caliphate. The leaders of the party, which included heroes of the Nationalist cause such as Rauf Orbay and Kazım Karabekir, were later arrested on charges of attempting to assassinate Mustafa Kemal and resurrect the Committee of Union and Progress. Both men were acquitted, but neither was allowed to re-enter politics until after Atatürk's death in 1938.

By no means was the Kemalist revolution driven by personal ambition and insecurity alone. Key components of Atatürk's revolution, such as language reform and the 'modernization' of Islamic practices and institutions, were long-established goals of the Turkish Hearth. As they had before the war, ideologues perceived Kemal's program as vital to the state's survival. The formal establishment of the Republic of Turkey allowed for the full realization of what many in the movement had pined for: a government that championed the ideals of an explicitly Turkish nationalism. Yet unlike the heady rhetoric of the Defense of Rights Association, Turkish newspaper editors and officials ultimately dispensed with the notion that Islam fueled the nation's sense of belonging or patriotism. Over time, ethnicities previously lauded as fellow Muslims or loyal Ottoman citizens – be they Kurds, Arabs or Albanians – became the objects of derision. Instead, many followed the lead of Mahmud Esad, who reimagined Anatolia's Turks as the historic victims of oppression at the hands of their Muslim peers. 'The old Ottoman Empire', he wrote in 1924, 'incessantly fought Arabs, Albanians and other Islamic elements for centuries and it suffered the greatest damage from them. All these [peoples] did not serve to strengthen the Turks, [but rather] caused their weaknesses'. More recently, he pointed to the Circassians who had resisted the National Forces on the behalf of the sultan. 'We think that there is no Turk left who will forget the Circassians, who call themselves Muslims, who did this or that in the most dangerous and mournful days of the Turkish fatherland'.[59]

Ideologues like Mahmud Esad spoke far less of non-Muslims and their place in the young Turkish Republic. Considering what had happened, there was little reason to. After the population exchange with Greece, Greeks were categorically forbidden from living in Anatolia or Thrace. Under the protection of the Treaty of Lausanne, Istanbul's native Greeks endured increasingly harsh conditions. Discrimination, as well as the threat of violence, would force many to leave the city in the ensuing decades. By 1935, Istanbul's Greek community was reduced to 113,000 people, which constituted roughly a third of its pre-1914 population.[60] As of 2020, it is estimated that only 2,000 native Greeks claim residency in the city.[61] Similar hardships confront Armenians still living in Turkey. Like Greeks in Istanbul, Turkish citizens of Armenian descent have labored to preserve their culture while combating popular suspicions of being traitors. Beyond the estimated 60,000 Armenians residing in Turkey today, it is possible that there are another 2 million people in the country who either conceal or are unaware of their Armenian heritage.[62] What relevance the end of the Ottoman Empire has had to these and other native Christians it is difficult to say.

Even with the empire's demise, ambiguities and difficulties beset Ankara's effort to fashion a more coherent Turkish nation. Among the earliest – and most indicative – of the challenges Turkish nationalists faced was the reception and integration of deportees coming from Greece. At Lausanne, Ankara's negotiators insisted that Turkey would only accept Muslims who spoke Turkish as potential migrants, a condition Athens accepted. With the arrival of hundreds of thousands of immigrants after 1923, officials discovered that large portions of these newcomers neither spoke nor understood Turkish. Many arriving Muslims knew only Greek or identified themselves as Albanians. Die-hard nationalists in Ankara accused Athens of trickery in sending Turkey 'foreigners' instead of 'true Turks'. Locals in various parts of the country also looked upon arriving migrants with suspicion or with outright hostility. '[Local people] said we were *gavur*s [unbelievers or Christians] and corrupted by the Greeks', one settler from Crete later explained, 'and yet we're the descendants of Ottoman soldiers, as well as the Barbarossas and Turguts [legendary Ottoman sea captains]'.[63] Ankara's ability to sort out Turkish from non-Turkish immigrants did not improve as time passed. Despite orders to forbid entry to non-Turkish asylum-seekers, border officials welcomed in hundreds of thousands of diverse migrants from Bulgaria, Yugoslavia, Romania and the Soviet Union. Why so many came to Turkey was often rooted in Ottoman precedents. Thousands of Crimean Tatars like Hüseyin Fehmi have come to settle in Turkey since 1923, seeking refuge from oppression. Larger numbers of Albanians and Bosnians, as well as Muslims from the Caucasus, have resettled in Turkey, hoping for a better life, particularly in the wake of the conflicts of the 1990s. In many ways, Ankara's inability to regulate, let alone integrate, these newcomers helped preserve a sense of imperial diversity. To this day, millions of Turks trace their roots to lands outside Anatolia. Many preserve a sense of belonging and identity rooted in the experiences of empire, not ethnicity.

Other attributes more integral to the country further undermined the contention that Turkey was home to a single and indivisible nation. By the late 1920s, Atatürk helped foster the belief that the armistice line of 1918 corresponded to the Turkish Republic's natural demographic frontiers. The political borders agreed upon at Lausanne, he contended, encapsulated the Turkish nation. International observers, as well as local dissidents and officials, knew this to be patently false. Not only were there Turkish speakers beyond the country's borders, the Republic of Turkey was inherently a land of many cultures and languages. Rather than embrace this diversity, senior leaders in the young republic saw Anatolia's cultural richness as a lingering threat to the state and nation. Drawing on plans first conceived under the CUP, officials in Ankara moved almost immediately to crush all expressions of Kurdish identity. 'In our times of weakness, a monolithic Kurdish identity is very likely to be incited', Kazım Karabekir warned in 1923. If Ankara did not take steps to assimilate and 'civilize' Kurds, it was very likely 'they will destroy themselves and hurt us'.[64] Through the course of Atatürk's reign, administrators resorted to a number of tactics meant to eradicate Kurdish culture, including forced relocation and settlement, language restrictions and collective punishment. The outbreak of multiple armed rebellions amplified the viciousness of this campaign. As in 1921, Dersim again became the scene of insurrection and mass repression. In an offensive that remains shrouded in official secrecy, Turkish security forces staged expansive operations against suspected areas of resistance in Dersim in 1937–8. Aircraft and other weapons ultimately exacted a terrible toll on the region's population. The terror inflicted by Turkish troops, as one private remembered, rivaled the depredations of Nurettin Pasha. 'Today the mountains and forests have been swept', he jotted in his diary. 'Our company brought the head of one of the notorious [rebels] ... There is a soldier named Ruşen in our unit. He cuts off all the heads. We've been so miserable here'.[65]

Remarkably, Kurds defied these assaults and conserved their culture. To some extent, Kurdish resilience mirrored a broader pattern of opposition and indifference to Ankara's campaign of nationalization. Throughout Turkey, everyday citizens found ways of circumventing the new cultural restrictions placed upon them. Ironically, among the institutions to outlive Mustafa Kemal himself was the Ottoman language. From the outset of the 1928 language reforms, people of all walks of life continued to communicate their thoughts in the Ottoman script as opposed to Latin letters. Even statesmen, such as postwar Prime Minister Adnan Menderes, continued to scribble down notes in Ottoman as opposed to 'modern' Turkish. Atatürk's efforts to impose his newly invented 'Turkicized' lexicon also struggled to gain traction as people continued to use words and phrases that derived from Arabic or Farsi. In the long run, however, Ottoman ceased to be a living language. As generations of Turks born after Kemal's death matured, older Ottoman expressions gave way to a more simplified 'modern Turkish' taught in schools. By the 1970s, the vocabulary of roughly 70 percent of newspaper articles was made up of real or invented words associated with the post-1928 reforms.[66] By the end of the twentieth century, it became impossible for most literate citizens to read, let alone fully grasp, the language of those who had grown up as Ottoman citizens. Today, the number of Turks fully capable of reading and understanding Ottoman constitutes a very small sliver of society as a whole. For most Turks, the ability to personally engage with how their ancestors spoke or saw themselves has been lost.

The death of the Ottoman language has had an even more profound effect upon people living outside modern-day Turkey. For Arabs and various peoples in the Balkans, much of the history of their communities remains encased in documents and books housed in the Republic of Turkey. While a trip to Istanbul's Ottoman archives may not be too prohibitively expensive, the number of people living outside Turkey capable of reading Ottoman sources is minuscule. These realities have exacerbated feelings of alienation seen among many peoples in the former empire. In most Middle Eastern and Balkan countries, the teaching of history in state schools is often anchored in depictions of the Ottoman past as a time of extreme backwardness and oppression. Be it in Greece, Armenia or Egypt, the reign of the sultans is often construed as a period of foreign rule, one no different to the British, Russian and French imperial regimes that dominated much of Asia and Africa. In countries like Iraq, Syria and Lebanon, this narrative became canonical within the first decades after the Ottoman Empire's formal dissolution. Ironically, many of those who helped enshrine this reading of history were scholars, officers and officials who had served in the Ottoman administration. Whether the first citizens of Syria, Iraq or Jordan immediately took to this interpretation of the past, or retained contrary views on the Ottoman Empire, is not entirely clear. Regardless, by the close of the Second World War, the politics of Arab nationalism commanded the attention and loyalties of most peoples living in the former Arab provinces of the empire. With the opening of the Cold War, Ottoman rule was broadly construed as a long, dark prologue before the establishment of the new states of the Middle East. Casting off the 'Turkish yoke' was only an intermediate step towards full Arab independence.

Few in Europe and the United States have sought to draw cautionary lessons from the Ottoman Empire's end. After all, the Treaty of Lausanne and the establishment of the Turkish Republic appeared to lay to rest the so-called 'Eastern Question' at long last. Meanwhile, the mandate states that had replaced the old empire fixed British and French interests in the Middle East for years to come. Churchill, for one, looked back proudly at his government's management of its interests in Anatolia. Though he readily conceded that London's faith in Greece was misguided, he was certain that Britain had fared well in holding onto the Turkish Straits as long as it did. Britain's 'strong action', as Churchill put it, laid the groundwork for the 'mutual respect' that had defined the negotiations at Lausanne.[67] Writing in

1929, he was certain that London's fortitude along the Dardanelles proved the British Empire's durability, not weakness. Neither he nor other great statesmen would remember the sultanate's dismemberment and dissolution as an omen for the future. The upheaval inspired by Ottoman resistance efforts in Asia and Africa faded from active memory as the Second World War began. The inability of the Allies to impose their absolute will upon Anatolia and the Levant after 1918 was also forgotten. Subsequent historical moments, such as the Suez Crisis in 1956, ultimately served as more defining lessons for ardent imperialists in Britain and France. Americans have equally failed to draw direct lessons from the politics of the Ottoman Empire's dissolution. More than a few presidents of the United States have cited Woodrow Wilson's vision for a more democratic world as an inspiration for Washington's policies in the Middle East and beyond. Wilson's specific failures in securing peace in the Ottoman lands, however, are rarely discussed in depth.

To say, however, that the Ottoman Empire lost all its relevance after its formal dissolution would be far from correct. Though Atatürk's reforms may have clouded aspects of Turkey's imperial past, they did little to undermine the affection many citizens had for the empire or its history. At the height of Kemal's rule as president, newspapers regularly featured stories recalling the heroism and triumphs of the Ottoman army. Venerable writers known for their pro-reformist politics penned works commemorating the martyrs and territories lost during the reign of the sultans. In his ode to the end of the Great War, poet Yahya Kemal expressed as much sadness for the loss of his country as he did for those killed at the front. 'Those who died, died', he wrote of the year 1918. 'We suffered with those who remained. We are now a despised community in the fatherland. Those who died were saved from this turmoil in the end. And behind their eyelids is the old fatherland'.[68]

The Ottoman Empire's rehabilitation progressed rapidly after the Second World War. As a time and a place representing both greatness and loss, the empire served as a well from which celebrants and critics drew inspiration. In 1953, state officials and private citizens were exultant in marking the 500th anniversary of Constantinople's capture by Sultan Mehmed II. Festivities around the occasion highlighted the country's historic military might, as well as the proposition that the city had remained Turkish at the expense of the Byzantines and Greeks. The early 1950s also ushered in a wave of revisionist histories lamenting the empire's collapse. Among the leaders of this resurgence was the poet and polemicist Necip Fazıl Kısakürek. As a staunch religious conservative and an opponent of Atatürk's reforms, Kısakürek vilified the Young Turks as unbelieving Freemasons who had sought to undermine the empire's Islamic character. In addition to lavishing praise upon Abdülhamid II as a symbol of Islamic unity and piety, he fervently defended Mehmed VI as an Ottoman patriot who, he claimed, had in fact helped launch and defend the National Movement. For these and other assertions, Kısakürek was tried for insulting Atatürk and the Turkish nation and imprisoned.

Recep Tayyip Erdoğan's understanding of the past borrows heavily from the writings and beliefs of Kısakürek. As both Prime Minister and president of the Turkish Republic, he has leaned heavily upon the proposition that the Ottoman Empire's fall was both a political and a moral catastrophe. The great sultans, as Erdoğan would have it, represented the height of Turkish power, sophistication and Islamic virtue. His romantic attachment to the Ottoman past, however, is not without internal inconsistencies. While lionizing the sultanate, he has never gone so far as to condemn the establishment of the republic. He instead maintains that the regime Atatürk founded was the continuation of an enduring Turkish state that dates back to the medieval Seljuk Empire (a proposition actively advanced by many of Mustafa Kemal's ardent supporters). Nor has Erdoğan ever cast doubt upon the validity or heroism of Kemal's National Movement. Yet, ironically, Erdoğan has touted his own reign as a genuinely 'new Turkey', one that stands in contrast to the failed policies of Atatürk's successors rather than to the Ottoman Empire. In looking to the present and future, he has long maintained that the same forces that humbled the Ottoman Empire in 1918 continue to threaten Turkey's survival. For Erdoğan, the 2016 coup that nearly toppled him commenced 'a second war of independence', a conflict that has pitted Turkey against the Greeks, the great powers of Europe and the United States as well as native traitors. The object of the July 2016 conspiracy, in his words, 'was an attempt to occupy the last piece of our land, which shrank to one-fifth [of its size] in the short period from 1912 to 1923'.[69]

International observers have not overlooked Erdoğan's fondness for the empire. After his decision to intervene militarily in the Syrian civil war in 2016, he has regularly spoken of Turkey's strategic interests in lands previously governed from Istanbul (or within what he euphemistically has called the country's 'spiritual borders').[70] Such contentions have led to a steady stream of foreign editorials and official statements accusing Erdoğan of possessing a 'neo-Ottomanist' agenda of territorial expansion. Regardless of what may drive Ankara's foreign policy agenda, what is clear is the degree to which Turkish citizens now look to the country's imperial history for inspiration. Since the 1970s, Turks have shown a steady willingness to embrace symbols of the Ottoman past. After Ankara's decision to restore Turkish citizenship to members of the Ottoman royal family, heirs to the throne have been welcomed back to Turkey as honored guests. Decades after their deaths, the bodies of both Enver and Talat Pashas were brought back to Istanbul and reinterred as heroes of the Turkish nation. Popular fascination with the Ottoman past has reached new peaks through the medium of television. Period dramas based on the conquests and intrigues of the early Ottoman centuries are now core staples of Turkish popular culture. Why this cultural turn has occurred is largely the product of relatively recent tensions and events. This radical shift towards imperial nostalgia, however, remains almost exclusively confined to the Republic of Turkey. Leaders in the Arab world have tended to look upon Ankara's casual allusions to the empire with indifference. In most of the Middle East, governments demonstrated little interest in marking the First World War's centennial. In 2016, Erdoğan went to great pains to celebrate the hundredth anniversary of the Ottoman victory over the British in Kut, in Iraq. The battle, he declared, was an example of 'how our nation took care of its fatherland despite all the impossibilities'.[71] Baghdad, however, neither responded to Erdoğan's boasts nor staged commemorations of its own.

The glories of the Ottoman past are not the only source of popular nostalgia. It is possible to find other expressions of yearning that do not pertain to the loss of the empire as a state. If one peruses Michael

Hagopian's interviews with survivors of the Armenian Genocide, one finds greater longing for families and communities left behind in the Ottoman lands. Many who allowed Hagopian to record them expressed bitterness over what they experienced. Many others, including those who survived the worst of the deportations, could still muster words of affection for Muslim neighbors they had known in their youth, as well as towns and villages. Aging Turkish residents in Izmir who spoke to anthropologists in the 1990s equally pined for what was lost. For Mehmed Ergun, who was eight years old when the empire ended, native Greeks were no less dismayed by the 1919 invasion. 'They, the older [Greek residents], said something like, "This dog [meaning the Greek army] should not be allowed to shelter here. We lived wonderfully in the Ottoman Empire. And this [dog] shattered our comfort."'[72] It is possible that Ergun's memories do not reflect the times as they were. His sentiments, however, were borne out by genuine experiences. Being an Ottoman citizen was something he lived and was obliged to remember.

Notes

Introduction

1. Robert Gerwarth, *The Vanquished: Why the First World War Failed to End* (New York: Farrar, Straus and Giroux, 2016), 61.
2. Hasan Babacan and Servet Avşar (eds.), *Meşrutiyet Ruznamesi Cavid Bey, 3. Cilt* (Ankara: Türk Tarih Kurumu Basımevi, 2014), 559.
3. Gwynne Dyer, 'The Turkish Armistice of 1918: 2: A Lost Opportunity: The Armistice Negotiations of Moudros', *Middle Eastern Studies*, 8.3 (1972), 337.
4. Ahmet Ağaoğlu, *Mütareke ve Sürgün Hatıralar* (Istanbul: Doğu Kitabevi, 2010), 48–9.
5. Leon Trotsky, *History of the Russian Revolution* (Chicago: Haymarket Books, 2008), 800, 818.
6. Andreas Kappeler, *The Russian Empire: A Multi-Ethnic History* (London: Routledge, 2014), 371.
7. Terry Martin, *The Affirmative Action Empire: Nations and Nationalism in the Soviet Union, 1923–1939* (Ithaca, NY: Cornell University Press, 2001), 5.
8. Peter Holquist, 'To Count, to Extract, and to Exterminate: Population Statistics and Population Politics in Late Imperial and Soviet Russia', in Ronald Grigor Suny and Terry Martin (eds.), *A State of Nations: Empire and Nation-Making in the Age of Lenin and Stalin* (Oxford: Oxford University Press, 2001), 111–44.
9. Peter Zarrow, *After Empire: The Conceptual Transformation of the Chinese State, 1885–1924* (Stanford, CA: Stanford University Press, 2012), 287.
10. TBMM, *Zabıt Ceridesi*, Devre: 1, Cilt: 24, 30 October 1922, 293.
11. Ibid., 1 November 1922, 311.
12. Karen Jungblut, 'Hagopian, J. Michael', USC Shoah Foundation Visual Archive Online, 4:20:28 http://vhaonline.usc.edu/viewingPage?testimo

nyID=54836&returnIndex=1, 23 June 2010 (consulted 6 November 2019).

13. 'Award-Winning Filmmaker J. Michael Hagopian Dies at 97', *Asbarez*, 13 December 2010.

14. Pelin Böke (ed.), *İzmir, 1919–1922: Tanıklıklar* (Istanbul: Tarih Vakfı Yurt Yayınları, 2006).

15. Mustafa Kemal Atatürk, *Nutuk*, ed. Bedi Yazıcı (Istanbul: n.p., 1995), 805.

16. Mustafa Oral, 'Türk İnkılap Tarihi Enstitüsü (1933)', *Ankara Üniversitesi Türk İnkılap Tarihi Enstitüsü Atatürk Yolu Dergisi*, 27–8 (2001), 329.

17. https://www.tccb.gov.tr/konusmalar/353/2988/1915-osmanli-imparatorlugunun-en-uzun-yili-sempozyumunda-yaptiklari-konusma (consulted 7 November 2019).

18. http://edam.org.tr/wp-content/uploads/2015/01/EdamAnket2015-1.pdf (consulted 7 November 2019).

19. https://www.tccb.gov.tr/haberler/410/105090/-amaci-hakikati-bulmak-olan-herkese-arsivlerimizin-kapilari-sonuna-kadar-aciktir- (consulted 7 November 2019).

1. 'Our Policies Have Failed': The Ottoman Empire by 1918

1. Brian Glynn Williams, *The Crimean Tatars: The Diaspora Experience and the Forging of a Nation* (Leiden: Brill, 2001), 227.

2. Kalusd Sürmenyan, *Harbiyeli Bir Osmanlı Ermenisi* (Istanbul: Tarih Vakfı Yurt Yayınları, 2015), 42.

3. 'Hard Times of the Sultan', *New York Times*, 19 May 1890.

4. Neil Gale, *The Midway Plaisance at the 1893 World's Columbian Exposition in Chicago* (Lulu.com, 2017), 11.

5. Selim Deringil, *The Well-Protected Domains: Ideology and the Legitimation of Power in the Ottoman Empire, 1876–1909* (London: I.B. Tauris, 1998), 160.

6. Ryan Gingeras, *Fall of the Sultanate: The Great War and the End of the Ottoman Empire, 1908–1922* (Oxford: Oxford University Press, 2016), 197.

7. Murat Özyüksel, *The Hejaz Railway and the Ottoman Empire: Modernity, Industrialisation and Ottoman Decline* (London: I.B. Tauris, 2014), 69.

8. Stefanos Katsikas, *Islam and Nationalism in Modern Greece, 1821–1940* (Oxford: Oxford University Press, 2021), 21.

9. Benny Morris and Dror Ze'evi, *The Thirty-Year Genocide: Turkey's Destruction of Its Christian Minorities, 1894–1924* (Cambridge, MA: Harvard University Press, 2019), 130–32.

10. Ahmet Reşit Rey, *İmparatorluğun Son Döneminde Gördüklerim Yaptıklarım (1890–1922)* (Istanbul: İş Bankası Kültür Yayınları, 2007), 29.

11. David Roessel, *In Byron's Shadow: Modern Greece in the English and American Imagination* (Oxford: Oxford University Press, 2001), 45.

12. W. E. Gladstone, *Bulgarian Horrors and the Question of the East* (London: J. Murray, 1876), 53.

13. İpek K. Yosmaoğlu, 'Counting Bodies, Shaping Souls: The 1903 Census and National Identity in Ottoman Macedonia', *International Journal of Middle East Studies*, 38.1 (2006), 62.

14. 'The Turk at Home', *Harper's New Monthly Magazine*, 1 December 1853, 798.

15. Selçuk Akşin Somel, *The Modernization of Public Education in the Ottoman Empire, 1839–1908: Islamization, Autocracy and Discipline* (Leiden: Brill, 2001), 262–3.

16. Roderic H. Davison, *Reform in the Ottoman Empire, 1856–1876* (Princeton, NJ: Princeton University Press, 1963), 3.

17. Niyazi Berkes, *The Development of Secularism in Turkey* (Routledge: New York, 1998), 222.

18. Murat Birdal, 'Fiscal Crisis and Structural Change in the Late Ottoman Economy', in Amal Ghazal and Jens Hanssen (eds.), *The Oxford Handbook of Contemporary Middle Eastern and North African History* (Oxford: Oxford University Press, 2021), 37.

19. Bernard Lewis, *The Emergence of Modern Turkey* (Oxford: Oxford University Press, 1961), 136.

20. Murat R. Şiviloğlu, *The Emergence of Public Opinion: State and Society in the Late Ottoman Empire* (Cambridge: Cambridge University Press, 2018), 244.

21. Fatma Müge Göçek, *Denial of Violence: Ottoman Past, Turkish Present, and Collective Violence against the Armenians, 1789–2009* (Oxford: Oxford University Press, 2015), 119.

22. Kemal H. Karpat, *The Politicization of Islam: Reconstructing Identity, State, Faith, and Community in the Late Ottoman State* (Oxford: Oxford University Press, 2001), 173.

23. The quote is from Namık Kemal, perhaps the most influential Ottoman poet and playwright of the nineteenth century. See Doğan Gürpınar, *Ottoman/Turkish Visions of the Nation, 1860–1950* (London: Palgrave Macmillan, 2013), 70.

24. Kemal H. Karpat, *Ottoman Population, 1830–1914: Demographic and Social Characteristics* (Madison, WI: University of Wisconsin Press, 1985), 215. This statistic is based on the averages recorded for the provinces of Erzurum, Adana, Ankara, Aydın, İzmit, Bitlis, Biga, Sivas, Trabzon, Konya, Hüdavendigâr, Kastamonu and Van.

25. Nicholas Doumanis, *Before the Nation: Muslim–Christian Coexistence and Its Destruction in Late Ottoman Anatolia* (Oxford: Oxford University Press, 2012), 80.

26. Banu Turnaoğlu, *The Formation of Turkish Republicanism* (Princeton, NJ: Princeton University Press, 2017), 100.

27. M. Şükrü Hanioğlu, *The Young Turks in Opposition* (Oxford: Oxford University Press, 1995), 187.

28. Steven W. Sowards, *Austria's Policy of Macedonian Reform* (Boulder, CO: East European Monographs, 1989), 76.

29. M. Şükrü Hanioğlu, *Preparation for a Revolution: The Young Turks, 1902–1908* (Oxford: Oxford University Press, 2001), 220.

30. Sürmenyan, 42.

31. Douglas Scott Brookes (ed.), *On the Sultan's Service: Halid Ziya Uşaklıgil's Memoir of the Ottoman Palace, 1909–1912* (Bloomington, IN: Indiana University Press, 2020), 229.

32. Bedross Der Matossian, 'From Bloodless Revolution to Bloody Counterrevolution: The Adana Massacres of 1909', *Genocide Studies and Prevention*, 6.2 (2011), 162.

33. Ismail Kemal, *The Memoirs of Ismail Kemal Bey* (London: Constable and Co., 1920), 366–8.

34. Hasan Kayalı, *Arabs and Young Turks: Ottomanism, Arabism, and Islamism in the Ottoman Empire, 1908–1918* (Berkeley, CA: University of California Press, 1997), 88.

35. TNA/FO 294/47/38, 28 August 1910. Also cited in Hans-Lukas Kieser, *Talaat Pasha: Father of Modern Turkey, Architect of Genocide* (Princeton, NJ: Princeton University Press, 2018), 86.

36. A. Holly Shissler, *Between Two Empires: Ahmet Ağaoğlu and the New Turkey* (London: I.B. Tauris, 2003), 159.

37. Masami Arai, *Turkish Nationalism in the Young Turk Era* (Leiden: Brill, 1992), 61.

38. Enver Pascha, *Um Tripolis* (Munich: Hugo Bruckmann Verlag, 1918), 10.

39. Feroz Ahmad, *The Young Turks: The Committee of Union and Progress in Turkish Politics, 1908–1914* (London: Hurst, 2009), 96.

40. Eyal Ginio, 'Constructing a Symbol of Defeat and National Rejuvenation: Edirne (Adrianople) in Ottoman Propaganda and Writing during

the Balkan Wars', in Stefan Goebel and Derek Keene (eds.), *Cities into Battlefields: Metropolitan Scenarios, Experiences and Commemorations of Total War* (Farnham: Ashgate, 2011), 97.

41. Erik-Jan Zürcher, 'The Young Turks: Children of the Borderlands?', in Kemal H. Karpat and Robert W. Zens (eds.), *Ottoman Borderlands: Issues, Personalities, and Political Changes* (Madison, WI: University of Wisconsin Press, 2003), 281.

42. BCA 272.14.75.24.6.21, September 1920.

43. Ahmad, 129.

44. 'Die Türkei nach dem Frieden', *Neue Freie Presse*, 18 May 1913 (found in PAAA R 13193, A 10191, 18 May 1913).

45. Ümit Kurt, *Türk'ün Büyük, Biçare Irkı* (Istanbul: İletişim Yayınları, 2012), 207.

46. Karpat, *Ottoman Population*, 188. According to Istanbul's own accounting, there were 1.7 million Orthodox Christian citizens still living in the empire in 1914.

47. 'Muhacirler', *Tasvir-i Efkar*, 1 January 1919.

48. Taner Akçam, *The Young Turks' Crime against Humanity: The Armenian Genocide and Ethnic Cleansing in the Ottoman Empire* (Princeton, NJ: Princeton University Press, 2012), 68.

49. Ronald Grigor Suny, *'They Can Live in the Desert but Nowhere Else': A History of the Armenian Genocide* (Princeton, NJ: Princeton University Press, 2017), 203.

50. Halil Menteşe, *Osmanlı Mebusan Meclisi Reisi Halil Menteşe'nin Anıları* (Istanbul: Hürriyet Vakfı Yayınları, 1986), 176.

51. Yiğit Akın, 'The Ottoman Home Front during World War I: Everyday Politics, Society, and Culture', PhD Dissertation: Ohio State University, 2011, 198.

52. Mustafa Aksakal, 'Not "by Those Old Books of International Law, but Only by War": Ottoman Intellectuals on the Eve of the Great War', *Diplomacy and Statecraft*, 15.3 (2004), 512.

53. Sürmenyan, 45.

54. Hüseyin Fehmi Genişol, *Çanakkale'den Bağdat'a Esaretten Kurtuluş Savaşı'na: Cephede Sekiz Yıl Sekiz Ay (1914–1923)* (Istanbul: Türkiye İş Bankası Kültür Yayınları, 2010), 3.

55. Mehmet Hacısalihoğlu, *Jön Türkler ve Makedonya Sorunu (1890–1918)* (Istanbul: Tarih Vakfı Yurt Yayınları, 2008), 147.

56. Kieser, 167.

57. Hikmet Özdemir, *The Ottoman Army, 1914–1918: Disease and Death on the Battlefield* (Salt Lake City, UT: University of Utah Press, 2008), 52.

58. 'Die Türkische Presse', *Osmanischer Lloyd*, 11 January 1916.
59. Yücel Yanıkdağ, *Healing the Nation: Prisoners of War, Medicine and Nationalism in Turkey, 1914–1939* (Edinburgh: Edinburgh University Press, 2013), 17.
60. Akın, 203.
61. Taner Akçam, 'When Was the Decision to Annihilate the Armenians Taken?' *Journal of Genocide Research*, 21.4 (2019), 477.
62. BOA.DH.MV 198/24. Reproduced in T.C. Başbakanlık Devlet Arşivileri Genel Müdürlüğü, *Osmanlı Belgelerinde Ermenilerin Sevk ve İskanı (1878–1920)* (Ankara: Sistem Ofset, 2007), 155–6.
63. PAAA R 14086, A19744, 25 June 1915.
64. Uğur Ümit Üngör, 'Orphans, Converts, and Prostitutes: Social Consequences of War and Persecution in the Ottoman Empire, 1914–1923', *War in History*, 19.2 (2012), 177.
65. Murat Bardakçı, *Talat Paşa'nın Evrak-ı Metrukesi* (Istanbul: Everest Yayınları, 2008), 81, 91.
66. Morris and Ze'evi, 486–8.
67. Sürmenyan, 66.
68. Ibid., 109.
69. PAAA R 13196, A12238, 9 May 1916.
70. PAAA R 13196, A8212, 29 March 1916. It is interesting to note that German authorities estimated that between 500,000 and 2 million Armenians had been killed by this point.
71. Linda Schatkowski Schilcher, 'The Famine of 1915–1918 in Greater Syria', in John Spagnolo (ed.), *Problems of the Modern Middle East in Historical Perspective: Essays in Honour of Albert Hourani* (Reading: Ithaca Press, 1992), 254.
72. Süleyman Beyoğlu, *İki Devir Bir İnsan: Ahmet Faik Günday ve Hatıraları* (Istanbul: Bengi Yayınları, 2011), 106; Abbas Kadhim, *Reclaiming Iraq: The 1920 Revolution and the Founding of the Modern State* (Austin, TX: University of Texas Press, 2012), 2.
73. Genişol, 15
74. Ibid., 37.
75. Ibid., 55–6.
76. Ibid., 84.
77. Ibid., 83.
78. 'Baku'nun Zabtından Sonra', *Tanin*, 25 September 1918.
79. A. Alp Yenen, 'The Young Turk Aftermath: Making Sense of Transnational Contentious Politics at the End of the Ottoman Empire, 1918–1922', PhD Dissertation: University of Basel, 2019, 67, 68.

2. 'A Comedy of Mutual Distrust': The Politics of Surrender and Occupation

1. TNA/FO 371/4157/82979, 2 June 1919.
2. Alan Sharp, *Consequences of Peace: The Versailles Settlement – Aftermath and Legacy 1919–2010* (London: Haus Publishing, 2010), 101–2.
3. TNA/FO 608/103/3626, 6 March 1919.
4. TNA/FO 608/103/3836, 10 March 1919.
5. Harold Nicolson, *Peacemaking, 1919* (New York: Grosset & Dunlap, 1965), 251.
6. Eleutherios Venizelos, *Greece before the Peace Congress of 1919: A Memorandum Dealing with the Rights of Greece* (New York: Published for the American-Hellenic Society by Oxford University Press, American branch, 1919), 23.
7. Awetis Aharonean et al., *The Armenian Question before the Peace Conference* (New York: Press Bureau, the Armenian National Union of America, 1919), 28.
8. Ibid.
9. Charles T. Thompson, *The Peace Conference Day by Day: A Presidential Pilgrimage Leading to the Discovery of Europe* (New York: Brentano's Publishers, 1920), 181.
10. David H. Miller, *My Diary at the Conference of Paris: With Documents*, Volume IV (New York, 1924), 297–9.
11. Andrew Patrick, 'Woodrow Wilson, the Ottomans, and World War I', *Diplomatic History*, 42.5 (2018), 909.
12. Andrew Patrick, *America's Forgotten Middle East Initiative: The King–Crane Commission of 1919* (London: I. B. Tauris, 2015), 49–50.
13. Briton Cooper Busch, *Mudros to Lausanne: Britain's Frontier in West Asia, 1918–1923* (Albany, NY: State University of New York Press, 1976), 126.
14. Edmund Burke, 'Moroccan Resistance, Pan-Islam and German War Strategy, 1914–1918', *Francia*, 3 (1975), 441.
15. Conor Meleady, 'Negotiating the Caliphate: British Responses to Pan-Islamic Appeals, 1914–1924', *Middle Eastern Studies*, 52.2 (2016), 188.
16. Stanford J. Shaw, *From Empire to Republic: The Turkish War of National Liberation, 1918–1923: A Documentary Study* (Ankara: Türk Tarih Kurumu Basımevi, 2000), Volume 2, 135.
17. Venizelos, 19.

18. Michael Llewellyn Smith, *Ionian Vision: Greece in Asia Minor, 1919–1922* (London: Hurst & Company, 1998), 65.

19. Nicolson, 346.

20. *Papers Relating to the Foreign Relations of the United States: The Paris Peace Conference, 1919*, Volume IV (Washington: United States Government Printing Office, 1943), 510 (https://history.state.gov/historical documents/frus1919Parisv04/d30).

21. Shaw, Volume 2, 417.

22. Ali Fuat Türkgeldi, *Görüp İşittiklerim* (Ankara: Türk Tarih Kurumu, 2010), 224.

23. Ahmet İzzet Paşa, *Feryadım: Cilt 1* (Istanbul: Nehir, 1992), 72. This was a comment specifically made of the organization's Russian-born members and of Ziya Gökalp, who was of Kurdish extraction. For greater discussion, see Chapter 5.

24. Ibid., 224.

25. Douglas Scott Brookes (ed.), *On the Sultan's Service: Halid Ziya Uşaklıgil's Memoir of the Ottoman Palace, 1909–1912* (Bloomington, IN: Indiana University Press, 2020), 79.

26. Murat Bardakçı, *Şahbaba: Osmanoğulları'nın Son Hükümdarı VI. Mehmed Vahideddin'in Hayatı, Hatıraları ve Özel Mektupları* (Istanbul: İnkılap, 2006), 31.

27. Gotthard Jäschke, 'Beiträge zur Geschichte des Kampfes der Türkei um ihre Unabhängigkeit', *Die Welt des Islams*, 5.1 (1957), 13.

28. Türkgeldi, 173.

29. Ibid., 81.

30. Ahmet İzzet Paşa, *Feryadım: Cilt 2* (Istanbul: Nehir, 1992), 9–10.

31. Donald Bloxham, *The Great Game of Genocide: Imperialism, Nationalism, and the Destruction of the Ottoman Armenians* (New York: Oxford University Press, 2007), 137.

32. A. Alp Yenen, 'The Young Turk Aftermath: Making Sense of Transnational Contentious Politics at the End of the Ottoman Empire, 1918–1922', PhD Dissertation: University of Basel, 2019, 66.

33. Tarık Zafer Tunaya, *Türkiye'de Siyasal Partiler, Cilt II: Mütareke Dönemi* (Istanbul: Hürriyet Vakfı Yayınları, 2003), 118.

34. Hasan Babacan and Servet Avşar (eds.), *Cavid Bey, Meşrutiyet Ruznamesi, 3. Cilt* (Ankara: Türk Tarih Kurumu Basımevi, 2014), 592.

35. 'İttihad ve Terakki İki İsmi', *İkdam*, 17 November 1918.

36. 'Hacı Adil Bey ve Çiftlikleri', *Alemdar*, 27 December 1918.

37. 'Anadolu Diyor ki', *Anadolu*, 8 November 1919. This passage can also be found in Osman Akandere, 'Damat Ferit Paşa Hükümetleri Döneminde

Kuva-yı Milliye Hareketine Yöneltilen İthamlar', *Atatürk Araştırma Merkezi Dergisi*, 24.70 (2008), 28–9.

38. Ayhan Aktar, 'Debating the Armenian Massacres in the Last Ottoman Parliament, November–December 1918', *History Workshop Journal*, 64.1 (2007), 251–2.

39. TBMM, *Meclisi Ayan Zabıt Ceridesi*, Devre: 3, Cilt: 1, 21 November 1918, 122.

40. TBMM, *Meclisi Mebusan Zabıt Ceridesi*, Devre: 3, Cilt: 1, 4 November 1918, 110.

41. Ibid., 103.

42. Raymond Kévorkian, *The Armenian Genocide: A Complete History* (London: I.B. Tauris, 2011), 783–4.

43. Yenen, 'The Young Turk Aftermath', 65.

44. TBMM, *Meclisi Ayan Zabıt Ceridesi*, Devre: 3, Cilt: 1, 14 November 1918, 90. These specific charges, it should be said, stemmed from an inquiry first submitted by a senior Ottoman officer.

45. Vahakn N. Dadrian and Taner Akçam, *Judgment at Istanbul: The Armenian Genocide Trials* (New York: Berghahn Books, 2011), 314.

46. Sharp, 111.

47. 'Vilson'nın Terazısı Doğru Tartiyorsa', *Tasvir-i Efkar*, 1 December 1918.

48. 'George Vashington', *Vakit*, 23 February 1919.

49. Nur Bilge Criss, *Istanbul under Occupation, 1918–1923* (Leiden: Brill, 1999), 53.

50. 'Hükümetin Muhtırası', *İkdam*, 3 March 1919.

51. Ahmet İzzet, *Feryadım*: Cilt 2, 56.

52. Türkgeldi, 211.

53. M. Tayyip Gökbilgin, *Milli Mücadele Başlarken, 1 Cilt* (Ankara: Türkiye İş Bankası Yayınları, 2011), 96.

54. *Papers Relating to the Foreign Relations of the United States: The Paris Peace Conference, 1919*, Volume IV (Washington: United States Government Printing Office, 1943), 511 (https://history.state.gov/historical documents/frus1919Parisv04/d30).

55. Ahmet Ağaoğlu, 'Siyaset: İktisadiyatımız ve Lisan', *Tercüman-ı Hakikat*, 3 March 1916.

56. Ahmet Ağaoğlu, 'Siyaset: Halka Doğru', *Tercüman-ı Hakikat*, 10 December 1917.

57. Halide Edip, 'Evimize Bakalım', *Vakit*, 30 June 1918.

58. Martin Hartmann, 'Der Aufbau Anatoliens', *Deutsche Levante Zeitung*, 7 (1916), found in PAAA R 13196 A 8212, 21 March 1916.

59. PAAA R 13196, A 18613, 14 July 1916.
60. 'Review of the Year's Work at Trebizond', *The Orient*, 3 March 1920.
61. Sinan Hakan, *Türkiye Kurulurken Kürtler (1916–1920)* (Istanbul: İletişim Yayınları, 2013), 54.
62. BCA 490.001.648.151.1, No. 32160, 26 August 1933.
63. M. Kemal Temel, 'The 1918 "Spanish Flu" Pandemic in the Ottoman Capital, Istanbul', *Canadian Bulletin of Medical History*, 37.1 (2020), 219.
64. Pelin Böke (ed.), *İzmir, 1919–1922: Tanıklıklar* (Istanbul: Tarih Vakfı Yurt Yayınları, 2006), 73.
65. Fuat Dündar, *Modern Türkiye'nin Şifresi: İttihat ve Terakki'nin Etnisite Mühendisliği (1913–1918)* (Istanbul: İletişim Yayınları, 2008), 418.
66. Ibid., 410.
67. HHSt PA XXXVIII, 14 October 1918.
68. 'Muhacirler ve Mülteciler', *İleri*, 3 February 1920.
69. TNA 371/4157/18850, 3 February 1919; TNA 371/4157/18851, 5 February 1919.
70. Kemal H. Karpat, *Ottoman Population, 1830–1914: Demographic and Social Characteristics* (Madison, WI: University of Wisconsin Press, 1985), 184; TNA/FO 371/4157/83004, 2 June 1919.
71. TNA/FO 371/4157/55062, 9 April 1919.
72. Karpat, *Ottoman Population*, 176; Ümit Kurt, 'Introduction', in Kevork Baboian, *The Heroic Battle of Aintab* (London: Gomidas Institute, 2017), xvii.
73. Ümit Kurt, 'The Making of the Aintab Elite: Social Support, Local Incentives and Provincial Motives behind the Armenian Genocide (1890s–1920s)', PhD Dissertation: Clark University, 2006, 171.
74. TNA/FO 371/4157/79408, 25 May 1919.
75. Karpat, *Ottoman Population*, 176; Venizelos, 36.
76. Venizelos, 24.
77. Mehmet Polatel, 'Geri Dönüş ve Emval-ı Metruke Meselesi', in Ümit Kurt and Güney Çengin (eds.), *Kıyam ve Kıtal: Osmanlı'dan Cumhuriyet'e Devletin İnşası ve Kolektif Şiddet* (Istanbul: Tarih Vakfı Yurt Yayınları, 2015), 491.
78. Adem Günaydın, 'The Return and Resettlement of the Relocated Armenians (1918–1920)', Master's Thesis: Middle East Technical University, Ankara, 2007, 61.
79. TNA/FO 371/4157/18835, 5 February 1919.
80. Lerna Ekmekçioğlu, 'A Climate for Abduction, a Climate for Redemption: The Politics of Inclusion during and after the Armenian Genocide', *Comparative Studies in Society and History*, 55.3 (2013), 527.

81. Zühtü Güven, *Anzavur İsyanı: İstiklâl Savaşı Hatıralarından Acı Bir Safha* (Ankara: Türkiye İş Bankası, 1965), 10.

82. Süleyman Beyoğlu, *İki Devir Bir İnsan: Ahmet Faik Günday ve Hatıraları* (Istanbul: Bengi Yayınları, 2011), 334.

83. Hasan Basri Çantay, *Kara Günler ve İbret Levhaları* (Istanbul: Ahmed Said Matbaası, 1964), 61.

84. Mustafa Ragıp Esatlı, *İttihat ve Terakki'nin Son Günleri: Suikastlar ve Entrikalar* (Istanbul: Bengi, 2007), 88.

85. Elif Mahir Metinsoy, *Ottoman Women during World War I: Everyday Experiences, Politics, and Conflict* (Cambridge: Cambridge University Press, 2017), 124.

86. Charles King, *Midnight at the Pera Palace: The Birth of Modern Istanbul* (New York: W. W. Norton, 2014), 148.

87. Yiğit Akın, 'The Ottoman Home Front during World War I: Everyday Politics, Society, and Culture', PhD Dissertation: Ohio State University, 2011, 168.

88. Elie Kedourie, 'Young Turks, Freemasons and Jews', *Middle Eastern Studies*, 7.1 (1971), 103.

89. PAAA R 13930, A 19923, 13 July 1919.

90. Eyüp Durukan, *Günlüklerde bir Ömür – IV: Meşum Mütareke ve Meşru Mücadele (1918–1922)* (Istanbul: Türkiye İş Bankası, 2018), 16, 25.

91. 'Zavalli Türkler', *Sabah*, 15 November 1918.

92. USNA RG 59, 867.00/855, 25 March 1919.

93. Sam Kaplan, 'Documenting History, Historicizing Documentation: French Military Officials' Ethnological Reports on Cilicia', *Comparative Studies in Society and History*, 44.2 (2002), 351.

94. Ephraim K. Jernazian, *Judgment unto Truth: Witnessing the Armenian Genocide* (New Brunswick, NJ: Transaction Publishers, 1990), 110–11.

95. Keith David Watenpaugh, *Being Modern in the Middle East: Revolution, Nationalism, Colonialism, and the Arab Middle Class* (Princeton, NJ: Princeton University Press, 2012), 142.

96. TNA/FO 371/4157/66819, 1 May 1919.

97. Sarkis Torossian, *From Dardanelles to Palestine: A True Story of Five Battle Fronts of Turkey and Her Allies and a Harem Romance* (Boston, MA: Meador Publishing Company, 1947), 202–3.

98. HHSt PA XXXVIII, 8 September 1913.

99. USNA RG 59, 867.00/859, 5 April 1919.

100. Umit Eser, 'All Loud on the Western Front: Ethnic Violence, Occupation, and the Ottoman Bureaucrats in Aydin Province (Vilâyet), 1919–1922',

PhD Dissertation: University of London, School of Oriental and African Studies, 2016, 45–6.

101. Böke (ed.), 136.

102. TNA/FO 608/103/9513, (?) May 1919.

103. Christopher Gratien, 'The Mountains Are Ours: Ecology and Settlement in Late Ottoman and Early Republican Cilicia, 1856–1956', PhD Dissertation: Georgetown University, 2015, 436.

3. The War Resumes: The Origins and Implications of a Resurgent Ottoman Empire

1. Victoria Solomonidis, 'Greece in Asia Minor: The Greek Administration of the Vilayet of Aidin, 1919–1922', PhD Dissertation: King's College, University of London, 1984, 52–3.

2. *Greek Atrocities in the Vilayet of Smyrna (May to July 1919)* (Lausanne: Permanent Bureau of the Turkish Congress at Lausanne, 1919), 20.

3. Ellinor Morack, 'Fear and Loathing in "Gavur" Izmir: Emotions in Early Republican Memories of the Greek Occupation (1919–22)', *International Journal of Middle East Studies*, 49.1 (2017), 72.

4. 'Galeyan Mili: Vilayetden Gelen Telegraflar', *Tasvir-i Efkar*, 19 May 1919.

5. Stanford J. Shaw, *From Empire to Republic: The Turkish War of National Liberation, 1918–1923: A Documentary Study* (Ankara: Türk Tarih Kurumu Basımevi, 2000), Volume 2, 619.

6. 'Yüz Bin Müslüman Sultan Ahmed Meydanında Muazzam bir Miting Akdedildi', *İkdam*, 24 May 1919.

7. M. Tayyip Gökbilgin, *Milli Mücadele Başlarken, 1 Cilt* (Ankara: Türkiye İş Bankası Yayınları, 2011), 97.

8. 'İzmir Hadisesi Münasebetiyle', *Alemdar*, 17 May 1919.

9. Eyüp Durukan, *Günlüklerde bir Ömür – IV: Meşum Mütareke ve Meşru Mücadele (1918–1922)* (Istanbul: Türkiye İş Bankası, 2018), 98.

10. Ibid., 117.

11. Yenibahçeli Şükrü et al., *Yenibahçeli Şükrü Bey'in Hatıraları* (Konya: Çizgi Kitabevi, 2011), 38.

12. Ibid., 39.

13. Ibid., 44.

14. Ibid., 44.

15. Hasan Babacan and Servet Avşar (eds.), *Cavid Bey, Meşrutiyet Ruznamesi, 3. Cilt* (Ankara: Türk Tarih Kurumu Basımevi, 2014), 667.

16. 'Bostancı Fedaisi Kurbanları', *İkdam*, 4 March 1919.

17. Rifat Yüce, *Kocaeli Tarih ve Rehberi* (İzmit: Türk Yolu Matbaası, 1945), 65.

18. TNA/FO 371/4157/62437, 5 April 1919.

19. Süleyman Beyoğlu, *İki Devir Bir İnsan: Ahmet Faik Günday ve Hatıraları* (İstanbul: Bengi Yayınları, 2011), 365.

20. Kazım Karabekir, *İstiklal Harbimiz* (İstanbul: Türkiye Yayınevi, 1960), 18.

21. Osman Selim Kocahanoğlu, *Atatürk–Karabekir Kavgası* (İstanbul: Temel Yayınları, 2013), 70.

22. Sadi Borak and Utkan Kocatürk (eds.), *Atatürk'ün Söylev ve Demeçleri: Tamim ve Telgrafları, Cilt V* (Ankara: Türk Inkılap Tarihi Enstitüsü Yayınları, 1972), 89–90.

23. Ibid., 92.

24. Ibid.

25. Gérard Tongas, *Atatürk and the True Nature of Modern Turkey* (London: Luzac & Co., 1939), 21.

26. Nilüfer Hatemi, 'Unfolding a Life: Marshal Fevzi Çakmak's Diaries', PhD Dissertation: Princeton University, 2000, 651.

27. Mustafa Kemal Atatürk, *Nutuk*, ed. Bedi Yazıcı (İstanbul: n.p., 1995), 72.

28. Yenibahçeli Şükrü et al., 108.

29. Osman Selim Kocahanoğlu (ed.), *Rauf Orbay'ın Hatıraları, 1914–1945* (İstanbul: Temel Yayınları, 2005), 198.

30. Ali Çetinkaya, *Askerlik Hayatım: Irak Cephesi, İşgal İzmir'i ve Ayvalık, 1914–1922* (İstanbul: Türkiye İş Bankası Kültür Yayınları, 2012), 6.

31. TNA/FO 371/4157/22090, 8 February 1919.

32. Çetinkaya, 347.

33. Adnan Sofuoğlu, 'İzmir İşgali Sonrasında Yunanlıların Batı Anadolu'da İşgali Genişletmeleri ve Bölgede Oluşan Milli Direniş', *Ankara Üniversitesi Türk İnkılâp Tarihi Enstitüsü Atatürk Yolu Dergisi*, 8.29 (2002), 137.

34. Çetinkaya, 442.

35. Hasan Basri Çantay, *Kara Günler ve İbret Levhaları* (İstanbul: Ahmed Said Matbaası, 1964), 16.

36. TNA/FO 608/103/20849, November 1919.

37. Atatürk, *Nutuk*, 886–7.

38. Kazım Karabekir, *Günlükler (1906–1948)* (İstanbul: Yapı Kredi Yayınları, 2009), 560.

39. Mazhar Müfit Kansu, *Erzurum'dan Ölümüne Kadar Atatürk'le Beraber* (Ankara: Türk Tarih Kurumu Basımevi, 1986), 20.

40. Cevat Dursunoğlu, *Milli Mücadele'de Erzurum* (Erzurum: Erzurum Kitaplığı, 1998), 96.

41. Ali Fuat Cebesoy, *Milli Mücadele Hatıraları* (Istanbul: Temel Yayınları, 2000), 199.

42. Ali Fuat Türkgeldi, *Görüp İşittiklerim* (Ankara: Türk Tarih Kurumu, 2010), 235.

43. Durukan, 182.

44. Ahmet İzzet Paşa, *Feryadim: Cilt 2* (Istanbul: Nehir, 1992), 74.

45. Kansu, 390.

46. 'İstanbul İntihabına Dikkat Edelim', *Tasvir-i Efkar*, 30 October 1919.

47. TNA/FO 371/4161/161867, 12 November 1919.

48. TNA/FO 371/5043/E-1363, 11 March 1920.

49. The sole non-Muslim to be elected in 1919 was Mişon Ventura, a Jewish law professor from Istanbul.

50. TBMM, *Meclisi Mebusan Zabıt Ceridesi*, Devre: 4, Cilt: 1, 31 January 1920, 50.

51. Ibid., 17 February 1920, 144–5.

52. Ibid., 9 February 1920, 72.

53. Ibid., 16 February 1920, 116.

54. TBMM, *Meclisi Ayan Zabıt Ceridesi*, Devre: 4, Cilt: 1, 16 February 1920, 67.

55. 'Arabistan', *Hakimiyet-i Milliye*, 10 January 1920.

56. 'Osmanlılık ve Türklük', *İkdam*, 30 January 1920.

57. Ibid.

58. PAAA R 13930, A 19923, 13 July 1919.

59. TBMM, *Meclisi Ayan Zabıt Ceridesi*, Devre: 4, Cilt: 1, 16 February 1920, 70.

60. Fatih Mehmet Sancaktar, 'Son Osmanlı Meclis-i Ayan'ında Damat Ferit Paşa Taraftarlarının Faaliyeti ve Anadolu Hareketine Etkisi', *Yakın Dönem Türkiye Araştırmaları*, o.9 (2006), 156.

61. Kemal Özer, *Kurtuluş Savaşında Gönen* (Gönen: Türkdili Matbaası, 1964), 60.

62. Hacim Muhittin Çarıklı, *Balıkesir ve Alaşehir Kongreleri ve Hacim Muhittin Çarıklı'nın Kuvayı Milliye Hatıraları, 1919–1920* (Ankara: Türk Inkılâp Tarihi Enstitüsü, 1967), 19.

63. Ibid., 24.

64. Özer, 60.

65. Muhittin Ünal, *Miralay Bekir Sami Günsav'ın Kurtuluş Savaşı Anıları* (Istanbul: Cem Yayınevi, 2002), 197.

66. TNA/FO 371/4158/105778, 27 June 1919.

67. Beyoğlu, 389.

68. Yenibahçeli Şükrü et al., 102–3.

69. Brad Dennis, 'Explaining Coexistence and Conflict in Eastern Anatolia, 1800–1878', PhD Dissertation: University of Utah, 2015, 99.
70. Nuri Dersimi, *Hatıratım* (Stockholm: Roja Nu Yayınları, 1986), 42.
71. *Memorandum on the Claims of the Kurd People* (Paris: Imprimerie A.-G. L'Hoir, 1919), 14.
72. Kazım Karabekir, *Kürt Meselesi* (Istanbul: Emre, 2004), 10.
73. Sinan Hakan, *Türkiye Kurulurken Kürtler (1916–1920)* (Istanbul: İletişim Yayınları, 2013), 152.
74. Andrew Mango, 'Atatürk and the Kurds', *Middle East Studies*, 35.4 (October 1999), 6–7.
75. Hakan, 309.
76. Edward Noel, *Diary of Major Noel on Special Duty in Kurdistan* (Basra: n.p., 1920), 26.
77. TBMM, *Meclisi Ayan Zabıt Ceridesi*, Devre: 4, Cilt: 1, 1 March 1920, 173.
78. 'Kürdler ve İslamiyet', *Tasvir-i Efkar*, 29 February 1920.
79. Noel, 24.
80. Çarıklı, 98.
81. Ünal, 218.
82. Ibid., 230–31.
83. BOA.DH.EUM.AYS, 29/45, 31 December 1919.
84. 'Anzavur Ahmed Bey', *Alemdar*, 3 December 1919.
85. Türk Cumhuriyet Genelkurmay Başkanlığı Harb Tarihi Dairesi, *Türk İstiklal Harbi: VI ncı Cilt, İç Ayaklanmalar (1919–1921)* (Ankara: Genelkurmay Basımevi, 1964), 66.
86. Taha Niyazi Karaca, 'Milli Mücadele'de Bozkır İsyanları', *Erciyes Üniversitesi Sosyal Bilimler Enstitüsü Dergisi*, 1.16 (2004), 172.
87. Faik Tonguç, *Birinci Dünya Savaşı'nda Bir Yedek Subayın Anıları* (Istanbul: Türkiye İş Bankası Kültür Yayınları, 2001), 386.
88. Ibid., 388.
89. 'Cengaver Çerkesler!' *Millet Yolu*, 26 April 1920.
90. Caner Yelbaşı, *The Circassians of Turkey: War, Violence and Nationalism from the Ottomans to Atatürk* (London: Bloomsbury Publishing, 2019), 56.
91. TNA/PRO 371/5043/E-1343, 9 February 1920.
92. TNA/PRO 371/5044/E-1917, 19 March 1920.
93. 'Mekteblere Beyanname', *İkdam*, 19 April 1920.

4. Towards a Sovereign State:
The Politics of Reconsolidation in the Ottoman Lands

1. Karnig Panian et al., *Goodbye, Antoura: A Memoir of the Armenian Genocide* (Stanford, CA: Stanford University Press, 2015), 152–4.
2. Der Nerses Babayan and Ümit Kurt, *Günlüğümden Sayfalar* (Istanbul: Tarih Vakfı Yurt Yayınları, 2017), 35.
3. Ibid., 38.
4. Ibid., 40.
5. Édouard Brémond, *La Cilicie en 1919–1920* (Paris: Imprimerie Nationale, 1921), 40.
6. 'Dans le Levant: La Situation en Cilicie', *Le Temps*, 17 March 1920.
7. Muktar el Farouk, 'La Question Indigène', *L'Ikdam*, 21 May 1920.
8. Paul C. Helmreich, *From Paris to Sèvres: The Partition of the Ottoman Empire at the Peace Conference of 1919–1920* (Columbus, OH: Ohio State University Press, 1974), 280.
9. TBMM, *Meclisi Mebusan Zabıt Ceridesi*, Devre: 4, Cilt: 1, 13 March 1920, 461–3.
10. Ibid., 12 February 1920, 99.
11. Mustafa Kemal Atatürk, *Atatürk'ün Bütün Eserleri: 1920, Cilt 7* (Istanbul: Kaynak Yayınları, 2002), 122.
12. TNA/FO 371/5047/E-3543, 23 March 1920.
13. Ali Fuat Türkgeldi, *Görüp İşittiklerim* (Ankara: Türk Tarih Kurumu, 2010), 260.
14. TNA/FO 371/5047/E3673, 8 April 1920.
15. Amit Bein, *Ottoman Ulema, Turkish Republic: Agents of Change and Guardians of Tradition* (Stanford, CA: Stanford University Press, 2011), 102.
16. Kemal H. Karpat, *Ottoman Population, 1830–1914: Demographic and Social Characteristics* (Madison, WI: University of Wisconsin Press, 1985), 172–3.
17. Mazhar Müfit Kansu, *Erzurum'dan Ölümüne Kadar Atatürk'le Beraber* (Ankara: Türk Tarih Kurumu Basımevi, 1986), 505–6.
18. TBMM, *Zabıt Ceridesi*, Devre: 1, Cilt: 1, 24 April 1920, 30.
19. Andrew Mango, *Atatürk: The Biography of the Founder of Modern Turkey* (New York: Overlook Press, 2002), 278.
20. TBMM, *Gizli Celse Zabıtları*, Devre: 1, Cilt: 1, 24 April 1920, 6.
21. Lohanizade Mustafa Nureddin, *Gaziantep Savunması* (Gaziantep: Kurtuluş Matbaası, 1974), 16.
22. Ibid., 16–17.

23. Ibid., 23.

24. Ali Saib Ursavaş, *Kilikya Faciaları ve Urfa'nın Kurtuluş Mücadeleleri* (Ankara: 1924), 23.

25. See Zekeriya Türkmen, 'İşgal Yıllarında İstanbul'daki Uygulamalar: Mütareke Döneminde Ermeniler Tarafından Türk Çocuklarının Kaçırılması ve Hristiyanlaştırılması', *KÖK Araştırmalar*, 2.2 (2000), 265–83.

26. Lohanizade, 26.

27. TNA/FO 371/5044/E-1784, 4 March 1920.

28. Robert Zeidner, 'The Tricolor over the Taurus: The French in Cilicia and Vicinity, 1918–1922', PhD Dissertation: University of Utah, 1991, 349.

29. TNA/FO 371/5044/E-1784, 4 March 1920.

30. Ursavaş, 115.

31. Ephraim K. Jernazian, *Judgment unto Truth: Witnessing the Armenian Genocide* (New Brunswick, NJ: Transaction Publishers, 1990), 118.

32. TNA/FO 371/5047/E-4513, 27 April 1920.

33. Babayan and Kurt, 41–2.

34. Lohanizade, 40.

35. Panian et al., 176.

36. TNA/FO 371/5048/E-5042, 20 May 1920.

37. Panian et al., 182–3.

38. Babayan and Kurt, 52.

39. Brémond, 61–2.

40. Lohanizade, 214.

41. Ibid., 265–6.

42. Kazım Karabekir, *Günlükler (1906–1948)* (Istanbul: Yapı Kredi Yayınları, 2009), 457.

43. PAAA R 11044, A 18188, 29 April 1918.

44. Karabekir, *Günlükler*, 475.

45. Ali İhsan Sabis, *Harp Hatıralarım: Birinci Cihan Harbi, Cilt IV* (Istanbul: Nehir Yayınları, 1993), 277.

46. Michael G. Smith, 'Anatomy of a Rumour: Murder Scandal, the Musavat Party and Narratives of the Russian Revolution in Baku, 1917–20', *Journal of Contemporary History*, 36.2 (2001), 228.

47. TNA/FO 371/5166/E-2610, 1 April 1920.

48. Alexander E. Balistreri, 'A Provisional Republic in the Southwest Caucasus: Discourses of Self-Determination on the Ottoman–Caucasian Frontier, 1918–19', in Yaşar Tolga Cora et al. (eds.), *The Ottoman East in the Nineteenth Century: Societies, Identities and Politics* (London: I.B. Tauris, 2016), 71.

49. TNA/FO 371/5165/E-1509, 15 March 1920.

50. TNA/FO 371/5166/E-2610, 1 April 1920.

51. Kazım Karabekir, *İstiklal Harbimiz* (Istanbul: Türkiye Yayınevi, 1960), 445.

52. Nejdet Karaköse, 'Askeri, Siyasi ve Silah Sanayicisi Kişiliği ile Nuri Paşa (Killigil)', PhD Dissertation: Dokuz Eylül University, 2010, 302.

53. George A. Bournoutian, *Armenia and Imperial Decline: The Yerevan Province, 1900–1914* (London: Routledge, 2018), 34.

54. Richard G. Hovannisian, *The Republic of Armenia, Volume II: From Versailles to London, 1919–1920* (Berkeley, CA: University of California Press, 1982), 6.

55. Ronald Grigor Suny, *Looking toward Ararat: Armenia in Modern History* (Bloomington, IN: Indiana University Press, 1993), 127.

56. Ari Sekeryan, 'The Armenians in the Ottoman Empire after the First World War (1918–1923)', PhD Dissertation: Oxford University, 2018, 182.

57. Karabekir, *İstiklal Harbimiz*, 473.

58. Karabekir, *Günlükler*, 627.

59. Richard G. Hovannisian, *The Republic of Armenia, Volume IV: Between Crescent and Sickle: Partition and Sovietization* (Berkeley, CA: University of California Press, 1996), 286.

60. Kalusd Sürmenyan, *Harbiyeli Bir Osmanlı Ermenisi* (Istanbul: Tarih Vakfı Yurt Yayınları, 2015), 112.

61. Ibid., 115.

62. Babayan and Kurt, 57.

63. Vahé Tachjian, *La France en Cilicie et en Haute-Mésopotamie: Aux confins de la Turquie, de la Syrie et de l'Irak, 1919–1933* (Paris: Karthala, 2004), 220.

64. 'The Evacuation of Cilicia', *The Orient*, February 1922.

65. Karpat, *Ottoman Population*, 176.

66. Tachjian, 258.

67. TBMM, *Gizli Celse Zabıtları*, Devre: 1, Cilt: 1, 24 April 1920, 3.

68. Theodor Wiegand and Cemal Paşa. *Alte Denkmäler aus Syrien, Palästina und Westarabien: 100 Tafeln mit beschreibendem Text* (Berlin: G. Reimer, 1918), 12.

69. Selim Deringil, *The Ottoman Twilight in the Arab Lands: Turkish Memoirs and Testimonies of the Great War* (Boston, MA: Academic Studies Press, 2019), 109.

70. Ibid., 44.

71. Djemal Pasha, *Memories of a Turkish Statesman, 1913–1919* (New York: George H. Doran Company, 1922), 206.

72. Deringil, *Ottoman Twilight*, 104.

73. Ibid., xxv.

74. Mesut Uyar, 'Ottoman Arab Officers between Nationalism and Loyalty during the First World War', *War in History*, 20.4 (2013), 538.

75. Djemal Pasha, 300.

76. Hasan Kayalı, *Arabs and Young Turks: Ottomanism, Arabism, and Islamism in the Ottoman Empire, 1908–1918* (Berkeley, CA: University of California Press, 1997), 29.

77. Djemal Pasha, 199.

78. Ibid., 61–2.

79. Deringil, *Ottoman Twilight*, 12.

80. PAAA R 14161, A21246, 29 October 1913.

81. USNA RG 59, 867.00/789, 3 August 1916.

82. Thomas Kühn, 'An Imperial Borderland as Colony: Knowledge Production and the Elaboration of Difference in Ottoman Yemen, 1872–1918', *MIT-EJMES*, 3 (Spring 2003), 7.

83. Ü. Gülsüm Polat, 'Osmanlı'dan Cumhuriyet'e Yemen ile İlişkiler (1911–1938)', *Atatürk Araştırma Merkezi Dergisi*, 33.96 (2017), 121.

84. IOR/L/PS/10/658, 'Arab Bulletin', no. 109, 27. See https://www.qdl.qa/en/archive/81055/vdc_100048056857.0x00000f (consulted 6 April 2022).

85. Polat, 'Osmanlı'dan Cumhuriyet'e', 134.

86. Ü. Gülsüm Polat, *Türk-Arap İlişkileri: Eski Eyaletler Yeni Komşulara Dönüşürken (1914–1923)* (Istanbul: Kronik Kitap, 2019), 303.

87. Polat, 'Osmanlı'dan Cumhuriyet'e', 135.

88. Alia El Bakri, '"Memories of the Beloved": Oral Histories from the 1916–1919 Siege of Medina', *International Journal of Middle East Studies*, 46.4 (2014), 711.

89. IOR/L/PS/10/658, 'Notes on the Middle East No. 3', 100. See https://www.qdl.qa/en/archive/81055/vdc_100048056858.0x000012 (consulted 6 April 2022).

90. 'The Arabs and the Caliphate', London *Times*, 30 April 1920.

91. Süleyman Beyoğlu, *İki Devir Bir İnsan: Ahmet Faik Günday ve Hatıraları* (Istanbul: Bengi Yayınları, 2011), 100.

92. IOR/L/PS/20/250, 'Reports of Administration for 1918 of Divisions and Districts of the Occupied Territories in Mesopotamia. Vol. I', 416. See https://www.qdl.qa/en/archive/81055/vdc_100038755287.0x000028 (consulted 6 April 2022).

93. Mahmut Nedim Kerkük, *Hatıratım, 1334 (1918)* (Ankara: Altınküre Yayınları, 2002), 39.

94. Arnold T. Wilson and Gertrude L. Bell, *Review of the Civil Administration of Mesopotamia* (London: His Majesty's Stationery Office, 1920), 127.

95. Ibid., 26.

96. Mustafa Kemal Atatürk, *Atatürk'ün Bütün Eserleri: 1915–1919, Cilt 2* (Istanbul: Kaynak Yayınları, 1999), 378.

97. 'Irak'ta', *Hakimiyet-i Milliye*, 14 January 1920.

98. TBMM, *Gizli Celse Zabıtları*, Devre: 1, Cilt: 3, 22 July 1922, 563.

99. Sabis, *Harp Hatıralarım*, 325.

100. Sinan Hakan, *Türkiye Kurulurken Kürtler (1916–1920)* (Istanbul: İletişim Yayınları, 2013), 130.

101. Ibid., 163.

102. 'Irak ve Kürdistan Ahvali', *Hakimiyet-i Milliye*, 2 February 1920.

103. TBMM, *Gizli Celse Zabıtları*, Devre: 1, Cilt: 3, 22 July 1922, 563.

104. Polat, *Türk-Arap İlişkileri*, 235.

105. Wadie Jwaideh, *The Kurdish National Movement: Its Origins and Development* (Syracuse, NY: Syracuse University Press, 2006), 194.

106. Hasan Kayalı, *Imperial Resilience: The Great War's End, Ottoman Longevity, and Incidental Nations* (Berkeley, CA: University of California Press, 2021), 151–2.

107. Zekeriya Türkmen, 'Özdemir Bey'in Musul Harekâtı ve İngilizlerin Karşı Tedbirleri (1921–1923)', *Atatürk Araştırma Merkezi Dergisi*, 17.49 (2001), 67.

108. Wilson and Bell, 58.

109. Binbaşı Vecihi, *Filistin Ricatı* (Istanbul: Matbaa-yı Askeriye, 1921), 12.

110. James L. Gelvin, *Divided Loyalties: Nationalism and Mass Politics in Syria at the Close of Empire* (Berkeley, CA: University of California, 1998), 171.

111. Keith David Watenpaugh, *Being Modern in the Middle East: Revolution, Nationalism, Colonialism, and the Arab Middle Class* (Princeton, NJ: Princeton University Press, 2012), 141.

112. 'Vilayat Arabiye'de', *İkdam*, 1 January 1919.

113. Phebe Marr, 'Yasin al-Hashimi: The Rise and Fall of a Nationalist', PhD Dissertation: Harvard University, 1966, 82.

114. Alp Yenen. 'Envisioning Turco-Arab Co-Existence between Empire and Nationalism', *Die Welt des Islams*, 61.1 (2021), 106.

115. Oktay Gökdemir (ed.), *İzmir'e Doğru* (İzmir: İzmir Büyükşehir Belediyesi, 2010), 112.

116. TBMM, *Gizli Celse Zabıtları*, Devre: 1, Cilt: 1, 24 April 1920, 2–3.

117. 'Tehlike Karşısındayız', *İrade-i Milliye*, 9 February 1920.

118. Elizabeth F. Thompson, *How the West Stole Democracy from the Arabs: The Syrian Arab Congress of 1920 and the Destruction of Its Liberal-Islamic Alliance* (New York: Atlantic Monthly Press, 2020), 173.

119. Stefan Winter, *A History of the 'Alawis: From Medieval Aleppo to the Turkish Republic* (Princeton, NJ: Princeton University Press, 2016), 252.

120. Robin Leonard Bidwell et al. (eds.), *British Documents on Foreign Affairs – Reports and Papers from the Foreign Office Confidential Print, Part II ... Series B ... Volume 2: The Allies Take Control, 1920–1921* (Frederick, MD: University Publications of America, 1985), 53.

121. TBMM, *Zabıt Ceridesi*, Devre: 1, Cilt: 26, 23 December 1922, 9.

122. Hasan Rıza Soyak, *Atatürk'ten Hatıralar* (Istanbul: Yapı Kredi Yayınları, 2004), 528.

123. TBMM, *Zabıt Ceridesi*, Devre: 1, Cilt: 1, 1 May 1920, 165.

124. TBMM, *Gizli Zabıt Ceridesi*, Devre: 1 Cilt: 4, 22 September 1923, 262, 270.

125. Ibid., 269.

5. 'Beyond the Reach of Scorn': A Fateful Year of Protests, Atrocities and Combat

1. 'Suikasd Mürettiblerinin Tevkifi', *Alemdar*, 1 June 1920.

2. Tarık Mümtaz Göztepe, *Mütareke Günleri* (Istanbul: Cümle Yayınları, 2017), 486–7.

3. TNA/FO 371/5050/E 8636, 27 May 1920.

4. '"Sultanahmet" ve "Aya Sofia" Arasında: Dünkü Tezahürat-ı Milliye', *İkdam*, 22 May 1920.

5. TNA/FO 371/5168/E 6631, 17 June 1920.

6. Andrew Ryan, *The Last of the Dragomans* (London: Geoffrey Bles, 1951), 173.

7. Briton Cooper Busch, *Mudros to Lausanne: Britain's Frontier in West Asia, 1918–1923* (Albany, NY: State University of New York Press, 1976), 228.

8. Zühtü Güven, *Anzavur İsyanı: İstiklâl Savaşı Hatıralarından Acı Bir Safha* (Ankara: Türkiye İş Bankası, 1965), 77.

9. 'The Local Press', *The Orient*, 7 July 1920.

10. Göztepe, *Mütareke Günleri*, 479.

11. Ibid., 495.

12. TBMM, *Gizli Celse Zabıtları*, Devre: 1, Cilt: 1, 25 September 1920, 138.

13. TBMM, *Zabıt Ceridesi*, Devre: 1, Cilt: 7, 20 January 1921, 332.

14. Mustafa Kemal Atatürk, *Atatürk'ün Bütün Eserleri: 1920, Cilt 9* (Istanbul: Kaynak Yayınları, 2002), 387.

15. 'Payitaht – Anadolu', *İkdam*, 5 October 1920.

16. 'Asya Tehlikesi', *Hakimiyet-i Milliye*, 2 February 1920.

17. Hüseyin Fehmi Genişol, *Çanakkale'den Bağdat'a Esaretten Kurtuluş Savaşı'na: Cephede Sekiz Yıl Sekiz Ay (1914–1923)* (Istanbul: Türkiye İş Bankası Kültür Yayınları, 2010), 105.

18. Ibid., 92.

19. Ibid., 215.

20. 'Mühim Vak'aların Hülasası', *Yeni Giresun*, 21 March 1922.

21. 'Eski bir İmparatorluğunun İnhilalı', *İkdam*, 7 November 1918.

22. Oktay Gökdemir (ed.), *İzmir'e Doğru* (İzmir: İzmir Büyükşehir Belediyesi, 2010), 63.

23. Yusuf Akçura, *Üç Tarz-ı Siyaset* (Ankara: Türk Tarih Kurumu Basımevi, 1976), 34.

24. Philip Hendrick Stoddard, 'The Ottoman Government and the Arabs, 1911 to 1918: A Preliminary Study of the *Teşkilat-ı Mahsusa*', PhD Dissertation: Princeton University, 1963, 117.

25. 'Bulletin du Jour: Abordez le Problème Turc!' *Le Temps*, 11 December 1919.

26. TNA/FO 371/4161/162140, 6 December 1919.

27. Busch, 195.

28. Azmi Özcan, *Pan-Islamism: Indian Muslims, the Ottomans and Britain (1877–1924)* (Leiden: Brill, 1997), 181.

29. Mahatma Gandhi, *Speeches and Writings of M. K. Gandhi* (Madras: G. A. Natesan, 1922), 493.

30. M. Naeem Qureshi, *Pan-Islam in British Indian Politics: A Study of the Khilafat Movement, 1918–1924* (Leiden: Brill, 1999), 180.

31. Ibid., 215.

32. 'Afganistan Sefiri Hazretlerinin Resim Kabulu', *Hakimet-i Milliye*, 26 April 1921.

33. A. Alp Yenen, 'The Young Turk Aftermath: Making Sense of Transnational Contentious Politics at the End of the Ottoman Empire, 1918–1922', PhD Dissertation: University of Basel, 2019, 426.

34. Israel Gershoni and James P. Jankowski, *Egypt, Islam, and the Arabs: The Search for Egyptian Nationhood, 1900–1930* (New York: Oxford University Press, 1987), 46.

35. Muktar el Farouk, 'La Question Indigène', *L'Ikdam*, 21 May 1920.

36. Michael Goebel, *Anti-Imperial Metropolis: Interwar Paris and the Seeds of Third World Nationalism* (Cambridge: Cambridge University Press, 2015), 253.

37. V.T., 'Maroc et Turquie', *L'Évolution Nord-Africain*, 1 April 1921.

38. Mustafa Kemal Atatürk, *Atatürk'ün Bütün Eserleri: 1920–1921, Cilt 10* (Istanbul: Kaynak Yayınları, 1999), 117–19.

39. İsmail Hakkı Kobakizade, *Bir Mübadilin Hatıraları* (Istanbul: Yapı Kredi Yayınları, 2008), 59.

40. 'Müslümanlarda Muhacirat Fikri Var Mı?', *Hak*, 28 October 1922.

41. Nurcan Özgür-Baklacıoğlu, 'Devletlerin Dış Politikaları Açısından Göç Olgusu: Balkanlar'dan Türkiye'ye Arnavut Göçleri (1920–1990)', PhD Dissertation, Istanbul University, 2003, 227.

42. Merve Dogan Kader and Seán Patrick Smyth, 'Neither Suvla nor Seddul-Bahr – When Harp and Crescent Intertwined', *History Ireland*, 28.2 (2020), 43.

43. Pierre Loti, 'Pour la Turquie', *L'Ikdam*, 12–19 March 1920.

44. Mustafa Kemal Atatürk, *Atatürk'ün Bütün Eserleri: 1921, Cilt 11* (Istanbul: Kaynak Yayınları, 1999), 230.

45. Barbara Gilmore, 'Albert Dewey', USC Shoah Foundation Visual Archive Online, 29:58, https://vhaonline.usc.edu/viewingPage?testimonyID=56392&segmentNumber=0, 22 March 1975 (consulted 30 October 2021).

46. Andrew Patrick, *America's Forgotten Middle East Initiative: The King–Crane Commission of 1919* (London: I.B. Tauris, 2015), 168.

47. Seçil Karal Akgün, 'Louis E. Browne and the Leaders of the 1919 Sivas Congress', in George S. Harris and Nur Bilge Criss (eds.), *Studies in Atatürk's Turkey: The American Dimension* (Leiden: Brill, 2009), 38.

48. 'Senate Rejects Lausanne Treaty', *New York Times*, 19 January 1927.

49. Yenen, 'The Young Turk Aftermath', 157.

50. 'Kızıl Tehlike Etrafında', *Hakimiyet-i Milliye*, 11 February 1920.

51. 'Türk Bolşevik İttifakı', *Hakimiyet-i Milliye*, 5 October 1920.

52. Mustafa Kemal Atatürk, *Atatürk'ün Bütün Eserleri: 1920, Cilt 9*, 272–3.

53. Bülent Gökay, *Soviet Eastern Policy and Turkey, 1920–1991: Soviet Foreign Policy, Turkey and Communism* (London: Routledge, 2006), 22.

54. 'Angora's Reliance on Lenin', London *Times*, 6 July 1921.

55. Hüseyin Cahit Yalçın, *İttihatçı Liderlerin Gizli Mektupları* (Istanbul: Temel Yayınları, 2002), 81.

56. İzzettin Çalışlar, *On Yıllık Savaşın Günlüğü* (Istanbul: Yapı Kredi Yayınları, 1997), 321.

57. Ibid., 327.

58. TBMM, *Zabıt Ceridesi*, Devre: 1, Cilt: 7, 8 January 1921, 228.

59. Berthe Georges-Gaulis, *Angora, Constantinople, Londres* (Paris: Armand Colin, 1922), 15.

60. Ziya Gökalp, *The Principles of Turkism* (Leiden: E. J. Brill, 1968), 53.

61. Necmettin Sılan, *İlk Meclis Anketi: Birinci Dönem TBMM Üyelerinin Gelecekten Beklentileri* (Ankara: TBMM Kültür, Sanat ve Yayın Kurulu, 2004), 191.

62. Ibid., 206.

63. Ibid., 213–14.

64. Ibid., 123–4.

65. Sabahattin Selek, *Anadolu İhtilali, II. Cilt* (Istanbul: Kastaş Yayınları, 2004), 518.

66. Emel Akal, *Milli Mücadelenin Başlangıcında: Mustafa Kemal, İttihat Terakki ve Bolşevizm* (Istanbul: TÜSTAV, 2002), 88.

67. İsmail Kandil, 'Türk Basınında Osmanlı Bağımsızlık Günü Kutlamaları', Master's Thesis: Istanbul University, 2010, 92–4.

68. Ioannis Nioutsikos, 'The Greek Military Strategy in the Asia Minor Campaign, 1919–1922: An Application of Clausewitz's Theory on Culmination', in Konstantinos Travlos (ed.), *Salvation and Catastrophe: The Greek–Turkish War, 1919–1922* (Lanham, MD: Lexington Books, 2020), 149.

69. '15,000 Muhacire Acılım ve Yardım Edilim', *Vakit*, 4 June 1921.

70. Arnold J. Toynbee, *The Western Question in Greece and Turkey: A Study in the Contact of Civilisations* (London: Constable and Company, 1922), 285.

71. 'Atrocities in Ismid and Yalova', *Manchester Guardian*, 20 August 1921.

72. See Mustafa Turan et al. (eds.), *Türkiye'de Yunan Fecayii* (Ankara: Berikan, 2003), xii–xv.

73. 'Marmara'nın Derdli Sahillerine Bir Nazar', *Tasvir-i Efkar*, 5 June 1921.

74. Toynbee, 282–3.

75. Victoria Solomonidis, 'Greece in Asia Minor: The Greek Administration of the Vilayet of Aidin, 1919–1922', PhD Dissertation: King's College, University of London, 1984, 170.

76. Ibid., 169.

77. İbrahim Ethem Akıncı, *Demirci Akıncıları* (Ankara: Türk Tarih Kurumu, 1989), 288.

78. Caner Yelbaşı, *The Circassians of Turkey: War, Violence and Nationalism from the Ottomans to Atatürk* (London: Bloomsbury Publishing, 2019), 112.

79. 'İzmir'deki Mahudlara bir Cevab', *Açık Söz*, 3 November 1921.

80. TBMM, *Gizli Zabıt Ceridesi*, Devre: 1, Cilt: 2, 4 October 1921, 269–70.

81. Türk Cumhuriyet Genelkurmay Başkanlığı Harb Tarihi Dairesi, *Türk İstiklal Harbi: VI ncı Cilt, İç Ayaklanmalar (1919–1921)* (Ankara: Genelkurmay Basımevi, 1964), 144.

82. USNA RG 59, 867.4016/454, 3 May 1922.

83. İsmail Akbal, *Milli Mücadele Döneminde Trabzon'da Muhalefet* (Trabzon: Serander, 2008), 265.

84. 'Hangings in Asia Minor', London *Times*, 18 October 1921.

85. 'The Greek Offensive', *Manchester Guardian*, 14 July 1921.

86. George W. Gawrych, *The Young Atatürk: From Ottoman Soldier to Statesman of Turkey* (London: I.B. Tauris, 2013), 146.

87. Andrew Mango, *Atatürk: The Biography of the Founder of Modern Turkey* (New York: Overlook Press, 2002), 321.

88. Zeki Sarıhan, *Kurtuluş Savaşı Günlüğü, IV* (Ankara: Türk Tarih Kurumu, 1996), 57.

89. Mustafa Kemal Atatürk, *Atatürk'ün Bütün Eserleri: Cilt 11*, 401–10.

90. Jean Schlicklin, *Angora: L'Aube de la Turquie nouvelle (1919–1922)* (Paris: Berger-Levrault, 1922), 40.

91. Georges-Gaulis, 106.

92. 'Munich and Angora', *Manchester Guardian*, 8 August 1922.

6. 'A New Kind of Turk':
The Ottoman Empire's Final Days

1. Victoria Solomonidis, 'Greece in Asia Minor: The Greek Administration of the Vilayet of Aidin, 1919–1922', PhD Dissertation: King's College, University of London, 1984, 137.

2. Rıfat N. Bali (ed.), *A Survey of Some Social Conditions in Smyrna, Asia Minor, May 1921* (Istanbul: Libra Kitap, 2009), 72–3.

3. A Resident in Smyrna for Thirty Years, 'The Greeks in Smyrna', London *Times*, 16 December 1921.

4. TBMM, *Zabıt Ceridesi*, Devre: 1, Cilt: 20, 15 May 1922, 56.

5. '15 Mayıs 335 Kara Günü', *İkdam*, 15 May 1922.

6. Michael Llewellyn Smith, *Ionian Vision: Greece in Asia Minor, 1919–1922* (London: Hurst & Company, 1998), 269.

7. 'Mr. Montagu's Defence', *Observer*, 12 March 1922.

8. 'Greece Seeks to Occupy Constantinople', *Manchester Guardian*, 31 July 1922.

9. Umit Eser, 'All Loud on the Western Front: Ethnic Violence, Occupation, and the Ottoman Bureaucrats in Aydin Province (Vilâyet), 1919–1922', PhD Dissertation: University of London, School of Oriental and African Studies, 2016, 141.

10. Cevdet Kerim İncedayı, *İstiklal Harbi (Garp Cephesi)* (Istanbul: Yapı Kredi Yayınları, 2007), 250.

11. *Lausanne Conference on Near Eastern Affairs, 1922–1923: Records of Proceedings and Draft Terms of Peace* (London: His Majesty's Stationery Office, 1923), 676.

12. TNA/WO 158/485/2489, 22 May 1922.

13. Emre Erol, *The Ottoman Crisis in Western Anatolia: Turkey's Belle Époque and the Transition to a Modern Nation State* (London: I.B. Tauris, 2016), 226.

14. J. Michael Hagopian, 'Antigone Raphael', USC Shoah Foundation Visual Archive Online, https://vhaonline.usc.edu/viewingPage?testimonyID=56638&returnIndex=0, 9:39, 19 July 1985 (consulted 17 November 2021).

15. Ellinor Morack, *The Dowry of the State? The Politics of Abandoned Property and the Population Exchange in Turkey, 1921–1945* (Bamberg: University of Bamberg Press, 2017), 182–3.

16. 'Atatürke Aid Hatıralar', *Cumhuriyet*, 30 January 1939.

17. Andrew Mango, *Atatürk: The Biography of the Founder of Modern Turkey* (New York: Overlook Press, 2002), 346–7.

18. Masami Arai, *Turkish Nationalism in the Young Turk Era* (Leiden: Brill, 1992), 60.

19. Erol A. F. Baykal, *The Ottoman Press (1908–1923)* (Leiden: Brill, 2019), 133.

20. Bülent Çukurova, 'Büyük Taarruz Günlerinde Ali Kemal ve Siyasi Görüşleri', *Atatürk Yolu Dergisi*, 6.23 (1999), 367.

21. Tarık Mümtaz Göztepe, *Mütareke Günleri* (Istanbul: Cümle Yayınları, 2017), 598.

22. Mahmut Esat Bozkurt, *Toplu Eserler, I* (Istanbul: Kaynak Yayınları, 2014), 264.

23. Ibid., 562.

24. Ahmet Ağaoğlu, *İhtilal mı, İnkilap mı* (Ankara: Alaeddin Kiral Basımevi, 1942), 35.

25. Jean Schlicklin, 'Une Interview de Mustapha Kemal', *Le Petit Parisien*, 18 May 1922.

26. M. Abdülhalik Renda, *Hatırat* (Istanbul: Yapı Kredi Yayınları, 2018), 243.

27. Ali Vasıb, *Bir Şehzadenin Hatıratı* (Istanbul: Yapı Kredi Yayınları, 2012), 113.

28. Andrew Ryan, *The Last of the Dragomans* (London: Geoffrey Bles, 1951), 159.

29. Ahmed Emin Yalman, *Yakin Tarihte Gördüklerim ve Geçirdiklerim* (Istanbul: Pera Turizm ve Ticaret, 1997), 700.

30. 'Une Visite à Mustapha Kemal', *Le Petit Parisien*, 17 May 1922.

31. 'The Two Chiefs', London *Times*, 3 October 1922.

32. Winston S. Churchill, *The World Crisis: The Aftermath* (London: Thornton Butterworth, 1929), 368.

33. Hasan Babacan and Servet Avşar (eds.), *Cavid Bey, Meşrutiyet Ruznamesi, 4. Cilt* (Ankara: Türk Tarih Kurumu Basımevi, 2014), 327.

34. A. L. Macfie, 'The Chanak Affair: September–October 1922', *Balkan Studies,* 20.2 (1979), 323.

35. Ibid., 321.

36. 'İstanbul'un Milli Hükümetimiz Mümessiline Yaptığı Hararetle ve Samimi İstikbal Resmi', *Vakit*, 20 October 1922.

37. Halit Kaya, *Refet Bele: Askeri ve Siyasi Hayatı, 1881–1963* (Istanbul: Bengi, 2010), 141.

38. 'Une Conversation de Mustapha Kemal Pacha avec l'envoyé spécial du "Petit Parisien" en Turquie', *Le Petit Parisien*, 1 November 1922.

39. TBMM, *Zabıt Ceridesi*, Devre: 1, Cilt: 24, 30 October 1922, 292–3.

40. Ibid., 1 November 1922, 300.

41. Ibid., 315.

42. Ibid., 311.

43. Nurullah Ardıç, *Islam and the Politics of Secularism: The Caliphate and Middle Eastern Modernization in the Early 20th Century* (London: Routledge, 2012), 263.

44. Erol Ülker, 'Turkish National Movement, Mass Mobilization, and Demographic Change in Istanbul, 1922–1923', in Meltem Ersoy and Esra Ozyurek (eds.), *Contemporary Turkey at a Glance II* (Wiesbaden: Springer, 2017), 191.

45. Christine M. Philliou, *Turkey: A Past against History* (Berkeley, CA: University of California Press, 2021), 127.

46. Göztepe, *Mütareke Günleri*, 661.

47. Ryan, 169.
48. Charles Harington, *Tim Harington Looks Back* (London: John Murray, 1941), 124.
49. Tarık Mümtaz Göztepe, *Gurbet Cehennemi: Mütareke Sonrası Hatırat* (Istanbul: Kopernik Kitap, 2018), 178.
50. 'Mehmed VI', *Le Temps*, 18 May 1926.
51. Kemal Atatürk, *Atatürk'ün Söylev ve Demeçleri, Cilt* 2 (Ankara: Türk İnkilap Enstitüsü Yayınları, 2006), 105–6.
52. 'The Return of Turkey', *London Times*, 14 October 1922.
53. 'Saw a New Turkey Born at Angora', *New York Times*, 26 August 1923.
54. Ameer Ali, 'The Caliphate', London *Times*, 7 November 1922.
55. Mahmut Goloğlu, *Devrimler ve Tepkiler* (Ankara: Turhan Kitabevi, 1972), 139.
56. 'Dil Bayramı', *Son Posta*, 30 September 1934.
57. 'Turkish Press Criticism of Kemalists', *Manchester Guardian*, 15 November 1922.
58. Ardıç, 295.
59. Bozkurt, 201.
60. Maria Christina Chatziioannou and Dimitris Kamouzis, 'From a Multi-ethnic Empire to Two National States: The Economic Activities of the Greek Orthodox Population of Istanbul, ca. 1870–1939', in Darja Reuschke et al. (eds.), *The Economies of Urban Diversity: The Ruhr Area and Istanbul* (Basingstoke: Palgrave Macmillan, 2013), 134.
61. https://www.ekathimerini.com/society/diaspora/258839/greeks-in-istanbul-keeping-close-eye-on-developments/ (consulted 9 January 2022).
62. Fethiye Çetin, *My Grandmother: An Armenian-Turkish Memoir* (London: Verso, 2012), ix; https://www.hurriyetdailynews.com/armenian-population-of-turkey-dwindling-rapidly-patriarch-151691 (consulted 9 January 2022).
63. Fahriye Emgili, *Yunanistan'dan Mersin'e: Köklerinden Koparılmış Hayatlar* (Istanbul: Bilge Kültür Sanat, 2011), 244.
64. Kazım Karabekir, *Kürt Meselesi* (Istanbul: Emre, 2004), 48.
65. http://www.agos.com.tr/tr/yazi/23286/dersim-soykirimi-ve-kotulugun-siradanligi (consulted 17 November 2021).
66. Geoffrey Lewis, *The Turkish Language Reform: A Catastrophic Success* (Oxford: Oxford University Press, 1999), 161.
67. Churchill, 437.
68. Yahya Kemal, '1918', in Yahya Kemal, *Kendi Gök Kubbemiz* (Istanbul: Yahya Kemal Enstitüsü, 1974), 79.

69. https://www.tccb.gov.tr/haberler/410/52441/15-temmuz-turk-milletinin-ikinci-kurtulus-savasidir (consulted 30 November 2021).
70. https://www.bbc.com/turkce/haberler-turkiye-37773388 (consulted 30 November 2021).
71. https://www.trthaber.com/haber/gundem/cumhurbaskani-erdogandan-1916da-kutul-amare-mesaji-247810.html (consulted 30 November 2021).
72. Pelin Böke (ed.), *İzmir, 1919–1922: Tanıklıklar* (Istanbul: Tarih Vakfı Yurt Yayınları, 2006), 137.

Bibliography

Archives

Başbakanlık Cumhuriyet Arşivi (BCA)
Başbakanlık Osmanlı Arşivi (BOA)
Haus, Hof und Staat (HHSt)
India Office Records and Private Papers (IOR) (consulted via the Qatar National Library)
Politisches Archiv – Auswärtiges Amt (PAAA)
The National Archive (TNA)
United States National Archives (USNA)
USC Shoah Foundation Visual Archive Online

Document Collections

Papers Relating to the Foreign Relations of the United States, Paris Peace Conference, 1919
Türkiye Büyük Millet Meclis (TBMM), *Gizli Celse Zabıtları*
Türkiye Büyük Millet Meclis (TBMM), *Gizli Zabıt Ceridesi*
Türkiye Büyük Millet Meclis (TBMM), *Meclisi Ayan Zabıt Ceridesi*
Türkiye Büyük Millet Meclis (TBMM), *Meclisi Mebusan Zabıt Ceridesi*
Türkiye Büyük Millet Meclis (TBMM), *Zabıt Ceridesi*

Periodicals

Açık Söz
Alemdar
Cumhuriyet

L'Évolution Nord-Africain
Hak
Hakimiyet-i Milliye
Harper's New Monthly Magazine
İkdam
L'Ikdam
İleri
İrade-i Milliye
Manchester Guardian
Millet Yolu
New York Times
Observer
The Orient
Osmanischer Lloyd
Le Petit Parisien
Sabah
Son Posta
Tanin
Tasvir-i Efkar
Le Temps
Tercüman-ı Hakikat
Times of London
Vakit
Yeni Giresun

Monographs and Other Published Materials

Ağaoğlu, Ahmet. *İhtilal mı, İnkilap mı*. Ankara: Alaeddin Kıral Basımevi, 1942.
———. *Mütareke ve Sürgün Hatıralar*. Istanbul: Doğu Kitabevi, 2010.
Aharonean, Awetis, et al. *The Armenian Question before the Peace Conference*. New York: Press Bureau, the Armenian National Union of America, 1919.
Ahmad, Feroz. *The Young Turks: The Committee of Union and Progress in Turkish Politics, 1908–1914*. London: Hurst, 2009.
Ahmet İzzet Paşa. *Feryadım*. Istanbul: Nehir, 1992.
Akal, Emel. *Milli Mücadelenin Başlangıcında: Mustafa Kemal, İttihat Terakki ve Bolşevizm*. Istanbul: TÜSTAV, 2002.
Akandere, Osman. 'Damat Ferit Paşa Hükümetleri Döneminde Kuva-yı Milliye Hareketine Yöneltilen İthamlar', *Atatürk Araştırma Merkezi Dergisi*, 24.70 (2008), 17–56.

Akbal, İsmail. *Milli Mücadele Döneminde Trabzon'da Muhalefet*. Trabzon: Serander, 2008.

Akçam, Taner. 'When Was the Decision to Annihilate the Armenians Taken?', *Journal of Genocide Research*, 21.4 (2019), 457–80.

———. *The Young Turks' Crime against Humanity: The Armenian Genocide and Ethnic Cleansing in the Ottoman Empire*. Princeton, NJ: Princeton University Press, 2012.

Akçura, Yusuf. *Üç Tarz-ı Siyaset*. Ankara: Türk Tarih Kurumu Basımevi, 1976.

Akgün, Seçil Karal. 'Louis E. Browne and the Leaders of the 1919 Sivas Congress', in George S. Harris and Nur Bilge Criss (eds.), *Studies in Atatürk's Turkey: The American Dimension*. Leiden: Brill, 2009.

Akın, Yiğit. 'The Ottoman Home Front during World War I: Everyday Politics, Society, and Culture', PhD Dissertation: Ohio State University, 2011.

Akıncı, İbrahim Ethem. *Demirci Akıncıları*. Ankara: Türk Tarih Kurumu, 1989.

Aksakal, Mustafa. 'Not "by Those Old Books of International Law, but Only by War": Ottoman Intellectuals on the Eve of the Great War', *Diplomacy and Statecraft*, 15.3 (2004), 507–44.

Aktar, Ayhan. 'Debating the Armenian Massacres in the Last Ottoman Parliament, November–December 1918', *History Workshop Journal*, 64.1 (2007), 240–70.

Arai, Masami. *Turkish Nationalism in the Young Turk Era*. Leiden: Brill, 1992.

Ardıç, Nurullah. *Islam and the Politics of Secularism: The Caliphate and Middle Eastern Modernization in the Early 20th Century*. London: Routledge, 2012.

Atatürk, Mustafa Kemal. *Atatürk'ün Bütün Eserleri: 1915–1919, Cilt 2*. Istanbul: Kaynak Yayınları, 1999.

———. *Atatürk'ün Bütün Eserleri: 1920, Cilt 7*. Istanbul: Kaynak Yayınları, 2002.

———. *Atatürk'ün Bütün Eserleri: 1920, Cilt 9*. Istanbul: Kaynak Yayınları, 2002.

———. *Atatürk'ün Bütün Eserleri: 1920–1921, Cilt 10*. Istanbul: Kaynak Yayınları, 1999.

———. *Atatürk'ün Bütün Eserleri: 1921, Cilt 11*. Istanbul: Kaynak Yayınları, 1999.

———. *Nutuk*, ed. Bedi Yazıcı. Istanbul: n.p., 1995.

Babacan, Hasan, and Servet Avşar (eds.). *Cavid Bey, Meşrutiyet Ruznamesi, 3–4. Cilt*. Ankara: Türk Tarih Kurumu Basımevi, 2014.

Babayan, Der Nerses, and Ümit Kurt. *Günlüğümden Sayfalar*. Istanbul: Tarih Vakfı Yurt Yayınları, 2017.

Bali, Rıfat N. (ed.). *A Survey of Some Social Conditions in Smyrna, Asia Minor, May 1921*. Istanbul: Libra Kitap, 2009.

Balistreri, Alexander E. 'A Provisional Republic in the Southwest Caucasus: Discourses of Self-Determination on the Ottoman–Caucasian Frontier, 1918–19', in Yaşar Tolga Cora et al. (eds.), *The Ottoman East in the Nineteenth Century: Societies, Identities and Politics*. London: I.B. Tauris, 2016.

Bardakçı, Murat. *Şahbaba: Osmanoğulları'nın Son Hükümdarı VI. Mehmed Vahideddin'in Hayatı, Hatıraları ve Özel Mektupları*. Istanbul: İnkılap, 2006.

———. *Talat Paşa'nın Evrak-ı Metrukesi*. Istanbul: Everest Yayınları, 2008.

Baykal, Erol A. F. *The Ottoman Press (1908–1923)*. Leiden: Brill, 2019.

Bein, Amit. *Ottoman Ulema, Turkish Republic: Agents of Change and Guardians of Tradition*. Stanford, CA: Stanford University Press, 2011.

Berkes, Niyazi. *The Development of Secularism in Turkey*. New York: Routledge, 1998.

Beyoğlu, Süleyman. *İki Devir Bir İnsan: Ahmet Faik Günday ve Hatıraları*. Istanbul: Bengi Yayınları, 2011.

Bidwell, Robin Leonard, et al. (eds.). *British Documents on Foreign Affairs – Reports and Papers from the Foreign Office Confidential Print, Part II . . . Series B . . . Volume 2: The Allies Take Control, 1920–1921*. Frederick, MD: University Publications of America, 1985.

Birdal, Murat. 'Fiscal Crisis and Structural Change in the Late Ottoman Economy', in Amal Ghazal and Jens Hanssen (eds.), *The Oxford Handbook of Contemporary Middle Eastern and North African History*. Oxford: Oxford University Press, 2021.

Bloxham, Donald. *The Great Game of Genocide: Imperialism, Nationalism, and the Destruction of the Ottoman Armenians*. New York: Oxford University Press, 2007.

Böke, Pelin (ed.). *İzmir, 1919–1922: Tanıklıklar*. Istanbul: Tarih Vakfı Yurt Yayınları, 2006.

Borak, Sadi, and Utkan Kocatürk (eds.). *Atatürk'ün Söylev ve Demeçleri: Tamim ve Telgrafları, Cilt V*. Ankara: Türk Inkılap Tarihi Enstitüsü Yayınları, 1972.

Bournoutian, George A. *Armenia and Imperial Decline: The Yerevan Province, 1900–1914*. London: Routledge, 2018.

Bozkurt, Mahmut Esat. *Toplu Eserler, I*. Istanbul: Kaynak Yayınları, 2014.

Brémond, Édouard. *La Cilicie en 1919–1920*. Paris: Imprimerie Nationale, 1921.

Brookes, Douglas Scott (ed.). *On the Sultan's Service: Halid Ziya Uşaklıgil's Memoir of the Ottoman Palace, 1909–1912*. Bloomington, IN: Indiana University Press, 2020.

Burke, Edmund. 'Moroccan Resistance, Pan-Islam and German War Strategy, 1914–1918', *Francia*, 3 (1975), 434–64.

Busch, Briton Cooper. *Mudros to Lausanne: Britain's Frontier in West Asia, 1918–1923*. Albany, NY: State University of New York Press, 1976.

Çalışlar, İzzettin. *On Yıllık Savaşın Günlüğü*. Istanbul: Yapı Kredi Yayınları, 1997.

Çantay, Hasan Basri. *Kara Günler ve İbret Levhaları*. Istanbul: Ahmed Said Matbaası, 1964.

Çarıklı, Hacim Muhittin. *Balıkesir ve Alaşehir Kongreleri ve Hacim Muhittin Çarıklı'nın Kuvayı Milliye Hatıraları, 1919–1920*. Ankara: Türk Inkılâp Tarihi Enstitüsü, 1967.

Cebesoy, Ali Fuat. *Milli Mücadele Hatıraları*. Istanbul: Temel Yayınları, 2000.

Çetin, Fethiye. *My Grandmother: An Armenian-Turkish Memoir*. London: Verso, 2012.

Çetinkaya, Ali. *Askerlik Hayatım: Irak Cephesi, İşgal İzmir'i ve Ayvalık, 1914–1922*. Istanbul: Türkiye İş Bankası Kültür Yayınları, 2012.

Chatziioannou, Maria Christina, and Dimitris Kamouzis. 'From a Multi-ethnic Empire to Two National States: The Economic Activities of the Greek Orthodox Population of Istanbul, ca. 1870–1939', in Darja Reuschke et al. (eds.), *The Economies of Urban Diversity: The Ruhr Area and Istanbul*. Basingstoke: Palgrave Macmillan, 2013.

Churchill, Winstons. *The World Crisis: The Aftermath*. London: Thornton Butterworth, 1929.

Criss, Nur Bilge. *Istanbul under Occupation, 1918–1923*. Leiden: Brill, 1999.

Çukurova, Bülent. 'Büyük Taarruz Günlerinde Ali Kemal ve Siyasi Görüşleri', *Atatürk Yolu Dergisi*, 6.23 (1999), 357–70.

Dadrian, Vahakn N., and Taner Akçam. *Judgment at Istanbul: The Armenian Genocide Trials*. New York: Berghahn Books, 2011.

Davison, Roderic H. *Reform in the Ottoman Empire, 1856–1876*. Princeton, NJ: Princeton University Press, 1963.

Dennis, Brad. 'Explaining Coexistence and Conflict in Eastern Anatolia, 1800–1878', PhD Dissertation: University of Utah, 2015.

Der Matossian, Bedross. 'From Bloodless Revolution to Bloody Counterrevolution: The Adana Massacres of 1909', *Genocide Studies and Prevention*, 6.2 (2011), 152–73.

Deringil, Selim. *The Ottoman Twilight in the Arab Lands: Turkish Memoirs and Testimonies of the Great War*. Boston, MA: Academic Studies Press, 2019.

———. *The Well-Protected Domains: Ideology and the Legitimation of Power in the Ottoman Empire, 1876–1909*. London: I.B. Tauris, 1998.

Dersimi, Nuri. *Hatıratım*. Stockholm: Roja Nu Yayınları, 1986.

Djemal Pasha. *Memories of a Turkish Statesman, 1913–1919*. New York: George H. Doran Company, 1922.

Dogan Kader, Merve, and Seán Patrick Smyth. 'Neither Suvla nor Sedd-ul-Bahr – When Harp and Crescent Intertwined', *History Ireland*, 28.2 (2020), 42–4.

Doumanis, Nicholas. *Before the Nation: Muslim–Christian Coexistence and Its Destruction in Late Ottoman Anatolia*. Oxford: Oxford University Press, 2012.

Dündar, Fuat. *Modern Türkiye'nin Şifresi: İttihat ve Terakki'nin Etnisite Mühendisliği (1913–1918)*. Istanbul: İletişim Yayınları, 2008.

Dursunoğlu, Cevat. *Milli Mücadele'de Erzurum*. Erzurum: Erzurum Kitaplığı, 1998.

Durukan, Eyüp. *Günlüklerde bir Ömür – IV: Meşum Mütareke ve Meşru Mücadele (1918–1922)*. Istanbul: Türkiye İş Bankası, 2018.

Dyer, Gwynne. 'The Turkish Armistice of 1918: 2: A Lost Opportunity: The Armistice Negotiations of Moudros', *Middle Eastern Studies*, 8.3 (1972), 313–48.

Ekmekçioğlu, Lerna. 'A Climate for Abduction, a Climate for Redemption: The Politics of Inclusion during and after the Armenian Genocide', *Comparative Studies in Society and History*, 55.3 (2013), 522–53.

El Bakri, Alia. '"Memories of the Beloved": Oral Histories from the 1916–1919 Siege of Medina', *International Journal of Middle East Studies*, 46.4 (2014), 703–18.

Emgili, Fahriye. *Yunanistan'dan Mersin'e: Köklerinden Koparılmış Hayatlar*. Istanbul: Bilge Kültür Sanat, 2011.

Enver Pascha. *Um Tripolis*. Munich: Hugo Bruckmann Verlag, 1918.

Erol, Emre. *The Ottoman Crisis in Western Anatolia: Turkey's Belle Époque and the Transition to a Modern Nation State*. London: I.B. Tauris, 2016.

Esatlı, Mustafa Ragıp. *İttihat ve Terakki'nin Son Günleri: Suikastlar ve Entrikalar*. Istanbul: Bengi, 2007.

Eser, Umit. 'All Loud on the Western Front: Ethnic Violence, Occupation, and the Ottoman Bureaucrats in Aydın Province (Vilâyet), 1919–1922', PhD Dissertation: University of London, School of Oriental and African Studies, 2016.

Gale, Neil. *The Midway Plaisance at the 1893 World's Columbian Exposition in Chicago.* Lulu.com, 2017.

Gandhi, Mahatma. *Speeches and Writings of M. K. Gandhi.* Madras: G. A. Natesan, 1922.

Gawrych, George W. *The Young Atatürk: From Ottoman Soldier to Statesman of Turkey.* London: I.B. Tauris, 2013.

Gelvin, James L. *Divided Loyalties: Nationalism and Mass Politics in Syria at the Close of Empire.* Berkeley, CA: University of California, 1998.

Genişol, Hüseyin Fehmi. *Çanakkale'den Bağdat'a Esaretten Kurtuluş Savaşı'na: Cephede Sekiz Yıl Sekiz Ay (1914–1923).* Istanbul: Türkiye İş Bankası Kültür Yayınları, 2010.

Georges-Gaulis, Berthe. *Angora, Constantinople, Londres.* Paris: Armand Colin, 1922.

Gershoni, Israel, and James P. Jankowski. *Egypt, Islam, and the Arabs: The Search for Egyptian Nationhood, 1900–1930.* New York: Oxford University Press, 1987.

Gerwarth, Robert. *The Vanquished: Why the First World War Failed to End.* New York: Farrar, Straus and Giroux, 2016.

Gingeras, Ryan. *Fall of the Sultanate: The Great War and the End of the Ottoman Empire, 1908–1922.* Oxford: Oxford University Press, 2016.

Ginio, Eyal. 'Constructing a Symbol of Defeat and National Rejuvenation: Edirne (Adrianople) in Ottoman Propaganda and Writing during the Balkan Wars', in Stefan Goebel and Derek Keene (eds.), *Cities into Battlefields: Metropolitan Scenarios, Experiences and Commemorations of Total War.* Farnham: Ashgate, 2011.

Gladstone, W. E. *Bulgarian Horrors and the Question of the East.* London: J. Murray, 1876.

Göçek, Fatma Müge. *Denial of Violence: Ottoman Past, Turkish Present, and Collective Violence against the Armenians, 1789–2009.* Oxford: Oxford University Press, 2015.

Goebel, Michael. *Anti-Imperial Metropolis: Interwar Paris and the Seeds of Third World Nationalism.* Cambridge: Cambridge University Press, 2015.

Gökalp, Ziya. *The Principles of Turkism.* Leiden: E. J. Brill, 1968.

Gökay, Bülent. *Soviet Eastern Policy and Turkey, 1920–1991: Soviet Foreign Policy, Turkey and Communism.* London: Routledge, 2006.

Gökbilgin, M. Tayyip. *Milli Mücadele Başlarken, 1 Cilt.* Ankara: Türkiye İş Bankası Yayınları, 2011.

Gökdemir, Oktay (ed.). *İzmir'e Doğru.* Izmir: İzmir Büyükşehir Belediyesi, 2010.

Goloğlu, Mahmut. *Devrimler ve Tepkiler.* Ankara: Turhan Kitabevi, 1972.

Göztepe, Tarık Mümtaz. *Gurbet Cehennemi: Mütareke Sonrası Hatırat.* Istanbul: Kopernik Kitap, 2018.

———. *Mütareke Günleri.* Istanbul: Cümle Yayınları, 2017.

Gratien, Christopher. 'The Mountains Are Ours: Ecology and Settlement in Late Ottoman and Early Republican Cilicia, 1856–1956', PhD Dissertation: Georgetown University, 2015.

Greek Atrocities in the Vilayet of Smyrna (May to July 1919). Lausanne: Permanent Bureau of the Turkish Congress at Lausanne, 1919.

Günaydın, Adem. 'The Return and Resettlement of the Relocated Armenians (1918–1920)', Master's Thesis: Middle East Technical University, Ankara, 2007.

Gürpınar, Doğan. *Ottoman/Turkish Visions of the Nation, 1860–1950.* London: Palgrave Macmillan, 2013.

Güven, Zühtü. *Anzavur İsyanı: İstiklâl Savaşı Hatıralarından Acı Bir Safha.* Ankara: Türkiye İş Bankası, 1965.

Hacısalihoğlu, Mehmet. *Jön Türkler ve Makedonya Sorunu (1890–1918).* Istanbul: Tarih Vakfı Yurt Yayınları, 2008.

Hakan, Sinan. *Türkiye Kurulurken Kürtler (1916–1920).* Istanbul: İletişim Yayınları, 2013.

Hanioğlu, M. Şükrü. *Preparation for a Revolution: The Young Turks, 1902–1908.* Oxford: Oxford University Press, 2001.

———. *The Young Turks in Opposition.* Oxford: Oxford University Press, 1995.

Harington, Charles. *Tim Harington Looks Back.* London: John Murray, 1941.

Hatemi, Nilüfer. 'Unfolding a Life: Marshal Fevzi Çakmak's Diaries', PhD Dissertation: Princeton University, 2000.

Helmreich, Paul C. *From Paris to Sèvres: The Partition of the Ottoman Empire at the Peace Conference of 1919–1920.* Columbus, OH: Ohio State University Press, 1974.

Holquist, Peter. 'To Count, to Extract, and to Exterminate: Population Statistics and Population Politics in Late Imperial and Soviet Russia', in Ronald Grigor Suny and Terry Martin (eds.), *A State of Nations: Empire and Nation-Making in the Age of Lenin and Stalin.* Oxford: Oxford University Press, 2001.

Hovannisian, Richard G. *The Republic of Armenia, Volume II: From Versailles to London, 1919–1920.* Berkeley, CA: University of California Press, 1982.

———. *The Republic of Armenia, Volume IV: Between Crescent and Sickle: Partition and Sovietization.* Berkeley, CA: University of California Press, 1996.

İncedayı, Cevdet Kerim. *İstiklal Harbi (Garp Cephesi)*. Istanbul: Yapı Kredi Yayınları, 2007.

Jäschke, Gotthard. 'Beiträge zur Geschichte des Kampfes der Türkei um ihre Unabhängigkeit', *Die Welt des Islams*, 5.1 (1957), 1–64.

Jernazian, Ephraim K. *Judgment unto Truth: Witnessing the Armenian Genocide*. New Brunswick, NJ: Transaction Publishers, 1990.

Jwaideh, Wadie. *The Kurdish National Movement: Its Origins and Development*. Syracuse, NY: Syracuse University Press, 2006.

Kadhim, Abbas. *Reclaiming Iraq: The 1920 Revolution and the Founding of the Modern State*. Austin, TX: University of Texas Press, 2012.

Kandil, İsmail. 'Türk Basınında Osmanlı Bağımsızlık Günü Kutlamaları', Master's Thesis: Istanbul University, 2010.

Kansu, Mazhar Müfit. *Erzurum'dan Ölümüne Kadar Atatürk'le Beraber*. Ankara: Türk Tarih Kurumu Basımevi, 1986.

Kaplan, Sam. 'Documenting History, Historicizing Documentation: French Military Officials' Ethnological Reports on Cilicia', *Comparative Studies in Society and History*, 44.2 (2002), 344–69.

Kappeler, Andreas. *The Russian Empire: A Multi-Ethnic History*. London: Routledge, 2014.

Karabekir, Kazım. *Günlükler (1906–1948)*. Istanbul: Yapı Kredi Yayınları, 2009.

———. *İstiklal Harbimiz*. Istanbul: Türkiye Yayınevi, 1960.

———. *Kürt Meselesi*. Istanbul: Emre, 2004.

Karaca, Taha Niyazi. 'Milli Mücadele'de Bozkır İsyanları', *Erciyes Üniversitesi Sosyal Bilimler Enstitüsü Dergisi*, 1.16 (2004), 169–90.

Karaköse, Nejdet. 'Askeri, Siyasi ve Silah Sanayicisi Kişiliği ile Nuri Paşa (Killigil)', PhD Dissertation: Dokuz Eylül University, Izmir, 2010.

Karpat, Kemal H. *Ottoman Population, 1830–1914: Demographic and Social Characteristics*. Madison, WI: University of Wisconsin Press, 1985.

———. *The Politicization of Islam: Reconstructing Identity, State, Faith, and Community in the Late Ottoman State*. Oxford: Oxford University Press, 2001.

Katsikas, Stefanos. *Islam and Nationalism in Modern Greece, 1821–1940*. Oxford: Oxford University Press, 2021.

Kaya, Halit. *Refet Bele: Askeri ve Siyasi Hayatı, 1881–1963*. Istanbul: Bengi, 2010.

Kayalı, Hasan. *Arabs and Young Turks: Ottomanism, Arabism, and Islamism in the Ottoman Empire, 1908–1918*. Berkeley, CA: University of California Press, 1997.

————. *Imperial Resilience: The Great War's End, Ottoman Longevity, and Incidental Nations*. Berkeley, CA: University of California Press, 2021.

Kedourie, Elie. 'Young Turks, Freemasons and Jews', *Middle Eastern Studies*, 7.1 (1971), 89–104.

Kemal, Ismail. *The Memoirs of Ismail Kemal Bey*. London: Constable and Co., 1920.

Kemal, Yahya. *Kendi Gök Kubbemiz*. Istanbul: Yahya Kemal Enstitüsü, 1974.

Kerkük, Mahmut Nedim. *Hatıratım, 1334 (1918)*. Ankara: Altınküre Yayınları, 2002.

Kévorkian, Raymond. *The Armenian Genocide: A Complete History*. London: I.B. Tauris, 2011.

Kieser, Hans-Lukas. *Talaat Pasha: Father of Modern Turkey, Architect of Genocide*. Princeton, NJ: Princeton University Press, 2018.

King, Charles. *Midnight at the Pera Palace: The Birth of Modern Istanbul*. New York: W. W. Norton, 2014.

Kobakizade, İsmail Hakkı. *Bir Mübadilin Hatıraları*. Istanbul: Yapı Kredi Yayınları, 2008.

Kocahanoğlu, Osman Selim. *Atatürk–Karabekir Kavgası*. Istanbul: Temel Yayınları, 2013.

————. (ed.). *Rauf Orbay'ın Hatıraları, 1914–1945*. Istanbul: Temel Yayınları, 2005.

Kühn, Thomas. 'An Imperial Borderland as Colony: Knowledge Production and the Elaboration of Difference in Ottoman Yemen, 1872–1918', *MIT-EJMES*, 3 (Spring 2003), 4–16.

Kurt, Ümit. 'Introduction', in Kevork Baboian, *The Heroic Battle of Aintab*. London: Gomidas Intsitute, 2017.

————. 'The Making of the Aintab Elite: Social Support, Local Incentives and Provincial Motives behind the Armenian Genocide (1890s–1920s)', PhD Dissertation: Clark University, 2006.

————. *Türk'ün Büyük, Biçare Irkı*. Istanbul: İletişim Yayınları, 2012.

Lausanne Conference on Near Eastern Affairs, 1922–1923: Records of Proceedings and Draft Terms of Peace. London: His Majesty's Stationery Office, 1923.

Lewis, Bernard. *The Emergence of Modern Turkey*. Oxford: Oxford University Press, 1961.

Lewis, Geoffrey. *The Turkish Language Reform: A Catastrophic Success*. Oxford: Oxford University Press, 1999.

Llewellyn Smith, Michael. *Ionian Vision: Greece in Asia Minor, 1919–1922*. London: Hurst & Company, 1998.

Lohanizade Mustafa Nureddin. *Gaziantep Savunması*. Gaziantep: Kurtuluş Matbaası, 1974.

Macfie, A. L. 'The Chanak Affair: September–October 1922', *Balkan Studies*, 20.2 (1979), 309–41.

Mahir Metinsoy, Elif. *Ottoman Women during World War I: Everyday Experiences, Politics, and Conflict*. Cambridge: Cambridge University Press, 2017.

Mango, Andrew. *Atatürk: The Biography of the Founder of Modern Turkey*. New York: Overlook Press, 2002.

———. 'Atatürk and the Kurds', *Middle East Studies*, 35.4 (October 1999), 1–25.

Marr, Phebe. 'Yasin al-Hashimi: The Rise and Fall of a Nationalist', PhD Dissertation: Harvard University, 1966.

Martin, Terry. *The Affirmative Action Empire: Nations and Nationalism in the Soviet Union, 1923–1939*. Ithaca, NY: Cornell University Press, 2001.

Meleady, Conor. 'Negotiating the Caliphate: British Responses to Pan-Islamic Appeals, 1914–1924', *Middle Eastern Studies*, 52.2 (2016), 182–97.

Memorandum on the Claims of the Kurd People. Paris: Imprimerie A.-G. L'Hoir, 1919.

Menteşe, Halil. *Osmanlı Mebusan Meclisi Reisi Halil Menteşe'nin Anıları*. Istanbul: Hürriyet Vakfı Yayınları, 1986.

Miller, David H. *My Diary at the Conference of Paris: With Documents*, Volume IV. New York, 1924.

Morack, Ellinor. *The Dowry of the State? The Politics of Abandoned Property and the Population Exchange in Turkey, 1921–1945*. Bamberg: University of Bamberg Press, 2017.

———. 'Fear and Loathing in "Gavur" Izmir: Emotions in Early Republican Memories of the Greek Occupation (1919–22)', *International Journal of Middle East Studies*, 49.1 (2017), 71–89.

Morris, Benny, and Dror Ze'evi. *The Thirty-Year Genocide: Turkey's Destruction of Its Christian Minorities, 1894–1924*. Cambridge, MA: Harvard University Press, 2019.

Nicolson, Harold. *Peacemaking, 1919*. New York: Grosset & Dunlap, 1965.

Nioutsikos, Ioannis. 'The Greek Military Strategy in the Asia Minor Campaign, 1919–1922: An Application of Clausewitz's Theory on Culmination', in Konstantinos Travlos (ed.), *Salvation and Catastrophe: The Greek–Turkish War, 1919–1922*. Lanham, MD: Lexington Books, 2020.

Noel, Edward. *Diary of Major Noel on Special Duty in Kurdistan*. Basra: n.p., 1920.

Oral, Mustafa. 'Türk İnkılap Tarihi Enstitüsü (1933)', *Ankara Üniversitesi Türk İnkılap Tarihi Enstitüsü Atatürk Yolu Dergisi*, 27–8 (2001), 321–33.

Özcan, Azmi. *Pan-Islamism: Indian Muslims, the Ottomans and Britain (1877–1924)*. Leiden: Brill, 1997.

Özdemir, Hikmet. *The Ottoman Army, 1914–1918: Disease and Death on the Battlefield*. Salt Lake City, UT: University of Utah Press, 2008.

Özer, Kemal. *Kurtuluş Savaşında Gönen*. Gönen: Türkdili Matbaası, 1964.

Özgür-Baklacıoğlu, Nurcan. 'Devletlerin Dış Politikaları Açısından Göç Olgusu: Balkanlar'dan Türkiye'ye Arnavut Göçleri (1920–1990)', PhD Dissertation: Istanbul University, 2003.

Özyüksel, Murat. *The Hejaz Railway and the Ottoman Empire: Modernity, Industrialisation and Ottoman Decline*. London: I.B. Tauris, 2014.

Panian, Karnig, et al. *Goodbye, Antoura: A Memoir of the Armenian Genocide*. Stanford, CA: Stanford University Press, 2015.

Patrick, Andrew. *America's Forgotten Middle East Initiative: The King–Crane Commission of 1919*. London: I. B. Tauris, 2015.

———. 'Woodrow Wilson, the Ottomans, and World War I', *Diplomatic History*, 42.5 (2018), 886–910.

Philliou, Christine M. *Turkey: A Past against History*. Berkeley, CA: University of California Press, 2021.

Polat, Ü. Gülsüm. 'Osmanlı'dan Cumhuriyet'e Yemen ile İlişkiler (1911–1938)', *Atatürk Araştırma Merkezi Dergisi*, 33.96 (2017), 113–54.

———. *Türk-Arap İlişkileri: Eski Eyaletler Yeni Komşulara Dönüşürken (1914–1923)*. Istanbul: Kronik Kitap, 2019.

Polatel, Mehmet. 'Geri Dönüş ve Emval-ı Metruke Meselesi', in Ümit Kurt and Güney Çeğin (eds.), *Kıyam ve Kıtal: Osmanlı'dan Cumhuriyet'e Devletin İnşası ve Kolektif Şiddet*. Istanbul: Tarih Vakfı Yurt Yayınları, 2015.

Qureshi, M. Naeem. *Pan-Islam in British Indian Politics: A Study of the Khilafat Movement, 1918–1924*. Leiden: Brill, 1999.

Renda, M. Abdülhalik. *Hatırat*. Istanbul: Yapı Kredi Yayınları, 2018.

Rey, Ahmet Reşit. *İmparatorluğun Son Döneminde Gördüklerim Yaptıklarım (1890–1922)*. Istanbul: İş Bankası Kültür Yayınları, 2007.

Roessel, David. *In Byron's Shadow: Modern Greece in the English and American Imagination*. Oxford: Oxford University Press, 2001.

Ryan, Andrew. *The Last of the Dragomans*. London: Geoffrey Bles, 1951.

Sabis, Ali İhsan. *Harp Hatıralarım: Birinci Cihan Harbi, Cilt IV*. Istanbul: Nehir Yayınları, 1993.

Sancaktar, Fatih Mehmet. 'Son Osmanlı Meclis-i Ayan'ında Damat Ferit Paşa Taraftarlarının Faaliyeti ve Anadolu Hareketine Etkisi', *Yakın Dönem Türkiye Araştırmaları*, 0.9 (2006), 129–70.

Sarıhan, Zeki. *Kurtuluş Savaşı Günlüğü, I–IV*. Ankara: Türk Tarih Kurumu, 1996.

Schatkowski Schilcher, Linda. 'The Famine of 1915–1918 in Greater Syria', in John Spagnolo (ed.), *Problems of the Modern Middle East in Historical Perspective: Essays in Honour of Albert Hourani*. Reading: Ithaca Press, 1992.

Schlicklin, Jean. *Angora: L'Aube de la Turquie nouvelle (1919–1922)*. Paris: Berger-Levrault, 1922.

Sekeryan, Ari. 'The Armenians in the Ottoman Empire after the First World War (1918–1923)', PhD Dissertation: Oxford University, 2018.

Selek, Sabahattin. *Anadolu İhtilali, II. Cilt*. Istanbul: Kastaş Yayınları, 2004.

Sharp, Alan. *Consequences of Peace: The Versailles Settlement – Aftermath and Legacy 1919–2010*: London: Haus Publishing, 2010.

Shaw, Stanford J. *From Empire to Republic: The Turkish War of National Liberation, 1918–1923: A Documentary Study*, 5 vols. Ankara: Türk Tarih Kurumu Basımevi, 2000.

Shissler, A. Holly. *Between Two Empires: Ahmet Ağaoğlu and the New Turkey*. London: I.B. Tauris, 2003.

Sılan, Necmettin. *İlk Meclis Anketi: Birinci Dönem TBMM Üyelerinin Gelecekten Beklentileri*. Ankara: TBMM Kültür, Sanat ve Yayın Kurulu, 2004.

Şiviloğlu, Murat R. *The Emergence of Public Opinion: State and Society in the Late Ottoman Empire*. Cambridge: Cambridge University Press, 2018.

Smith, Michael G. 'Anatomy of a Rumour: Murder Scandal, the Musavat Party and Narratives of the Russian Revolution in Baku, 1917–20', *Journal of Contemporary History*, 36.2 (2001), 211–40.

Sofuoğlu, Adnan. 'İzmir İşgali Sonrasında Yunanlıların Batı Anadolu'da İşgali Genişletmeleri ve Bölgede Oluşan Milli Direniş', *Ankara Üniversitesi Türk İnkılâp Tarihi Enstitüsü Atatürk Yolu Dergisi*, 8.29 (2002), 131–42.

Solomonidis, Victoria. 'Greece in Asia Minor: The Greek Administration of the Vilayet of Aidin, 1919–1922', PhD Dissertation: King's College, University of London, 1984.

Somel, Selçuk Akşin. *The Modernization of Public Education in the Ottoman Empire, 1839–1908: Islamization, Autocracy and Discipline*. Leiden: Brill, 2001.

Sowards, Steven W. *Austria's Policy of Macedonian Reform*. Boulder, CO: East European Monographs, 1989.

Soyak, Hasan Rıza. *Atatürk'ten Hatıralar*. Istanbul: Yapı Kredi Yayınları, 2004.

Stoddard, Philip Hendrick. 'The Ottoman Government and the Arabs, 1911 to 1918: A Preliminary Study of the Teşkilat-ı Mahsusa', PhD Dissertation: Princeton University, 1963.

Suny, Ronald Grigor. *Looking toward Ararat: Armenia in Modern History*. Bloomington, IN: Indiana University Press, 1993.

———. *'They Can Live in the Desert but Nowhere Else': A History of the Armenian Genocide*. Princeton, NJ: Princeton University Press, 2017.

Sürmenyan, Kalusd. *Harbiyeli Bir Osmanlı Ermenisi*. Istanbul: Tarih Vakfı Yurt Yayınları, 2015.

Tachjian, Vahé. *La France en Cilicie et en Haute-Mésopotamie: Aux confins de la Turquie, de la Syrie et de l'Irak, 1919–1933*. Paris: Karthala, 2004.

T.C. Başbakanlık Devlet Arşivileri Genel Müdürlüğu. *Osmanlı Belgelerinde Ermenilerin Sevk ve İskanı (1878–1920)*. Ankara: Sistem Ofset, 2007.

Temel, M. Kemal. 'The 1918 "Spanish Flu" Pandemic in the Ottoman Capital, Istanbul', *Canadian Bulletin of Medical History*, 37.1 (2020), 195–231.

Thompson, Charles T. *The Peace Conference Day by Day: A Presidential Pilgrimage Leading to the Discovery of Europe*. New York: Brentano's Publishers, 1920.

Thompson, Elizabeth F. *How the West Stole Democracy from the Arabs: The Syrian Arab Congress of 1920 and the Destruction of Its Historic Liberal-Islamic Alliance*. New York: Atlantic Monthly Press, 2020.

Tongas, Gérard. *Atatürk and the True Nature of Modern Turkey*. London: Luzac & Co., 1939.

Tonguç, Faik. *Birinci Dünya Savaşı'nda Bir Yedek Subayın Anıları*. Istanbul: Türkiye İş Bankası Kültür Yayınları, 2001.

Torossian, Sarkis. *From Dardanelles to Palestine: A True Story of Five Battle Fronts of Turkey and Her Allies and a Harem Romance*. Boston, MA: Meador Publishing Company, 1947.

Toynbee, Arnold J. *The Western Question in Greece and Turkey: A Study in the Contact of Civilisations*. London: Constable and Company, 1922.

Trotsky, Leon. *History of the Russian Revolution*. Chicago: Haymarket Books, 2008.

Tunaya, Tarık Zafer. *Türkiye'de Siyasal Partiler, Cilt II: Mütareke Dönemi*. Istanbul: Hürriyet Vakfı Yayınları, 2003.

Turan, Mustafa, et al. (eds.). *Türkiye'de Yunan Fecayii*. Ankara: Berikan, 2003.

Türk Cumhuriyet Genelkurmay Başkanlığı Harb Tarihi Dairesi. *Türk İstiklal Harbi: VI ncı Cilt, İç Ayaklanmalar (1919–1921)*. Ankara: Genelkurmay Basımevi, 1964.

Türkgeldi, Ali Fuat. *Görüp İşittiklerim*. Ankara: Türk Tarih Kurumu, 2010.

Türkmen, Zekeriya. 'İşgal Yıllarında İstanbul'daki Uygulamalar: Mütareke Döneminde Ermeniler Tarafından Türk Çocuklarının Kaçırılması ve Hristiyanlaştırılması', *KÖK Araştırmalar*, 2.2 (2000), 265–83.

———. 'Özdemir Bey'in Musul Harekâtı ve İngilizlerin Karşı Tedbirleri (1921–1923)', *Atatürk Araştırma Merkezi Dergisi*, 17.49 (2001), 49–79.

Turnaoğlu, Banu. *The Formation of Turkish Republicanism*. Princeton, NJ: Princeton University Press, 2017.

Ülker, Erol. 'Turkish National Movement, Mass Mobilization, and Demographic Change in Istanbul, 1922–1923', in Meltem Ersoy and Esra Ozyurek (eds.), *Contemporary Turkey at a Glance II*. Wiesbaden: Springer, 2017.

Ünal, Muhittin. *Miralay Bekir Sami Günsav'ın Kurtuluş Savaşı Anıları*. Istanbul: Cem Yayınevi, 2002.

Üngör, Uğur Ümit. 'Orphans, Converts, and Prostitutes: Social Consequences of War and Persecution in the Ottoman Empire, 1914–1923', *War in History*, 19.2 (2012), 173–92.

Ursavaş, Ali Saib. *Kilikya Faciaları ve Urfa'nın Kurtuluş Mücadeleleri*. Ankara, 1924.

Uyar, Mesut. 'Ottoman Arab Officers between Nationalism and Loyalty during the First World War', *War in History*, 20.4 (2013), 526–44.

Vasıb, Ali. *Bir Şehzadenin Hatıratı*. Istanbul: Yapı Kredi Yayınları, 2012.

Vecihi, Binbaşı. *Filistin Ricatı*. Istanbul: Matbaa-yı Askeriye, 1921.

Venizelos, Eleutherios. *Greece before the Peace Congress of 1919: A Memorandum Dealing with the Rights of Greece*. New York: Published for the American-Hellenic Society by Oxford University Press, American branch, 1919.

Watenpaugh, Keith David. *Being Modern in the Middle East: Revolution, Nationalism, Colonialism, and the Arab Middle Class*. Princeton, NJ: Princeton University Press, 2012.

Wiegand, Theodor, and Cemal Paşa. *Alte Denkmäler aus Syrien, Palästina und Westarabien: 100 Tafeln mit beschreibendem Text*. Berlin: G. Reimer, 1918.

Williams, Brian Glynn. *The Crimean Tatars: The Diaspora Experience and the Forging of a Nation*. Leiden: Brill, 2001.

Wilson, Arnold T., and Gertrude L. Bell. *Review of the Civil Administration of Mesopotamia*. London: His Majesty's Stationery Office, 1920.

Winter, Stefan. *A History of the 'Alawis: From Medieval Aleppo to the Turkish Republic*. Princeton, NJ: Princeton University Press, 2016.

Yalçın, Hüseyin Cahit. *İttihatçı Liderlerin Gizli Mektupları*. Istanbul: Temel Yayınları, 2002.

Yalman, Ahmed Emin. *Yakin Tarihte Gördüklerim ve Geçirdiklerim*. Istanbul: Pera Turizm ve Ticaret, 1997.

Yanıkdağ, Yücel. *Healing the Nation: Prisoners of War, Medicine and Nationalism in Turkey, 1914–1939*. Edinburgh: Edinburgh University Press, 2013.

Yelbaşı, Caner. *The Circassians of Turkey: War, Violence and Nationalism from the Ottomans to Atatürk*. London: Bloomsbury Publishing, 2019.

Yenen, A. Alp. 'Envisioning Turco-Arab Co-Existence between Empire and Nationalism', *Die Welt des Islams*, 61.1 (2021), 72–112.

———. 'The Young Turk Aftermath: Making Sense of Transnational Contentious Politics at the End of the Ottoman Empire, 1918–1922', PhD Dissertation: University of Basel, 2019.

Yenibahçeli Şükrü et al. *Yenibahçeli Şükrü Bey'in Hatıraları*. Konya: Çizgi Kitabevi, 2011.

Yosmaoğlu, İpek K. 'Counting Bodies, Shaping Souls: The 1903 Census and National Identity in Ottoman Macedonia', *International Journal of Middle East Studies*, 38.1 (2006), 55–77.

Yüce, Rifat. *Kocaeli Tarih ve Rehberi*. İzmit: Türk Yolu Matbaası, 1945.

Zarrow, Peter. *After Empire: The Conceptual Transformation of the Chinese State, 1885–1924*. Stanford, CA: Stanford University Press, 2012.

Zeidner, Robert. 'The Tricolor over the Taurus: The French in Cilicia and Vicinity, 1918–1922', PhD Dissertation: University of Utah, 1991.

Zürcher, Erik-Jan. 'The Young Turks: Children of the Borderlands?', in Kemal H. Karpat and Robert W. Zens (eds.), *Ottoman Borderlands: Issues, Personalities, and Political Changes*. Madison, WI: University of Wisconsin Press, 2003.

Acknowledgments

This book would have never been written without the support of Mark Mazower. It was due to Mark that I was introduced to the gracious editor of this work, Simon Winder. While I have long tinkered with the idea of writing a history of the post-1918 Ottoman Empire, I am confident that I would not have come up with the basic framework of this book without Simon's help. 'The end of the Ottoman Empire', I roughly remember him saying, 'is something we often read about after plodding through a very long study encompassing decades or centuries of history. It would be really helpful just to understand how it all unfolded at the very end'. This recommendation stuck with me throughout the crafting of this narrative. And I cannot say how happy and grateful I am for the way the book ultimately turned out.

The production and refinement of this work were genuinely a team effort. This book's development is indebted to the guidance I first received from Virginia Aksan and Hasan Kayalı as a graduate student. Their input was instrumental in encouraging me to take on the post-1918 era many years ago. Others have certainly helped me along the way. Among those who especially helped me in a moment of need was Ümit Kurt, who gave me timely advice on sources, and Ron Suny and Ari Şekeryan, who invited me to speak about the crafting of this book at the annual meeting of University of Michigan's Center for Armenian Studies. I would specifically like to thank Yaşar Cora for allowing me to reprint his personal copies of the photographs of Kalusd Sürmenyan. Equal thanks also go to representatives of Türkiye İş Bankası Kültür Yayınları for allowing me to reproduce the image of Hüseyin Fehmi Genişol, another critical figure whose memoirs are vital to the telling of this story. My gratitude also extends to the Levantine

333

Heritage Foundation for permission to use their extensive collection of photos as well. Last, but by no means least, I would like to express my heartfelt thanks to Kit Shepherd. Never in my career have I had the pleasure of working with such a diligent and dutiful copyeditor. Many times I found myself truly humbled by the amount of attention Kit put into the manuscript. It is a far better work due to these efforts.

None of what was accomplished here would have been done without the love of my family. My wife Mariana, my children Amaya and Sebastian, and my mother Dedee never fail to inspire me to proceed forward. In closing, I would like to especially dedicate this book to someone who played an early role in putting me on the path that I have followed thus far. Janet Davis was my teacher and mentor for much of my high school years. As a student of hers for three of my four years at the University of San Diego High School, I had the pleasure of learning much about the history of Europe and Asia. It was in her classroom that I heard my first lectures about the Ottoman Empire. It was because of Mrs Davis that I came to understand how rewarding being a historian and teacher could be. I hope she accepts this work as a small token of my eternal gratitude.

Index